Y0-DKO-716

McGRAW-HILL SERIES IN MANAGEMENT
KEITH DAVIS, *Consulting Editor*

Business Management

McGRAW-HILL SERIES IN MANAGEMENT

KEITH DAVIS, *Consulting Editor*

KEITH AND GUBELLINI: Business Management

BUSINESS MANAGEMENT

Lyman A. Keith

PROFESSOR AND CHAIRMAN
DEPARTMENT OF BUSINESS MANAGEMENT
NORTHEASTERN UNIVERSITY

Carlo E. Gubellini

ASSOCIATE PROFESSOR
DEPARTMENT OF BUSINESS MANAGEMENT
NORTHEASTERN UNIVERSITY

1958 New York Toronto London
McGRAW-HILL BOOK COMPANY, INC.

BUSINESS MANAGEMENT

Library of Congress Catalog Card Number 57-10908

Preface

There is probably no field of human endeavor that is more important to our general well-being today than that of business management. Management as a science is relatively new; it has emerged since the turn of the century and now occupies a leading position in our business society. In the years ahead we can expect that demands on management will be rising steadily and steeply owing to the pressures of our highly competitive civilian economy and of a cold war of unknown duration. During this period America will need the highest caliber of business leadership to enable it to maintain, and where necessary retain, its position as a world power. Superior and continuously improved management is our only protection against slipping to the role of a secondary power.

The purpose of this book is to describe for the novice student of business just what management means and what it involves. The field of management is extremely broad and encompasses a multitude of interrelated factors. As a result, there is no single starting point for a study of management; rather, a logical sequence of topics is adopted, and from this the entire range of management functions and considerations is developed. By the time he completes his study of the book, the reader will have been exposed to the over-all role of management from its conception of an idea to make or sell something through the fulfillment of its goals. To indicate the nature and extent of management's functions this book will present many of the problems encountered in the organization and operation of a business venture, and approaches to their solution.

Business Management should be considered as a broad statement of the problems and functions with which management is concerned, presented in a manner that can be easily understood by the beginning student. It is a forerunner to a more detailed examination of the science of management.

The authors are indebted to countless sources for information used in this book. To them, our sincere thanks. Especially the authors wish to express their gratitude to Prof. Thomas J. Cavanagh of our staff for his efforts in editing and typing the manuscript and for the preparation of the Index. Whatever success this book may enjoy is due in large measure to the assistance and inspiration of others.

Lyman A. Keith
Carlo E. Gubellini

Contents

Introduction

The word "management" implies control or direction. A study of business management, therefore, would include a study of the functions involved in the controlling and directing of a business enterprise; more specifically, in its organization and operation. Management is the force that integrates men and physical plant into an effective operating unit. Good management greatly enhances the possibility of a profitable business operation; poor management can by itself cause the strongest or best-conceived business to fail.

The terms "management" and "owner" are considered synonymous by many; this interpretation was probably true when businesses were small and most operations were carried on under one roof. With the growth of a firm, which many times involves acquisition of subsidiary plants in other areas, owners are no longer able to personally provide the necessary direction and control. The corporate form of business makes possible the combination of thousands of individual owners into an autonomous self-perpetuating organization. Whenever there is a large number of owners, there is a need to separate the functions of ownership from those of active management of the business. The more than one million stockholders of the American Telephone and Telegraph Company, for example, could not join together effectively to manage this billion-dollar corporation by themselves; rather the stockholders elect directors, who in turn hire the managerial talents needed to run the organization.

Management, then, has become a specialized function designed to obtain the same degree of coordination, direction, and control in large organizations that formerly was possible only in small ones. In larger organizations the functions of management cannot be performed directly by the owners. Either the organization is too large and the owners are unable to cope with its attendant complexities or, as in the case of corporate ownership, there may be too many owners to allow each of them to play a direct part in management. The two terms "management" and "owner," therefore, must have different meanings.

In smaller organizations one person or a few can effectively supervise all aspects of business provided they possess a moderate amount of managerial ability. The development of modern large-scale business enterprise has necessitated greater emphasis on direction and control, or management. In nearly all fields of private business, competition between business organizations is very keen; each company seeks an advantage over the other. If one company can perform an operation more efficiently and effectively or is better managed than another, it can gain a competitive advantage. The advantage may take the form of better product design, better merchandising techniques, lower costs of operation, or some other facet of business activity. To reduce the possibility of a competitor's gaining an advantage, management must adopt the best methods and procedures for doing things—methods and procedures that are more effective than those of its competition. Management possesses no device that will indicate in advance that one course of action is positively superior to all others. However, through a scientific approach to its problems management may reduce the risk of uncertainty.

Scientific Management

In the fields of physical science, such as physics or chemistry, it is known that if certain ingredients are combined in a certain sequence, in certain proportions, under certain conditions, a specific result will be obtained. It is also known that this same result will be forthcoming each and every time the same experiment is conducted.

Because the scientist is so successful in obtaining the same result over and over again simply by following a well-planned and well-defined procedure, management turns to the scientist to obtain a foundation for the procedure it should employ in conducting experiments in the field of business management. Wherever possible, management develops and applies standardized procedures to the more or less standardized situations. Frequently, however, management finds that each time an analysis is made the ingredients of the study and their proportions vary so that each situation must be appraised largely on its own merits rather than on a standardized procedure for all. Business management, therefore, must be considered a quasi science.

When the solution to a problem of management is obtained by guesswork, opinion, hunch, or as the result of a single past experience, there is no reason to believe that such a solution is scientific or correct. If, on the other hand, the solution to a problem is reached through sound reasoning based on facts organized and analyzed systematically and without bias, the chances are that such a solution is reasonably scientific and sound. This, then, is the meaning of "scientific management." In the fields of social science which, of course, includes business management, it is difficult if not impossible to get an exact answer to a problem that deals with future events. The scientific method is used to determine the area wherein the true answer to a problem lies, thus preventing management from making decisions that are basically wrong—decisions that could cause irreparable damage to the future of the enterprise.

Scientific management involves the application of a scientific approach in the solution of such management problems as purchasing, setting of sales or production goals, locating the organization, preparation of budgets, determining the prices of commodities, and a host of other areas.

Responsibilities of Business Management

The owners of an enterprise and the public at large commonly view the profitability of a business venture as the principal yardstick of achievement, large profits denoting greater achievement than small. Yet in its approach to everyday and long-run problems management finds its task complicated by the fact that it cannot always set its goals in terms of the highest possible profit. To be sure, an enterprise must make a profit in order to continue its existence unless it is subsidized. However, management cannot always take the path that leads directly to greatest profits. Factors other than profits must guide the modern business organization. Observation of many well-managed business organizations offers convincing evidence that important management decisions are constantly being made that are not based strictly on the profit motive. Over the long run a single goal of profits is not strong enough to keep business management operating at the pressure level to which we have become accustomed. Management decisions are often based on noneconomic motives such as prestige, competitive reputation, regard for employees, or simply the social philosophy of top management.

In addition, management has a responsibility to groups other than itself which may interfere with the profit-making process. It has an ever-increasing responsibility to its work force. Modern laws and customs require that management devote itself to paying good wages, wages which will increase the worker's standard of living; to providing better working conditions; and to providing a greater degree of economic security to the workers. Management has a responsibility to the stockholders of the business to maintain the value of their investment and to provide a fair return on their stock. In conducting its affairs, management must consider the community in which it operates and the society that it serves with its products. It must provide the things that people want at prices that are within reason, and it should conduct itself in a manner that will not disrupt the life of the community wherein it is located. Management has a responsibility to make sure that its actions will promote the American system of free enterprise, leaving no opportunity for government intervention and socialism. The degree of skill and wisdom with which management accepts and discharges its responsibilities in the years ahead may well determine the destiny of the American system of business. Indeed, the field of business management is both complicated and challenging.

PART ONE

Basic Planning

The first chapter of Part One is devoted to a discussion which describes the evolution of a business enterprise. The purpose of this discussion is to present the reader with a picture of just what is involved in organizing and operating a business venture. This picture is presented in broad terms and in a sequence that is logical and easily understood.

The remaining chapters in Part One are designed to elaborate on specific portions of the over-all discussion of business management. These chapters will deal with four general areas that need consideration during the basic planning stage of business. Specifically, these areas are basic market considerations, basic product considerations, product research, and planning the nature and extent of production.

Before management can logically consider the specific requirements of its organization, size of plant, manufacturing methods and facilities, number and type of employees, and the like it must first obtain a picture of markets in general and the specific market in which it will compete. Similarly, a general knowledge of product characteristics is needed, for they in turn have a decided influence on the nature and extent of production and the entire operating plan.

Part One is essentially a discussion of orientation and basic planning. It answers the questions: What, in general, is involved in organizing and operating a business and what broad and basic areas must be considered prior to making decisions regarding the firm's operating plan?

CHAPTER 1

The Evolution of a Business Enterprise

In the United States there is a favorable combination of circumstances that provides a stimulant for entry into business. With but few limitations, our government protects the right of every citizen to enter any business he sees fit. The inalienable right to life, liberty, and the pursuit of happiness as proclaimed in our Declaration of Independence continues to dominate our thinking in the field of business enterprise. We as citizens, therefore, have the right to pursue any lawful business or vocation in any manner not inconsistent with the equal rights of others. As a result, each day a wide variety of new business ventures, promoted and operated by people from all walks of life, are added to the nearly 4½ million business organizations already in existence. While no two business ventures are exactly alike, all have at least two features in common. In each new business venture there is the desire for and the anticipation of profit; profit must be the underlying goal of all private business activity. Secondly, there is the desire for self-satisfaction by the owners of a business. Owning a business is a sign of achievement; the more successful the business, the higher the achievement.

THE ENVIRONMENT FOR BUSINESS

Only those who are familiar with business history realize that the relation of business to society as it exists in the United States is a relatively new and different concept; a concept applied in few countries of the world. Prior to the eighteenth century, freedom of business organization and operation was nonexistent. Business, such as it was, was controlled by the guilds and the church and dominated by the manorial system. It was not until the latter part of the eighteenth century that any real break in this relationship occurred. In 1776, Adam Smith in his work, *The Wealth of Nations*, expounded a new philosophy, the philosophy of *laissez faire* which proposed a minimum of government interference with the lives of people. Under this philosophy the government would act primarily as a referee over the actions of people rather than as a dictator of policy. His writings were instrumental in the development of this new philosophy and are important to us for they opened the door, at least, to a new system of business—the system that we live by today.

In this treatise, Smith set forth what he believed were the proper functions of any government. To quote from his works:[1]

> According to the system of natural liberty, the sovereign has only three duties to attend to . . . simple to common understanding: I, the duty of protecting the society from the violence and invasion of other societies; II, the duty of protecting as far as possible every member of society from the injustice and oppression of every other member of it, or the duty of establishing an exact administration of justice; and III, the duty of maintaining certain public works and public institutions, which it can never be for the interest of any individual, or small number of individuals, to erect and maintain, because the profit could never repay the expense to any individual or small number of individuals, though it may frequently do more than repay it to society.

It may appear on the surface that the philosophy of our government toward business is basically different from that implied in the doctrine of *laissez faire*. It is true that our governments exercise a great deal of control over business organizations and business activity. Every day, management, whether employing one or one thousand workers, must share a part of the working day with bureaucracy. There is no division of business activity which is not directly or indirectly subject to rules and regulations of our Federal government. But this condition is due primarily to the very complex nature of our society rather than the philosophy of the government. Controls are exercised only when it is to the benefit of society to have certain types of activity controlled. In comparison with other countries, America allows the businessman the most freedom in organizing and operating his business. The distinction between the American philosophy of business enterprise and that of many other countries is well illustrated by a statement made by Leon Jolson, which appeared in *Reader's Digest*.[2] Mr. Jolson is perhaps best known as the man who introduced the Necchi sewing machine to America. "In some countries a man like myself would have to wait months, maybe years, for government permits and licenses to start operating. But here, one day you decide to sell sewing machines and the next morning you're in business." While this statement perhaps oversimplifies the actual conditions

[1] Adam Smith, *The Wealth of Nations*, book IV, chap. 9.

[2] Oscar Schisgall, "He Stitched Himself a Dream," *Reader's Digest*, October, 1953.

surrounding the start of a new business venture, it does point out, at least, the relative simplicity of entry into business in the United States.

The Basic Institutions

It is possible for us to enjoy this freedom of entry into business because of the underlying philosophy of our government described above and the existence of three basic institutions which characterize the American way of life. To effectuate our basic philosophy toward entry into business we honor the institutions of private property, freedom and security of contract, and free enterprise.

The framers of our Constitution were careful to protect the property rights of individual citizens. The Fifth Amendment and the Fourteenth Amendment both guarantee that no person shall be deprived of property without due process of law. "Due process of law" has been construed to mean both according to the wording of the law and that the law itself must be just and reasonable. The Fifth Amendment guarantees that private property shall not be taken for public purposes without just compensation to the owner. The effect of these amendments is to prevent the arbitrary taking of one's property by force or by any means other than legal sale, gift, or bequest. The institution of private property guarantees that whatever property a man owns is his to use as he sees fit and without interference by others. With this guarantee there is an incentive for individuals to accumulate property beyond their immediate needs because it is assured that this property can be retained for future use. The institution of private property therefore encourages the accumulation of surplus goods which ultimately become the capital needed in developing business enterprise. Without the institution of private property there could be no accumulation of capital except by force; without capital there could be no business enterprise.

To use and develop one's capital effectively, it is often necessary or at least desirable to contract into the future for goods and services. The inherent interdependence of business organizations dictates that this be done. Contracts would never exist unless there was some guarantee that the parties to the agreement would have to perform according to the prescribed terms. Without freedom and security of contract, modern business could not operate. Freedom of contract means that an individual is at liberty to contract with others as he sees fit. The courts have interpreted "deprived . . . of liberty . . . without due process of law" to include liberty, or freedom, of contract. That a contract will remain secure until fulfilled is guaranteed in Article I, Section 10 of our Constitution which provides that no state shall pass any law that will impair the obligation of contract. Inasmuch as contract law is basically state law, this provision is of great significance. Thus if a businessman contracts with a supplier today for a carload of steel to be delivered in three months, both parties are assured that no law will be passed that will allow one party to violate the contract at the expense of the other. Freedom and security of contract encourage planning into the future by giving assurance that certain of these plans will ultimately mature—an essential to sound business management.

However, essential as the institutions of private property and freedom and security of contract are to our system of business, they do not in themselves permit free entry into business. Entry into business is closely regulated by the government in several countries that recognize these institutions. The third institution, free enterprise, is the right of a person to make whatever he wants and to use his capital and his abilities as he sees fit. Free enterprise allows a person to enter any business or profession he may desire without interference by others. If a man wants to open a machine shop rather than a shoe store as a means of using his capital and abilities, he is quite free to do so. As a result, an individual may pursue that particular endeavor which will best utilize his talents and bring the greatest possible reward to himself and society.

It must be realized that there are certain prohibitions against the use of goods or abilities in a manner that would jeopardize the health, safety, and welfare of others. A man is not allowed to burn his house, even though he owns it, because of the inherent danger to others. Likewise there are certain contracts that are not enforcible before the law. Contracts made under duress, gambling contracts, contracts by minors, and contracts in restraint of trade are not enforcible in our courts. While our government does dictate the conditions to which contracts must conform to be enforcible, they are for our protection as individuals and should not be considered infringements on this right. Recognition must also be made of the fact that there are certain restrictions on free enterprise. The practice of medicine, law, and many other trade and professional occupations may be subject to regulation by Federal, state, or local government. However, any restrictions so placed on members of society are usually imposed for failure to live up to desired standards of conduct and are not real infringements on this institution. We must also realize that during periods of national and perhaps local emergency these privileges may be temporarily suspended.

Private property and freedom and security of contract supply the incentive for business activity, while free enterprise insures that the road to business opportunity will always remain open. These are the basic ingredients of the American system of business enterprise.

Essential to our concept of business as these basic ingredients may be, they do not of themselves constitute the requisites for a successful business venture. There are many other factors to be considered. There must be some motivating force which will make people take advantage of this opportunity for easy entry into business. Every business organization must have a product or service to make and/or sell, a product or service for which there will be a demand. There must exist production facilities and production know-how to create the product or service to the satisfaction of the consumer. A plan of production must be formulated to utilize men, materials, and other facilities in such a manner that the product or service is produced when consumers want it and at a price they are willing to pay. An effective selling organization must be created to market the product or service and arrangements completed to finance the business activity. Whether the business is large or small, a management structure must be developed as a coordinating force to give full effect to all operating facilities. As the business venture is formed and operated, constant attention must be given to the future course of the enterprise to guard against the business risks inherent in any dynamic society. Attention must be directed constantly to the influence of unions and government in a wide area of management activity.

Each of the factors mentioned above plays a vital role in the development and growth of a business enterprise. Any or all of these factors could be a serious stumbling block to a successful business venture unless steps are taken to satisfy the requirements in each of these areas of activity. The following paragraphs will be devoted to a more detailed explanation of these factors.

Why People Enter Business

People enter business for a wide variety of reasons, but the underlying motive, as indicated above, must always be the desire for profit modified perhaps by some other drive.

The most frequently mentioned reason for entry into business is the desire to be independent. For many individuals even a big salary cannot compensate for the satisfaction of being one's own boss. Too, there is great security in knowing that you cannot be fired, that your destiny is in your own hands. If a person has had an especially unsatisfactory work experience while working for someone else, he may be tempted to go into business for himself just to be rid of the ennui that surrounded past employment. In many instances the motivation to be independent is so strong that the obvious hazards of business enterprise are overlooked in an attempt to satisfy what might have been a lifelong desire or ambition. While this motivation is both powerful and widespread, it is not by itself a justifiable reason for investing time and money in a business venture. There is no reason to believe that a business motivated solely by this force will be successful.

Many individuals organize their own business because self-employment affords the opportunity for them to more fully utilize and develop their abilities. In many instances, especially in medium- or large-size organizations, it may take an employer a considerable period of time to discover the abilities of each of his workers. Maximum individual development is a major goal of management's personnel program, but individual abilities cannot always be recognized immediately, and they may go unnoticed indefinitely unless the employer has some technique that he can use to locate and measure them. Thus there are many instances where a person is hired for a clerical task, which he can adequately perform, whereas his real ability lies in the field of sales or sales promotion. Frequently, too, it may be that an employer has no use for the specific abilities of each of his workers. Referring to the illustration above, if the employer has no use for the sales or sales promotion talents of this worker, they may go unused until he changes his job. In either event, the desire for individual development is strong enough to prompt many workers to leave their employer and form a business of their own. A business venture motivated by the desire to more fully utilize and develop one's abilities will have a much better chance of success than one motivated simply by the desire to be independent.

The dynamic nature of our society creates innumerable instances where there is a large demand for a product or service and an absence of facilities to adequately satisfy this demand. Since demands must be recognized, these instances invite new enterprise to exploit or take advantage of the unsatisfied demand. A housing project located in a previously undeveloped area or the construction of a new highway might open new retail opportunities. The enactment of a law requiring the installation of emergency lighting equipment in buildings where people congregate after dark or a law requiring directional signals on all automobiles could open new manufacturing and selling opportunities. Whenever there is a deadline for compliance with the law, as there may be in the above situations, the opportunity for exploiting the demand is magnified. The temptation to enter business under these conditions is very great because there is, for a time at least, an absence of normal competition, and meager management ability can operate profitably. The danger is that sooner or later the advantage of limited competition will cease, and such ventures are doomed unless their managements learn to operate in a competitive market.

Many people enter business to capitalize on a new product that they have developed. Perhaps a person has invented a new carburetor for automobiles and has decided to form a business to produce and market it rather than to sell the idea to an established firm. In this instance the basic motivation comes from a product, and there may or may not be a satisfactory market; and the promoter may or may not have the necessary managerial talents. The mere existence of a new and useful product, however, does not guarantee a successful business venture; there is a risk in every business venture regardless of the motivation. Management must manufacture the product efficiently, market it wisely, and constantly strive to improve it, else competition will force it to the sidelines. This situation can be illustrated through reference to the ball-point pen industry. One of the first ball-point pens to hit the market enjoyed immediate success because of the newness of the product and its many desirable or different features. This pen dominated the market for many months and experienced little or no direct competition. Success in the future seemed assured. Because of the fertile nature of the market many other manufacturers introduced their line of ball-point pens embodying new and better design and operating features. Within a relatively short period of time after competition entered, the original pen was overshadowed by the new and better lines. Today, the original ball-point pen is just a memory, the victim of more efficient and effective business management. Few business organizations enjoy continued success in today's market simply because of the physical characteristics of their products; the product is but one of the requisites for a successful business venture.

Finally, there are many instances where a person enters business for family reasons; to perpetuate a family institution. When a person inherits or takes over the management of a going business, there are generally far fewer problems to face than when starting from scratch. The business is established, has a market and a product or service to sell, and it may have produced many experiences that have been recorded to serve as a guide for future policy formation.

Factors in Business Success

We have now developed two very significant requisites to the formation of new business; the freedom of opportunity guaranteed by private property and free enterprise and the desire of individuals to enter business. It appears that the only additional requirement for starting a business is money. This is true. However, the fact that a large number of business ventures fail during their first year of operation and many more fail in succeeding years (see below) indicates that something more is required to make a success of a business venture. Success in business can be realized only through the application of sound principles of management to a host of related areas. The following paragraphs will outline many of these areas.

A Product. The object of all business activity is the satisfaction of human wants; production or distribution that does not satisfy a want must be considered waste. It is vital that there be an existing or potential demand for a product or service before an attempt is made to formally set up and operate a business. It is a simple task to select a product that can be manufactured, a service that can be performed, or a line of goods to stock a retailer's shelves, but quite another matter to select a product or service for which there will be a satisfactory demand. Launching a new product or service on the business scene can be a costly venture; therefore, any businessman or potential businessman should examine the market for a good or service to estimate the chances of success and to recognize the more dangerous elements of risk that threaten new business ventures. An examination of the market should be made to reveal its size, its location, and the types of buyers that would purchase the product or service. In addition, the examination should uncover the nature and extent of competing or related products. A clear-cut decision of management's course of action can be made only after complete information about the market has been obtained and analyzed.

While management is in the process of developing a product or service, attention must be given continually to a wide range of legal considerations. Patent and copyright laws must be investigated to ascertain that any new product or service does not infringe upon what others might have done previously. Licensing and tax problems must be examined, as well as state and local laws relative to health, safety, and welfare. Often a product must be modified in terms of existing patents or safety laws. It is wise practice to investigate these many areas before any attempt is made to actually manufacture a product. Considerable time and money may be saved and legal complications avoided.

Determining Production Needs. Production needs consist of materials, machines, manpower, and other facilities necessary to satisfy production requirements. These needs cannot be planned until the market analysis has been made, since it is the product that determines production needs. The product, in turn, is designed to comply with the findings of the market analysis. Management must determine how the product is to be made and what materials and machines are needed for the manufacturing process. Manpower requirements both in numbers and specific skills must be measured. A location for the business must be chosen, and its housing requirements satisfied. All these needs should be considered prior to formal business operation.

Operating the Production Facilities. A product in demand and the best production facilities do not guarantee a successful business venture. Often success or failure is determined by the way management uses its facilities in its everyday operations. Management must acquire the necessary personnel, train them, and supervise them at their work. Management must mold its work force into a well-coordinated production team and provide the incentive needed for a continuous high level of performance.

Operating a business involves the purchasing and controlling of a wide variety of materials and supplies in such a manner that production will never be subject to delays for want of things to work with. Management must set and maintain standards of performance as a means of controlling the rate of production and production costs. If management obtains the proper production tools and uses them intelligently, then efficient production will result.

Sales Management. It has been established that there is a market for the product in question, production needs have been fulfilled, and a production plan completed. Attention must now be turned to selling the product. The best-conceived products often fail to sell because they are improperly presented to the consumer. Sales management must determine sales outlets, selling methods, and the price that the consumer is willing to pay for the product. Distribution channels must be established to ensure an efficient movement of the product from the maker to the consumer. Finally, the product must be advertised and promoted to make the consumer feel that this product can satisfy his wants better than any other competing product. Great care should be taken in creating and operating the sales organization, for the success of any business venture depends heavily on the efficacy of sales management.

Financial Management. The promoters of a business must constantly give consideration to the ways and means of financing the venture. As the requirements for production, men, materials, machines, and housing are determined, a picture of the financial needs of the enterprise evolves. After the plan for distribution has been approved, the entire financing problem comes into view, and there is then a sound basis for measuring specific money needs. Specific money needs cannot be ascertained until a complete picture of what the business plans to do has been developed. We must assume that the promoters of the venture have some idea of the feasibility of financing it; otherwise there would be no purpose in carrying through to this point. There are several sources available for financing a business. Those who form the business undoubtedly will personally provide a large portion of the initial financing requirements. Public sale of securities may provide additional funds. Banks, insurance companies, and certain government agencies may be resorted to for borrowing. The promoters should recognize that to obtain the necessary financing they may be required to relinquish control of the business. There is no one means of satisfying financial requirements. If the venture is well conceived and is in the hands of qualified and determined individuals, financial problems may be more easily solved.

The Structure for Management. As each of the factors of business success is considered, it will become apparent that a particular type of business ownership may be most preferable. If the business is small and local in its area of activity, perhaps a single proprietor type of ownership may be adequate. In many instances varied talents are needed to operate a business, or more money is needed than one man can raise. In this case a partnership arrangement might be desirable. When a new business venture requires large amounts of capital and a wide variety of managerial abilities, a corporate type of ownership may be used. The attributes of the various types of ownership are discussed in greater detail in Chapter 22.

Every business organization needs a coordinating force in the form of an internal organization structure that will put the responsibility for running the enterprise into proper and qualified hands. Authority must be delegated to certain individuals within the company, and they must be held responsible for the performance of their delegated tasks. In most business organizations the boss is not able to supervise and control every phase of business activity. He must then rely on others to perform many of the necessary functions. How well these functions are coordinated is very often determined by the quality of the internal organization structure.

Measuring and Evaluating Performance. It has often been said that "the proof of the pudding is in the eating." So, too, the effectiveness of a business organization is determined through measuring and evaluating performance. Every business should have an over-all goal, either general or specific, preferably specific. This over-all goal can be achieved only through adherence to several lesser goals. An over-all goal must be broken down into a production goal, a sales goal, a financial goal, and a goal for the development of the work force. Actually there is a goal for nearly every factor in business success.

Management must measure and evaluate its performance in terms of each of these goals. Whenever there is any deviation from a well-conceived goal, it is a sign that operations do not measure up to standard. Management should study and evaluate such weaknesses, develop and apply corrective measures to prevent recurrence of any substandard performance. Only through measuring and evaluating performance can management be assured that its goals are satisfactory and that proper steps are being taken to reach these goals.

We can be sure, however, that not every new business venture has evolved through analysis of all of the elements as discussed above. Often many important considerations are set aside during the formation of a new business as not needing attention because of certain preconceived ideas. If a business promoter plans his activity on the premise that his product is better than all others, that there is a market for it, or that consumers will pay a particular price for it without first ascertaining that each of these is true, then the entire operation may be headed in the wrong direction.

The factors of business success mentioned above combine as the essential ingredients for a profitable business venture. Some factors will be of more significance than others in specific situations, but none should be dismissed as irrelevant in any event. "An ounce of prevention is worth a pound of cure," and the best time to develop and apply preventive measures is at the start of a venture. A thorough study of any situation is fundamental to an intelligent decision.

The Future Role of the Enterprise

Should a business be allowed to grow, should its operations be restricted, should it reduce the scope of its activities, or should it suspend operations entirely? Periodic appraisals of these alternatives are a prerequisite for planning the future role of the enterprise. Many organizations are not allowed to grow because management feels inadequate to the task of solving the problems associated with growth. Other organizations grow because growth may be essential for the preservation of the organization's competitive position. There are many business organizations that fail because of growth while others fail because they are not allowed to grow. The decision to grow or not to grow is an important one and should be frequently analyzed in the light of the environment in which the business operates. Management should remember that a decision not to grow may be as fatal as a decision to attempt growth at an excessively rapid rate.

Growth should not take place until management has assurance that the existing organization is properly managed and capable of handling the problems associated with growth. These problems will be quite similar to those encountered in the formation of a new business. Growth requires motivation, capital, a new product, or a larger market, or larger production facilities. Each of these in turn requires consideration of the other factors of business success. Whether growth is accomplished by adding to a line of products, expansion of existing facilities, or acquisition of additional plants, problems similar to those encountered when the business was first conceived must be met and solved.

Consideration of Unions and Government

Since 1935 and the passage of the National Labor Relations Act, unions have grown rapidly in numbers and in strength. Every year unions demand additional concessions from management for their members. There is every reason to believe that unions will continue to demand more and more in the future. Management must realize that unions are a permanent part of the labor-management aspects of business and prepare to deal with them in a manner that is best for itself, the workers, the union, the stockholders, and the general public.

In the past a few business organizations have operated in a manner opposed to the best interests of the American public. As a result, certain restrictive legislation has been enacted to prevent recurrence of these situations. It is to the benefit of any businessman to investigate these areas of government regulation, for they reach into every conceivable area of business activity. While making a search of these restrictions on business, it is also worthwhile for management to look into the evergrowing number of aids that our government provides for business. A businessman often finds that the answers to his problems have already been published by one of our large number of government agencies.

A NOTE OF CAUTION

Every year there are thousands of individuals in this country who decide to enter business of some sort, either by themselves or in company with others. History shows that a large percentage of these businesses do not survive for their first anniversary and that a significant percentage fail in the following years. The life of the average business, especially small business, is quite short. Nearly 60 per cent of the concerns that failed in 1954 had been in business less than five years. In most instances when a business fails it leaves a trail of economic waste, tragic disappointment, and great personal debt. The magnitude of this problem of business failure is illustrated in Table 1–1. The average liabilities of each

TABLE 1–1
BUSINESS FAILURES IN THE UNITED STATES, 1948–1956

Year	Number of failures	Liabilities (000 omitted)
1948	5,252	$310,566
1949	9,246	308,037
1950	9,162	248,283
1951	8,058	259,467
1952	7,611	283,314
1953	8,862	394,153
1954	11,086	462,628
1955	10,969	449,380
1956	12,704*	552,418*

* Estimated.
SOURCE: U.S. Department of Commerce, *Survey of Current Business*, 1949–1957.

failing business in 1956 was more than $43,000 per establishment. Either the owners or other businessmen who dealt with the failing firm must bear this loss.

Every year as many as 80,000 applications for patents are received by the Department of Commerce in Washington; yet no more than one-half as many patents are issued. It is conservatively estimated by the Small Business Administration that as few as five patented inventions in one hundred ever repay even the cost of securing the patent. It appears then that there are many unwarranted entries into business every year and that many of the new ideas conceived are not worthy of development. Although thousands of new businesses are started every year, the total number of business establishments in this country increases very slowly because of the high rate of failure. The reason so many fail to survive is simply that the people who start them are ill prepared in one way or another. But the very factors that make private business such a tough race for them multiply the chances of success for the educated, ambitious man or woman with proper resources.

Causes of Business Failure

Just as a businessman may feel that certain of the factors which make for business success do not apply to him, he may also feel that in his case there is no need to consider the causes of business failure. The wise move is to consider why others have failed and take precautionary measures to prevent a similar situation.

More business ventures fail because of poor management than for any other single cause. Poor management can be described as the failure to pay proper attention to the factors in business success. Frequently a businessman will blame his plight on "economic conditions" over which he has no control, but it cannot be emphasized too strongly that in a vast majority of cases business failures are human failures.

Poor management is perhaps too general a statement of the causes of business failure. Specifically, most business failures stem from the product or service that is being offered; failure to relate the product or service to the entire organization and the market; and failure to determine the role that the product plays in the satisfaction of human wants. It is for this reason that the discussions in the following chapters will be centered around the product, its market, and an organization to produce and distribute it in an effective manner.

Business failure is often caused by insufficient capital; a business does not have sufficient funds for its needs. There are many reasons why businessmen get into financial difficulty. Perhaps the business began with too little capital; capital requirements may have been underestimated; or perhaps sufficient capital was not available to the promoters. If money is taken from the business by the owners faster than it is being earned, financial difficulties are bound to arise. When a businessman has the bulk of his funds invested in fixed assets or slow-moving inventory items, he may become financially embarrassed and be unable to meet his obligations as they mature. These are illustrations of insufficient capital, but it can be easily seen that the underlying cause of trouble is poor planning by poor management.

Many business organizations fail because the owners or managers do not have adequate knowledge concerning the progress of the firm. In other words, because of inaccurate or inadequate records management has no sound basis for making intelligent decisions relative to the proper course of action for the firm. Record keeping is a tedious task for any business, and unfortunately, the value of good records is often not recognized until a businessman finds himself in difficulty. Once it was the boast of some successful businessmen that they carried their offices in their hats. True, a clever businessman can carry an amazing number of facts and figures in his head and frequently feels justified in keeping track of his business affairs in this manner. Sooner or later the time will come when, either because of the passage of time and/or the growth of the business, this method will prove unsatisfactory.

Records are essential to control, and a business cannot prosper and grow without proper controls. Cash, receivables, sales, inventories, expenses, and payables are a basic minimum of records that a businessman should keep. Without cost-selling price relationships, inventory data, credit sales volume, credit purchases volume, and other records a businessman cannot know where he stands or where he is headed.

Finally, failure in business can be attributed to poor organization and poor leadership. Whether a business is large or small, proprietorship, partnership, or corporation, it is essential that there exist the intangible asset of leadership. The basic plan for executive and administrative action will rest on the ability and personality of the chief executive. The chief executive of any organization should be willing and able to subject himself to a self-examination that will reveal the strong and weak points in his business make-up. Since it is highly desirable to have the affairs of a firm in competent hands, the chief executive should be able to determine those areas of activity that he can properly handle by himself and then obtain help in performing those duties that lie beyond his capabilities. This means that in some situations the chief executive would be just the promoter and only a figurehead. The actual running of the business would be entrusted to that group of individuals he has gathered about him, each having a special talent vital to the successful operation of the business.

On the other hand there is a class of business executive known as the "captains of industry." This group would include the Schwabs, the Carnegies, the Swifts, the Chryslers, and many of our contemporary business leaders. Each of these individuals was blessed with an extraordinary measure of business sense. Organization, product development, market characteristics, production problems, financing, and distribution—these men had an almost uncanny ability to make sound decisions in all of these areas. On the surface it appears that these men could run their giant corporations singlehanded. However, these men were not great because of their innate knowledge; rather they were able to see the real nature of problems as they arose; they were able to pin-point the role that each member of the organization was to play in the making of business decisions and, through the guidance of their staff, to determine the best policy to follow. The giant corporations in this country, and all successful business organizations, are built not through the efforts of an individual but through leadership that knows how to utilize the abilities of others to best advantage. Good management always requires that duties and responsibilities be so dispersed throughout an organization that the loss of a single individual will not result in the loss of leadership and the ability to make sound decisions. Business failures can many times be avoided through good organization and effective leadership.

SUMMARY

The preceding discussions have shown in general terms the evolution of a business enterprise from its conception through the stage of successful operation. The discussions apply to manufacturing, retailing, service, or wholesaling activity. The same basic problems face all types of business activity.

Nowhere else on earth do a group of people enjoy the privilege of owning their own businesses as we do in the United States. The firmly established principles of private property, freedom and security of contract, and free enterprise guarded by our Constitution and the courts are the foundation for the most liberal philosophy of government and business in the world today.

Ours is a creative society in which we encourage constant change by striving competitively to improve our goods, services, and processes. Yet we have been able to make progress through the encouragement of change while keeping intact the basic institutions which have always characterized our political and economic system. Business, like any other institution that hopes to endure, must adjust itself to the goals of the people it serves. Should business fail to do this, it will be challenged by new business eager to capitalize on the mistakes of others. As cruel as this philosophy may appear to be at times, it has enabled us to increase our standard of living to a higher level than that of any other nation on earth.

The fact that many business ventures fail in this country may be looked upon as a sign of weakness in our economic system. On the contrary, failures can be desirable. In the United States a person is limited basically only by his initiative if he desires to become an entrepreneur. However, success in business is not guaranteed. Adapt or perish is an inexorable law of life in American business; a business organization must fulfill a need for society or perish.

QUESTIONS

1. What is management? What is scientific management?
2. What is the meaning and significance of *laissez faire*?
3. What are the proper functions of any government according to Adam Smith? Is his philosophy applicable today?
4. Define free enterprise and private property. Why are both essential to free entry into business?
5. What is meant by freedom and security of contract? Why is this so essential to business enterprise?
6. For what basic purpose does our government control business?
7. What are the requirements for a successful business venture?
8. What are the major causes of business failure?
9. For what reasons do people enter business for themselves?
10. What is leadership and why is it so important to business success?

CHAPTER 2

Basic Market Considerations

A businessman must know something about the economic climate in his sphere of activities. The competition which he must meet each day is rendered more or less powerful depending upon two factors. The first of these is the extent of knowledge which the businessman possesses—knowledge, that is, not only of the day-to-day operational procedures of his firm, but also of the many factors of the business world which have their influence upon the course of his enterprise. Second, and equally important, is the manner in which the entrepreneur analyzes and interprets the myriad factors and fancies which represent the past and present and thereby provide, possibly, a guide to the road which should be followed into the future. The hope is that the road he chooses to travel will lead to the preservation and enhancement of the competitive position of the business firm.

EVALUATING AND FORECASTING

The man who undertakes a business venture is confronted with two different tasks as he attempts to portray the future. The first task is that of gathering pertinent data, and the second task is that of formulating a sound decision as to his future course of action. This decision is at least in part, if not wholly, based upon the interpretation of the available data. This interpretation is fundamentally a subjective process. Regardless of what information may be available, any final decision made on the basis of such facts is a reflection of the capabilities and the skill of the individual rendering such a decision. Always, in the final sense, the businessman must sit down, look at the mass of data, and then by some internal process hit upon what he considers a sound conclusion or pronouncement. As those of the business world seek to make all aspects of business decisions more precise and scientific, the procedure of fact-gathering and analysis becomes more and more regimented into an orderly approach to the analysis of problems.

The Paradox of Evaluation

Each day of business existence the managers are called upon to render decisions in a host of varied matters. Each decision must eventually be precisely, even though erroneously, stated. There is no provision in business for a price to be quoted in the final sense as being "around $50." Nor is there the possibility that an order can be placed for "around one thousand units" without the need for a final specific number being shipped by the vendor. Somewhere along the line the decision must be handed down. These day-to-day answers to business questions and problems represent the meat and potatoes of business operations. They are the things which management thrives on, and because of, gains or loses. Yet, in the light of a proved need for a "yes or no" answer, it is necessary for management to venture into decision making which involves "may be or could be" as part of the answer. The attempt to understand the great economic environment is beset principally by the plague of a host of intangible variables which must be considered in the forecasting of economic activity. The available information concerning these variables and the method of interpreting this information raises serious doubt in the minds of many businessmen who conclude that the task of making a business forecast on the basis of statistical facts is beyond the range of human ability. Therefore, they feel that such activity is best left to the judgment of experience.

Such forecasts rendered by experience have often matched the forecasts expressed by professional economists. The businessman must admit that the bases for his decision must certainly have paralleled, if not duplicated, the factors which were considered by the economist.

On the one hand, management is involved in situations which demand specific and quantitative answers; whereas, on the other hand, there are areas of consideration which at best can be measured only in terms of estimates. Both types of decision must be made today, and both types are pertinent to the profitability of the business. Today's decision reaps today's profits. Today's estimate of tomorrow provides the basis for a course of business action which will set the stage for the everyday decisions which will have to be made by future managers. Many of the managers of today are gathering profits, a good part of which one might say were really earned in the past. Even as they do so, they are busy evaluating prospects in the hopes of originating or developing new areas for future profit taking. Many millions of dollars and twelve years of research went into the development of nylon by Du Pont. During all these years and before, a succession of estimations and decisions had to be made. A great time gap exists between the origination and the authentication which profitability gives to decision.

The Economic Factors of Evaluation

What are the economic factors with which the businessman should be concerned? Does it make any difference whether his line of business is manufacturing, selling, or the performance of services? What if the product or service which he is dispensing is meant for the personal use or satisfaction of individuals as opposed to goods or services which are intended to satisfy some business need? One businessman may consider the possibility of investment in a baby diaper service; another may be concerned with the possibility of developing a new golf course. On the other extreme, the steel industry is contemplating additional capacity for steel production. Even as these positive acts are occurring in such widely diverse fields, we read of negative aspects of business life such as business failures and liquidations. There must certainly be raised the question of what relationship, if any, exists between these positive and negative aspects. Is there a common denominator which may be useful in the interpretation of the economic activity which occurs about us? Are there possibly different common denominators depending upon whether an inquiry concerns goods for personal use as opposed to those for business use? If search should disclose the existence of such denominators, then certainly we shall have answered a query raised above which concerns the discovery of the economic factors with which the businessman should be concerned.

At this point we can only admit that a general knowledge of economic conditions is a basic necessity. The businessman cannot first place his emphasis upon a set of specific economic facts, for prior to pinpointed examination there must be an appreciation of the general economic conditions or factors of the business economy which call the turn of business in general. The evaluation of the future for a particular business enterprise must be viewed in terms of general business conditions, then industry conditions, and finally the setting for the particular venture. Because of the increasing influence of general economic conditions on the well-being of an enterprise, the businessman must watch carefully the economic activity on a national basis. No longer can the firm concern itself solely with the task of satisfying its customers in an essentially local market. Such an attitude in earlier days would have been the very key to business success. Today, however, the entrepreneur must recognize that competition, market size, purchasing power, population, politics, general business activity, and government regulation all have their influences upon the environment within which the particular firm will carry on its activities.

The eventual offshoot of the inquiry into and evaluation of general economic factors is the development of a picture of the demand which may exist for the product of the industry. The businessman is then concerned with the nature of the market for his particular product or service and whether it is likely to change in size during the next year or during the next five, ten, or twenty years. Will the demand be concentrated during a particular season of the year? Will the bulk of sales be concentrated within one or more geographic areas? What companies are already engaged in providing the particular products or services? What changes may occur in respect to the nature of competition and the number of competitors within the field? On what basis must a company meet competition? Price? Quality? Performance?

These are but some of the questions which are pertinent to the planning of a proposed venture or the continuance of a going concern. It is hoped that in the search for answers to such queries management will gain a broader perspective and a detailed insight of economic factors both on a general and a specific industry basis. The familiarity and understanding which the businessman may have with economic matters provide the bases upon which he may enter into the analysis of his particular business problem.

The "Turns of Business"

Business behavior has historically demonstrated the prevalence of certain measurable characteristics which are useful in the understanding and forecasting of business activity. These characteristics appear in the form of business fluctuations which occur either regularly from year to year and are classified as seasonal variations or those which show up as deviations from the normal level of activity which has been established for the business. These latter deviations may occur irregularly owing to temporary maladjustments in business activity, such as oversupply or shortages, or they may persist for extended periods of time prior to re-establishment of the normal level of activity. This form of business fluctuation is identified as the "cyclical swing" in business which occurs for reasons which are not yet precisely catalogued. In addition to these fluctuations of economic activity, there is a third measurable characteristic which may be used by those who seek to measure the future. This measurement is termed the "secular trend" and is a portrayal of the long-term change in business activity. This long-term change may be one of either growth or decline in activity. In general, therefore, we see three patterns of business activity with which the businessman should be acquainted.

Seasonal Variation. If the activity of the business firm or industry shows a consistent pattern of variation in its volume of sales or production from year to year, it may be concluded that there is an inherent seasonal factor involved. Department store sales are notoriously seasonal.

This is shown by the great increase in sales which occurs regularly each year during the Christmas shopping season. Obvious examples, such as beach concession activities and ski lodge operations, easily indicate the essence of seasonal operations. Canneries and packers, similarly, find that their activities are dependent upon crop maturities.

Seasonal variations are very much subject to managerial attention which is aimed at minimizing the impact of such variation upon the firm or industry. The seasonal factors of industry pose the problems of fluctuating employment levels and idle equipment during the so-called "off season." Successful attempts have been made by management in reducing the impact and the extent of seasonal variations of specific industry groups.

In addition, sociological and economic changes have their influences. The increase in home ownership has made for less of a seasonal-minded approach to home improvements and repairs. The prevalence of larger families and wider income distribution have respectively forced and allowed the consuming public to deviate from accustomed spending habits both as to time of spending and amount of spending. The improvement in the status of the wage earner and security of income has created a new array of wants. It has made the pursuit of pleasure and leisure a year-round occupation and has reduced the impact which seasonal income would have upon buying habits.

The prospective businessman should not find it too hard to understand and determine the nature of the seasonal problem with which he may be faced. Recognition of this factor is not the important aspect, for of greater concern are the problems of financing, employment, procurement, and inventories which may come about as a result of seasonal irregularities in business. Seasonality must also be viewed from the point of view of suppliers of the firm and that of complementary industries, for the seasonal problem of a supplier or of the industry with which the particular firm has product association becomes the problem of the firm itself.

Business Cycles. The examination of a chart which shows graphically such business data as sales, production, shipments, or prices over a period of years may show a series of wavelike movements. Such undulations in the graphic plot of business activities represent the phases of prosperity, recession, depression, and recovery which have occurred. These phases of "boom and bust" represent the periodic expansions and contractions which involve maladjustments and readjustments and which also involve the idea of rhythm in business activities. It is with the business cycle, its nature and causes, that the businessman has greatest concern. The future of the enterprise is tied to this cycle of activity; therefore, the potential cyclical movements are an area of keen investigation by management. Unrelentingly the search proceeds for an explanation of the occurrence of cyclical variations; and at the same time the search persists for some device or technique of analysis and projection which will allow the forecasting of future levels of business activity. This approach to a look-see into the future, it is hoped, will provide the basis for planning which will allow one to take advantage of future conditions. On the other hand, if the view of the future course of business activity is less than desirable, the availability of an adequate forecasting technique may provide the basis for lining up defenses against or offenses to prevent the possible chaos which analysis may indicate is imminent.

The business cycle has certain observed characteristics which may be combined to present a picture of the nature of a cyclical swing. If we may start our picture at the beginning of a period of business recovery, we may find the following developments as part of the cyclical scene:

1. Rising stock prices
2. Increasing price levels
3. Increasing production
4. Increasing sales
5. Increasing inventories
6. Increasing credit and interest rates

This is not an all-inclusive listing of developments, nor are they presented in order of occurrence or importance. These are merely some of the indicators of business activity, and their trends usually conform to the general trend of economic activity. These indicators continue to show increased activity until a peak is reached. This peak is one of the indeterminables which confront the analyst who is attempting to predict its occurrence. At this stage, economic activity in the form of production, consumption, etc., is in high gear when for some yet elusive reasons, the trend of activity reverses itself. Each of the indicators listed above likewise has a trend reversal which is tantamount to a general slowdown in economic activity. If the situation is left to run its course, we find widespread unemployment of men and production facilities, a decrease in price levels, national income level, and purchasing power, and the resulting curtailment of sales, depending upon the nature of the goods involved.

These indicators do not necessarily vary in the same direction or to the same degree at any one time. Even from cycle to cycle their behavior patterns vary. Regardless of this inconsistency there is still very fundamental and important usage of these indicators; for each, in general or particular, is representative of the current or future activity in a segment of the economy. These are the pieces of the puzzle of the future which the businessman attempts to put together in the form of a clear picture of events to come.

Secular Trend. If a month-to-month comparison of the statistics of business activity were to be made, the long-time trend would most likely be imperceptible because of its very gradual change during such short periods of time. However, the irregular variations which occur on a day-to-day basis are most readily seen; and the seasonal fluctuations may be seen if one takes the year's perspective. Cyclical variations and the secular trend show themselves only when activity is viewed on a long-range basis. The long-term trend is the smooth and regular increase or decrease which occurs in a given series of economic data during a period of years. The trend is a measurement of the long-term average level of production, sales, income, population, or other economic or social activity. The trend of any particular company's activity may or may not conform

FIGURE 2–1

THE MOVEMENTS OF BUSINESS ACTIVITY

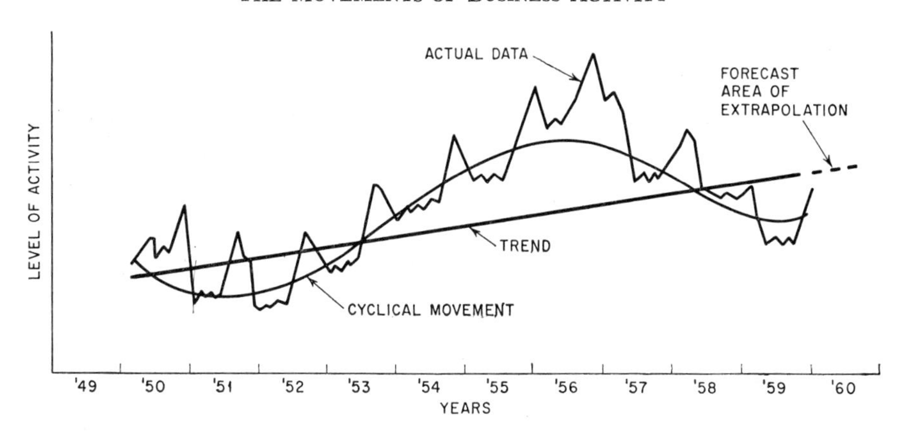

to that of its industry which, in turn, may or may not conform to the trend of general economic activity.

The comparison of a series of data with its own trend allows one to determine the range of fluctuation above and below the average level and thereby fix the range within which the future activity may most likely occur. In addition, the secular trend provides a basis for extrapolation. If there is reason to believe that there are no factors which may force a change in the trend as evidenced, it is possible to extend the long-time trend for a short period into the future as an estimation of the average level of the future activity.

The chart in Figure 2–1 portrays the measurements which may be made of business activity. The fluctuations of the actual data about the curve depicting cyclical movement are due to seasonal factors or irregularities which may occur for various reasons.

The trend depicted is positive over a ten-year period. Barring any forces to the contrary, it may be possible to consider that an extension of the trend line as shown on Figure 2–1 may be a valid assumption of the average level of future activity. The business is still concerned with evaluation of the level of this future activity in terms of the extent of its fluctuations about the trend line.

Basic Economic Indicators

There are several measuring sticks which have been devised or established as being significant in the measurement and understanding of the current and prospective levels of economic activity. Although no particular data can be singled out as being uniquely pertinent to a firm's planned activities, there are many basic economic indicators which do assist in the problem of business forecasting. Some of the more important uses for these indicators are: (1) measures of the economic status of the economy, of a geographic region, of an industry, or of a company; (2) guides for the initiation of government or business activity; and (3) the basis for forecasting. The nature and use of several indicators are discussed below.

Wholesale Price Index. This index, prepared by the U.S. Bureau of Labor Statistics, measures the average rate and direction of movements in commodity prices at primary market levels. These prices represent all sales of goods by or to manufacturers or producers or those in effect on organized commodity exchanges. These are not the prices charged by wholesalers, in spite of the title. This economic indicator is used to measure the economic health of the nation in so far as price levels of commodities are indicative of healthy trading activity. The index is also used for comparison with series of individual business data. A businessman may check up on his prices for materials and the extent to which their relative variations conform to those of the wholesale price index.

Consumers' Price Index. This index, also of the Bureau of Labor Statistics, is a measure of the changes in prices for goods and services purchased by wage earners and their families. It serves to measure the purchasing power of the dollar, and has served as a basis for wage-rate escalator clauses wherein payments to workers were varied in accordance to the direction and extent of movement of the consumer price index. This index, when used in conjunction with others, becomes useful in showing what influence the continued restriction or increase in purchasing power may have upon the consumption of specific goods and services. Since it is known that the consumer will allocate his purchasing power first to the area of necessity spending, the businessman who seeks profits in the area of goods and services which are not classified as necessities must recognize the importance of the variations which occur in purchasing power as a result of price changes. Such variations will serve either to release purchasing power or restrict it.

Industrial Production Index. This index, published monthly by the Federal Reserve Board, is a measurement of the changes in the physical output of factories and mines. Its major use is as an indicator of the economy's output. It answers most closely the questions, "Is production increasing or decreasing?" and "In which industries are major increases or decreases occurring?" The index is presented for the two basic categories of mining and manufacturing with the manufacturing category then broken down into those of durable and nondurable goods. The indices are reported for several major manufacturing groups and mining groups. This breakdown allows for specific use of the data in that a firm may compare its position and trend with that of its comparative industrial or mining group. In addition, the indicators of activity in the durable and nondurable areas become a basis for administrative decisions.

National Income and Product. The estimates of Gross National Income and Gross National Product represent a summary of the receipts and expenditures of all governments, businesses, and individuals in the economy. These estimates are the results of rather complicated procedures, and their major value lies in their use as indicators of the income from current national output. In so far as the estimates of income —its amounts, sources, and means of disposal—are realistic, then such components are valuable in the appraisal of the well-being of a specific sector of the economy. Specifically, the knowledge of whether the share of income had by employee groups is rising or falling, or is showing tendencies in either direction, is of specific concern to those businessmen who find a market for their products among these employees. The tendency or indication of change for that share of income which represents business's share or profits is the type of information which is vitally important to the businessman who sells to industry.

Average Work Week in Manufacturing. Variation in the average work week may be precedent to a lowering or increase in the tempo of business activity. Since the income of the nation is spent significantly for manufactured products, it necessarily follows that in the anticipation of a reduction in the sales levels of manufactured products there will be first a reduction in the working hours or employment level of the industries involved. In such cases the manufacturer may be concerned with the avoidance of excessive inventory accumulations, and in that event the average work week will be reduced. On the other hand, in anticipation of improving sales, the firm will seek additional output to meet the need, and therefore the average work week should increase. This variation in work week should not be considered valuable in itself, for as it is with all indicators of economic activity, any variation in one is an expression of an effect for which one should seek the causes. Variation in work week, therefore, occurs not only because of restriction or expansion in desired production levels, but also because of such a factor as increased efficiency in production.

Business Failures. The number of business failures is a sensitive indicator of business health. This series is used as a barometer of general business recovery and decline. The record of failures by industry groups and by geographical regions is useful to the businessman who is contemplating a business venture.

Residential Building Activity. Building activity normally has such wide influence that its trend will always have much significance. The greater this activity, the greater the demand for the crafts and materials of the construction industry and its suppliers. The erection of dwelling units creates demand for appliances, power tools, and other products which are needed in the home. In general, building activity in terms of its ups and downs leads the general business cycle.

The Timing of Statistical Indicators

For decades there has been continuing research effort to uncover the magical business data which have significant forecasting value. Business management fully recognizes the importance of planning as a means of enhancing if not ensuring the profitability of operations. The increasing use of professional economists as members of the managerial team is proof of the great significance which business attaches to the understanding and interpretation of economic evidence. Among the many series of statistical data which are recorded and available, several have been singled out as regularly leading or following the turns which occur in business activity. These data have shown themselves to be sensitive to general economic conditions and show signs of change which precede or follow the general change in business activity. A big problem which confronts those who seek to use such indicators as forecasting devices is that of determining which of the variations that do occur are really indicative of a pending turn of general economic activity and which are merely the meanderings of the series itself. Success, therefore, depends largely upon the ability of management to analyze existing conditions and to evaluate their meaning in terms of the particular business firm.

In the attempt to define more precisely the relationship between specific statistical series and general economic conditions, time relationships have been explored in order to establish the lead and the lag characteristics of specific economic indicators. This work has been carried out in the hopes of developing a means of more adequately or more accurately "calling the turns" of business. In this pursuit several series of data have been classified in terms of the average timing of their turns relative to the general business cycle. Some series turn before the general business cycle and are called "leaders." Others turn after the general business cycle and are called "laggers."

Summary of Forecasting

The art of forecasting or anticipation of the future may differ as to the degree of anticipation and as to its certainty. The businessman may be sometimes concerned with tomorrow's prices and conditions, or his task may be to foretell the course of activity in general during the next year or five years or more. In one case the only indication necessary may be that the trend will be up or down or good or bad for a particular venture. On another occasion it may be essential to forecast much more precisely in order that specific committals may be made. Often, if the businessman knows what current conditions are, he knows enough. At any given time, the extent of misinformation of the current situation may be so extensive that the person who recognizes the truth of existing conditions has for all practical purposes made a forecast. For certain, under such prevailing conditions he would know the truth in advance of others. A clear understanding of the present is a prerequisite to the making of day-to-day decisions and to a clearer look-see into the future, for sound forecasting must involve an accurate analysis of existing conditions and their causes as a basis for interpretation of the trends which may therefore logically be anticipated. The desirable end of the forecasting attempt is to provide management with the knowledge which will allow it to compete most favorably for the market which exists for the product or service offered. At best, in the first stages of forecasting of general economic activity, management may be assured only of the existence of conditions favorable to its line of business or to the economy in general. There yet remain other avenues for investigation in order to define more precisely, if possible, the future environment and potential for the particular firm.

MARKET MEASUREMENT

The measurement of any market is the attempt to determine the total demand for a product or service which will exist in some future period. The technique of business forecasting converges upon this single focus. All of the measurements and attempts to read the economic indications are steppingstones to the final evaluation of demand potential. Without demand for the products and services of industry, expansion is certainly not warranted and contraction is inevitable.

The need for a measurement of market demand may exist in order to justify the production of a contemplated article or to establish a production goal which will not lead to oversupply or deficiency in satisfying the demand situation. In either case commitments for investments and operating plans must be made on the basis of demand estimates.

The question of total demand must first be answered, but also it is necessary that this total demand be analyzed in terms of what portion will be had by a specific company. To further complicate the analysis it may be necessary to define demand in terms of geographic areas in order that the areas may be earmarked for special analysis or concerted action. Here again, the businessman will want to know what portion of the regional demand is to be his.

The approximate sales which have been made of a commodity or service may be determined with the aid of census data of the United States. These commodity sales data present information as to the extent of sales of commodities according to their nature, the kind of business making the sales, or geographic area of the sale. On the basis of such reported data it may be possible to estimate future demand. The amount of this demand which a particular firm may get for itself depends upon many factors. The question as to what amount may be quickly resolved by some rule-of-thumb method or by an involved statistical technique. If the businessman can determine his past percentage share of the total market for his product, he may assume that his share of the future market may be in the same relationship and accordingly set his production plans and sales campaign in the light of such an estimate. On the other hand, a new firm has no such basis of establishing its potential share of the market. In this case, it would be important for the firm to recognize not only the extent of the market and its geographic distribution but also the nature and extent of the competition in the market. Business population statistics are available which classify trade groups according to the items which they handle and their methods of operations. It is possible for manufacturers of electrical goods, for example, to determine what classes of wholesalers sell electrical goods, where such wholesalers are located, and how important such commodities are to their business. All this information is available from basic United States Census data. A new firm therefore may at least step into the business ring knowing what the opponent has to offer. An alternative after this evaluation is, of course, not to sign up for the match. In any event, with an indication of the strength or weaknesses of competition, the size of the competing firms, and the extent of the market, a potential entrepreneur may then plan his approach to the market. He will test and evaluate competition as best he can in order that he may be able to develop operational and product features which will best gain for him a market entry.

Potential and Effective Demand

The economist may define demand as the number of units of a good that would be purchased at each of various possible prices in a given market and during a given period of time. This definition assumes that money is available and would be used for these purchases, for we must recognize the difference between demand and desire. Desire we each have for many things. Without the necessary funds to make the purchase, our desire is ineffective. The businessman who recognizes that each housewife desires a device which will automatically keep her home free of dust has recognized an area of potential demand. This means little until and unless some advance is made in the direction of a satisfaction of this desire. If the desire is eventually satisfied, we then have the existence of real demand as expressed via the act of a purchase being made. The demand for the products of the electronic and home appliance industries is real in the sense that there are ready customers for the products, who at the right prices will purchase with available funds the goods which are offered by the industry. There does exist for each of these industries a potential demand for the products in those areas wherein electrical facilities may not yet be sufficiently developed or where income is not yet high enough to release purchasing power beyond the level of necessities. Potential demand may exist, for wherever there are homes there is potential demand for the products of the electronic and appliance industries. In the field of business goods the situation of effective and potential demand likewise is apparent. Electronic "brains" capable of extreme variation of data handling are certainly potentially applicable in many more areas of business than can currently afford to own or operate such devices. The myriad of office activities which are performed repetitively from day to day in countless offices across the nation is testimony to the existence of potential markets for electronic "brains." The continuing problem at this time is that of reducing the price of the product or service to such a level that a firm with limited need may be able to afford the service. In this manner potential demand may be converted into effective demand.

Today's business managers are constantly attuned to tomorrow. The area of potential demand is most assuredly an element of the nature of dynamic management. The concern of today's management is not confined to current quantitative limitations, but rather there is the attitude that an area holds a potential as yet untapped, and herein lies the market measurement and the target for development efforts.

Population and Demand

All business activity, in the final sense, depends upon the number of buyers available. Naturally, population and its trend and characteristics therefore may serve as a single basis on which a general forecast of future economic activity may be rendered. The increasing population of the United States is viewed in terms of its rate of increase in order that estimations of future levels may be made. In addition, the nature of the increase and the basic characteristics of population are subjected to continuing scrutiny in order that changes in composition may be recognized. These changes in composition of the population are just as important as the over-all increases or decreases which may occur.

The birth rate as a characteristic of population is significant in that it indicates the demand which may be made on the facilities of those industries which cater to infant needs. It also indicates the demand which will be made in a few years upon those who cater to juvenile needs in terms of clothing, toys, schooling. As the results of the birth rate of any particular year are extended into the future, we are able to project the future population of various age categories and thereby have gained an insight into the potential demand which is had within each group. The size of future labor forces, school and college enrollments, and changes in the population category which is classified as retired are each important indications to the businessman as he sees each group having its impact upon the economy in general and upon specific business activities.

Without also considering the need for purchasing power as part of the picture, there would seem to be an incompleteness in the importance of population as a single factor for evaluation. Potential demand only measures what may be, while we as businessmen are vitally concerned with effective demand, and this in turn cannot be ours unless purchasing power is available to the population. To clear this dilemma we must refer to that area of business forecasting which believes, or at least promotes, the theory that business activity is of a self-generating nature. This theory attempts to explain the activity of business in general along the lines that positive actions determine positive results. Applying this thought to the indications which population analysis gives, the businessman who finds that population tendencies will provide him a potentially great market will act to make the most of this potential market by converting it into effective demand for his products. In so doing, he must make use of labor, money, materials, and any factor which is currently available and suited to his purpose. This activity in itself is a bootstrap operation which promotes general well-being and maintains the momentum of the times as the potential market is being approached. Furthermore, a greater measure of success may result, because the initial approach was one which allowed no room for the consideration of a loss or nonexistence of the potential market. We saw a mirage upon the horizon and steered a course which would lead to it.

The Demand for Durable and Nondurable Goods

In any event, each businessman should attempt to determine the significance of his business unit as a part of the industrial group to which he belongs. As a part of this determination, he needs to understand how large his industry group is. In order to make some headway into the problem of demand analysis, he must also recognize the nature of the products and services which are offered by that particular industrial group.

If a firm is engaged in the mass production of vacuum tubes or automobiles or refrigerators, there will be little problem in identifying that firm with a specific industrial group; as a matter of fact, we can quite precisely enumerate the firms which comprise the group. In many cases, great numbers of smaller firms find their sole hope for survival rests upon the performance of a basic service or upon the manufacture and sale of a few basic or standard products which may be used by many differing industrial groups. These smaller operators also seek to identify themselves with particular industrial groups in order to determine who their friends, neighbors, and competitors are. In some cases this gives rise to the formation of trade associations among such firms. On the other hand, in every case, whether or not specific industrial association can be discerned, there is a basis on which the individual firm may be able to recognize its counterparts. This basis of recognition is in terms of the categories of product and is expressed in terms of whether the products fall into the classifications termed "durable" or "nondurable." These classifications are intended to denote the life span in usage which may be an attribute of the products under consideration. Durable goods are those which have extended life and therefore represent a long-term investment either by the business firm or by a consumer. Examples of durable goods in the business field would include machinery, transportation equipment, fixtures, and any of the many items which fall into the general category of equipment. Nondurable goods for the businessman would be those items which are basically classified as supplies for maintenance of plant or office or those categories of raw materials which are considered to be perishable and therefore are not customarily held for long periods of time. The consumer durable goods consist of the line of household appliances and automobiles and include lesser durables, such as clothing. The nondurables in the consumer group include again the perishable items, which fall principally into the food category.

The individual firm is therefore in a position to recognize itself as part of a specific industrial group and/or as part of a general group of business firms which cater to the market in terms of basic product attributes. The importance of this type of association is realized only if the nature of demand and demand activity for the durable and nondurable classifications is known.

The Deferrability of Demand

Depending upon whether the businessman is associated with a nondurable or a durable product line, he is able to identify the extent to which the demand for his product may be deferrable. The more durable the product, the longer its life in use. The more nearly the product approaches the luxury category, the greater the possibility that potential customers can make do with what they have, or can at will, decide to postpone purchasing. If the product is nondurable, and in addition is of the necessity category, consumers cannot postpone purchase for long. Such purchases must be made repetitively and with little if any variation possible in the quantity of purchase. There may be a switch to substitutes, such as more meat and less potatoes.

It is evident, therefore, that depending first upon the basic life in use, and second the extent to which the product is a necessity, we may be able to isolate the basic characteristics of the demand which exists for such a product.

The Demand for Deferrable Goods

For the businessman deferrable goods consist of such items as plant and equipment, each of which represents investment. Since the value of such investment lies in the efficiency with which it may be used over a long period of time, a businessman may hesitate to purchase unless the prospects of business activity are favorable. For the individual consumer, deferrable goods are those which would be considered luxury items, or those which fall into appliance categories. Residential construction is also a deferrable good.

The demand for such deferrable goods fluctuates violently over the course of the business cycle. If business is good or is expected to be good, the demand for these deferrable items increases, and at a much more rapid rate than does the demand for items which the customer cannot put off buying. If an unfavorable level of business activity is expected, the demand for such deferrable items is quickly reduced. In addition, the demand for the labor, materials, power, and all other factors involved in the production of such items is likewise subject to a reduction in demand.

Because of the great variation which may occur in the demand for

FIGURE 2–2

PATTERN OF CYCLICAL ACTIVITY—
DURABLE AND NONDURABLE GOODS

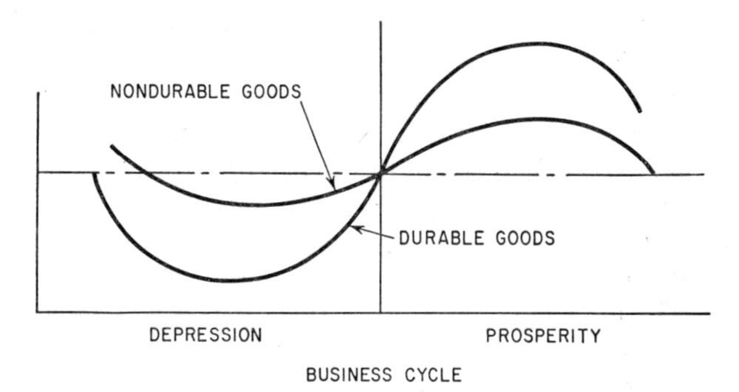

deferrable products, we find that at times the demand which exists cannot be satisfied by the facilities which are immediately available. On other occasions, the demand is inadequate to support the facilities which could be put to the task.

The Demand for Nondeferrable Goods

On the other extreme, we find that the very nature of the nondeferrable category forces constant purchasing upon the customer. The items which make up this category are, as we have indicated, necessities. As a result of this, the variations which can occur in the demand for nondeferrable items is, of course, limited. There is a limit to the extent that a man can pull in his belt and reduce his consumption of food regardless of the level of economic activity. There is a lesser restriction upon the reduction which may occur in the purchase of clothing, for this product is of a more durable, thus deferrable, nature. Nevertheless, because of the necessity of goods, there is a lesser degree of fluctuation which can and does occur in the cyclical activity of these consumer nondurable goods.

The Elasticity of Demand

As was mentioned above, demand involves the consideration of a price. In addition, we must recognize the relationship which exists between the number of units of a product which will be sold and the price at which the product is offered.

As the businessman seeks to anticipate the size of his market, he must measure it in terms of its elasticity, which is another way of indicating that at different price offerings on his part he may either gain or lose customers. The relationship between the number of units which may be sold and the price at which they are offered is not only a measurement of the demand characteristics but may also be an indication of the extent to which the producer should consider either increasing or restricting the volume of his output.

It is evident that if the prices of many household appliances were lowered sufficiently, many potential purchasers would be converted into effective purchasers, for the reduction in price would be sufficient to overcome the deferrability features of their demand. The question that is raised by the businessman is that of the extent of price reduction necessary to convert this potential demand into actual sales.

In the case of some products, a change in price either up or down may have little if any effect upon the demand. If the refiners of salt or sugar were today to announce that their prices per unit of product were either doubled or halved, although there would possibly be some demand change, for the most part consumers would alter but little their past habits of consumption of this product. If the manufacturer of a popular automobile were to cut the price of his product in halves, we could in this case expect a significant change in the demand for his products. Whether this change would involve merely a shift of customers from some other brand to his or whether it would involve an increase in the number of cars demanded of the auto industry as a whole must be considered.

The businessman who is playing with the factor of price and attempting to measure potential changes and their effects must always keep in mind that greater sales at a lower price do not necessarily result in greater profits. The concern with the concept of demand elasticity revolves about the extent to which a variation in price will affect demand and thereby have its final influence upon the income of the firm. If the number of firms in the industry is limited and the potential market is great, it is possible that a higher rather than a lower price offer will provide management with better income levels. The opposite may also prevail, for there is never the assurance to the businessman that the buyer must make a particular purchase.

SUMMARY

Although historical evidence is in plentiful supply and allows the businessman to view the meandering of economic activity, there is no pattern which can be so diagnosed and whose elements can be so stated as to establish the causes of these same meanderings. The constant search continues to discover a means whereby better insight into the economic future may be had. Any insight is not necessarily better than none, but being handicapped with ignorance as we are, we can best approach the measurement of the future armed with what we have observed of the past and fortified by our ability to fit together the pieces of the puzzle. Many statistical tools and techniques have been devised which assist at least in understanding what has happened if not also in anticipating what might happen if certain conditions were not variable. It is these variable factors which continually concern the businessman and which prove him a good guesser or an unfortunate loser.

As the individual entrepreneur reaches out to feel the pulse of his market area, he is much concerned with the company he keeps both from the point of view of competition and that of product characteristics. The very nature of the industry of which he is a part may dictate that he conform to certain patterns of economic activity; it may also give him cues as to what he may expect of business fluctuations because he is a member of a particular group.

His product characteristics also determine to a great extent the nature of activity which he may experience. If the product is durable, he has slow replacement sales. If the product is nondurable, his replacement sales may be daily. Depending again on these two extremes of product classifications, he may find that his fluctuations in business activity may be more or less severe depending upon the phase of the business cycle.

An inherent element of the product is its feature of demand elasticity. The businessman is certainly concerned with the increase in sales that may come about with a decrease in price. Such knowledge, if measurable, will allow him to consider levels of operations as being either desirable or nondesirable. This depends upon the income to the firm which results from price and related demand variations.

The process of anticipating the future for business in general, and finally for the firm in particular, is beset with an array of variables and intangibles. Managements of today can exist only by setting their sights upon tomorrow. It is the future which holds the profits of the firm and the measure of its success. Today's leaders in industry recognize continually the importance of tomorrow and base the decision of today upon future effects. If the future holds promise, the management is then justified in applying itself to the details which will eventually wring the measure of success from the business environment.

QUESTIONS

1. The businessman is confronted with two tasks as he attempts to portray the future. What are these two tasks?

2. Management is involved in making decisions in matters which pertain to the future or to the immediate situation. What is the difference in the nature of such decisions?

3. What are some positive and negative aspects of business life?
4. Why must the businessman of today be concerned with economic activity on a national rather than a local basis?
5. In general, there are three patterns of business activity with which the businessman should be acquainted. What are these three patterns?
6. What is seasonal variation?
7. What problems may arise because of seasonal variations?
8. What is the nature of a cyclical swing?
9. What is secular trend?
10. What is an economic indicator? What are its uses?
11. What are leaders and laggers? How may they be used?
12. What is market measurement?
13. How may the United States census assist the potential entrepreneur?
14. What difference is there between potential and effective demand?
15. Why is population the most important consideration when viewing future economic activity?
16. In what way(s) do durable and nondurable goods differ?
17. What is demand deferrability? How important is this to the producer of durable goods? Of nondurable goods?
18. What is elasticity of demand?
19. How may price variations influence the volume of sales? The amount of sales income? The amount of profits?

CHAPTER 3

Basic Product Considerations

Inasmuch as all business activity involves the making and/or selling of a particular product or service, it is safe to say that the basic problems of business management stem initially from the product or service involved. In the discussions that follow when reference is made to a "product" or "good," it is intended that the discussion apply to a service as well. The exact nature of management's problems and their solution cannot be determined until a businessman attempts to relate his particular product to a specific market and to his own organization. However, a good idea of the problems of a business venture may be obtained by relating the product in general terms to a market and the organization. Products are made and services rendered to satisfy different types of markets, each with its own peculiarities and problems. A study of the characteristics of these different markets may reveal many of the general problems that must be solved by business management. The following paragraphs will describe different types of products and their markets, and will point out certain problems and peculiarities associated with each.

BUSINESS AND CONSUMER GOODS

The output of business and industry can be described as being either business goods and services or consumer goods and services. Business goods are those used in producing other goods and services or in the operation of a business enterprise. Thus a punch press used in a metal fabricating plant or the cash register used at the local store should be classified as business goods. Commodities and services used by individuals and households for final consumption, such as a pair of shoes or a suit of clothes, are consumer goods. However, it is not the product itself that distinguishes it as being a business good or a consumer good, but rather the use that is made of the product. A drill press used in a machine shop is a business good because it is used to produce other goods. The same type of drill press is a consumer good when used in a basement hobby shop. We are interested in making this distinction between business goods and consumer goods primarily because of the differences in the markets that are served.

The Business Goods Market

The basic characteristics of the business goods market and those which distinguish it from the consumer goods market are discussed below. Since there are far fewer business organizations in this country than ultimate consumers, there are far fewer potential buyers of business goods than of consumer goods. In addition, the bulk of the sales of many business goods are made to a very small number of establishments. For example, if a particular business good is to be used solely in the manufacture of automobiles, it is conceivable that a supplier would have only five potential customers for his product: General Motors, Ford, Chrysler, American Motors, and Studebaker-Packard. If the businessman cannot sell his product to any one of these companies, he may have no market at all for it. The above illustration is perhaps an extreme one. The market for most business goods is not nearly so limited. There are hundreds of thousands, maybe millions, of potential customers for adding machines, typewriters, cash registers, and office supplies. However, the business goods market is quite limited when compared to the market for consumer goods. As a result of the limited number of customers in the business goods field, each one assumes greater importance to the vendor and the loss of a single customer could prove disastrous. Because of the limited nature of the business goods market, it is both difficult and costly to obtain new customers.

Most of the buyers of business goods are located in manufacturing centers since manufacturers are the major consumers of business goods. As a result, the seller of business goods generally can find his customers more easily than can one who sells consumer goods. It is also a much simpler task to locate sales offices and warehouse facilities and to direct sales efforts.

Another factor which distinguishes the business goods market is the size of the individual purchase. A single order placed by the buyer of business goods very often involves many thousands of dollars and may account for a large percentage of the vendor's annual sales volume. Because of the importance of each sales transaction, there is a tendency to deal directly with each customer rather than employ middlemen. This is in direct contrast to the consumer market where mass-distribution techniques employing middlemen are relied on heavily.

Because business goods are used in the production of additional goods and in the operation of a business enterprise, technical considerations assume great importance. Many times a sale of business goods depends upon the ability of a vendor to design and produce a product that will meet the specific requirements of the buyer. It is a source of pride to be able to advertise one's ability to engineer his products to the specific needs of the buyer. The technical aspect of the business goods market requires a high quality of sales personnel. In addition, an engineering staff must be employed and made available to assist salesmen in determining and satisfying customer requirements. The technical nature of the business goods field does not reduce competition; rather it creates many instances where large sums of money are invested in trying to obtain an order only to have it go to a competitor who has come up with a better solution to the customer's problem.

The purchaser of business goods generally buys on the basis of need or anticipated need and will buy no more or no less than requirements dictate. Initial cost, performance, obsolescence, depreciation, and maintenance costs are common considerations when purchasing a business good. Purchases are made on dollar-and-cents comparisons that will indicate management's best buy. Finally, the purchaser of business goods is, or should be, a skilled buyer who has the ability to make the best purchase consistent with the company's need and who is not swayed by the psychic value of product features.

The Consumer Goods Market

A potential market for consumer goods may exist wherever people are to be found, and the market for any particular good may extend from border to border. The decision to buy consumer goods is often based on want rather than need. Needs are rather specific, but human wants, or desires, are unlimited and vary from person to person and from one area to another. An item that sells poorly in Cleveland might have an excellent market in Savannah and vice versa. The manufacturer of consumer goods must produce goods in advance to satisfy wants he is not sure exist. The greatest variety and perhaps the most difficult marketing problems are found in the consumer goods field.

The user of consumer goods is not a skilled buyer and frequently cannot tell whether or not a wise purchase was made since he seldom makes an attempt to compare and evaluate the attributes of all competing brands. Consumer goods are frequently purchased on the basis of appearance, convenience, or what a neighbor has or has not purchased. The differences in the characteristics of the business and consumer goods markets can be brought into focus through the following illustration. When a person buys an automobile for family use, he is interested primarily in performance, appearance, and special features that make ownership of a particular brand more gratifying. Power assists, color combinations, horsepower, upholstery fabrics, and style are often more important to the consumer in deciding his purchase than initial cost, depreciation, and operating cost. A businessman who buys an automobile for business purposes, such as a taxi, is interested primarily in operating costs and depreciation and the provision of services for customers, and he displays little interest in the special features so appealing to the ultimate consumer.

The Demand for Goods

Since the object of all business activity is the satisfaction of human wants, it follows that the demand for business goods is determined by the demand for consumer goods. The output of the blast furnaces of Pittsburgh and the foundries of Detroit must be determined in the long run by the demand for consumer goods. As consumer wants change from one type of goods to another, the products of industry and the services rendered by business must also change to conform to this new demand. In a competitive economy the consumer is king.

The businessman who deals with consumer goods has an opportunity to create a demand for his products to a much greater degree than one who deals with business goods. Demand creation includes all efforts by a manufacturer, his distributors, and the retailers to stimulate a desire for goods with the ultimate objective of a profitable sale. Trade journals, magazines, newspapers, radio, television, billboards, and direct contact with the potential buyer afford opportunities to create demand. Through demand creation the consuming public or business is made to buy two of a product rather than one, to buy one product instead of another, to spend money rather than save it, or to buy from retailer A instead of retailer B. In the business goods field, efforts to create demand will many times fail, since there may be no justification for a purchase. Business buyers will not or should not make a purchase unless requirements, immediate or future, make it necessary. Demand creation in this field must be related closely to business needs.

The needs of a particular business establishment, as indicated above, are quite specific and measurable at any given time, and a rather scientific approach can be made to their solution. Not so with the ultimate consumer, for although his needs are specific, they are not completely measurable. Consumers need food, shelter, and clothing, but it is not known how much or what quality of each is demanded by a particular family.

Basically, the consumer has two problems associated with the spending of his income. The first is deciding the particular product or service that will be bought. For most consumers the broad general classes of goods to be purchased are determined by their limited income. However, there is considerable variation between consumers having like incomes in the proportion of their respective income spent for such things as food, clothing, and shelter. Some families through choice or need spend heavily on food and sacrifice on shelter and clothing, while others react in quite the opposite way. Some families feel that they must have a new automobile every other year; others buy a car with the intention of "running it into the ground." The consumer, because of the unlimited nature of his wants, will always face the problem of deciding which products to buy with his limited income. Secondly, after a decision has been made to spend income in the purchase of a particular commodity, there is the problem of deciding how to make the wisest purchase. Which brand of vacuum cleaner, for example, should be purchased and from what retailer?

Since the consumer is invariably faced with solving either or both of these problems and since the consumer is not a clever or skilled buyer, he is quite vulnerable to suggestions from others. There will be a constant struggle among businessmen to win the consumer's favor. Through demand-creation efforts the consumer is made to buy a new home and stop renting, to buy brand A instead of brand B, and to buy from one retailer instead of another. In the consumer goods field the limitations of human imagination are the only boundary to the area of demand creation.

Durable and Nondurable Goods

In addition to this classification of products, goods may, as we have seen in Chapter 2, be classified as either durable or nondurable, whether intended for the business goods or the consumer goods field. Again we are interested in making this distinction between types of goods because of the differences in the market to be served.

Durable goods are generally more costly than nondurables; and it is more than likely, especially in the consumer goods field, that their purchase will be financed. In many instances it is more difficult to stimulate the demand for durable goods. A person who buys a new refrigerator for his home today, or for his business, will not be in the market for another refrigerator for five or ten years despite the attempts of manufacturers and retailers to convince him that the newer models are vastly superior to the old. It is far easier to convince madame that she needs a new chapeau or frock even though she may have several of each in her wardrobe.

The demand for a good is affected significantly by the replacement factor for that good. "Replacement factor" refers to the speed with which products are replaced. If replacement came frequently, a relatively small group of customers could provide an adequate market for a businessman. The corner variety store prospers with a limited group of customers because they return to the store several times a week. An automobile dealer or the manufacturer of industrial equipment must cater to a much larger group of customers because a single purchase today may satisfy customer requirements for a long time to come.

Standard and Custom Goods

A final comparison of goods distinguishes them as being either standard or custom goods. Most business organizations deal with standard goods, goods manufactured with no particular customer in mind. The bulk of the production of automobiles, foods, clothing, appliances, and many other fields are standard goods. Custom goods result when a customer asks to have something made to his own specifications. Frequently custom goods are nothing but a modification of some standard good. We are interested in this distinction between standard and custom goods for two basic reasons—the nature of the market for each of these and the production problems associated with custom goods.

People ask for custom goods because standard goods do not meet their requirements. We care not whether these requirements be real or imaginary; the demand is present in either event. In the consumer goods field, custom goods are frequently made to satisfy a person's desire to be different, to be able to tell friends and associates, "I had this made to my own specifications." In the business goods field manufacturing or administrative processes often require something different for the effective performance of a task. Industry seldom buys goods just to be different. Custom goods are used in business if they will do a better job than standard goods.

In general, custom goods are more costly than similar standard goods because they are not produced and sold in volume. Many times custom goods must be made on a job-order basis with machines not specifically designed for the job. To illustrate, a person asked the superintendent of a job-order machine shop to make two special bolts for his stock car. The requirements for length, diameter, head size, and thread could not be matched by any available standard bolt. The cost of these two machine-shop-made bolts was $26, whereas similar standard bolts could be purchased for less than 50 cents a pair. The reason for this great difference in price may not be apparent. A specific machine setup had to be made to turn a rod to the proper diameter and to turn the threads. A die could not be used to make the threads because they were not standard size. The special heads had to be milled, which required another machine setup. Several hours were required to make these bolts because the machines used were not specifically designed for this type of work. Similarly a custom-tailored suit is much more costly than one made by mass-production methods.

The market for custom goods is, of course, very limited—limited to those who need or who can afford something different. In the business goods field it is often more desirable to use custom goods, while in the consumer goods field custom goods are to a great extent luxuries, and the demand for them depends on the existing level of prosperity. During periods of recession or depression the market for custom goods suffers in favor of the less expensive standard goods.

DIVERSIFICATION

Diversification involves the addition of new products, new models, sizes, qualities, or colors to a company's line of goods. The basic reason for following a policy of diversification is to add variety to a line of goods with the expectation that a larger and more profitable share of the market will result. Through diversification a businessman tries to meet the consumer's wants more satisfactorily than can his competitor. At the same time a better utilization of production and distribution facilities may result which can enhance the company's competitive position. Basically speaking, diversification is a plan for growth, but the manner through which a program of diversification will be effected depends upon the underlying reasons for adding to a company's line. In certain instances diversification will result from circumstances within the company, such as surplus funds or idle capacity, while in others the impetus may come from the market.

Reasons for Diversification

1. Consumer Demand for Variety. The underlying reason for diversification is the fact that consumers demand variety in the things that they buy. They want several color combinations to compare before they finally decide; they want an opportunity to be different from their neighbors without paying the extra cost of custom-made goods. The keener the competition for any type of good, the greater will be the efforts of businessmen to lure new customers through the offering of greater varieties.

2. Price Appeal. Diversification may be practiced to create price appeal. Many consumers buy to a price; that is, they decide to spend a particular amount for a commodity and seek out the merchant who can satisfy their price goal. A person may decide to spend $5 for a new hat, by choice or necessity, and will pay no more or no less despite the fact that a better buy is available at a higher or lower price. Because consumers may buy to a price, many manufacturers will make their products in a wide variety of sizes or models to satisfy the broad range of prices demanded by the consumer.

3. Consumer Quality Demands. Similarly, many people buy quality rather than price. Some consumers demand little quality in the things they buy, while others demand the best. As a result, manufacturers must offer a variety of products, each having different quality to satisfy the consumer's quality demands. Price and quality generally go hand-in-hand, but the distinction here is that certain people demand much or little quality with price a secondary factor.

4. New Market. Diversification may be caused by the emergence of a new market which a businessman wishes to exploit. Radio manufacturers diversify through the addition of television; tire manufacturers through adding foam-rubber mattresses; and so on. In each instance above there was a new area of demand or a new product. Existing business diversifies to satisfy this demand and at the same time to meet competition.

5. Market of Limited Nature. The limited nature of a market may force a business to diversify. All markets are limited, but to varying degrees. Some markets will exist indefinitely, while others are for a limited time only. There is, of course, an inherent danger in producing and/or selling a single product or a narrow line of products, since sales and success are then dependent on a narrow area of demand. Should the market for a single product disappear, the business must stop and start over again or pass out of existence. Additional products can provide a very desirable type of insurance against the hazards of constantly changing markets.

Diversification has as one of its goals a balanced line of products that will cover a wide area of demand. There may be, however, a danger in producing and selling too wide a range of products. When a company produces or sells a single product, techniques can be standardized and the greatest operating economies realized. As a line of products grows and requires constant change in the use of facilities, it is quite possible that manufacturing methods will revert to job-order production with its relatively high costs of operation. This is especially true of the small or medium-sized concern. How soon this takes place in any organization is determined by the extent of diversification and the facilities available to the company. In determining the proper degree of diversification, management must weigh the gains from this practice against the increased costs that may arise.

Goals of Diversification

Management usually seeks one or more of the following goals through a program of diversification:

1. Production Economies. These may be effected through better utilization of facilities. From time to time most manufacturers are faced with the problem of idle machinery and idle facilities. Retailers and distributors have similar problems. Idle time adds to the cost of doing business. When sales volume increases, unit costs of operation are forced downward. The addition of new products to a manufacturer's, distributor's, or retailer's line may, through more complete utilization of facilities, result in lower costs of operation and greater profits.

2. *Selling Economies.* More effective use of distribution and promotional facilities may result in selling economies. Many times the addition of new products to a line does not add to the cost of selling; it may be possible to sell and promote two or more products with a single effort. This is especially true when the additional products are related to the existing line. A well-known manufacturer of razors and blades operated for many years with this narrow line of products. Lately the company has added shaving cream to its line. Because these products are so closely related in their use, it is possible to promote and sell the three products with little additional effort beyond that required for the original two. It is conceivable that the addition of new products would decrease selling and promotion expense by creating a more attractive sales atmosphere. This is in keeping with the ultimate goal of diversification—increasing sales volume without a corresponding increase in the costs of doing business.

3. *Protection of a Market.* As consumer wants increase or change, new markets appear. The producer of a successful product may be forced to add new products to his line simply to protect what he has. The same is true of distributors and retailers. To illustrate, company A has the most popular coffee on the market. The same coffee prepared in different grinds is the company's sole product. Instant coffee becomes extremely popular. Company A is forced to develop an instant coffee simply to protect its product popularity. Frequently distributors and retailers may pressure a manufacturer to diversify by threatening to drop a limited line in favor of a competitor's broader line of products.

4. *Compensation for Seasonal Changes.* Most businessmen must face the problems associated with seasonal fluctuations in business activity. Seasonal influences are exerted on the production, consumption, and price of goods. They magnify the problem of making full use of production and distribution facilities and increase the risk associated with price changes. Experience will show, for example, that production or consumption of a particular product will be higher than average during certain months of the year and lower than average at other times. These changes in activity that recur each year at about the same time are called "seasonal fluctuations." They occur with great intensity in agriculture, ore mining, and the construction trades; and to a lesser degree in the consumption of food, cigarettes, and countless other items. Seasonal variations cause a disparity in the supply and demand relationships of a commodity, which causes a change in price. The greater the disparity, the greater the price change. Many businessmen suffer great losses because of price changes. Generally, no one businessman is powerful enough to

alter a seasonal pattern of business activity; rather, he accepts it, analyzes it, and adjusts his business to coincide with the changes.

Fortunately for the businessman, seasonal fluctuations in activity can be measured and predicted with reasonable accuracy. Since this is possible, a businessman can commit himself to alternative uses for his facilities during off seasons. The seasonal problem is determined initially by the magnitude and duration of the seasonal change. If seasonal changes are great and for an extended period, an additional product or line of products may provide the solution to the problem of idle facilities. If the off season is of short duration, perhaps vacations can be taken at this time or maintenance work scheduled. Diversification appears to be the most widely used device to conquer the seasonal problem.

Increased Costs from Diversification

The more positive aspects of diversification discussed above clearly indicate that this is a means of protecting profits and competitive position. It is true, however, that the diversifying business must subsidize the development and marketing of a new product with the profits earned on its old ones, through additional investment, or through borrowing. Diversification, then, can impair as well as protect the status of a business because of the incurring of additional costs. The increased costs of diversification will vary from company to company depending on the extent of diversification and the facilities available. The following cost changes should be anticipated as a line of products grows:

1. A Larger Investment in Inventory. It is quite possible that a better utilization of raw-material inventory will result from diversification, but an increased investment in finished goods inventory is almost certain to result owing to the larger number of products carried. This is equally true of manufacturer, wholesaler, or retailer.

2. Increased Storage Costs. The additional inventory referred to above must be stored and will increase storage costs if additional space is required. When diversification allows for better utilization of storage facilities, savings in storage costs will result.

3. A More Elaborate Inventory Control System. A small inventory can be controlled adequately through rather simple techniques. As an inventory grows in size, the control problem is magnified. Because a larger inventory investment results from diversification, it is more important that accurate knowledge of inventory be maintained. An inventory control payroll can be substantial.

4. Increased Costs of Production. Diversification may result in using the same equipment and personnel to produce several products. The resulting shorter runs of production, setting up for new production, and training workers for new jobs can become a significant cost factor.

SIMPLIFICATION

Simplification refers to the elimination of items from a company's line of products; it is the antithesis of diversification. Manufacturers, wholesalers, and retailers alike may from time to time follow a policy of simplification. In order to satisfy varying wants of buyers or to meet the desires of consumers for something different, manufacturers, wholesalers, and retailers add to their line of products. When one businessman adds a product to his line, competition is likely to follow suit and extend the line. Studies often reveal that a large portion of sales is concentrated on a small number of items and that many items are seldom sold and are not required to satisfy the legitimate needs of the great bulk of buyers. Regardless, management should make frequent audits to determine whether the need for a broad line of products still exists. Accounting and inventory records should provide the information for evaluating this situation. Sales volume and costs of a particular item are not the only factors to consider in determining the desirability of carrying a product. Attention should be given to the fact that many times a large volume of sales of one product is dependent on the existence of certain slow-moving products.

Simplification begins with a careful analysis of existing products to determine the ones that might be eliminated to allow for greater production and/or selling economies and at the same time have the least undesirable effect on sales and profits. When management does decide to eliminate products from its line, a special effort should be made by the sales department to sell customers on the virtues of the remaining products. Actually, the sales approach that led to diversification must be reversed when simplification sets in. The gains through simplification are basically a reduction of the costs of diversification discussed above.

STANDARDIZATION

To standardize means to cause to conform to certain uniform specifications; standards give products or parts certain known characteristics. Standardization includes the basic principles of simplification; that is, a reduction of sizes, styles, and special features. However, it embodies much more. Standardization is applied to the size and form of manufactured products. There are standards of excellence or quality, engineering and production standards, standard materials, standard methods and performances, standard tools, standard conditions, and many other types of standards. Standardization is an attempt toward uniformity in terms of these features so that the buyer of a product or the user of tools, materials, etc., will be able to evaluate them prior to their purchase or use. Through standardization a manufacturer may be able to reduce the number of parts required in his assembly and his investment in tools and inventory. Through standardization it may be possible for a manufacturer to carry on diverse production without encountering the increased costs of diversification mentioned above. To the extent that new products are developed largely through a different combination of standard parts, production economies of simplification can be largely retained.

Sources of Standards

The term "standard," or "standardization," can have a very broad meaning as indicated above. Some standards have world-wide application, while others may be limited to a particular department of a business organization. Some standards are adhered to voluntarily by businessmen while others are enforced through law. An indication of some of the different sources of standards is presented below.

1. Government Standards. Government agencies become involved with standards in many different ways. Most common of government standards is our uniform system of weights and measures. In addition there is the National Bureau of Standards of the Department of Commerce. For many years this agency has cooperated with industry in an attempt to reduce the types and sizes of many products and to set uniform quality standards for certain basic commodities.

2. Professional Groups and Trade Associations. Many of the standards used today have been adopted by professional groups and trade associations whose membership comes largely from business and industry. Standards are set by these groups, and industry formally or informally adopts them. Some of our more common standards developed by these groups include hardness tests for metals (Rockwell test), viscosity tests for lubricants (Society of Automotive Engineers), the Boiler Code of the American Society of Mechanical Engineers, thread sizes, measures of surface finishes, and countless other characteristics needed by business, industry, and the public to gage the identity of parts, materials, or products.

3. Company Standards. Standards are set within a company to facilitate production and reduce production costs. For example, speedometers, wheels, motors, and body parts used in the manufacture of a particular automobile are largely interchangeable. Likewise, products may be designed to be used in several different products. The same type of generator can be used on certain models of both Ford and Mercury automobiles.

4. Commercial Standards. The adoption by manufacturers of uniform quality, quantity, performance, or some other product characteristic leads to the establishment of a commercial standard. The existence of a commercial standard implies that a particular product, regardless of manufacture, will embody the same attributes. Automobile tires, electric-light bulbs, pipe, pipe fittings, and many others products are made by different manufacturers, and yet each product conforms to the established standard and is, therefore, greatly interchangeable.

Advantages from Standardization

Regardless of the nature of standardization—whether it pertains to size, quality, or quantity—there are certain inherent advantages that accrue to business and society.

1. Avoidance of Misunderstanding. Standardization removes the possibility for misunderstanding between the maker and the user of a product. When a buyer asks for a brass bushing having a 32 finish, he is sure to get what he wants, because this degree of smoothness has been specifically defined in smoothness standards adopted throughout industry.

2. Simplifying of the Buying Function. When quality, quantity, and size of a particular good are known, price and terms of sale are the only remaining factors to consider in consummating the sale. Since standardization implies a reduction in the variety of goods offered by vendors, the buying function is thereby simplified.

3. Creation of a Favorable Buyer Attitude. Standardization creates a favorable buyer attitude toward a product by enabling the satisfied user to buy the product again and with the assurance that it has not changed. However, if the standards are unacceptable to the consumer, it will hinder repeat sales of the item.

4. Encouragement of Significant Differences. Standardization may be an indirect advantage in that it forces manufacturers to develop significant differences in their products. The manufacturer of a product using standard parts can hardly claim a product superior to that of his competitor who uses the same parts. Parts of automobiles such as tires, batteries, glass, body shells, and many others may be the same from one brand of automobile to another. The significant differences in the product are where they count most in such major components as the power plant, chassis, and so on.

Limitations to Standardization

Just as there is a limit to the extent to which a manufacturer should simplify his line of goods, there is also a limit to the amount of standardization that should take place. As mentioned above, each businessman seeks a satisfactory competitive position by making his company different from other business in his field. Standardization should be avoided when it begins to interfere with the basic selling features of a product. There is mutual agreement as to the necessity for and the value of standardization of articles of strict utility such as a plow, a hoe, an automobile tire, or a railroad train; but there are certain products that preclude standardization. Few people would be satisfied with a standard house, standard furniture, or a standard picture over the fireplace. Consumers are willing to accept standardization in some things that they buy but not in others. The extent of standardization should be decided through a formal market study.

MANAGEMENT IMPLICATIONS

The problems of business management are determined to a great extent by the variety of goods or services offered. The greater the variety of goods and services offered, the greater and more complex the problems; this is generally true. Some businesses are designed to produce and sell a single product that is used in a single market; others deal with a wide variety of goods and services for both home and business consumption. A machine shop may be set up to machine a specific type of casting for a single customer; others operate on a job-order basis and perform a wide variety of operations on many types of material for many different customers. Likewise, a retailer in one instance sells only men's dress shoes in a limited price range, while another carries footwear for the entire family and for every purpose.

In a business organization that handles a single product or a closely related line of products, management may specialize and become more

FIGURE 3–1

NONSPECIALIZED MANAGERIAL ORGANIZATION

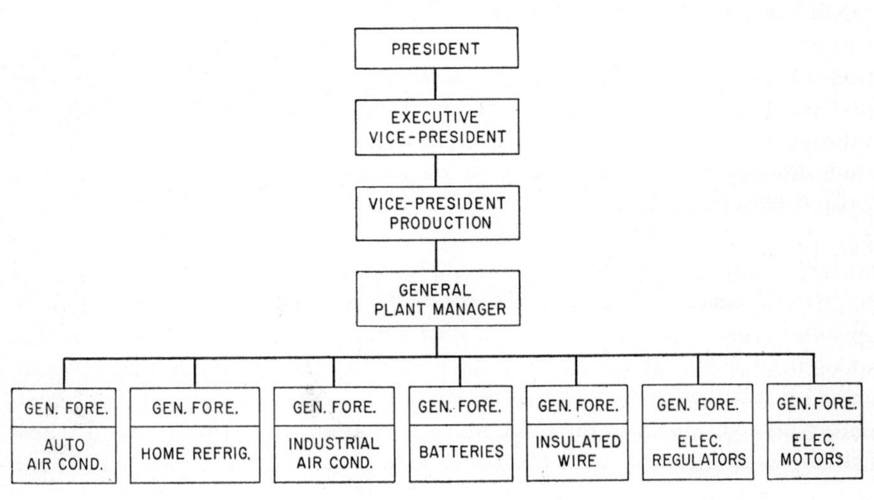

effective. As the variety of activity under a single management team broadens, the management group must also broaden its range of abilities to cope with new situations as they arise. Eventually, however, this management team may find itself dabbling in many unrelated fields too varied for it to deal with effectively. One of the most difficult decisions faced by business management is determining when and how to diversify. It is a particularly difficult decision because it centers largely on a management's appraisal of itself; specifically, on whether it has the ability to manage any more than it already has to manage.

Once it has been ascertained that management is making the most of its existing operation, a specific plan for managing a more diversified business must be developed. To avoid the spreading of management

FIGURE 3–2

SPECIALIZED MANAGERIAL ORGANIZATION

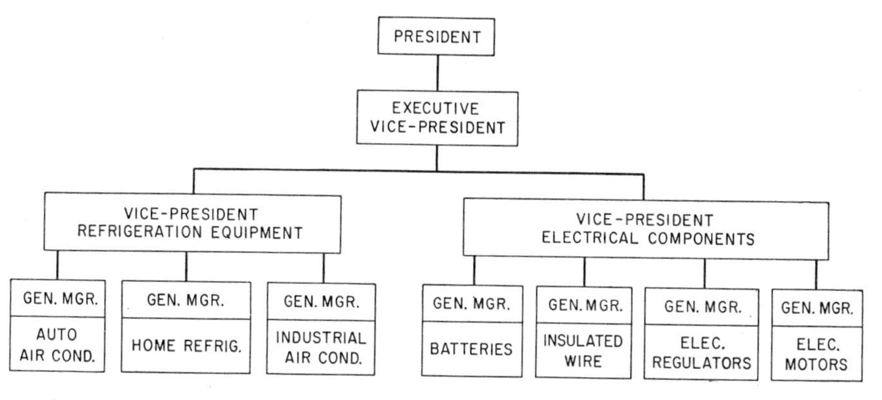

talents over too broad an area, a plan embodying the aspects of running the specialized business may be adopted. Figure 3–1 illustrates a situation where upper management is called upon to cover a broad area of activity. Both the vice-president and the general plant management must supervise production of diverse areas. Their problems will magnify as each division adds to its line of products.

In Figure 3–2 management is more specialized. The production vice-president for refrigeration can forget about batteries and electric motors and concentrate on problems related to the field of refrigeration. He builds a management team around him which includes specialists in the specific aspects of refrigeration, such as industrial air conditioning. These specialists are far better able to make intelligent decisions in their respective areas than is a general plant manager. Many of our larger business concerns are organized to gain the advantage of the simplified management that may result from specialization. The vast General Motors Corporation is broken down into several operating divisions, each producing a line of related products and each having its own separate management responsible, of course, to top company management. Thus the Frigidaire Division produces refrigerators and allied refrigerating equipment, and the Delco Division produces mainly electrical products. When these divisions add new products to their line, a new management structure is developed to supervise production and distribution. The management of these divisions can become specialized since all problems pertain to products having similar characteristics. With this type of organization there is less danger that management will become top-heavy —management can grow with the business.

The principle of specialized management illustrated above is not confined to the field of manufacturing; it is also widely applied in retailing and other phases of distribution. Years ago in this country the general store was popular—a retail establishment that carried a highly diversified line of goods. The owner of the general store bought, sold, priced, and displayed the entire line of merchandise; no attempt was made to specialize since the basic purpose of the store was to supply a wide variety of goods. By modern standards the general store was inefficient and, except in certain areas, it has virtually disappeared from the retail scene. Experience has shown that the retail function can be performed more effectively and efficiently through the use of specialized management. Today the specialty shop is a common type of retail establishment. This retailer devotes his energies to merchandising a rather narrow line of goods. The largest of our retailers, the department store, also uses specialized management by breaking its merchandising division into separate departments such as furniture, furs, appliances, men's clothing, and the like. Each department has its specially trained management whose responsibility is limited to a department. In addition, department stores employ specially trained buyers, advertising and display specialists, and many others who possess unique skills. As a result, the department store can effectively merchandise a highly diversified line of goods.

When an ever-changing variety of goods is produced or sold under a single management, it becomes difficult to standardize the task of managing. Management must exercise many more controls over its operations since new situations requiring management action continually arise. A businessman must be careful not to extend his limited managerial ability over too wide a range of production or distribution. If he does, something, somewhere along the line, is bound to suffer from the lack of adequate management. The list of organizations that have failed because they "bit off more than they could chew" is long, and it continues to grow despite the experiences and warnings of successful businessmen. A business organization should never try to include more products or production in its program than it can properly manage; a business should diversify only as rapidly as the management that directs it.

SUMMARY

The risks of business enterprise stem basically from the fact that no one knows what the future holds. If a businessman knew specifically what was to happen tomorrow, he could take the necessary steps to exploit the future or to protect himself from impending dangers. Such is not the case. However, because a businessman *is* engaged in a particular line of activity, it may be possible for him to determine the general nature of the problems that will arise. The problems that confront any business, manufacturing or distribution, must stem from the product involved in the operation. Basic product knowledge will provide part of the answer to the problems that arise. The balance of the answer will depend on the circumstances surrounding the specific problem.

The business goods market is different from the consumer goods market. The demand for business goods stems from need; for consumer goods, from need and want. Because of this, the demand for consumer goods can be stimulated much more than the demand for business goods. The market for durable goods is different in many respects from that for the nondurable. Custom goods involve many problems in production and selling not found in the standard goods field. If a businessman recognizes the distinguishing characteristics of the market for different types of goods, he can prepare to solve many of his problems before they arise. The major task of any businessman is to satisfy a market. The greater the number of market characteristics that are known, the easier it becomes to do this.

In their search for greater profits or greater prestige many business organizations move to a program of diversification. Whether or not a policy of diversification will result in greater profits rests on the wisdom of management in selecting a line of products and on the ability of management to recognize and solve the problems associated with an expanding business venture. Success for a business organization depends not on the product or line of products involved, but rather, on the quality of management which directs it.

QUESTIONS

1. Distinguish between a business good and a consumer good.
2. Point out the distinguishing features of each.
3. Why are custom goods generally more costly than standard goods?
4. Justify the statement that the problems of management stem from the product.

5. What is meant by demand creation? How is it accomplished?
6. How can the demand for business goods be stimulated?
7. Distinguish between a need and a want.
8. Why is the market for custom goods so limited?
9. What are the causes of diversification?
10. What are the goals of diversification?
11. What increased costs usually result from diversification?
12. How would you simplify a line of goods?
13. Distinguish between simplification and standardization.
14. How can a manufacturer save through standardization?
15. How does the consumer gain through standardization?
16. How does diversification increase the number and complexity of management's problems?
17. Define specialized management.

CHAPTER 4

Product Research

Few people appreciate the brand of courage displayed by a businessman each time he puts a new product or a new line of products on the market. Research, design, development, field testing, and tools for production can absorb hundreds of thousands of dollars or more before the first unit comes off the production line. All of this is done with no positive assurance of getting back the money invested in spite of the most careful advance market study. Until orders actually come in, the element of risk remains.

However, before substantial sums of money are invested in any new product, a preliminary market evaluation, as described in Chapter 2, can be made, which will indicate the general market characteristics and whether or not a potential market exists for the product. That there is a market for a particular product is not enough. We all know that there is a tremendous market for automobiles, television sets, vacuum cleaners, and thousands of other items; yet there is no proof that a particular brand of vacuum cleaner, for example, will be successful. Management must go much further than the preliminary market evaluation; it must determine in specific terms the design features of its products, the price, style, color, and the like which will be considered by the consumer as he plans his purchase. Product research then involves the study of new products and relating them to the consumer and, of course, the facilities of the organization.

The American public is impatient and demanding. Business in the past has provided the consumer with new and better products at an ever-increasing rate, and he has become accustomed to this luxury of plenty. In an economy such as ours where free enterprise flourishes, if established business does not continually improve its products and services, new business will be formed to take advantage of such consumer wants as have been disregarded. It is through product research and the resulting improvements in product design and operation that businesses prosper and grow. No attempt is being made to ignore or minimize the importance of good selling and sales promotion. It is understood that the best conceived products may fail because of inadequate sales and promotion efforts. Through product research the desires of the consumer may be more closely achieved in the products of industry. This in turn makes the task of selling easier and less costly.

Product research is a function that should be performed continuously, not simply when a new product is contemplated. Management must realize that there are several forces constantly at work attempting to undermine the continued success of any product. Competition, technological change, obsolescence, and changes in consumer desires are but a few of the forces that will ultimately destroy the value of any product. The iceman, the blacksmith, and the general storekeeper—so vital to our society a few decades ago—are today faint images of the past, victims of progress. The Auburn, the Graham, the Hupmobile, and the Reo —all popular motor cars in the thirties—have long since passed from the scene, unable to keep pace with the dynamic and demanding market. More than 2,500 makes of automobiles have been made in this country; yet less than two dozen remain. Why is it that a relatively small number of products prosper and so many fail? The answer is quite simple. Some products are geared to the specific wants of the consumer while others are not; some products are sold aggressively and intelligently while others, in many cases, must actually sell themselves.

Basically, a businessman has but three alternatives at his disposal to gain a profitable share of a market. First, he may make a better product than his competitor; secondly, he may sell his product more aggressively and intelligently than his competitor; and third, he may sell his product for less than his competitor. Product research, therefore, should be focused on one or a combination of these alternatives.

AREAS OF PRODUCT RESEARCH

The over-all purpose of product research is clear. However, a program of product research may be applied to one of several different areas of activity. The reader should note the direct relationship between product research and the earlier discussion of diversification and the later discussion of growth.

Product Improvement

Progressive management will constantly strive to improve its products through reviewing the costs of production, product uses, and consumer desires. Through a breakdown of production costs, management may be able to locate weaknesses or waste in its production plan. Material costs can often be reduced through the use of new and less expensive material substitutes; cheaper plastics are often used in place of metals without reducing the quality of the product and often improving its appearance. Labor costs may be reduced through improved methods of fabrication and assembly. Management may be able to improve its market position simply by improving production of its existing products. As time passes, there may be certain product features that should be abandoned and new ones added because the consumer has altered his use of the product. Any change should be aimed at making the product more acceptable to the consumer and, if possible, more profitable to the company. Obviously a product that is more useful will have greater consumer appeal and hence a greater market, unless the improvements add prohibitively to its price.

Development of New Products

As time passes by, many new materials and ideas come into being providing a basis for the development of new products. There is undoubtedly more risk involved in bringing a new product on the market than in simply modifying or improving an existing product. New products, however, have the potential for opening new markets and bringing greater profits than are obtainable simply through product improvement; as indicated above, the consumer is impatient and wants new things. Automobile transmissions were constantly improved until about 1940 when additional improvements in an old idea became hard to find. Attention was then devoted to a new product, the automatic transmission, which in turn will be continually improved. The new product gave automobile manufacturers a new selling point and a potentially larger market.

Management develops new products basically to cover any one of three situations. Because of seasonal variations in sales or a decline in the demand for a product, management develops new products to make better utilization of facilities. Management also seeks new products as a means of expanding the business and finally as a means of investing surplus funds. Often the growth of a firm is limited or restricted when it deals with a single product or a narrow line of products. Product research, then, is essential to growth and the maintenance of competitive position. Funds not needed for existing operations may be wasted unless diverted to new product development. Product research reaches into the vital phases of management activity.

Acquisition of New Products

Acquisition of new products from external sources is a fairly popular alternative to company development of products. There is always considerable risk and time involved in product research and development. As indicated above, there is no real assurance that new ideas and new products will be successful until they are sold. To reduce this risk and to save time, management may buy out an existing manufacturer or his products or obtain use of an existing patent right. Product research then may be applied to products not owned by the company. The Gillette Safety Razor Company has expanded through the acquisition of the Toni home permanent and the Paper Mate pen. In cases such as these, product research is aimed at the future possibilities of existing products and need not be so involved as in the development of a new product.

OBJECTIVES OF PRODUCT RESEARCH

The over-all objective of product research has been described above: to develop new or improved products that will enhance a company's competitive position. To achieve the over-all objective attention must be focused on two specific objectives—determining the basis for consumer acceptance and relating the product to the enterprise.

Determining the Basis for Consumer Acceptance

It is almost trite to say that if a product meets the needs of the consumer it will be more acceptable than one that does not; yet very often manufacturers will make no attempt to relate their products to consumer desires or even attempt to determine them. Before a product is developed, an investigation should be made to determine those features most frequently looked for by the consumer when buying a particular type of good, whether it be food, clothing, or household appliances. Through market analysis some hints, clues, and tentative directives may be found that will greatly enhance the chances of a successful operation.

At this point it should be remembered that there are many different types of products to be sold and different types of buyers to buy them. What satisfies one consumer may not satisfy another; what holds true for one product will not necessarily be true of others.

The characteristics of the business goods market are discussed above in Chapter 2 and indicate in general terms the basis for the business goods purchase. At this point we shall explore more fully the features looked for by the ultimate consumer as he plans his purchase. It will be noted that some of these apply to the purchase of business goods also.

Utility. As a businessman designs his products, one of the first requisites to be examined should be the utility, or usefulness, of the product under consideration. In other words, what is it good for? Why will people buy it? Why is it more useful than some other product? What modifications could be made to make it more useful and acceptable? The refrigerator that will both freeze and refrigerate is more useful than one that refrigerates only. The mixer that will prepare cake batter, juice oranges, and grind meat is more useful than a mechanized egg beater. The station wagon is more useful, in the eyes of thousands at least, than the conventional sedan. Utility features can be selling features, and the more selling features built into a product, the greater are the possibilities for consumer acceptance.

Convenience. Closely related to the feature of utility is the improved convenience of the product. Today's consumer does not like to be inconvenienced; he generally prefers to take the easiest way out of any situation even though it may be more costly. Flour manufacturers have developed a tremendous new market for their products through prepared mixes. Frozen foods are in many instances more convenient to use than fresh foods. The consumer generally acts favorably to convenience innovations.

Size. Size, shape, and weight features also have a direct bearing on the acceptability of a product. If an item is too large, it may be unwanted; if an item is too light or too heavy, the consumer may rebel and seek something more suitable to his needs; to wit—light, heavy, and regular-weight razors are now produced by a single manufacturer to satisfy more shavers and to keep large numbers of people from changing their brand of shaving implements. Size, shape, and weight features may have considerable bearing on product development itself. Smaller tubes and substitute transistors have enabled manufacturers to produce compact pocket and car radios. At General Electric Company where "Progress Is Our Most Important Product" a new line of electric motors has been developed that average 31 per cent smaller and 33⅓ per cent lighter than their predecessors; yet they equal the old design in performance. A ¼-hp motor, for example, has been reduced in weight from 69 lb in 1903 to 16 lb in 1955. Reductions in size and weight may increase the usability of a product and enhance its market potential.

Beauty and Style. At one time the consumer was willing to accept an ugly product provided it was useful and convenient to use. Today the consumer demands beauty and style in virtually every product purchased. The difference between success and failure of many goods depends upon this one feature. Common household items such as mops, brooms, stools, irons, are now designed with a modern flair. One should never assume that style and beauty are not needed in a product. Where it is difficult to beautify a product, such as cigarettes or detergents, package improvement may add to product appeal. The importance of package appeal can be illustrated by the change in the design of the Philip Morris cigarette package. Market research studies revealed that the drop in cigarette sales for the company was caused largely by the drab appearance of the package. The company expended $250,000 in cash plus a considerable amount of management effort in the design and styling of the new package. It is expected that sales will rise because of the improved appearance of the package.

Price. Price should be an important consideration in designing and making a product, yet we are certain that a moderate or low selling price alone will do little toward making a product successful. On one hand, a low selling price may be taken as an indication of low quality; while on the other, high price will drive some potential customers from the market. The problem is to create a price that will appeal to the consumer and yet safeguard the prestige of the product.

How much should be charged for a product? How much will consumers pay? Are there enough consumers to make a profitable sales volume? The price finally given a product is usually determined after consideration of several interrelated factors. Generally, though not always, a businessman wants a price high enough to cover his costs and allow for a profit. If this is the only factor involved in setting the price for a product, the accountant alone can determine the proper price. There is, of course, no assurance that the product will sell at this price.

Price must be related to product design just as product design must be related to the consumer. Products are often designed to appeal to specific classes of consumers; therefore the prices of such products should also be set so they will appeal to these customers. The producers of electric-light bulbs and sugar in this country, for example, do not set their prices to suit any one particular group of consumers, for they cater to virtually all classes of customers. A manufacturer of silverware or furniture or the retailer of men's clothing, however, would price his product at a level that will exclude certain people from his market and attract others. Competitors' prices for similar products must be considered, especially if consumers regard them as a standard of "fair" price. Traditional prices must also be considered. It seems that the most acceptable price for a razor blade or a package of gum is five cents. Few if any manufacturers have been able to convince consumers that a higher price is justified.

Another aspect of price that must be considered during the development process is the general price field of competition. The price of a product determines to a large degree the nature and extent of competition. The competition faced by the Ford Motor Company with its Continental automobile differs in many respects from that of its Ford automobiles. The Continental market is discriminating and not price conscious. Few people will buy this car because of trade-in allowances or cost of operation; rather, they will buy because of "pride of possession." Management must decide its price field of competition early in the planning process because of the effect of price field on other planning aspects. If management's decision is to make a high price, high quality product, it follows that—

1. The workers producing the product must possess a high degree of skill and maintain pride in their workmanship.

2. The machinery used in production will have less skill; the workers, more. Lower-priced products are often made with high-cost specialized automatic equipment that requires only the services of an unskilled operator. High-quality goods often are the result of skilled hands working with hand tools and general-purpose equipment. Custom shoe manufacturing illustrates this situation very well. Thus the investment in machinery, the quality of raw materials, and the caliber of the work force should be determined by the price field of competition.

3. The nature of the distribution system must be considered. Generally, a manufacturer should expect to have a high degree of control over the distribution of his product if it is of high quality. The impression that people have of a product is determined in part by the place where the product is sold, the nature of advertising and promotion, and the adherence to a rigid price policy. A high-quality product can easily lose its prestige if it is sold through a poor type of retailer, if retailers sell it on a price basis by cutting prices, and if questionable promotion is used in merchandising. Management must create a distribution system to guard the prestige of its product. If, on the other hand, the product is being made for a mass market, the distribution policy should be aimed at reaching as many people as possible, and management cannot be so selective in determining retail outlets and selling policies.

If management selects a price field of competition where a low-price, low-quality product is made and sold, then the results will be somewhat the opposite of the above considerations.

Durability. Durability and cost of operation are primary considerations in the purchase of business goods, as explained earlier, and are of concern to the ultimate consumer. An important consideration here is that a good can have too much durability as well as too little. People like change, yet they may be reluctant to change when a product "still has a few good years left." Generally, too, durability and cost of operation have a significant bearing on price. Through study, management must discover whether or not the consumer prefers the quality of durability or a lower price.

Relating the Product to the Enterprise

A program of product design and research can originate in an organization from any one of a series of forces. It may be management's policy to have a continuing program of design or redesign and development that will give its products a reputation for leadership. The goal may be the best improvement that can be found through the process of research within a limited budget and within a limited period of time, or management might follow a program whose purpose is to make changes only when dictated by the forces of competition. A policy of continued research is more likely to ensure continued success than any alternative plan.

Often a program of research and development evolves from the demands of the selling department for new and better products. This is quite natural and to a certain extent desirable, since the selling department has constant contact with the markets being served by the company's products. However, the initiative for product research should come from management and not from the sales department, because it is management's responsibility to keep abreast of market changes independent of any single department of the organization. In its quest for a highly diversified and well-rated line of products, the sales department might overlook an important aspect of research and development—cost. The production departments seek to develop the most efficient method for producing a product and, realizing that any change in design disrupts a going method of doing things, is reluctant to make any changes. The same condition exists when a new product is added to the company's line. Any change that requires alteration of a going order of relationships and necessitates the perfection of new manufacturing methods is disliked by production men. Since the sales department thrives through constant change and manufacturing divisions are interested in a production *status quo*, it falls on top management to determine the extent to which a company's line of products will be changed.

To illustrate the above situation, in the manufacture of automobiles the sales department would welcome drastic changes in design and operating features from year to year, or more often. Rapid changes in the design of a product stimulate consumers to buy new models. A great number of people buy new cars each year simply because they are new, not because they are needed. Changes in body and power-plant design often cost several millions of dollars. Modest changes involve a minimum of retooling, revision of assembly techniques, and lapses in production during the change-over period. Drastic changes from year to year would cause the price of automobiles to rise out of the reach of the bulk of purchasers since the cost of one change in design should be recaptured via price before another change is made.

The task of design, research, and development becomes a problem of determining what changes can be made in a product that will satisfy the sales department and the consumer and still not cause major disruptions in established production methods. The reason why automobiles change so little from year to year is not that Detroit has run out of ideas (automobile designs and features are set many months or years in advance of actual production); rather, only those changes are made that will not cause any major variation in the price of any automobile from year to year. Any major changes or innovations from year to year, such as an air-conditioning system for automobiles, are offered as optional equipment for those who wish to pay the increased cost of this change.

Research and development engineers are essentially creative individuals who commonly think in terms of engineering or mechanical aspects of a product. Because of this their work must constantly be attuned to several other basic considerations:

Consumer Demand. As indicated above, products are made to satisfy consumer desires and, therefore, should be designed with the consumer in mind.

The Cost Element. The cost of research and development of a product must be recovered through the sale of the product, else the profits from the sale of other products must be used to cover these costs. As is implied above, the longer a product is on the market, the greater are the possibilities that it will be replaced by some new and better competing product. Naturally, the more limited the market life of a product appears to be, the faster its development costs should be recovered. While the exact costs of research and development cannot be known until a normal level of production is reached, cost information can be gathered so that a reasonably accurate estimate can be made. A projected estimate of sales revenue should be made based on the market analysis that was made prior to starting the venture. This figure should be compared with the estimate of costs to determine whether or not it seems likely that the monies invested will be recovered.

Effect on Existing Lines. Changes in product design or the introduction of new products into a company's line should have the effect of bolstering the company's competitive position. Great care should be taken to make certain that any changes in products will not destroy or interfere with that phase of company operation upon which the success of the business rests. Many manufacturers through a careless evaluation of production costs, the market, and individual consumer desires, have added products or made changes that proved detrimental to the company. The manufacturers of the Pierce-Arrow automobile, once a leader in the quality-car market, developed a car of revolutionary design in the early 1930s. This car was expected to set a new standard and startle the market. This model, the Silver Arrow, was an automotive masterpiece but was far too extreme for the times. Mechanically and aerodynamically it perhaps bordered perfection, but it just was not the type of automobile that the consuming public wanted—it was not designed with the consumer in mind. Shortly after this episode the company ceased auto manufacturing entirely. The Chrysler Corporation and the Packard Motor Car Company both introduced new lines of cars in the 1930s; Chrysler introduced the Airflow series, and Packard a line of moderately priced cars. It was hoped that these new lines would strengthen the company's market position, but in both instances the lines were abandoned because of their detrimental effect on the company's regular line of cars and the company reputation in general. Much of the market lost twenty years or more ago by these companies has never been regained.

As a side light, the reader might wonder why such frequent reference is made to the automobile industry. There are several reasons for this: (1) the industry is large in scope and produces a product used by all; (2) the industry is conducive to many types of illustration; and (3) there perhaps is no single product of industry for which the consumer spends more money than automobiles.

Effect on Manufacturing Methods. Any program of research and development should be aimed first toward a better utilization of existing facilities; this program may well be a part of a program of diversification. Through the complete use of company facilities, costs can be lowered and the competitive position of the concern improved. When products are added to a line that require new production methods or facilities for a manufacturer or new distribution facilities for a retailer, the same economies may not result. While it is very often a desirable policy to add to facilities, it is more risky than the former policy and perhaps should not be explored until existing facilities are being employed most profitably.

Effect on Selling Methods. Similarly, if the new products added to the company's line can be sold through existing channels of distribution with existing personnel, selling economies may result and sales effort may be more productive. A manufacturer of safety razors and blades who adds shaving cream to his line of products, as indicated above, can achieve selling economies since both products are distributed through the same channels. If, on the other hand, this manufacturer had added typewriters to his line, the same selling economies probably would not be forthcoming since typewriters are sold through different channels of distribution.

SUMMARY—AREAS AND OBJECTIVES

The management of a business organization must many times feel like the fisherman who remarked "I know they're in there, but they just ain't bitin'." Surveys may indicate that there are fish in the pond, but it remains for the fisherman to determine when they will bite and the type of bait most likely to lure them from their hiding places. Studies may reveal that there is a market for a particular type of product, but unless the most careful pains are taken to design a product that meets specific consumer wants, the market potential may never be realized. A plan of product research and development can improve product design and operation, broaden markets through greater customer acceptance, enhance the prestige of the company, and provide a safeguard for future sales and profits.

LEGAL ASPECTS OF RESEARCH AND DEVELOPMENT

An important consideration in product development is the assurance of control over those features of operations which are fundamental to business success. Control may result from securing the legal position from which one has assurances that others may be prevented from usurping or even competing with the proposed projects of the enterprise. Patents, copyrights, and trade-marks, once acquired, may provide this assurance of maintained control.

The Constitution of the United States provides the Federal government with the sole control over patents and copyrights. A patent is a monopoly right granted to the patentee by the Federal government to control a new invention and its manufacture, use, and sale for a period of seventeen years from the date the patent is granted. Renewal of a patent, except for extensions to veterans, is possible only by special act of Congress. A copyright confers, upon registration with the Federal government, a monopoly control to the creator of artistic or literary works. Copyright protection is granted for a period of twenty-eight years and may be renewed for a like period. A trade-mark is a distinctive word, emblem, symbol, or device, or a combination of any of these, used to identify the manufacturer or the seller of goods. Trade-marks that have been used in interstate commerce may be registered in the Patent Office. The certificate of registration is given for twenty years and is renewable. Although the registration of a trade-mark does not confer ownership, it does serve as prima-facie evidence of ownership. The Federal patent and trade-mark laws are administered by the Patent Office of the United States Department of Commerce.

Patents

If business activity is founded upon a new and useful invention, it may be desirable to secure a patent to protect the enterprise from the commercial exploitation of the product by others. The extent of the protection which a patent affords depends initially upon the patent description. The problem of creating this description is twofold: first to create one which is not in conflict with any previous patent, and second, to create a description which is broad enough to prevent modified forms of the patented device from being entered upon the market by competitors.

Patent life may be extended beyond the original life of seventeen years by developing and patenting improvements to the original patent or by associating a trade-mark or other distinguishing feature with the product which will render any attempt at duplication more difficult. This is, of course, a function of product research and development. In this latter manner, the patentee is not really extending patent life but is instead preserving the market position of his product by impressing buyers with the product identification rather than the product itself. The invention becomes public property at the expiration of the patent and is subject to duplication by other manufacturers. However, the trade value of a distinctive feature remains the device of the original patentee and serves to maintain the market contact.

To be patentable an invention must have the following characteristics:

1. It must not have been in public use or sale in this country for more than two years prior to the filing of the application.
2. It must be useful.
3. It must be workable. A mere idea which has not been worked out is not patentable.

The matter of patents most certainly cannot be considered as belonging predominantly within the province of big business operations. Many small businessmen would undoubtedly lose their sole competitive advantage were it not for the exclusive rights conveyed to them as patentees of inventions upon which their businesses are based. This fact seems to be borne out by the activity of the smaller businessmen in denouncing attempts to propose legislation which was aimed at creating a compulsory licensing law. This law would force the patent-holder to license others to use his invention upon their payment of royalties as set by some designated office or officer.

The right to exclude others from making use of a patented invention serves to protect the risk capital necessary to promote the development of new things. It stimulates competitors in their search for something better. It provides a reward for the patentee which has a direct relationship to the value of his invention to the users.

Invention which serves as the foundation of business operations is a valuable property right and is entitled to protection. The safest procedure to ensure this protection is as follows:

1. Establish and preserve proper records of the invention.
2. Have a search made of the Patent Office records for prior patents and publications which are significant.
3. Perfect the invention and file application for a patent under the guidance of a competent patent attorney.

The applicant for a patent must expect to wait many months before his application is processed and acted upon. At the time of this writing the Patent Office had a backlog of approximately 220,000 applications that had not been processed.

Copyright

Copyrights are usually the basis for protection of the enterprise when the business is founded upon publications or motion pictures. The copyright gives to the owner certain exclusive rights to print, reprint, publish, copy, and sell the work. The strictness of the rule governing the copying of another's work is governed by the rule of "fair use." The exclusive right to sell copyrighted articles applies only to the original sale and in no way pertains to the resale of the article.

There is no search involved in the procedure for securing a copyright. If an application is in correct form and the material is of such nature that it can be copyrighted, the claim will be registered by the Copyright Office. The procedure is simple, and it is not necessary to employ legal talent in securing the registration of a copyright.

Trade-marks

Most firms seek to achieve uniqueness in their product. This individuality may come about in part through the identification features which are attached to the product. The trade-mark serves as the device which manufacturers or sellers attach to their goods to distinguish them from the goods of others. The trade-mark may often be a combination of a name plus a symbol or device of some sort. The purpose of the trade-mark is not only to establish a readily recognizable feature of the product but also to indicate the origin or nature of the goods.

The principle of prior use determines ownership of a trade-mark. The registration procedure serves to establish the time of first use of a particular mark, and therefore, in the event of controversy, the burden of proof of prior use rests on the party who has not registered. After a mark has been registered for five years, ownership by the registered holder shall be uncontestable. Federal registration of the trade-mark places the jurisdiction in the hands of the Federal courts which are more familiar with the nature of trade-mark cases than are the state courts.

Registration cannot be obtained for any mark which consists of scandalous or immoral material. No mark may be registered which consists of a flag or some symbol which may be used by a governing body in the United States or by some fraternal groups or institutions. Restrictions are also imposed upon the registration of a mark which because of resemblance to another may cause the public to become confused.

Both the Federal and state governments share in the power to provide for registration and protection of trade-marks. The Federal government is concerned with those marks which are used in interstate commerce, whereas the states have provided for registration of marks used in intrastate commerce. Some states will register labels; others will register slogans. There is considerable variation in the state laws that govern trade-marks.

SUMMARY—LEGAL ASPECTS

Congress, "to promote the progress of science and useful arts by securing for limited times to authors and inventors the exclusive right to their respective writings and discoveries," has created laws to protect individual property rights and to foster free enterprise.

As time passes by, it may become more difficult in many fields of activity to develop products and identifying marks that do not interfere with what others have done. Notwithstanding, a businessman must investigate those aspects of the law that restrict his activity and at the same time protect his new ideas or uniqueness. Failure to do this may result in suits for damages by those injured. In any event, a businessman stands to lose if he fails to investigate the law before launching a new product on the market.

QUESTIONS

1. What can be revealed through a preliminary market evaluation?
2. Why should product research be a continuous rather than an intermittent function?
3. To what different areas is product research applied? Illustrate what management hopes to accomplish by studying these areas.
4. Under what conditions would you as a businessman prefer to acquire an existing product in preference to developing a new product?
5. What are the two broad objectives of product research?
6. What types of goods can be made and sold with no regard to beauty and style?
7. What factors should be considered when establishing the price of a product?
8. What is a traditional price?
9. What is meant by relating the product to the market?
10. What is meant by relating the product to the enterprise?
11. Why should the initiative for product research come from top management?
12. How do production men react to product changes? Why?
13. What gains can be forthcoming from a program of product research?
14. How does a patent differ from a copyright?
15. Of what value is a trade-mark? How can a businessman obtain one?
16. What features must a product have to be patentable?
17. Why is it desirable to register a trade-mark?

CHAPTER 5

Planning the Nature and Extent of Production

Between the origin of the idea of a new product and its manufacture a vast amount of planning and preparation must take place. The general characteristics of the market to be served must be analyzed to ascertain that the venture is headed in the right direction. As indicated above, some markets, because of the elastic nature of demand, may lend themselves to expansion more than others. Some markets possess only a short-run demand potential, while others may have an indefinite life. Too, some markets are affected by seasonal fluctuations more than others.

It is within this setting that management formulates its ideas of product characteristics. Perhaps as a result of its general market analysis, management decides to produce a consumer good rather than a business good, a durable good rather than a nondurable, and a standard rather than a custom-type product; the market analysis shows that the best opportunity lies in this direction. Let us assume that the product decided upon is a lawn mower. A lawn mower would be selected perhaps because its sales follow a particular seasonal pattern, the pattern desired by management. Perhaps also the market for lawn mowers offers opportunities for growth, expansion, and continued sales consistent with management's over-all objectives. A lawn mower, then, more than any other product fits into management's general plans for a product. It is in this manner that management decides what product to make.

Now that management has decided to produce and sell a lawn mower, it must turn its attention to the specific design characteristics of the product. The problem of product design must be considered in the light of three important factors. The first relates to functional design. The lawn mower must be able to cut grass, it must be reasonably durable and easy to operate. Secondly, the product must have consumer appeal. That it will cut grass is not enough; it must incite consumer demand. It must look modern and neat and give the appearance of a fine piece of machinery, for, after all, it will be displayed before the critical eyes of neighbors and passers-by. The third aspect relates to cost. Perfection in the first two respects will prove meaningless if it cannot be achieved at reasonable cost. Excellence in design incorporates functional perfection, market appeal, and production costs which remain relatively low. Any compromise of these factors is made at the risk of injuring excellence in design.

Plans for production cannot be considered in specific terms until the design question has been answered. The above paragraphs are included in the discussion at this point as a review of the groundwork required prior to planning production methods. After production specifications have been agreed upon, management must turn its attention toward setting manufacturing specifications. What materials are to be used, metals or plastics, and what quality? What tolerances will be allowed in the dimensions of component parts and in the finished product? What degree of perfection does management want in the product? These and countless other manufacturing specifications constitute management's production goal and serve as a basis for planning the production process.

With the manufacturing specifications in mind, management can plan in detail for the methods of production it will use. What component parts are needed? How will they be made? Will component parts be made within the company or purchased from outside sources? How will the parts be assembled? In what sequence? Will mass-production techniques be employed or some alternative method? What controls will be exercised over quality? Over cost? Over individual worker output? Questions of this nature must be answered before the concrete plans for production are formulated.

PLANNING OBJECTIVES

Before management decides on a particular production method, it should give consideration to several basic planning objectives which are discussed below.

Time

Time may be of great importance in the introduction of a new product or a new model of a product. Seldom can a company take "its own sweet time" in planning production, for competition too may sense the need for a new product and rush to get the first entry into the market. Since many markets are seasonal in nature, production may have to be planned to coincide with the product's seasonal demand. A college textbook published in October will have a very limited market for that college year because such books are generally adopted by early summer. A retailer may buy his Christmas toys in August and his bathing supplies in January. If the supplier does not have these goods ready at the time purchases are normally made, the buyer may go elsewhere. This situation is true of a great number of consumer goods and perhaps to a lesser degree of business goods.

Cost

There can be a great variation in the costs of producing a good depending upon the methods used. Certain methods may produce small quantities at low cost yet become high-cost methods as volume increases. The reverse is also true. It may well be that the best production method will be high-cost at the outset only to become low-cost as sales and production volumes increase. Estimates of demand for a product can be converted into an estimate of income which, in turn, serves as a guide for production costs. Suppose an item is designed to sell at retail for $10. If the retailer needs a markup on retail of 40 per cent and the manufacturer wants to earn a profit of 10 per cent on his selling price while administrative and other nonproduction costs amount to 25 per cent of his selling price, the total cost of production is limited to $3.90. To illustrate:

$10.00	Retail price
4.00	Retailer's markup
6.00	Retailer's cost and manufacturer's selling price
.60	Manufacturer's profit
1.50	Administrative and nonproduction costs
3.90	Balance left for manufacturing costs

If, in this case, production is planned at 10,000 units per month, total production costs can be no more than $39,000. The task becomes one of dividing the $39,000 among labor costs, machine and facilities costs, and all other costs involved in the manufacturing process. If there isn't enough to go around under one set of conditions, more economical methods must be found. If more economical methods cannot be found, then the selling price must be raised unless economies can be found in administration or unless profit is sacrificed. It is well to note that increases in manufacturing costs tend to become magnified when reflected in the final retail price. If the cost of manufacture increased by 10 cents to $4 in the above illustration and the same relationships existed, as they very well might, the retail price would increase by 26 cents. The answer to economical production may lie in selecting production methods that involve higher total costs of operation yet produce so much more that unit costs are lowered. If the demand for the product in the above illustration should increase to allow for the production of 13,000 units at a total cost of $48,000, management would be better off on a unit-cost basis than it was when producing 10,000 units for $39,000. Certain methods of production are inherently more costly than others. The selection of appropriate production methods is essential to economical operations.

Use of Subcontractors

As management plans its production needs, it should consider the possibility of engaging qualified subcontractors. There may be existing business organizations that are better equipped to produce certain component parts or perform vitally needed services. Painting, anodizing, finishing, assembly, forging, machining, or even selling operations may be profitably sublet to outsiders. Through the use of subcontractors management can utilize a much wider variety of production and management skills; it can shorten its production cycle and reduce the over-all time required to get into production. Subcontracting has widespread application today and is used profitably by the largest as well as the smallest manufacturer. The great danger in subcontracting lies in engaging assistance from undependable or unqualified sources which may add to the production-cycle time and cause unnecessary expense to the businessman. Subcontractors should be specialists who, because of their equipment, facilities, and man power, can perform an operation most effectively. A more complete discussion of this topic is presented below under "To Buy or To Make."

Flexibility in Production

Since changes in product design are inevitable, management should plan its production methods with an eye to possible changes that may occur. Quite often the most efficient production method requires the use of specially designed, single-purpose equipment; that is, equipment that will perform one operation well but has no alternative use. As we have seen above, management may desire to diversify its line of products to make better use of facilities. Production methods which afford some flexibility make the problem of change easier and less costly. Somewhere between extreme specialization and its economies and complete flexibility and its high costs of operation there is a point of balance where production can be both reasonably economical and flexible. Management must find this point—the sooner, the better. It is well to remember at this point that flexibility in production can often be achieved through the use of subcontractors, as mentioned above.

Stabilizing Operations

In many fields of business activity it is not possible or feasible for management to stabilize its operations throughout the year. This is especially true of activity related to agriculture, where raw materials are available for a very short period of time. Here a year's production may be completed in a few weeks' time. In other fields, where style is a significant product feature, production may need to be deferred until the last minute to increase the possibilities of selecting the "right" style. On one hand, there is a series of forces dictating that production should fluctuate violently with the seasons. On the other hand, there is a growing concern for the worker who suffers from the irregular employment caused by irregular production levels. Today as in no other period in our history employers are expected to stabilize their production to provide steady employment. In several instances employers must guarantee earnings to employees for at least twenty-six weeks per year whether they work or not. It seems quite logical to assume that wherever possible employers in the future will be expected or forced to pay an annual wage to the bulk of the workers. We are certain that few employers are willing to pay workers for work not done; rather, it seems, production will be adjusted to conform to a rather even pattern throughout the year. Production facilities will be considered more in terms of normal rather than peak production requirements, for the peaks will be leveled off. Facilities must be flexible and workers more adaptable in many instances. Regardless, the time has come for management to consider production in terms of worker requirements as well as its own.

Satisfying Current Requirements

Perhaps it goes without saying that production methods and facilities should satisfy both current and long-run product goals. Through market analysis and product research it has been determined that a certain volume of a particular type of good could be sold. Production methods must be designed to build into each unit the features and the quality that the consumer desires. The immediate production goal must be achieved before long-run goals become a reality. It is good practice to set one's sights on the future but certainly not at the expense of destroying the present.

Growth Possibilities

Most businessmen hope that their product will appeal to an expanding market. Growth can be both desirable and necessary. Desirable because sales, profits, and prestige may increase with growth. Essential, for growth may be requisite to the maintenance of the company's competitive position. General Motors accounts for more than 50 per cent of the production of automobiles and about 76 per cent of all diesel locomotive production, yet the company continues to expand to satisfy an expanding market. When a manufacturer fails to grow as the demand for his products increases, he must expect vigorous competition from others seeking to reduce his competitive position. Since growth may be vital to continued success, production facilities should be designed to allow for greater levels of activity without sacrificing product quality and production costs.

PROCESS ANALYSIS

After the objectives of planning have been considered separately and in relation to one another, management is in a position to plan specifically for men, machines, and facilities. Just how will the product be made? To answer this question the product must be broken down into its component parts, and for each component part management must ask: What is the best method for making this part? What operations are required to make this part? What machines are best adapted for doing this work? In determining the best method for making a product, management should first conduct a study of the basic types of production processes. It may well be that management has no alternative when establishing production methods. In many instances there may be but one type of process suitable for the production of certain goods. The basic types of production processes are described below.

The Continuous Process

A continuous process involves an uninterrupted flow of production from raw material stage to the completion of the product. This production is accomplished by the continual movement of materials through a fixed series of operations. There is, customarily, no provision for the shutdown of the production line as is normally the case in the plant which sends its workers home at the five o'clock whistle. The continuous process usually involves round the clock operation or, at least, an uninterrupted time period once a batch of production has started. This feature may be a necessity for various reasons. The technical requirements of the process may involve such characteristics as chemical reactions which make it impossible to shut down production at will. Another reason may be that very high costs would be incurred if the process were shut down. These costs may arise because of the need to clear production lines and equipment before the process can be restarted, and during this down time there exists added cost in the form of lost production time and output.

Examples of the continuous type of process are sugar refining, blast-furnace operation, petroleum refining, and chemical production. It is evident that the processes listed above are each of such a nature that it involves a specific production procedure and thereby virtually commands that certain types of equipment be used and that this equipment be arranged in a rather rigidly defined pattern of layout. Once such processes are established, it becomes difficult to change them, and they are usually viewed as a long-run setup.

No continuous process can be considered as being in perpetual operation. Regardless of nature, every process at one time or another must be capable of shutdown if for no other reason than that of maintenance and repair of the productive facilities.

The nature of the manufacturing equipment employed in continuous-process work is very specialized. Since the product demands a fixed sequence and type of operation in order that it be correctly manufactured, the equipment used is usually specially adapted to the process and highly integrated. Thus the entire manufacturing cycle may be completely enclosed and automatically controlled by the equipment itself. The only human attention which may be necessary is that of inspection or check on the process as it functions.

The Repetitive Process

A repetitive process is typified by what is commonly referred to as the assembly line. In this case, production usually involves a series of operations, each of which is repetitively performed on successive units of the product. Each operation in the series adds, in some way, to completing the item being manufactured. A given product will, at a given time, be produced by traveling through a fixed series of work stations. However, this series of operations is variable to the extent that the same finished product could possibly be manufactured by other methods and machines and with a different sequence of operations if necessary. As a result, the manufacturing process is not so rigidly defined as may be the case with the continuous process.

The repetitive process is of greatest value when a large volume of production of a standardized product is required. If we consider an assembly line as an example of the repetitive process, we see the product always on the move from one operation to the next. This continuity of flow of production is one of the factors which enable the repetitive process to achieve its high volume of output at a relatively low cost. To the extent that production flow is maintained, the repetitive process resembles the continuous process. The difference between the two exists in the fact that the assembly line can, for the most part, respect the five o'clock whistle, and operations may be halted without worry over the uncompleted portion of the work which remains on the line. Production can start again on the following morning at the point where it left off the previous day.

The repetitive process makes best use of what is termed the single-purpose or special-purpose machine. Since a basic objective of the process is the achievement of a high volume of production, this can be best accomplished by using machines into which specific skills have been built and which have high output rates. The human element is of lesser importance in a situation such as this, for since the skill has been assigned to the machines, the operator becomes fundamentally a feeder of materials to the machine. A piece of equipment may be designed and constructed so as to do a particular operation repetitively and to do this with consistent accuracy, thereby eliminating the need for the worker to exercise excessive skill or judgment in terms of the particular operation.

The assembly of electrical appliances, the manufacture of automobiles, ready-to-wear garments, the manufacture of shoes, and the manufacture of many food products all involve, in varying degrees, some aspects of the repetitive process. Many items must be produced through the repetitive process described above to achieve the economies in production required in catering to a mass market.

The Intermittent Process

The intermittent process involves manufacture of a number of different products at the same time or over a period of time. Each product will follow its own peculiar production sequence. There may or may not be any relationship between products except that the nature of the production equipment used may be common to all products made. This is a stop-and-go type of production, wherein there is no maintained series of production stages through which each product must pass. In most cases production is initiated on receipt of an order from a customer. This order may call for any quantity of any one of many products which the firm may be capable of producing with the equipment at its disposal. Therefore, the process is not influenced by the need to achieve production of any one particular item.

The intermittent process is typified by the shop engaged in custom manufacture. In this case there is endless variety in the detail of operations which the shop may perform. It is usually uneconomical for such a shop to make its investment in equipment which has limited or specialized use in production. The typical custom shop would use equipment which would be for the most part general purpose in nature. This type of machine is capable of performing a variety of operations dependent upon the skill of the operator and the extent to which a variety of setups are possible with the machine.

The made-to-order or custom manufacturer may find that some of the items which he produces have sufficient demand to warrant his setting up a production method which will specialize in producing the particular item. Once this situation occurs, the shop no longer presents the picture of intermittent process. It now consists of both intermittent and repetitive processes. It is quite common to find this picture of mixed setup. The machine shop or cabinet making shop which produces to the order of the customer would usually involve a pattern of intermittent operations.

In conclusion, it appears that a businessman must conform to a particular type of process depending upon what he intends to produce. Within each of these basic processes there remains adequate opportunity for variation and improvement.

Operation-process Chart

The operation-process chart is a graphic device used to portray a process. It best serves to show the relationships which exist between the many operations or series of operations of which the process may consist. The chart, by means of special symbols which serve as a production shorthand, graphically presents the flow of materials or parts as they enter into the process and as they proceed through the various operations and inspections which make up the complete process.[1]

○ a large circle which denotes that an operation is being performed on the product.

□ a square which signifies the performance of an inspection function.

Such a chart, Figure 5–1, aids in quickly visualizing these relationships within the process. It presents an easily interpreted picture of operations, defines the nature and frequency of each type of occurrence, and also may include data defining time and location features involved. The operation-process chart may be made with due consideration of particular machines and facilities. It is an effective device which may assist in identifying the weaknesses and areas for improvement which exist in any proposed sequence of operations. Management, in the attempt to improve the process, raises the following questions regarding the operations and their relationships:

1. Can any steps be eliminated?
2. Can any steps be combined with another? Should any steps be divided? Should the sequence be changed?
3. Are there some steps which could be simplified?

A full knowledge of production and consumer requirements must be had before the process is modified to any extent. However, with these requirements in mind, management may discover, on raising the above questions concerning the process as it is currently set up, that there exist areas wherein beneficial changes could be made without sacrificing quality or quantity aspects of production.

The time and location features of the process are considered from the point of view of increasing production and decreasing cost. The time

[1] For a more detailed discussion of the process chart refer to Chap. 8, Layout Planning.

in process may be reduced in part as a result of changes which come about after analysis of the original process. Such changes may involve revision of the process and the adoption of different methods and equipment. An important consideration at this time is the effect that changes in one part of the process will have on others.

FIGURE 5–1

OPERATION PROCESS CHART

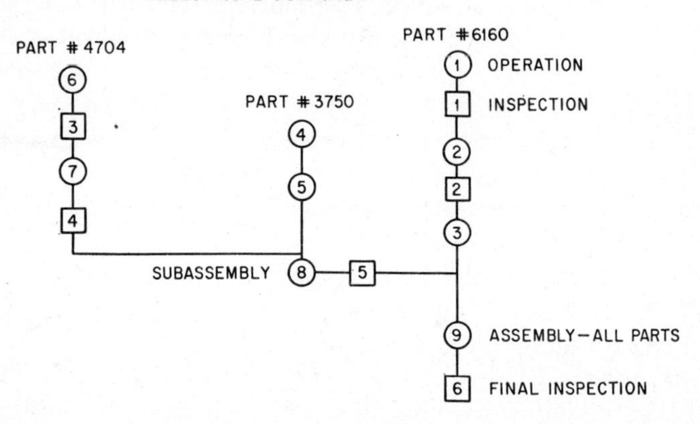

It is through continuous study and analysis of methods of production that management finally achieves a plan that is in harmony with over-all company objectives. Frequently the best methods cannot be ascertained until production actually begins. However, through preplanning the chances of establishing a poor method of production are greatly reduced.

REQUIREMENTS FOR PRODUCTION

Whatever the product to be manufactured, its specific requirements as to quality, quantity, and time of delivery must be ascertained. The required quality features will determine the nature of raw materials which must be used, the labor skills and the machine needs, and the specific types of inspection tests which the product must undergo during and upon completion of production. The quantity to be produced can be translated into hours of labor and machine time and volume of raw materials necessary.

Machine and Equipment Needs

The process of manufacture will delineate the nature and extent of man and machine skills which are needed to do a particular job. As indicated above, intermittent production implies that general-purpose equipment will be used, such as lathes, milling machines, band saws, and the like, that can be used in the production of a wide variety of products. Repetitive processes utilize specially designed equipment that, for example, might rough-bore, finish-bore, and hone the cylinders of an automobile engine. Based on the job to be done, management determines the machines needed and, considering planned volumes of production, decides on the number of machines to buy and the auxiliary equipment needed for effective production.

Material Needs

As the requirements for each product are analyzed, the features pertaining to types and amounts of needed raw materials must be stated as follows:

1. Specifications which state the physical characteristics and the inspection tests to which the materials must be subjected
2. Data as to quantities required
3. Time schedules of requirements

The above data must be prepared for all the material components which will be needed in production. Raw materials and parts which will be produced by the company or will be purchased from outside suppliers are considered. This may involve the question of "buy or make." The amounts of required materials are first checked as to sources and availability. Information as to when materials are needed for production is a prerequisite to the planning and storing of purchases. It is necessary that planned schedules of material usage be known by all parties concerned, and as a result, a coordinated material flow will occur.

Manpower Requirements

The product made and the machines used in the process indicate in rather specific terms the jobs that need to be done, the general types of labor that will be needed, whether skilled or unskilled, and the numbers of workers needed for production. If production is to be performed by general-purpose machines, the chances are that rather highly skilled operators will be needed. If specially designed equipment with built-in skills is used, then perhaps semiskilled or unskilled manpower will be used. Before management can satisfactorily fulfill its worker requirements, a rather comprehensive study of jobs must be made. There are three major procedures involved in the study of jobs—(1) job analysis, (2) job description, and (3) job evaluation. Job analysis may be defined as the discovery and study of the essential components of each job so that it can be fully described and evaluated. It is the initial determination of the exact tasks that comprise the job. The skill, knowledge, abilities, and responsibilities which are required of any worker who performs the job are brought into view through this process.

From the job analysis comes the job description. The information so obtained is sifted and weighed; and from this a written record of the duties, responsibilities, and requirements of a particular job is prepared; this is the job description. Eventually management must fill all jobs. The job description tells management what type of worker is needed for the different jobs and provides a basis for matching men with jobs.

Job evaluation compares one job with another. Its basic purpose is to determine the relative worth of all jobs or, in other words, how much should be paid to the worker who adequately performs this job. With these three tools management can determine exactly what jobs need to be done, can properly select individuals to fill the jobs, and pay wages commensurate with the value of the job to management.

TO BUY OR TO MAKE

Most manufacturers, whether they be large or small, find that they must make certain purchases of parts, materials, and services outside the company. There are few if any companies today that are so integrated that they are not dependent on outsiders. The decision to buy or to make will many times determine the basic nature of the manufacturing operation. The establishment that purchases the great bulk of its component parts from outsiders may well be just an assembler and not a manufacturer. The question, then, is not whether a company should buy goods and services on the outside, but what work will be done by outsiders. As a result of specialization in industry many times parts, materials, and services can be contracted for outside the company at a lower cost than they could be produced for in the plant. In some instances company departments that can produce parts are expected to compete with outside organizations for the company's business. At one time the Ford Motor Company manufactured tires for its cars and even owned rubber plantations. It later abandoned this practice because to produce tires required manufacturing skills, production facilities, and sources of raw materials that were foreign to the main Ford line. Currently Ford has several hundred suppliers all over the country who supply various parts and accessories needed in the manufacture of automobiles and trucks. For many years the Chrysler Corporation and the Packard Motor Car Company purchased automobile body shells from the Briggs Manufacturing Company; evidently it can be profitable to have outsiders perform certain work for this industry. This practice is certainly not confined to the production of automobiles; in fact, all manufacturers go outside their plants for some things.

It would be impossible to state what parts a particular manufacturer should make himself and what parts should be purchased from others. This decision depends on the general nature of the manufacturing organization. It is possible, however, to reach a general conclusion on the subject. Major components of the assembly should be produced in the plant; or at least their production by outsiders should be highly controlled. Not every manufacturer produces all his major components, yet this policy is followed by a large majority of business organizations. The most successful automobile manufacturers produce their power plants, although none of them produce the tires.

In today's competitive market each producer seeks to make his product different from that of his competitors. This is perhaps the easiest way to circumvent competition. Manufacturers try to build features into their products that will make them appear to be different from and better than all others. To maintain these competitive features a manufacturer should control them. Management should at least control that area of production that adds distinction to its product—the features that make it sell. Other general conclusions are mentioned below.

When to Make

Generally a manufacturer should make parts under the following conditions:

1. When the process or product contains a secret element that the company desires to retain for itself. The success of Coca-Cola lies partly in the formula used in making the syrup. Many outsiders have tried to duplicate this product without success. If this formula were known to others, it could be duplicated; and one of the major competitive advantages of the company would be lost.

2. When a high degree of quality needs to be maintained. Very often the old adage "if you want something done right, do it yourself" applies. A manufacturer sets his quality standards and must always be in a position to enforce them. There are many instances, however, where specialized tools or skills are needed to make a product or part. If a company does not have them, it will have to find an outsider who does. Close control must be maintained over the subcontractor.

3. When the product, part, or service can be produced in the plant at lower cost. This is perhaps the basic reason why management produces parts and services. This is especially true when a company has excess men and machines. It can be seen now that the decision to buy or to make may change based upon the extent to which company facilities are being utilized. Often it is better to make parts in the plant at a higher cost than outsiders would charge simply to keep men and machines occupied.

4. When sources of supply are uncertain in terms of delivery, thus raising a question as to whether or not the production schedules can be maintained.

5. When the problems of scheduling production are complex and complete coordination of activities within the plant is necessary.

When to Buy

Generally management will go outside its plant for parts and services under the following conditions:

1. When, because of specialization, outsiders can do a better job and at a lower cost. Borg-Warner produces automatic transmissions and overdrive units for some of the largest automobile manufacturers. This company was a pioneer in the field and probably possesses more knowledge of this product than anyone else.

2. When time is an important factor and the outside specialist is already set up for production of the part. An organization which specializes in grinding highly accurate plug gages used in inspection work can produce these gages faster and more economically than the machine shop that might use them.

3. When the demand for the part or service is temporary. In such a case the problem of obsolete facilities can be avoided by having someone else do the work. Generally management will not invest in facilities unless it can foresee a volume of production adequate to absorb this investment. It may be a better alternative to have outsiders make a part than accept the risk of obsolescence.

4. When funds for capital expenditures are limited. Many times a businessman has no alternative; he must engage others to perform certain work because he cannot afford to buy the necessary equipment. In the long run this is not a desirable alternative because the businessman will pay excessively for his parts and at the same time lose control over their production.

5. During periods of high or intense competition. In such circumstances a buyer can often take advantage of a seller's predicament and make a satisfactory purchase. One should not depend on these instances for a supply of parts.

Because of this practice on the part of most manufacturers of letting work out, the smaller business establishment is given a tremendous lift. There are thousands of small shops all over the country that exist solely to supply parts and services to others. They may be foundries, machine shops, metal fabricators, plastic molders, or any of a hundred or more different classifications. This is one reason why there are so many small establishments in the manufacturing field.

PLANNING RETAIL OPERATIONS

Just as business managers in the past have emphasized the production aspect of management, there is a tendency to do likewise in any discussion of business management. We must not lose sight of the fact that service organizations and middlemen of all types have problems similar to those of a manufacturer. The following paragraphs point out some of the similarities in the problems of a manufacturer and a retailer and in general are indicative of the problems faced by all businessmen. As a retailer plans his operation, he must face the same planning objectives as the manufacturer—time, cost, use of subcontractors, flexibility, stabilizing operations, satisfying current requirements and growth possibilities.

The retailer's problem of timing his purchases is just as vital a consideration as the manufacturer's problem of timing production. It must be so for frequently the manufacturer plans his production to satisfy the requirements of the retailer. If a retailer does not have merchandise for his customers when they want it, they are quite likely to go elsewhere. Retailers have a cost problem similar to, but perhaps somewhat simpler than, that of a manufacturer. A retailer must decide how much his customers will pay for different goods and, after determining his costs of operation and the desired profit, calculates how much he can pay for different items. Thus if a retailer's cost of operation equals 35 cents of each sales dollar and he desires to earn 3 cents on each sales dollar, he can spend 62 cents of each sales dollar for goods that he buys. A handbag retailing for $10 and costing $6.20 leaves $3.50 for operating expenses and 30 cents profit. If the retailer pays more than $6.20, he must raise his price, lower his expenses, or be satisfied with less profit.

A retailer tries to be flexible in his operation, just as does the manufacturer. There is a certain amount of fixedness in a retail operation, especially in terms of inventory and operating facilities. There may be certain franchise agreements with manufacturers also. Each of these tends to limit the retailer's freedom of operation. Retailers who are flexible can take advantage of new opportunities as they arise far better than the retailer who is committed to a fixed plan of operation.

It is perhaps self-evident that retailers desire a stable sales volume. Retailers seek to stabilize their sales activity by carrying a diversified line of goods and at the same time not causing a disproportionate increase in the costs of operation.

Not all retailers or manufacturers are interested in growth of their business. Frequently older owner-managers are content to let their business grow at a very slow pace or not at all, since they have no desire to face the problems normally associated with growth. Nevertheless the retailer may find growth both desirable and essential, as did the manufacturer. Growth can result in greater profits and enhanced prestige for the retailer and at the same time protect his competitive position.

The "to buy or to make" decision applies in a different manner to a retailer than to a manufacturer. This is because the retailer buys all of his goods from outsiders and makes none. Retailers often enlist the services of outsiders in the operation of many store departments. Sooner or later, as retail stores grow in size and increase the variety of merchandise they handle and the resulting number of departments they must operate, management is confronted with the problem of operating all these departments or leasing some of them to qualified outsiders. The following lists summarize the pros and cons of department leasing. They contain factors that are similar to those considered by the manufacturer as he makes his "to buy or to make" decision.

Advantages of Leasing Departments

1. It allows the store owner to expand his lines of merchandise without adding to his investment.
2. It provides an opportunity to use special skills and abilities in departments that are notoriously difficult to manage.
3. Because of the special skills and abilities of personnel, the risk of merchandising certain types of goods is greatly reduced.
4. By observing skilled leased department personnel, management may receive valuable training in new methods of retailing.
5. It may result in more profitable operations.

Disadvantages of Leasing Departments

1. The lease arrangement is complex. It is difficult to determine what a lessee should pay for the use of the store and the services that are provided by the owner.
2. The advantage of centralized control may be lost to the store. No matter how carefully the lease agreement is written, the lessee may operate to the detriment of the store by failing to create good will or simply by not cooperating with store management.
3. A lease agreement usually sets limits to the amount of income available to the store. If the department is very successful, it may be impossible for the retailer to gain additional income that may be warranted by the increased sales and profit of the department.

SUMMARY

As a result of its study of the market, management determines the characteristics of the market and decides whether or not a demand exists for a particular product. Through product research the specific design features of the product are formulated. At this point management has, on paper at least, a product that will sell in sufficient quantity to make for a successful business venture. The next problem facing management is to decide how the product will be made, adhering to the original design features and keeping costs at a reasonable level.

In planning for production, management must explore all possible methods and determine which method of production in the long run will prove best for the company. As management plans, it should study the possibility of utilizing the talents of outside specialists who in the past have aided others in the development of a profitable business.

To a degree all businessmen face the same basic problems whether they are manufacturers, retailers, middlemen, or managers of service establishments. The economical methods developed by manufacturers may have a similar application in retailing, and valuable lessons learned in retailing may be applied in modified form to manufacturing establishments.

QUESTIONS

1. What basic questions must be answered by management prior to planning the nature and extent of production?
2. What are the requirements of excellence in design?
3. What are the objectives of planning?
4. Why is time an important planning objective?
5. Why is cost an important planning objective?
6. What factors must be weighed in determining the extent to which production should be stabilized?
7. Why is growth desirable for an enterprise?
8. Why may growth be essential for an enterprise?
9. Distinguish between the continuous and the repetitive production process.
10. What type of business enterprise is likely to use the intermittent type of production process?
11. Of what value is the operation process chart?
12. How does management determine its machine and equipment needs?
13. How does management determine its material needs?
14. How does management determine its man-power needs?
15. Distinguish between job analysis and job evaluation.
16. Under what conditions should management make component parts?
17. Under what conditions should management buy component parts from others?
18. Compare the similarity of the retailer's and the manufacturer's problems in starting a business venture.
19. Why should a retailer lease departments in his store?
20. What disadvantages are inherent in department leasing?

PART TWO

Planning for Physical Facilities

Part Two of this text considers the problems associated with locating the enterprise, providing for suitable housing, and laying out the plant to allow for efficient production or operation.

The earlier consideration of the market provided an indication of the groups that management considers its future customers and also where they are located. The analysis of the company's product and its method of manufacture provided a basis for determining the relative importance of the various factors of production—men, materials, machines, and the like. With this knowledge management can determine whether it should locate with primary regard for its market, raw material sources, man-power skills, or some other factor. In addition, the basic planning for the product and the nature and extent of production provided a basis for evaluating housing requirements—housing for a job shop versus housing for an assembly-line type of manufacture, for example.

The establishment of physical facilities is, of necessity, an aftermath of the basic planning stage discussed in Part One. However, the significance of this next stage, Part Two, must not be lost because of its major emphasis on specific physical items. The concern of management is not only that of establishing facilities in keeping with product and market goals but also that of recognizing the varying importance of alternatives which, though adequate in a purely physical sense, fall short of the mark because they require an excessive amount of investment or involve a high degree of economic risk.

Because the establishment of physical facilities requires money investment, management is bound to a relatively long-term commitment. The sounder the initial plan of facilities, the greater is the assurance that the commitment will prove profitable.

CHAPTER 6

Location of the Enterprise

A businessman must consider his problems individually, to be sure, but also as they relate to one another. Thus the problem of location could be the number one problem of one businessman and of less significance to others. When locating his organization, a businessman asks this question: "All factors considered, where is the ideal spot for my business?" Most frequently the location finally selected is not ideal but represents a compromise wherein less of one desirable feature is obtained to get more of another desirable feature. The whole discussion of location breaks down quite logically into two separate problems: locating the smaller type of establishment and locating the larger type of establishment.

LOCATING THE SMALLER ESTABLISHMENT

As implied above, some factors might be of major concern to some businessmen and of less concern to others. Some factors that are of great importance to larger organizations might be of little importance to the small establishment. The reverse is also true. The basic considerations that should be studied in locating a smaller establishment are discussed below.

Market

Every businessman must consider the market from which he plans to derive his income when he locates his establishment. The small businessman usually approaches the problem of location by first setting up a given area within a certain radius of his home; he then redefines the problem of location by asking: "Where within this defined area, all factors considered, is the ideal spot for my business?" A large percentage of Americans tend to spend their lives within a rather limited area, near the place where they were born and have spent the earlier years of their lives. Their reluctance to move makes the problem of location much simpler, but it quite often results in the selection of a location that is far from being ideal.

The individual and his product are each factors that make for success of the small establishment. If a small businessman is the manufacturer of a product or service used by other business, he perhaps has a dozen or so customers all located within a rather limited distance from his shop. These few customers will comprise his market. The manufacturer seeks out his market; his customers perhaps do not come to him. The small manufacturer finds that he can satisfy his market whether located one block or one mile or more from it because of adequate transportation and communication facilities. His customers are more interested in the total service that this businessman offers than in the single factor of immediate accessibility.

A retailer, on the other hand, is more interested in locating in a spot where there will be a large number of potential customers passing by his door. He finds that his volume of trade is determined by this traffic, and therefore, he must locate on or near the "beaten path." We must realize that there are some retailers who, because of their unique status, may locate in out-of-the-way areas and still draw customers into their store. Generally this type of retailer is the exception, not the rule.

A location away from a small manufacturer's market need not be a major problem since the problem of communication can be met in many different ways. But the retailer who is located away from the traffic patterns must use costly devices to get people to go out of their way to trade with him. The adage based on "build a better mousetrap" cannot be depended upon in retailing today. A retailer can overcome the drawbacks of a poor location by offering substantial price reductions and by putting on a strong campaign of advertising and promotion. However, it is generally a costly proposition to try to make people change their normal buying habits. Since price concessions and promotion are tools used by all retailers, these devices are less effective when used in the same proportions by the retailer located off the beaten path. In the majority of instances, the location of a retail establishment must be considered in the light of the movement of potential customers.

In summary, the small manufacturer has considerable latitude in selecting a location for his business since he can adequately serve his market from a variety of locations while the small retailer must select a location where there is a flow of traffic adequate to sustain a profitable sales volume.

Housing

The selection of a business location is further complicated by the problem of suitable housing. The housing problem is more easily solved for a small manufacturer than for a small retailer. Since, as noted above, exact location is not demanded of the small manufacturer, there is greater opportunity for him to select a building having the features that are needed to engage in economical production and distribution. Currently, with the trend of larger establishments away from the urban areas and the migration of industrial plants to other areas where they are housed in new construction, buildings become available to the smaller manufacturer. In some communities buildings formerly used by large business are divided into small usable areas for smaller business. Locations that are no longer satisfactory for big business may be adequate for smaller business units.

The small retailer faces a different problem; he wants to locate in a thriving market where there is an abundance of customers. He finds that there are other retailers who want to locate in the same area. The better the trading area or the better the location, the more serious is the housing problem. Since the turnover of retail housing often results because the former tenant found the spot to be a poor location, it is quite possible that the same spot will be a poor location for a new tenant. The difference between a good and a poor retail location can be a matter of a few feet off the beaten path. Since there is a limit to the number of locations that can be on the beaten path, and since they are, of course, the most costly, the smaller retailer often winds up selecting a poor location or selecting inadequate housing in a location that has an adequate volume of traffic. Either solution is far from satisfactory.

It is assumed that most small businessmen will prefer not to finance the construction of a new building to house their business. Capital is always limited, and the ownership of a building simply creates another area of work for a usually overburdened management. Once the small businessman has narrowed down the possible areas where he might house his business, he faces the problem of either buying the property or leasing it under one of many possible lease agreements. However, it may be that he has no alternative. If housing is scarce, the current property owner might dictate the terms and require that the businessman buy or lease. If the real estate market is overloaded, then the businessman may have an opportunity to dictate the terms and specify whether he wishes to buy or lease. Some of the possible arrangements that can be used to acquire housing are discussed later in this chapter.

The housing requirements for any two or more establishments will probably differ, yet the same considerations must be studied by all businessmen in selecting their "home." The building itself should do much more than house the business; it should aid the business in performing those activities that are vital to its success. A manufacturer might have as a goal producing a product at the lowest possible cost. He then would select a building that gave him a low occupancy cost and would disregard many other building features. Boston's well-known department store, Raymond's, began business in 1893 when Mr. Raymond went out and bought up the bankrupt stock of other merchants and close-outs of merchants who wished to retire. He sold this merchandise at low prices. The store operated on this principle: Buy out another fellow's stock and sell at low prices. Naturally, one would not expect this kind of merchandise to be sold in the salon type of retail establishment. Instead, one would expect it to be sold in an older type of building where layout is awkward and services held to a minimum. Raymond's continues in their old "house" and the many people who trade with Raymond's accept this type of arrangement and cannot quite imagine it being otherwise.

Other retailers might enter a trading area desiring to create an impression of high service, high quality, sedateness, and staidness. To aid them in performing according to their plan, retailers should select housing that is in keeping with the ideals that they set. Manufacturers, as well as retailers, have a better chance to achieve their goals through selection of a proper type home.

Buying the Property. There is much to be said for the merits of buying the property that will house one's business, whether it be manufacturing or retailing. It is generally the cheapest way to provide for housing if it is intended that the business will occupy the premises for a long period of time. Landlords assume risks, earn profits on their investments, and expect to bc paid for the services that they perform. Over a long period of time it must be cheaper to own a building than to rent it, or else there would never be people in the business of renting commercial property. If the business is one that requires frequent changes in the internal layout of the building, the occupants must be free to make the necessary changes. Only through ownership can the businessman be relatively sure that changes can be made as and when he desires them. The landlord wants his building to be kept in condition that will provide for the largest possible number of prospective tenants; it enhances his possibility of renting at desirable rates. Anyone who has rented industrial, commercial, or residential property knows that landlords are reluctant to approve changes in their property. Thus for the sake of flexibility it is desirable to own rather than rent.

Lease agreements can be written to cover any period of time desired by the parties. After a lease expires, a new agreement is needed. The new agreement might be just a continuation of the old agreement, or the landlord might spell out an entirely new arrangement that would be to his satisfaction and not to the satisfaction of the business. The tenant then is never certain that he can occupy the same building as long as he desires. For the sake of a permanent home for a business, the best alternative is to buy.

Lease Agreements. Buying a building is all well and good for the businessman who can afford the investment, but what will the person with limited capital do? There are many different types of lease agreements offered to businessmen. These agreements can contain any number of provisions that landlord and tenant desire. Two different types of lease arrangements, the net lease and the gross lease, are described below. It should be remembered that there can be many modifications of these.

The net lease is an agreement between landlord and tenant, whereby the landlord agrees to provide the building and only the building. All services will be provided by the tenant and, of course, can be provided in such proportions as are necessary for the most efficient operation possible within the limitations of the building. These services would include heat, light, power, maintenance, janitor service, and perhaps even remodeling to some degree. This arrangement gives the tenant quite a bit of latitude in adjusting the building to serve his purposes. However, it does require him to invest his funds in someone else's property, and some of the property installed by the tenant becomes the property of the landlord; the tenant cannot take everything from the building when he decides to leave.

The gross lease is an agreement between landlord and tenant, whereby the landlord agrees to provide the building along with certain services as outlined in the lease. The landlord could then provide all the services mentioned under the net lease above that are performed by the tenant and as many more or less as the two parties can agree upon. This allows the tenant to enter and start business with a smaller investment than under the net lease. If the landlord is a specialist in providing these services, it might also result in time saved in starting the venture. The main drawbacks to this arrangement are first, cost, for the landlord seeks to make a profit on all services rendered; second, fixedness in terms of operation, for the businessman must scale his operation to the services provided by the landlord. The ideal situation is to provide services in terms of the business needs and not to adjust business activity to the services provided. The gross lease is a convenient way for a person to go in and out of business in a hurry without tying up large amounts of capital. Over the long run, however, this technique is generally a second-rate arrangement at best.

Labor

Unless a businessman intends to operate his business alone or with the help of family and friends, he must seek out a labor supply. Just as businessmen are reluctant to leave home in choosing a location, so are workers reluctant to move any great distance to seek employment. The small businessman generally must draw his labor force from the community near his business. Unless great financial rewards are present, the average worker will prefer to work within a few miles of his home. In recent years, however, many people accustomed to the constant change generated by World War II have been lured to the West and Southwest. Since the small businessman needs only a few workers for his labor force, locating in a special type labor market is not of major concern. The small businessman can offer the worker a congenial place in which to work, close association with management, and an opportunity for self-expression. One of his major problems is to lure good workers away from the larger establishments that can offer the worker more security than the small businessman. Workers in large plants are often covered by union contracts which provide for retirement benefits, insurance protection, and perhaps a guaranteed income. Larger organizations generally have the strength to weather financial storms. Workers are reluctant to seek employment in the establishment that cannot guarantee any degree of security. Therefore, the small business must sell itself to the worker, especially if there is a shortage of labor.

Other Location Factors

In addition to the factors of location mentioned above, a small businessman must consider other requirements of his business, such as power, transportation, banking facilities, and the community. However, most communities have adequate banking facilities to meet the needs of any small businessman. Our transportation system is so highly developed that it reaches into just about every community with adequate services and at reasonable cost. The same is true of our electric power system. Securing raw materials might be of major concern to some small businessmen, and they should give adequate consideration to this problem before finally selecting a location for their business. In general, the small businessman has but three major factors to consider in locating his business—the market, housing, and labor. The other factors of a desirable location are generally present in any area that would be given consideration.

LOCATING THE LARGER ESTABLISHMENT

In locating a larger business, the problem may involve finding the most desirable spot on the West coast, the East coast, or perhaps anywhere in North America. The problem of locating the larger establishment may be complicated initially by a great barrage of promotional material coming from development committees of just about every section of the country. Canadian organizations also try to lure American industry north of the border. In a single issue of a prominent business publication there appeared the following advertisements: "Canada . . .

Giant in Chemicals. Current building programs in Canada's expanding chemical industry will top $96 million. . . . This headline-making land to the north is fast emerging as one of the world's major producers of petrochemicals. Bank of Montreal . . . your gateway to Canada. . . . If you want to take advantage of a unique combination of natural resources, low-cost power, stable labor conditions, and favorable climate, let Canada's First Bank clear your path to Canada. . . ." Also in the same issue: "Before you make plans to locate new chemical processing plants, read the results of what Oklahoma offers you. . . . Here is a comprehensive analysis of Oklahoma raw materials such as natural gas. . . . Also, possible plant sites and markets relating to petrochemicals. . . ." South Carolina advertises: "Industry Succeeds in South Carolina." The Minneapolis Gas Company states: "Good living and business go hand-in-hand in Greater Minneapolis." The West Penn Electric advertises the "basic needs for manufacturing success" in the area served by that power company. Kansas City, Lewistown, Pennsylvania, and Louisiana industrial-development groups all had advertisements in the same issue. This is not an isolated case. Other issues of this magazine and other magazines and media are used to publicize the various sections of the country in hopes of attracting new industry to the respective areas. This battle for the smokestacks is progressing in earnest and is certain to continue in the years ahead. To be sure, all of this publicity is well meant; it is only natural for areas to want the maximum economic growth feasible. It does present a problem for the businessman; and while these agencies do a great deal to inform businessmen about the merits of a particular area, they say little or nothing about the drawbacks of the area. The businessman must sift the wheat from the straw and obtain additional evidence before reaching any decision on the matter.

The purpose of these organizations can be summed up in a statement from *An Open Book*, a publication of the Massachusetts Development and Industrial Commission:

> You as an industrialist have little time to make the comprehensive studies you might wish concerning possible locations for your manufacturing plant. We, as representatives of the Development and Industrial Commission of Massachusetts, feel that it might be to our common advantage to assist you in knowing more of what this Commonwealth offers in industrial advantages and opportunities. You will find this *Open Book* a summary, within reasonable limits, of some factual reasons why old industries continue to be satisfied with their choice of Massachusetts as a state in which to have their roots deep-sunk; why newcomers to Massachusetts' industrial population have chosen this state as one answering their demands for opportunity and expansion.

Industry appears to be constantly on the move. Year in and year out large numbers of organizations move to new locations. There can be many reasons for this movement; the original location might have been a poor one, or perhaps over the years conditions changed, making the original location undesirable. In selecting a business location, it must be remembered that the factors which determine a good location are ever-changing. Some areas increase in population much faster than others. Businessmen who must locate in or near their market are forced to relocate in accordance with their shifted market centers. Requirements for labor in terms of both quantity and skill are constantly changing because of the introduction of new machines and processes. New products are constantly being developed in American industry; some of these will take the place of other products, making them obsolete. Private business and the government are expanding power supplies, thus making possible the location of industry in certain areas where before it was impossible. The development of hydroelectric power in our Northwest has opened the door for the location of aluminum-producing plants in this area that knew little heavy industry a generation ago. A businessman must try to estimate the changes that might take place as they would affect the value of a particular location. A location that is desirable today may be undesirable tomorrow.

Factors Involved in Locating the Larger Establishment

The selection of a location for the larger manufacturing establishment is generally accomplished in a much more impersonal manner than for the smaller organization. The larger establishment puts much more attention on the economic factors of location and much less on the psychic. The larger establishment must be more careful than the smaller ones in selecting a location because it is often investing huge sums of money that have been entrusted to it. If the small businessman makes a mistake in location, he can quite often rectify the error by just moving to another location and through trial and error, if necessary, find the most desirable spot. The larger organization cannot do this as readily since it must invariably invest its funds in items of a more fixed nature.

The larger organization often asks the question: "Where in the United States is the ideal spot for this business?" The answer must be developed through three separate stages. First, in what general area shall we locate the business; second, in what community shall we locate; and finally, what site within this community.

Before the process of selection begins, attention must be given to the relative importance of each location factor. Location near the market might be of prime importance to the businessman who manufactures aluminum combination doors and windows, while location near the source of raw material might be of prime importance to the meat packer, and so on. The important considerations in locating the larger establishment together with an indication of the problems involved are discussed below. When evaluating the general area in which to locate, there are several factors that merit consideration. Again, to some businessmen each is of vital importance; to others, only a few of these factors may apply.

Soil. This is a factor of major importance for the agricultural and related establishment. It deserves consideration by other establishments inasmuch as the type of soil in an area determines to some degree the cost of land, especially if the land has alternative uses. Soil must also be considered as it influences building foundations and drainage problems.

Climate. Climate is probably of little significance in these times as a factor in the location of a business that needs a particular climatic environment for its manufacturing process. It has been claimed that one reason why the textile industry located in New England was that the relative humidity was satisfactory for weaving and related processes. With the advent and perfection of air-conditioning systems which regulate temperature and humidity, this area lost one of its location advantages, and the industry has gradually relocated elsewhere to take advantage of other location factors. Climate is still a factor in determining certain human characteristics that might have a bearing on the caliber of the workforce. Climate affects not only one's mode of living but his desire to work.

Raw Materials. Not every business establishment needs to locate near the sources of raw materials, for raw materials might be only a minor cost item in some types of manufacture. Business that depends on extractive industry still locates near the source of raw materials. One would expect to find a sawmill near the timber supply since the costs of transporting timber are so great and since a large portion of the raw material does not wind up as lumber. The automobile industry is located near its basic raw material, steel. However, much of the machine-tool industry is located away from its basic raw material, steel, since the costs of steel are a relatively minor part of the total costs involved in producing machine tools. Business locates near to or apart from raw material sources depending on how vital raw material costs are in terms of total costs.

Power Supply and Rates. Power costs and availability vary tremendously from area to area. If power is to be a major consideration for a businessman, he should study and compare the relative merits of alternative areas. The reasons for variation in power costs are: (1) ownership, of the power-producing establishment; and (2) method of producing power. In areas where the Federal government has erected power-producing facilities the cost of power is generally much lower than in areas where private capital has been used. The government uses tax revenue or borrows against tax revenues to get funds to construct its plants, while other producers use private funds for which interest or dividends must be paid. Tax concessions to government agencies account for more of the difference in the costs of government versus privately produced power. In 1952, for example, 22 per cent of the gross income of Southern power producers went to pay various types of taxes, while only 3 per cent of the gross income of government-owned power plants in the same area was spent for taxes. Interest, dividends, and taxes which the government-sponsored power plant does not have to pay can account for a great difference in power rates.

Some areas are blessed with an abundant water supply which can be turned into relatively low-cost power as in the Buffalo–New York area. Power in Boston, Massachusetts, is produced by coal-fired steam boilers. The production of steam requires coal which is costly, especially when it must be transported a thousand miles or more. Thus the difference in costs can be attributed to the method of producing power.

The small businessman generally need not consider the problem of power availability since there is undoubtedly an adequate supply for him in any area that has electric service. The total amount of power available for business use is definitely limited. The larger organization that will use considerable quantities of power must consider the availability of power in the area where it intends to locate. Since water supplies are unpredictable, those areas that depend on water as a source of power to generate electricity cannot guarantee the amount of current that can be produced. (Our Northwest depends heavily on water as a source of power, and there just isn't enough water available to produce unlimited quantities of power for industry.)

Markets. Few newly formed business organizations attempt to cater to a nationwide market. Generally, a business organizes to satisfy a local or regional market which is known to exist. As the market grows, the problems of satisfying customers in terms of delivery, services, etc., increase in magnitude. It is not always necessary or desirable to locate production facilities in or near the market. The problem of locating to satisfy a market is basically a problem of transportation and communication. The better the lines of communication between producer and consumer and the better the transportation facilities, the less significant is the exact location of a plant. Location can then be made with greater emphasis on other factors.

We know that a business located in one area can satisfy a distant market. This can be done through a well-organized sales and service staff. It should be remembered that the problem of communication is directly tied in with transportation since transportation is a part of communication.

If methods of reaching the consumer or market are well developed and coordinated, the major problem of locating to serve a market boils down to the cost of transportation. If goods, owing to their nature, are costly to move, then a location near the market may be necessary. If transportation costs represent a small percentage of the value of goods being shipped, the business can locate in terms of factors other than markets. Razor blades, for example, are produced in Boston, Massachusetts, and sold in every state in the union economically and effectively because of good communication and the relatively low cost of transportation.

On the other hand, the manufacturer of automobiles faces an entirely different problem. During the 1930s it cost in the vicinity of $100 to transport an automobile from Detroit to Boston. This transportation cost represented 10 per cent or more of the value of the product, obviously a high percentage. To overcome this high cost and to better serve the markets, assembly plants were constructed at strategic points throughout the country. Component parts which are relatively cheap to move were shipped over the rails from local suppliers to the assembly plants, resulting in great savings to the manufacturer and perhaps the consumer.

The factor of time must also be considered when locating to satisfy a market. True, air transportation has cut down the distance between our cities, but there are many instances where the market will demand immediate service. If time is an important factor in satisfying a market, the business must locate near the market or introduce some devices such as sales offices or warehouses to meet market demands.

Transportation. Transportation as it relates to markets was discussed briefly above. Some additional considerations of transportation are mentioned below. Most of us take our vast transportation system for granted since most of us have lived during the period when transportation facilities were available nearly everywhere in the United States. While our transportation system is second to none in the world, the businessman must still consider, as a basic problem of location, the movement of goods into and out of his plant. He must have materials to work with when needed, and he must be able to ship his goods to meet customer requirements. The location of manufacturing industries today is not fixed by Nature; there is still sufficient freedom of choice in selecting a location to make transportation costs a very significant aspect of the problem.

The businessman is concerned with an adequate system of transportation, one that will allow him to ship and receive goods at any time and preferably through a choice of carriers. While nearly every hamlet in the

United States is served with some form of transportation, some areas have more frequent service than others and a wider variety of carriers at varying costs.

Not all businessmen view an adequate system of transportation in the same light. To some businessmen adequate transportation could be parcel post and Railway Express, while others might need direct rail or water facilities. Adequate transportation is a relative term; what might be considered adequate for one businessman might be inadequate for another. The greater the number of carriers serving an area, in total and by type, the greater the probability that transportation will be adequate to meet business needs.

For most businessmen the choice of carrier boils down to either rail or motor truck. If the products used and sold by a business must move by rail, then location must be in terms of railroad accommodations. Motor-truck transportation is much more flexible than rail and is most frequently used in short- and intermediate-distance hauling.

Cost is another aspect of transportation that must be considered. The peculiarities of the freight-rate structure in this country exert a profound influence on the location of industry. Freight-rate structures are made under the supervision of Federal and/or state government agencies and are not determined by how much is carried over any given distance by a particular type of carrier. If certain towns are granted special rates lower than those granted to other towns, they may become important industrial centers. Manufacturers in other towns may have to give in to their better-located rival towns. The practice of grouping points of origin or destination, which gives all towns in the group the same rate, equalizes transportation costs to and from all towns in the group. The grouping of all rates to and from all points in New England when the point of origin or destination is in the West has equalized freight costs throughout New England. Thus, the freight cost from a western point to Portland, Maine, or Providence, Rhode Island, would be about the same. Some areas are blessed with equalized freight rates, while others are not. There are many other factors which affect freight costs to and from given areas. These factors are far too technical for discussion here. For exact information on freight costs anywhere in the United States, it is suggested that information be obtained from the Interstate Commerce Commission. The significant point is that transportation costs vary with the mode of movement and the geographic location.

Labor. No business can prosper unless it can obtain and maintain a productive labor force. In spite of the developments in modern machinery, which in many instances reduce the importance of skilled labor, no process has been developed to operate without man power. The key to success in any business organization is the human factor; workers can make or break any organization.

In considering labor, management faces three problems: first, the quantity of labor available in a given area; second, the quality of this labor; and finally, the cost of labor in the area. In mass-production assembly-line types of manufacture where workers can be trained cheaply and quickly, the quality of labor is not of great importance. However, many businesses require workers with particular skills learned through years of experience. Not every area in this country has an adequate supply of workers who possess the specific skills that management needs for efficient operation. If management seeks skilled workers, it must locate where they are, import them from another area, or train unskilled workers to perform skilled operations. Management must weigh these alternatives carefully since the cost of labor runs high. It must also be recognized that the costs of labor possessing the same skills will vary greatly from area to area.

Water and Disposal. Many manufacturing processes, such as those which produce aluminum, steel, paper, textiles, and other products, require enormous quantities of water for the process or for the production of electric power. Generally, a municipal water system could not meet such industry-process requirements. Therefore, business must locate in an area where an adequate water supply is or can be made available.

Water supply becomes a greater problem as time passes. In many areas the increase in population has exerted such demands on water facilities that rationing must be resorted to during dry months. Since human requirements must be satisfied first, industry finds less and less water available for its purposes.

A similar problem exists with the adequacy of waste-disposal facilities. Systems designed to provide residential service are often inadequate for industrial use. Adequate facilities may be available only at a major cost.

Taxes. Federal tax provisions are applied uniformly throughout the United States. Therefore, there is no preferential location which will favor a business firm with a reduced burden of Federal taxes. However, many types of taxes which are levied by the states vary considerably from one state to another. Some states levy corporate income taxes; others do not. Those which do levy such a tax vary considerably in the rate of taxation. Real estate taxes vary within a state from municipality to municipality. There are such variations in real estate taxation that a property tax in one area might be much greater or less than the tax on equivalent property in another area. Motor vehicle taxes, incorporating fees, sales taxes, and other types of taxes vary from area to area. Some states, although recognizing that taxes are perhaps not a key factor in the problem of plant location, do offer tax concessions to new industry as an inducement. The island of Puerto Rico now offers 100 per cent tax exemption to new industry. Federal taxes do not apply, and the Commonwealth offers full exemption from local taxes.

SELECTING THE COMMUNITY

After the above factors have been evaluated separately and in relation to one another, the general area of location can be determined. The next problem involves the selection of a community within which to locate. The problem of selecting a community involves a choice between the industrialized community as opposed to the nonindustrialized community. Each type of community has its strong points. A statement of the strong points of each type follows:

The Industrialized Community

1. Possibility of being near related or complementary industry which might produce materials, parts, and supplies.
2. A large labor pool with diversified talents.
3. More adequate transportation facilities.
4. More adequate public services.
5. More opportunity for a local market.

The Nonindustrialized Community

1. Lower costs for land.
2. Better opportunities for physical expansion.
3. Greater flexibility in building design because of lower land costs. This results in better layout of production processes.
4. Generally lower real estate taxes.
5. Generally lower labor costs resulting from lower costs of living. This factor tends to become less significant over the years as industry moves out of larger cities to suburban locations.
6. A better opportunity for good public and personnel relations.

With these guides in mind, the businessman compares his needs with the offerings of the particular community and selects the type which offers the greatest possibility of business success. Many of the advantages of both types of community are found in the industrial district discussed below.

The Industrial District

The industrial district is a tract of land which is subdivided and developed according to a comprehensive plan for the use of a community of industries and, to a lesser degree, retailers. Streets, rail-lead tracks, and utilities are installed before sites are sold or leased to prospective occupants. The planned industrial subdivision is a logical response to current trends in business location. It is well adapted to the continuing decentralization of industrial and business operations, the increased use of horizontal-line production methods best housed in land-consuming one-story plants, and the emphasis on aesthetics in building design. It recognizes the scarcity and high cost of in-town sites and the space requirements for future plant expansion, off-street loading docks, and employee and customer parking.

Management often wants to avoid the problems and delays attendant upon finding and developing raw sites and in arranging for utilities. Management also wants to be assured that its investment will be protected and that it will have compatible neighbors. A location in a planned district generally meets these requirements. By choosing a district location, a businessman can be assured that needed facilities and conveniences will be there when he moves in, that he will not be faced with zoning problems and possible indignation meetings of abutting residential property owners, and that control will be exercised over the type of activity and architectural design of the plants around him.

Although many of the larger business organizations are well equipped with plant-location experts, engineers, lawyers, and the like, smaller establishments would like to be spared the cost and inconvenience of plant-location surveys. From the viewpoint of this group the organized district is the answer to many locational problems. If desired by the individual businessman, the district may even provide a package or turn-key type of service. The package plan offered to a business is based upon the now-proved concept that a single company, whose business it is to service industry, is best able to locate the site, develop the land, design and engineer the building, construct and finance the building, and provide maintenance if needed—all in one package. In this way the many problems encountered by a firm desiring a new facility are eliminated, and the management of the operating company can be free to conduct its normal business affairs without being distracted by location problems.

Subdividers often insist upon the maintenance of high-standard protective restrictions to preserve the character of the centers. With these protections, the growth of industrial slums is eliminated, and the desirability of these prepared centers is perpetuated. The prestige gained from the quality of the development itself and from the type of company which it attracts is more than an intangible feeling. In terms of dollars and cents it means that a building within the center actually possesses a higher value than one in an isolated unrestricted development.

The organized industrial district came into being in the United States about the turn of the century (Chicago's Clearing Industrial District began in 1899), but has experienced its greatest growth since the end of World War II. There are more than one hundred of these districts in operation today with the greatest concentration in the north-central and northeast section of the United States. They vary in size from the five-acre Cambridge Parkway development in Massachusetts to the more than 19,000-acre development at Crab Orchard Lake in southern Illinois. In general these areas, especially in the northeast, are restricted to light or medium manufacturing, warehousing, distribution, and services, with a few allowing unrestricted heavy industry. In some areas retail activity is conducted in connection with warehousing.

SELECTING THE SITE

The final problem in plant location is the selection of the site. The selection of a site is often determined by a single factor, such as available buildings, access to water or rail transportation, topography, or available land. The careful attention given to the selection of the general area and the community must not be wasted through careless selection of a site. In selecting the site, management must consider those factors which may contribute to success or failure in the operation of its facilities: the building, movement of materials, parking facilities, neighborhood characteristics, and others.

THE SHOPPING CENTER

The enormous growth of population in the United States since 1940 has opened tremendous new markets. The significant aspect of this growth is that nearly half of the 28 million increase in population has taken place, or is now located, in residential suburban areas 10 to 40 miles away from the traditional big-city shopping centers. Thus to win the customer's dollars, retailers, too, must follow the consumer to the suburbs. Important also is the change in the nature of the suburban market. The do-it-yourself atmosphere of the suburbs has opened a new market for many household items. Washing machines, lawnmowers, freezers, power tools, and the like find a more fertile market in the suburbs. Suburban families are younger, have more children and a higher income than city families. They are, therefore, potentially bigger spenders and better customers than their urban counterparts.

The shopping center operates in much the same way as the industrial district; that is, developers buy and clear a site and set the pattern for store design, facilities, and the general "tone" of the center. Occupants are selected to make for a well-rounded shopping center offering a maximum of service to the area.

The growth of the suburbs has changed the pattern of United States retail trade so much that few new stores are being constructed in the center of big cities. Old established city retail stores are forced to build in the suburbs to offset the loss of sales to the shopping centers. There is little doubt that the move will continue, and as suburbs fill up, the migrants from the city and today's suburbs too will move farther out, spawning a new boom in yet undeveloped areas.

SUMMARY

The locating of a business organization presents a three-fold problem: selecting the general area, the community, and the site. To be sure that a proper location will be made, management should spell out in specific terms the needs of its business in terms of location, evaluate various available locations in terms of their offerings, and select that location that comes nearest to meeting current and future demands of the business.

To succeed, an organization must do a better job than its competition. A business in a location that offers the best combination of factors has this initial advantage over the improperly located plant. The poorly located business, in order to survive, must surpass its competitors by means of economies of operation.

The answer to a location problem can be based on a factual dollars-and-cents comparison of the costs of locating in different areas. Comparative labor costs, site costs, building costs, taxes, transportation costs, and the like, can be determined for each area under consideration and serve as a basis for a sound location decision.

QUESTIONS

1. What is meant by the statement that one location factor may be of greater importance to one businessman than another?
2. Why does the small manufacturer have so much leeway in selecting a location?
3. What is the major factor in selecting the location for a retail store?
4. What is meant by the statement that a building should do much more than just house a business?
5. How can a retailer overcome the drawbacks of a poor location?
6. Is it always cheaper to buy rather than lease a building? Discuss.
7. Distinguish between the net lease and the gross lease.
8. What is meant by the statement that the individual and his product are each factors that make for success in the small establishment?
9. What advantages can the small business offer a worker that are not obtainable in a larger establishment?

10. Do you agree that in general the small businessman need consider only three basic location factors and that the others are nearly universally available?
11. Discuss what is meant by "the battle for the smokestacks."
12. What are the major reasons for variations in power costs from one section of the country to another?
13. What is meant by "adequate" transportation?
14. What factors contribute to the differences in freight rates from one section of the country to another?
15. What three problems face management when discussing labor as a location factor?
16. What tax advantage would a business have by locating in your home state?
17. What advantages does the industrialized community possess?
18. What advantages does the nonindustrialized community possess?
19. What is an industrial district?
20. Why does the industrial district have strong appeal to the smaller establishment?
21. What factors are involved in the selection of a site?
22. Specifically, how can a business gain through a good location?
23. Can a plant location problem be answered objectively? Discuss.

CHAPTER 7

Housing the Enterprise

The structure which the businessman selects to house his entrepreneurial activities is an important consideration because of its influence upon the cost and effectiveness of operations and also because of the degree to which it assists in establishing a desirable attitude in the minds of workers and clientele. A manufacturer needs housing which is suitable as a setting for operations and which helps maintain efficient work flow and worker morale. A merchant or professional man needs housing which is most representative of the impression which the business is intended to convey and which will also serve to invite and adequately service the customer. In many cases, standards of structure, appearance, and condition must be fulfilled because of legal requirements or because of custom or practice which has been established within the trade field. In this regard the customer expects certain services or facilities to be available to him in a downtown department store, whereas he is less inclined to assume that these same facilities should be available in the small local shop. A buyer, in dealing with large industrial organizations, anticipates certain levels of reputation and physical structure of his vendor firms. In the event that this anticipation is not borne out, there may be a weakening of the relationship between the plant and its customer. In many cases, the nature of the production process or servicing activity which is to be carried on dictates that the housing be of certain design and size to adequately serve the requirements of the process

APPROACH TO THE EVALUATION OF HOUSING

Our consideration of the housing of an enterprise will of necessity involve an unrealistic approach, for as in so many other areas of business decision, there is no single line of approach to the examination and consideration of the many factors which must be explored. As is usual, we will deal with each of several factors of physical facilities, and should currently bear in mind that each factor must be considered in the light of its interrelationship with all the others. Therefore, if our discussion enters into the examination of the space which particular housing may provide, we must evaluate this space not only in terms of its amount, but also in respect to its serviceability for storage purposes, manufacturing purposes, the movement of personnel, and the nature and flow of transportation or handling devices which must be employed in the area. When we consider the allocation of space to the various departments, we must at the same time bear in mind the interrelationship of these departments in terms of flow of work and personnel. The perfect building or housing for the enterprise does not exist. For a brief moment during drawing-board stages, it would appear that an ideal mating of physical facilities and business operational needs has been accomplished. However, in most cases, as soon as facilities are put to use, "bugs" appear which show up the inadequacies. In many cases, even before a structure is completed or remodeling done, it is already in part outmoded. Such inadequacies may be the result of insufficient consideration of the housing problem by management. This, therefore, presents a basic challenge, and we shall seek to reduce the problem to a statement of basic considerations which will provide a starting point for more adequate evaluation of the housing problem of an enterprise.

Our approach is founded upon an understanding of the basic purposes which housing should serve. Once these basic purposes or requirements are established, a more detailed recognition of specific constructional, operational, and economic details may be entered into. The housing problem has a common starting point whether the enterprise involved is one which deals in the manufacture or the sales of a product or both, for all classifications of business enterprise can be reduced to the category of a process or procedure which is established to accomplish a specific task. Herein is the common denominator of our approach, for the housing of the business activity should be considered only in so far as it serves the purposes of the basic procedure or process which it is intended to contain.

PURPOSES WHICH HOUSING SERVES

A structure which is designed to house a business enterprise must be viewed as a tool created to serve the basic needs and purposes of the business. These purposes may be stated as follows:

1. *The structure must serve as a storage area.* It should be capable of fulfilling the space and security requirements necessary for economical operation of the enterprise.

2. *The production-process flow must not be hampered by deficiencies in physical features and adequacy of housing.* "Process flow" refers to the

movement of materials, paper-work flow, movement of people, and any other form of movement or communication.

3. In many cases it is most desirable that housing serve as an attraction. This feature is readily appreciated in connection with retailing enterprises which use physical features of their facilities, as well as prices and other devices, to attract customers. The manufacturer also recognizes the significance of the appearance of his plant since it may serve to create a more favorable impression upon workers and customers.

4. It is most advantageous to secure housing which serves adequately and does so at a reasonable cost. The availability of desirable and necessary features of a particular housing arrangement must finally be measured in terms of costs of acquisition and operation. The expenditure to maintain the premises and provide the many services necessary for production are very significant to competitive management. If the housing costs of the firm are relatively higher than those of the firm's competitors, management must then seek greater efficiency in the operation of other areas of the business, such as procurement or the use of labor.

Within the framework of the four purposes stated above we may amplify our discussion of housing by referring to more detailed considerations which are significant to the understanding, measurement, and accomplishment of each of the purposes.

HOUSING DETAILS

Determining Space Requirements

As a preliminary to the evaluation of the space availability of any structure, management must have a prior estimation of its needs. The manufacturer must first recognize that the production equipment and its proper functioning will depend upon there being ample spatial allowance in the premises which he contemplates using. Many times this preliminary decision as to basic space requirements comes about as a result of rather naïve estimation. It is true that the space necessary for the locating of machinery and equipment is readily ascertainable; however, the gross area which must provide for the storage and traffic needs of the plant are not so readily determined. Experience has indicated that in many cases of planning the spatial needs of a manufacturer the space occupied by machines and equipment has amounted to as little as 20 to 25 per cent of the total space required for the whole factory. This would mean that the space factor would be 4.0 to 5.0. Therefore, if 1000 square feet were necessary for machines and equipment, the total floor space required for the plant would amount to from 4000 to 5000 square feet.

An approach to determining space requirements which is as simple as the above is of value only after ample consideration has been given not only to the concept of a space factor but also to the influence which variations in floor plans have upon the effectiveness with which the gross area of a building may be used. In some cases it may be preferable to have a rectangular area as opposed to a square area. In other cases an L-shaped area may be quite appropriate for use. In each of these cases, the variation in shape of available premises may or may not allow for the most efficient use of space. Therefore, the concept of space factor must include such a consideration. In addition, due regard must be had for the requirements for aisle space to handle the traffic flow. This need for area is determined not only by the nature and volume of traffic but also by the rate of flow.

Storage

Each cubic foot of area provided by a building may be viewed in terms of its potential use as a storage facility for materials, equipment, records, and people. This space may also serve as a "matching and distribution" base wherein the company products or services are earmarked upon receipt of orders and are arranged for efficient handling as part of the scheme of product distribution.

The housing must provide ample facilities to allow for the stockpiling of raw materials, for goods which are already in various stages of processing, and for those goods which are finished and in storage pending sales or shipment. In addition, the nature of the operating equipment, its size, weight, and portability, enter into our consideration of storage facilities. The question which arises at this point concerns the adaptability of the area to variations in the location of production equipment. Variations in the quantity of storage of raw materials and finished goods must also be considered. The need for space for storage of materials is of more significance to the firm which deals in products which have seasonal aspects of production or sales. Floor-loading restrictions, because of the nature of building structure, may limit both the amount and location of storage.

The discussion must eventually get to the significance of a safety margin in space requirements. The advisability of securing housing with excess area as against less spacious premises may be resolved more or less to management's satisfaction. The measurement of the cost to maintain excess space until such time as it becomes necessary to use it as against the alternative cost of moving or seeking additional space at some later date provides a comparison of the potential saving or loss which is involved. No answer to any problem of this sort is ever any better than the significance of the information which enters into the calculation. The real value of such an approach is more often found in the fact that it forces management to weigh the alternative considerations. The chances of arriving at a conclusion which will serve management advantageously are therefore more likely.

Spatial Efficiency

When evaluating or comparing premises on the basis of floor area, it is highly significant to recognize the extent to which the gross area of a structure may not be indicative of the efficiency with which the area may be used. The ratio of spatial efficiency is related to the construction features of the area. These features may limit the percentage of over-all

FIGURE 7–1

SINGLE-STORY AND MULTISTORY FLOOR PLANS

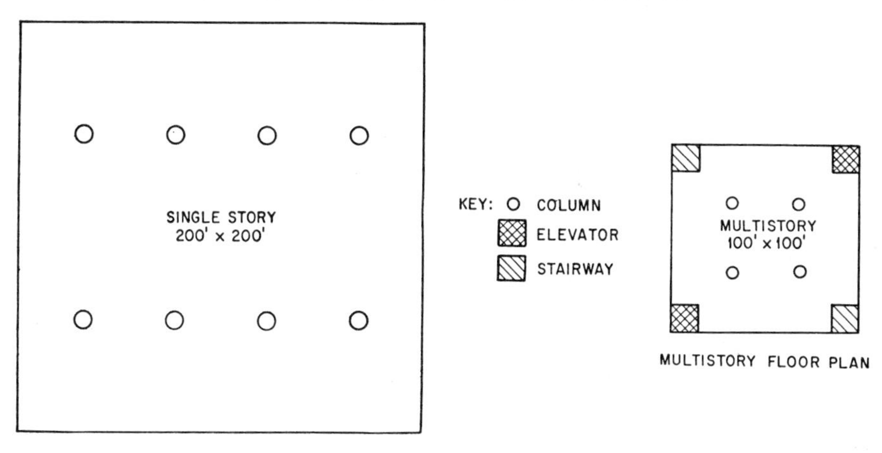

or gross area that may be used for manufacturing or servicing purposes.

As an illustration we may consider two buildings which are available for lease. Each has the same cubical and gross square-foot areas. One of these buildings is single-story and the other is multistory. We will find that because of the nature of building construction the single-story building provides more area for productive uses.

The need for stairways, elevators, supporting columns, and other construction features serves to detract from the efficiency with which space may be used. Naturally, the less use that can be made of the area for which a rental or ownership cost must be paid, the greater is the burden of paying its way which is put upon the plant's productive area.

The single-story structure in Figure 7–1 consists of an area 200 feet square, a total of 40,000 gross square feet. The multistory building is four stories high, and each floor is 100 feet square. This building also has a gross floor area of 40,000 square feet. Each of the diagrams gives indications of that area of floor space which is not usable because of construction features; and, therefore, the percentage of gross area which remains usable is the basis for determining the spatial efficiency of each of the buildings. It is assumed that in any event, regardless of the mathematical approach to measurement of efficiency, if in actual practice a sound use is not made of any premise, all calculations pertinent to its theoretical efficiency are of no avail.

Since income is determined by the extent of production and sales, the less the spatial efficiency of the plant, the less is the area available for productive use and servicing facilities; and thereby a restriction is imposed upon the quantity of production available from the area. The illustration below is a means of determining the percentage of gross area of a plant which is usable and then stating the fact in terms of a percentage of spatial efficiency.

DETERMINATION OF SPATIAL EFFICIENCY

Building type	Multistory	Single-story
Gross area	40,000 sq ft	40,000 sq ft
Productive area lost owing to:		
Elevators	1,000 sq ft	none
Stairways	1,200	none
Approaches	2,000	none
Columns	450	250 sq ft
Misc., heating, plumbing	1,000	800
Total area lost	5,650 sq ft	1,050 sq ft
Remaining usable area	34,350 sq ft	38,950 sq ft
Spatial efficiency (percentage of gross area which is usable)	$\frac{34,350}{40,000} = 85.9\%$	$\frac{38,950}{40,000} = 97.4\%$

In the event that management may wish to evaluate different structures or possible business locations which are not of the same general size or shape, the measurement of spatial efficiency as illustrated above is a handy means of stating each structure's efficiency in relation to the others. The dollars which are paid for ownership or rental represent payment for space and the location of the structure. In any event, management must be concerned with finding out which of a series of possible premises affords the opportunity for greatest space usability per dollar of cost.

Gravity-flow Features

The feature of gravity flow involves the extent to which a building may allow the use of the gravity principle in the movement of materials.

This feature may have little application in some cases, for the very nature of the product or material being handled may not allow for the use of gravity-flow procedure. Granular, fluid, or lightweight products may be easily handled via gravity devices, such as pipes, chutes, and conveyors. On the other hand, bulky and heavy objects would not be considered suitable for transport on a gravity system.

The multistory building may readily lend itself to gravity-flow use and thereby provide a cost-saving feature for management. Since mechanical power is replaced by the laws of gravity, the investment in material-handling equipment and the cost of operating this equipment may be reduced. Many plants start the manufacturing process in the upper stories of the building, and as successive operations are performed, the product moves to the lower floors by gravity flow, and finally the product is stored or shipped from the ground level of the structure.

FIGURE 7–2

USE OF GRAVITY FLOW IN SINGLE-STORY PLANT

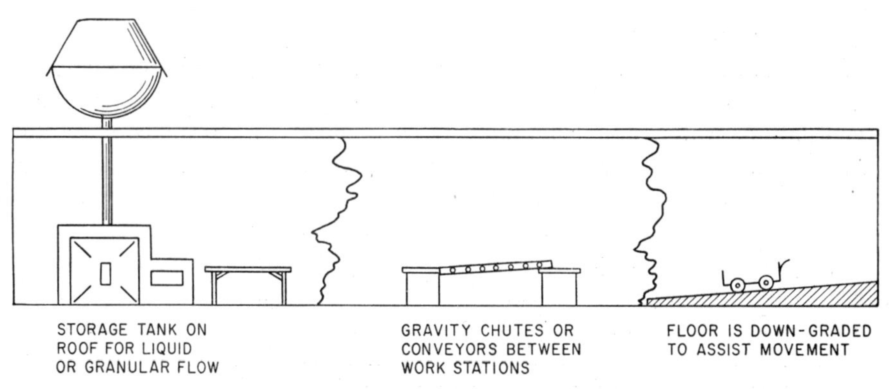

The single-story plant may make for a more limited use of gravity flow. The floor of the plant may be moderately graded in the direction in which production flows, in order that materials in transit may run a downhill route. If the materials are being manually or mechanically transported in wheeled trucks, the slight downgrade in the direction of travel will allow the use of less effort or power. The gravity principle may be applied to the movement of materials or goods between specific work stations on the production floor or throughout the production line. These situations are illustrated in Figure 7–2.

Chutes, ramps, pipelines, and other devices which may be used for gravity-flow handling of materials may help in the reduction of production costs. Such facilities, if available in premises which are being considered for occupancy, warrant extra consideration.

Other Handling Facilities

The route of flow of materials from the point of entrance into the premises, through the various operational areas, and to the final storage area prior to shipment must be considered basic in the analysis of any building which is to be put to industrial use. The existence of elevators, their capacity, and their locations may make the difference between smooth and regular flow of work as against erratic flow involving time-consuming delays which may be brought about by the inadequacy of such handling facilities. We must also consider the location and adequacy of means of entrance and egress and the extent to which mechanical or manual devices may be employed at these points to assist in the work of material handling. Many times the work to be done makes it necessary that specialized handling equipment or devices be used. In this case it is readily seen that a prime factor to consider in the evaluation of housing may well be the question of whether such equipment can be efficiently applied to the job.

Service Facilities

The services which are necessary for the operation of the plant or business include electricity, steam, compressed air, gas, lighting, heating, ventilation, water, and communications devices. The responsibility for maintaining these services usually falls upon the company engineering division, but the supply of these services is a concern of those who are involved in the selection of suitable housing for the enterprise.

Electricity. The requirements of the equipment and fixtures which are to be used by the firm must be known in terms of the quantity of electrical energy which will be needed, the voltages at which the electricity must be provided, and whether both A.C. and D.C. are necessary. On many occasions when management undertakes to use an existing building to house the firm, it is necessary to engage in extensive overhaul of the existing electrical system to provide ample and correct types of service. Newer construction does not usually carry with it this particular problem with respect to electrical-power availability. Present-day building construction quite often provides for great variation in both the nature and location of various plant electrical services which may be demanded.

Lighting. Some industrial buildings have been constructed to make full use of whatever natural lighting advantages there are to be had. These buildings rely upon windows and skylights and variations in roof structure to provide the maximum of natural lighting. (See Figure 7–3.) Some firms rely solely upon artificial lighting and carry on their work under "controlled conditions" of lighting. The typical firm makes use of both natural light and artificial lighting in so far as each serves a purpose. Under any circumstances, the nature of the lighting depends upon two considerations: what one wishes to see and what one wishes to show. Therefore, the manufacturer would want lighting facilities adequate enough to assist his work force in maintaining efficient visual perception. The retail merchant thinks of lighting which will highlight his features and displays and create the mood and atmosphere which he feels will most please and attract the customer. In each case, lighting incorrectly applied can cause serious financial loss.

Any given building or space being considered for business use must be measured in terms of its lighting advantages or disadvantages as in-

FIGURE 7–3

ROOF STRUCTURES AND ENTRY OF NATURAL LIGHT

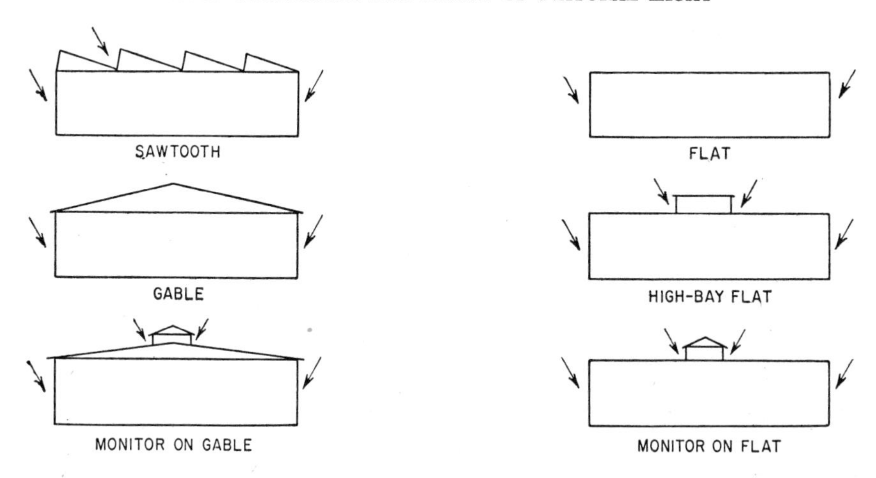

dication of possible influence upon the cost of operating within the premises. Several advantages accrue to a good lighting system.

1. Greater accuracy of work
2. Greater work volume
3. Possibility of better and fuller use of area
4. Promotion of more effective maintenance and cleanliness of plant
5. Improved morale among employees because of better conditions
6. Fewer accidents

It is generally accepted that good illumination does contribute to more effective performance of work and thereby to a reduction of costs. The problem of eye fatigue is eliminated, and the contribution of poor lighting to the accident rate is reduced. Although lighting is not the prime cause of industrial accidents, it is a contributing factor in a significant percentage of cases.

The lighting system of a building must be viewed as to general lighting facilities and supplementary lighting facilities. General lighting is that which provides the base or minimum quantity throughout a room, while supplementary lighting is that which is provided for a particular work area where extra illumination is needed. A warehouse primarily needs general lighting facilities, while a machine shop has need for both general and supplementary facilities. In addition, the versatility of the lighting arrangements is worthy of note in the event that use of the premises may involve frequent revisions in the physical layout of the machines or fixtures.

Ventilation. Adequate circulation is required within the plant, for it has been observed that inadequate ventilation can have an adverse effect upon the mental and physical activity of the work force. In the case of a retail or service organization the resultant discomfort from such inadequacy may cause clientele to take their business elsewhere. The nature of a structure, because of its size and shape, may create problems as to adequate ventilation which can be overcome only by expenditure of both time and money. Ventilation is usually more easily accomplished in the multistory building. Dead air spots are more likely to occur in the wide floor areas which are more common to the single-story structure. The dead spots may be overcome by the installation of ventilating equipment.

Many times the process of manufacture creates objectionable fumes or dust which must be vented from the building. Herein we have a practical reason for investigating the ventilation situation. When clearing the inside of the building of fumes and dust, it is necessary to consider the outside area into which the dust and fumes are vented. Unless care is taken to see that the solution of the venting problem does not interfere with the general surroundings or neighboring plants in particular, legal actions may arise because of inconvenience and damages suffered by innocent parties. This brings to mind the case of the local manufacturer who vented his paint-spray booth to the roadway adjacent to the plant. Needless to say, local parkers were soon aroused by the damage caused to their vehicles by the descending paint particles.

Heat. The individual worker's efficiency depends in part upon the maintenance of a proper temperature in the work area. An increase or decrease from the appropriate temperature will tend to aggravate the accident rate, for both mental and physical fatigue will tend to increase. The building must have ample heating facilities consistent with the requirements of the workers. Just what these requirements may be will depend upon the nature of the work which has to be done. Heavy work will require a relatively low temperature, while light work or mental work will require a higher degree of temperature. As the premises are being checked for heating facilities, it is best to visualize the area as it will be used in order that the work which is to be carried on can be related to the various areas and heating facilities.

The capacity of the heating plant must be checked for possible increase in the heating needs, and also it must be checked for the extent to which it is capable of meeting the heating needs which may be part of the production process. Certainly, the heating requirements for production may be much more important when considering premises than are the working conditions for the employees. Temperature variations and extremes can influence adversely the performance of a production process as well as that of an individual. Management must establish the more important consideration and evaluate housing accordingly.

Personnel Facilities. The need for personnel facilities exists whether the firm is to employ few or many people. The extent of these facilities depends upon the number, sex, and needs of the employees as may be dictated by the nature of the job or the status of labor relations. The laws of the various states govern the location, equipment, and sanitary provisions of personal facilities.

The evaluation of prospective housing must include the examination of available personnel facilities, such as lockers, washrooms, and eating areas. In the event such facilities are not available, consideration must be given to potential locations and cost of installation. If female workers are to be employed, special consideration of their needs is necessary. Although the law pertinent to sanitary facilities for female employees is about the same as that for male employees, it is necessary to consider the location of such facilities and how they may interfere with an otherwise favorable use of space.

The larger the firm, the greater the space allocation for personal-service areas. There is a need for basic sanitary facilities; and in addition there must be provided a great variety of service areas, such as dispensary, rest rooms, dressing rooms, and cafeteria. Each additional use of available space for provisions such as these adds to the cost of housing, for greater plant area is needed or less plant area becomes available for productive purposes. This additional cost may be justified by virtue of the worker's greater satisfaction with his place of employment, which may evidence itself by better production results. A negative approach to justification may cause us to realize that without plant service areas our work force may be less than adequately concerned with turning in a good performance. Such service features as mentioned above may be necessary as inducements to attract employees or to keep employees from escaping to a labor competitor. If the nature of the business involves the receiving of the public or plant visitors in professional capacities, then it certainly speaks well for management and its desire to serve if ample consideration of the establishment of personal facilities for such people is in evidence.

Noise Control. All the noise which interferes with worker performance does not originate within the walls of the plant. It is necessary to seek out possible noise sources in the neighborhood which may create annoyance of the work force. This problem of noise may also originate within the plant as a by-product of the production process. In either case, the possibilities of noise abatement must be viewed. The internal layout of the plant must be made with consideration of controlling noise and minimizing its adverse effects. In the event that the work to be done by the firm involves considerable noise annoyance, the possibility of breaking antinoise ordinances and the legal liability that may arise from hearing injuries should be investigated.

Building Protection. Protection against the entry of thieves and other unauthorized persons may be very important as a factor in the evaluation of housing. Fencing, burglar alarm systems, floodlighting, and other plant protection devices must be checked as to their availability and need as factors appropriate to both the nature of the business and its needs for security provisions.

Housing must also be viewed in relation to provisions for fire protection. Sprinkler systems, hydrant locations, both inside and outside of the building, fire-resistant construction, and other fire protection devices add to the security of operations and also reduce the cost of fire insurance coverage.

If the process or operations to be carried on within the building involve fire hazards, it is necessary to consider the need for special building design or alterations which will minimize possible catastrophe. Paint shops, welding and heat-treating areas, flammable materials storage and handling areas, are subject to greater than average fire hazards and should be enclosed or isolated from other work areas.

Each of the features which are desirable as protective devices adds to both the cost of premises and the relative advantages of one contemplated housing over another. Many times it is advisable to consider neighboring structures and neighboring firms, for the hazards associated with the processes which they house may well be of concern to all the residents in the area.

Parking Facilities. The management of today's plants is often faced with the problem of providing parking facilities for both customers and for employees. The city building is usually at a disadvantage in this respect, for space is at a premium, and on either rental or purchase basis is quite costly. The suburbanization of industry and commerce has to a great extent alleviated this problem. The greater land availability in the suburbs allows for parking facilities and for ample access areas to the building. If the building is not serviced by a railway spur line, all material deliveries will probably be made by motor vehicles; and these need space for access to and exit from the building so that the cargo can be delivered with a minimum of delay and inconvenience. In this regard it is sometimes quite desirable, if space permits, to separate the receiving and shipping area from the general parking area. The total space required for employees or customers will exceed plant area by many times and should be calculated with due consideration of the workforce size and the potential customer volume.

Conditions Affecting Supervision. The shape and size of the premises being considered may serve to assist or offer hindrances in the matter of personnel supervision. If, because of the way in which the building is constructed, the various departments cannot be laid out in an orderly and unbroken pattern, then we may find that supervision of these departments is less effective. Preferably, the area to be supervised should be readily viewable from one or several vantage points. Irregular shape of the area or division of the supervised unit will make it more difficult to maintain the degree of surveillance which may be desirable.

The variations in building design, namely the L, T, E, U, and other shapes do in particular circumstances afford advantages but only in so far as there is no great sacrifice of supervisory needs.

The Cost of Housing Requirements

The alternatives of buying property and leasing property have been discussed in some detail in Chapter 6. The questions of purchase versus lease, net-lease, and gross-lease arrangements have each been explored.

Whatever financial arrangements are entered into when management secures its housing, it must be recognized that the business is being burdened with a cost which is fixed in nature. The rental charge or the costs of ownership are dollars which must be paid out regardless of the efficiency with which the premises are put to use. The evaluation of adequate housing cannot be made solely on the basis of a charge for the premises, for this charge becomes less significant as more and more efficiency is had in the use of the premises.

In some cases, rental charges may be made in direct relation to the gross sales of an enterprise. This provides a more flexible basis for operation, for management does not have a fixed financial burden but pays in accordance with the use to which the facilities are put.

Flexibility in Housing

Except for some continuous type processing a basic goal to which intermittent and repetitive type manufacturing should subscribe is the inclusion of great flexibility and ease of conversion of plant facilities. The continuous processing industry, once it has established its housing requirements, has the expectation of making use of the facilities without need for conversion for a long period of time. Since great investment is made in processing equipment and its setup, it is necessary that the product have a long-term market and standardized production and design characteristics. On the other hand, changes in the demand for the product, the product itself, the process of manufacture, and the like, are inevitable in most other cases, and to maintain efficient production it is necessary that rearrangements be made. The particular housing which the manufacturer seeks must be viewed to see if it will serve the possible need for flexibility. As a means of adding to the flexibility of housing arrangements, the following considerations should be examined:

1. *Internal Structural Features.* Features such as number and location of supporting columns should be considered. These serve to hinder effective use of floor space.

2. *Ceiling Heights and Floor-load Capacities.* Ceiling height is important in terms of clearances for equipment and also because of the possibility of ceiling stacking as part of the plant storage procedure. Floor-load capacities unless sufficient will limit the placement of machinery.

3. *Service Facilities.* These facilities should afford greater capacity than is currently needed, and it is desirable that service lines for power, heat, gas, etc. be easily available throughout the structure.

4. *Opportunity for Expansion.* In general, it is desirable that the premises afford plant area beyond present needs. Adjoining land area on which additional buildings may be erected or adjacent structures which may be adaptable to the firm's purposes are the means whereby area for expansion may otherwise become available.

HOUSING FOR THE RETAILER

The retailer sees his building primarily as a selling instrument. This is in contrast to the viewpoint of the manufacturer or distributor, who may see his building as housing pure and simple. Currently the discount merchants are plying their trade in premises which are not unlike industrial housing and which, in many cases, are actually converted plants or warehouses. These vendors are sacrificing the sales merits of housing with the desire to provide customer service through lower prices, and possibly some convenience of location, rather than attractive and comfortable surroundings.

When the retailer considers the selection of housing, some of the features which he must bear in mind are as follows:

1. Exits and entrances.
2. Ease of access to entrances.
3. Building location and the possibility of entrances on two streets, as preferable to a corner location.
4. Number and size of show windows.
5. Ceiling height.
6. Nature and finish of floor.
7. Lighting system—for display purposes and general lighting.
8. Interior-space allocation possible for aisles and display.
9. If multistory, the means of traffic movement from floor to floor.

If the housing is to assist in the sale of merchandise, it must serve to attract the customer, and it must provide easy access. Once the customer is within the doors, there must be maximum viewing of the floor area and ready means of customer traffic to the various locations within the building.

SUMMARY

The housing which management selects is usually regarded as much less important than it actually is. More often than not, housing is considered as another "necessary evil," which becomes important only in so far as its cost can be reduced. It is much more realistic, however, to consider the premises which the firm occupies in their real role as an active, operating part of the business structure. Housing provides cover, or protection. It should have facilities for servicing the needs of the enterprise. It should provide these things at a reasonable cost. Since the operations of the firm are varying and therefore make changing demands upon facilities and premises, it becomes impossible to view housing as a passive area of the business scene.

If management is faced with making a choice from several possible housing arrangements, there are customarily a variety of approaches to the decision. In some cases, management may be guided solely by personal reasons and thereby select housing in an area with which they are familiar or which is not too far from some desirable residential area wherein they may locate their private residence. This is the least scientific way but it has great appeal to many businessmen. In other cases, the housing is selected on the basis of the ease with which it may be occupied, for it may offer little in the way of a moving or initial financial problem. A much more desirable approach to the evaluation of alternative housing would involve evaluation of both premises in terms of each of the four purposes which we propose that housing must serve. This evaluation is most readily understood if each location is measured in terms of cost for various services and the degree to which the features which management held desirable were respectively available in each case. With this sort of approach we attempt to reduce the comparison to a final objective measurement which becomes a basis for final evaluation.

QUESTIONS

1. Housing serves different purposes for different types of businesses. Discuss.
2. Housing serves four purposes. What are these?
3. The concept of "space factor" may be used as a guide in the determination of spatial requirements. What is its value and what are its limitations?
4. It is desirable to view storage space from the point of view of cubical area rather than just square footage of area. Discuss.
5. The gross area of a structure is but the starting point in the determination of its spatial efficiency. Discuss.
6. What restriction(s) does the nature of the materials impose upon the use of the gravity-flow principle in materials handling?
7. What are some of the services which are necessary for plant operations?
8. What advantages accrue to the use of a good lighting system?
9. What features must management seek in its housing which will enhance the safety and security of the plant?
10. How do building shape and construction features influence the supervisory task?
11. What features must be borne in mind by the retailer as he considers suitable housing for his enterprise?
12. When management is concerned with appraising the flexibility of housing provisions, what conditions should be examined?

CHAPTER 8

Layout Planning and Material Handling

Plant layout deals with the arrangement of the physical facilities and the manpower which are required to manufacture a product or perform a service. It is necessary that management devote some time to the consideration of the physical arrangement of facilities and the layout of work areas in order to promote the efficiency of their operations. The manufacturer is vitally concerned with the use of space in so far as he must position men and machines in such relationship as to foster production; the store merchant is concerned with the arrangement of counters, shelves, aisles, display racks, etc., and other devices which assist in the presentation of goods to the customers and which also cater to the traffic needs of his clientele; the office manager must tend to the placement of files, desks, other office equipment, and the location of working personnel so as to promote smoother work flow. In every case, of which these three are but illustrative, it is necessary to isolate the peculiar needs of the situation which must be catered to and to keep in mind the physical limitations of space and equipment.

Good Layout

A good layout should be planned so that the handling of materials is reduced to a minimum. Many times it is also desirable that personnel movement be kept to a minimum so as to reduce the amount of non-productive time. There exist, however, those who prefer a relaxation of this viewpoint on the grounds that the introduction of movement about the work area or plant as part of the task adds to the on-the-job satisfaction by relieving the monotony otherwise attendant. Good layout involves the use of the correct equipment, the right method of doing a job, and the location of the activity to allow for the most effective production of goods or services in the shortest practical time period and involving the least practical amounts of material handling, distance of movement, and costs. The above, as an indication of what is meant by "good layout," undoubtedly leaves one somewhat cold, for the significance of the repeated use of the word "practical" certainly cannot be overlooked. More often than not, one man's concept of a practical approach differs from another's. Because of this, there cannot be said to exist a perfect solution to the layout problem of any particular firm. As is usual, the final result is subject to the whims and interpretations of individuals as fortified by intelligent understanding but hampered by lack of knowledge or of physical accompaniments which would be necessary or desirable for effective layout.

The chances of accomplishing a successful layout increase as due attention is given a systematic approach to the planning of layout. The systematic approach certainly appears more valid if an understanding is had of the advantages which may result from sound layout practice. These may be enumerated as follows:

1. Lower-cost operations
2. Shortening of the production-cycle time
3. Increases in the volume of activity, greater production from existing facilities
4. Reduction in working capital requirements
5. Improved work-force morale

Each of these possible advantages will be brought into clearer focus in this chapter and the following one.

LAYOUT PROCEDURE

Goals of Production

In order to accomplish the basic objective of plant-layout activity, it is necessary that men and machines be integrated. However, integration cannot be effectively approached unless we first establish the basic goal or goals which management holds foremost. Customarily we pronounce that management is seeking efficient production. What is efficient production? The answer depends upon the nature of the activity and the nature of management's goals. For one firm efficient production may have the single meaning of the highest possible quantity of production. Thus the cooperation between men and machines must be one which reduces to a minimum the time factor involved in production. Herein we find that our approach to layout must therefore hold paramount the criterion of time. Another firm may establish as its definition of efficient production the ability of the firm to produce a variety of products. In this case the use of men and machines and the approach to plant layout must keep uppermost in mind the goal of versatility and flexibility. Yet another firm may consider quality to be its indicator of efficient production. In this case the production facilities and their arrangement cater primarily to those features of the process which add to or maintain the desirable quality features, and the use of space is less important in terms of cost and time. It is the extraordinary circumstance when some degree of importance is not attached to the significance of cost of operations and the influences which layout has upon this cost. Regardless of the primary goal, we usually find it necessary to place emphasis upon cost considerations.

The businessman does not usually establish a single goal for his venture. Although at any given time one goal may be of primary importance, each of the others mentioned above is customarily considered. The layout must be conceived and built around these basic goals, for without such a centralizing force the work effort expended in creating the layout would travel in diverse directions.

These basic goals of a producing unit may be finally stated as follows:

1. A large volume of output
2. A low cost per unit of output
3. Variety of output
4. Quality of performance

Process Analysis

Once management has firmly fixed in mind the basic goals which it seeks, the planning of a layout next involves an analysis of the process of work. This analysis involves the decision as to necessary operations and the order in which they are to be performed. The order of performance may then serve to indicate the location of machines, personnel, or departments—whichever may be engaged in the performance of the respective process steps. If the manufacture of a product calls for the making of many parts which are to be finally assembled into the finished product of the firm, it is necessary first to obtain a parts list from the product-engineering department and then to proceed with process analysis for each part. Whenever the process of manufacture involves several parts or processes of work, it becomes necessary to establish the layout in view of the interrelationship which each part or process has with the others. The task of layout planning differs in the case of the firm which carries on but one or a few processes of work as against the firm which involves itself in the handling of many varying processes of work which change from day to day. In the former case the firm would be concerned with establishing a layout pattern which would provide a large volume of production, while in the latter case the layout pattern must cater to the variety which is demanded of the production facilities. Since we must at the outset recognize these two diverse approaches to the establishment of the layout of physical facilities, it would seem best to assign their respective titles to the situations. The pattern which caters to limited variety of product, possibly a single product, is called "line layout." The inference is that the facilities are set up in a line, or predetermined order. The other form, which caters to variety of products, is called "process layout"; and in this case the physical plant is laid out by grouping facilities according to the nature of work performed rather than according to product worked on.

Process analysis is also significant in that it provides specific information as to the materials, machine, and equipment requirements necessary to perform the operations called for. Customarily we find the following information derived from the procedure of process analysis:

1. Bill of materials, list of parts
2. Equipment and machine listing
3. Labor-skill requirements
4. Sequence and schedule of operations

The process analysis is customarily set up in the form of a flow-process chart. This is a graphic device which is used to portray the details of any process. If the work involves the assembly of several parts, each manufactured by the firm, the process of manufacture for each part will first be set up in chart form. Then the relationship of each part to the others may be shown by an assembly chart which graphically shows how the various parts go together, which parts make up each subassembly, and how the various components flow through the production area and finally emerge as a finished product. This type of chart presents an over-all picture of the manufacturing and assembly process. (See operation process chart, Figure 5–1.)

Flow-process Chart

This device serves to portray in detail the process of work. It makes use of a series of symbols. The basic symbols used in this type of analysis are presented below. There are additional symbols in use. Some of them represent combined activities, such as an operation and a storage occurring simultaneously; others represent operations peculiar to the particular area of work being studied. The charting of an office procedure involves the use of specialized symbols in order to indicate adequately the nature of the various operations.

◯ Denotes an operation being performed on the product.

○ Denotes transportation, or movement.

□ Denotes an inspection.

▽ Denotes storage.

D Denotes a delay.

The flow-process chart is illustrated below. It defines the nature and frequency of each type of occurrence and also includes data as to the time and distance features involved in the particular operations being performed. The chart is usually prepared prior to the actual layout activity. We, however, will use the flow-process chart in connection with an existing or proposed layout in order that distance and time features may be realistically included in the illustration.

The flow-process chart, Figure 8–1, depicts the operation nature, the time involved per lot of 100 units at each process step, and the distance of movement, horizontal or vertical. Management, in the attempt to build more efficiency into the process, asks certain questions which are basic to all process analyses:

1. Can any steps be eliminated?
2. Can any step be combined with another? Should any step be divided?
3. Are there some steps which could be simplified?

The time-and-distance features of the process are considered from the point of view of cutting down the over-all time and limiting the distance which a unit must travel during the process. The time in process may be reduced, in part as a result of changes which come about after analysis.

Further time and distance reduction may occur as a result of revision of layout and the adoption of different handling methods or equipment. An important consideration at this time is the effect that changes in one department will have in terms of the other departments which are concerned with the production of the same item. This raises the question of equated capacity in production.

The management which is concerned with the process as illustrated in the flow-process chart may consider the following features worthy of appraisal and indicative of desirable changes:

1. Is there real need for quality and quantity inspection in operation #1? Would a standard method of stacking units on trucks eliminate the need for a full count (quantity inspection)?
2. Can rough-finish inspection be eliminated?
3. Can delays at elevator be minimized? Is a schedule of use possible with the elevator? Is more than one truckload of material handled per trip or can it be? Must these parts go into storage? How long will they be in storage?
4. Is a different layout of machines possible so as to limit time and distance?
5. Do volume of production and potential savings warrant the use of new handling methods and equipment? Conveyorize?

Since we are considering a situation of repetitive production, we will

FIGURE 8–1

FLOW-PROCESS CHART (BEFORE)

PROCESS: FINISH OPERATION ON PART X
LOCATION: DEPARTMENT 42

LOT SIZE: 100 UNITS

OPER. NO.	SYMBOL	EXPLANATION	TIME MINUTES	DISTANCE FEET
1	□	INCOMING MATERIAL INSPECTED FOR QUALITY AND QUANTITY	30.0'	
2	○	TRUCK TRANSPORT TO WORK STATION #304	.4'	40.0'
3	◯	ROUGH FINISH OPERATION	50.0'	
4	○	TRANSPORT TO INSPECTION	.6'	50.0'
5	□	INSPECT FOR QUALITY	20.0'	
6	○	TRANSPORT TO WORK STATION #405	.6'	50.0'
7	◯	FINE-FINISH OPERATION	50.0'	
8	○	TRANSPORT TO INSPECTION	.6'	50.0'
9	□	INSPECT FOR QUALITY	40.0'	
10	○	TRANSPORT TO ELEVATOR	.4'	30.0'
11	D	WAIT FOR ELEVATOR	.5 - 3.0'	
12	○	TRANSPORT TO STORAGE	.4'	VT. 30.0'
		TOTAL TIME/LOT	193.3– 195.8	
		TOTAL DISTANCE/LOT		220 HOR. 30 VT.

SUMMARY

◯ 2 ▽ 0 □ 3 D 1 ○ 6

assume that the market for the product will be long-term and, therefore, will warrant investment in improvements. Therefore, also assuming that certain inspections could be eliminated or handled by other means and that layout was revised, a resultant flow-process chart could appear as in Figure 8–2. It is evident that the time-and-distance savings as a result of the revisions are substantial. Management has gained costwise and productionwise.

The development of the final layout plan is the result of testing and improving upon each suggested pattern. However, approval is not rendered solely on the basis of flow-process-chart analysis. Other devices

FIGURE 8–2

FLOW-PROCESS CHART (AFTER)

PROCESS: FINISH OPERATION ON PART X (REVISED)
LOCATION: DEPARTMENT 42
LOT SIZE: 100 UNITS

OPER. NO.	SYMBOL	EXPLANATION	TIME MINUTES	DISTANCE FEET
1	○	CONVEYOR FROM PRECEDING DEPARTMENT TO STATION #304	.3'	30.0'
2	◯	ROUGH-FINISH OPERATION	50.0'	
3	○	TRANSPORT TO STATION #405	.3'	30.0'
4	◯	FINE-FINISH OPERATION	50.0'	
5	○	TRANSPORT TO INSPECTION DEPARTMENT	.4'	40.0'
6	□	INSPECTION	40.0'	
7	○	TRANSPORT TO STORAGE	.8'	40.0' VT. 30.0'
		TOTAL TIME/LOT	141.8'	
		TOTAL DISTANCE/LOT		140 HOR, 30 VT.

SUMMARY

◯ 2 ▽ 0 □ 1 D 0 ○ 4

must be used which will depict visually the layout form being considered. In this way potentially weak traffic arrangements and poor spatial relationships become evident.

Flow Diagram

After an assembly or flow-process chart has been set up for the process of work, it is necessary to consider the flow-of-work pattern. Although the flow-process chart fixes what management feels is the best sequence of operations, it does not solve the question of physical location of the various work stations. The process fixes the sequence, or route, of production in terms of order of events. It is now necessary that each step be planned to accomplish the movement of materials and/or manpower in as direct a path as possible through the plant. The start and finish of the process,

FIGURE 8–3

FLOW DIAGRAM (BEFORE)

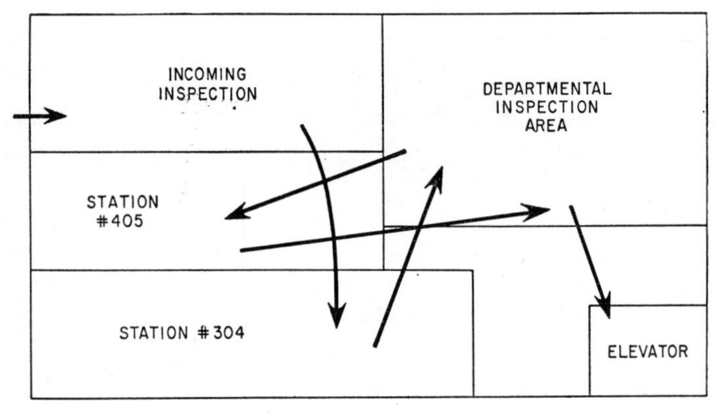

both on a departmental and a plant basis, must be viewed in terms of handling facilities and economies. The ideal situation is one in which the equipment is laid out to suit the process and the plant itself is designed around the layout. In most cases, however, the flow of work must be fitted into an existing area and possibly around existing facilities.

The flow diagrams Figures 8–3 and 8–4 represent the "before" and "after" of departmental layout as a result of the process revisions. The purposes served by the flow diagrams are to depict the traffic flow and to indicate areas where production routine may be hampered by crowded conditions.

Figure 8–3, the "before" situation, readily shows up the excessive hauling distances, the backtracking of the product in transit, and potential troubles with traffic flow as indicated by the crossing flow lines. The

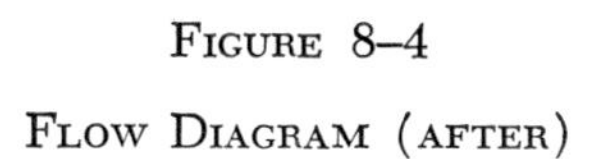

FIGURE 8–4

FLOW DIAGRAM (AFTER)

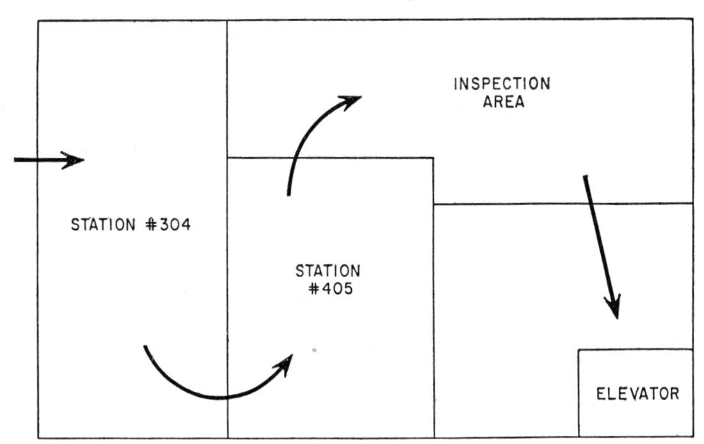

"after" situation, Figure 8–4, presents a much more orderly picture of flow and has eliminated the difficulties which previously existed.

The flow diagram points out those areas on the production floor where consideration must be given to roadways for the movements of men and materials. This type of diagram will indicate where it is best to make provisions for aisle space and in what amount, depending upon the volume and the nature of the movement being carried out.

If several products are being handled in the same area, each product path may be indicated on the same diagram by means of a different colored or different type of line. The greater the concentration of lines of flow in any particular location, the greater the need for adequate consideration of the flow problem.

As each layout revision is being considered, a flow diagram should be prepared so that the necessary traffic data such as distance of movement, concentration of movement, and need for space may be established.

Many factors affect the flow pattern. If the products consist of few parts, the flow planning is easier. The fewer the operations to be performed, the easier the flow planning. The number of subassemblies, the shape of the space available for working area, the size and weight of the raw materials—each is the concern of those who are responsible for the planning of production layout. The question may be raised whether the materials should be moved to the machines or vice versa; should parts be moved to subassemblies or vice versa? If the product being made increases in weight as it is processed, it might be wiser to move raw materials and parts greater distances. If the product decreases in weight and/or size as a result of processing, it becomes easier to handle; and therefore it may be moved with progressively more ease.

If the consideration of layout involves the use of the devices mentioned above and in addition uses them as tools of measurement and critical appraisal of the alternatives which may be available, then most assuredly a better layout will evolve.

The flow chart and process analysis are but the basis of layout planning. We must remember that the greatest operating efficiency is reached only when the process of work is accomplished in the shortest practical time. The longer the process time, the higher the cost of the process.

Templates and Models

Simultaneous with the development of the process and flow of work it is a good idea that each layout plan be represented by a model or templates or simple line diagrams.

Unlike the ordinary housewife who rearranges furniture by pushing each piece about the room several times until a satisfactory arrangement is had, the businessman who is in the process of arranging his machines and equipment makes use of paper cutouts or dimensional models to assist him in evaluating the various possible arrangements.

Templates are cutouts to scale of the various machines, the equipment, the product itself, or any other physical item which is necessary to the process of work and which must be assigned space. Templates are two-dimensional; models are three-dimensional. These templates and models include in their dimensions the space necessary for the worker who will tend the machine or work area; storage and aisle space which is necessary adjacent to the machine for tools, personnel, or materials; and area necessary for swinging or moving parts of the machine when it is in operation. Scale models of men, machines, and all the physical units which enter into the layout problem are intended to achieve the same purpose as templates but do so more realistically.

Each suggested revision or improvement in process and layout may be quickly demonstrated by shifting the templates or models about on a scaled floor diagram of the area in which the work is to be done. Alternatives to this procedure are the preparation of a series of scale drawings, one for each proposed layout pattern or, even as by the housewife, the repeated shifting about of pieces of equipment. This last method is out of the question in most industrial situations.

In any event, photographs of proposed layouts or revised layouts can be made for purposes of comparison. With these various visual aids to layout practice, space relationships are more easily viewed and potential trouble spots are more readily located.

BASIC LAYOUT PATTERNS

Whether the approach to layout is concerned with the revision of an old layout or the creation of a new one, the final solution must represent a joint effort in planning. Those who are to be responsible for operations within the area being laid out should be consulted with and cooperated with to the extent, at least, that their ideas concerning layout are considered by the planning department and evaluated on a par with all other ideas. Final layout should be decided upon only after multiple considerations. Every purpose cannot be fully served, but ample investigation and revision upon revision will undoubtedly add up to a more desirable final layout. The decision as to this final form rests with top management.

In preparing the layout, due emphasis should be placed on the provision for plant expansion. If the present location does not allow for an expansion factor, the business may at some future time be inconvenienced with moving or construction costs which possibly could have been avoided by adequate planning.

Since the individual firm must consider its layout goal in the light of its own needs, layout practice will vary according to circumstances. Our approach to defining the types of layout patterns will be based on the assumption of extreme or widely differing production goals on the part of management.

We shall first consider a layout form which has as its primary goal the production of a large quantity of a particular good. The second example of layout form will be one which has as its primary goal a variety of production. It should be understood that in either case both cost and quality goals, each according to its own merits, are the secondary goals which must be considered.

A high volume of production of single or of few products is a characteristic of the form of layout which is called "line layout."

If the goal of layout is to provide a variety of products, the process layout is the form which best provides the necessary versatility in production.

Line Layout

Line layout, or production-line layout, is the form best used when the manufacturing process is repetitive or continuous. There are two aspects involved: first, a volume of production of a particular product; and second, a fixed sequence of operations through which each unit of production must pass. Usually there is minor, if any, variation possible or necessary in terms of the finished product or the series of production stages through which the product must pass.

For any particular item being manufactured, the management will set up what it believes to be the most practical and efficient series of production steps. Two companies, each manufacturing the same product, may establish different sequences of production steps. Each company would necessarily be restricted or aided in establishing this series by the extent to which physical facilities and personnel were available.

The sequence in which the operations are to be performed is called "the process."

Line layout attempts in principle and practice to effect an orderly and logical arrangement of productive facilities that will be consistent with a large production volume. It would seem that this goal can be best achieved by placing the equipment which does the work in the same order of physical arrangement that is indicated by the process. This is fundamentally the procedure followed.

If a particular process consisted of four steps, each of which involved the use of a machine, the graphic picture of this layout would be as shown in Figure 8–5.

FIGURE 8–5

PATTERN OF LINE LAYOUT

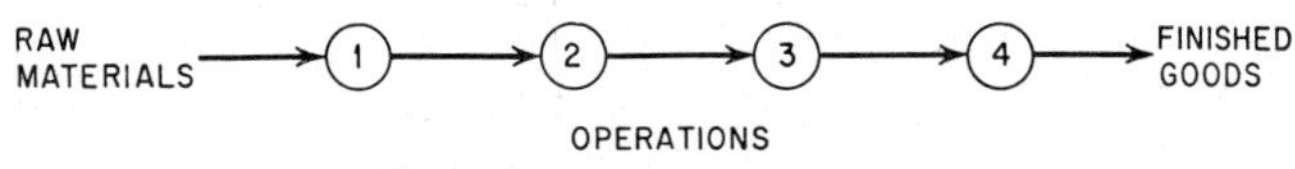

Let us assume that the machines used for each operation are as follows:

Operation #1 Table saw, Model S
" #2 Wood planer
" #3 Table saw, Model S
" #4 Sanding machine

It is evident that the machines which perform operations #1 and #3 are alike. In order to effect continuous forward movement, it is necessary that two machines of the particular type be used.

Several questions should be raised by the student even at this early point. With the types of machines indicated, cannot several possible items be produced? If this is so, what makes this layout pattern unique in terms of a large output of any particular product? Is it possible that the machine used in operation #1 could also take care of the work volume which is, according to the layout diagram above, being done by a duplicate machine at operation #3? Does line layout mean that the machines must be arranged in a straight line? Can the line curve? Does production necessarily move from a single machine setup to another single machine setup, or may two or more machines be fed by a single machine or some such variation?

Process Layout

This form of layout is best used when the products of the firm are of very varied nature as to type, quality, and quantity of production at any given time. Process layout form would be found in the shop of the custom manufacturer, who will produce only if and when items are ordered by customers. Since there is no one product around which the layout pattern may be built, it is necessary that some other basic aspect of production be used as a guide for layout practice. The basis used must be that which is the least variable element in the production activity.

By the elimination of quantity, quality, and nature of products, each because of its extremely variable nature, we have but the machines and labor left to consider. Even with these elements there will be variety,

FIGURE 8–6

PROCESS LAYOUT—MACHINE SHOP

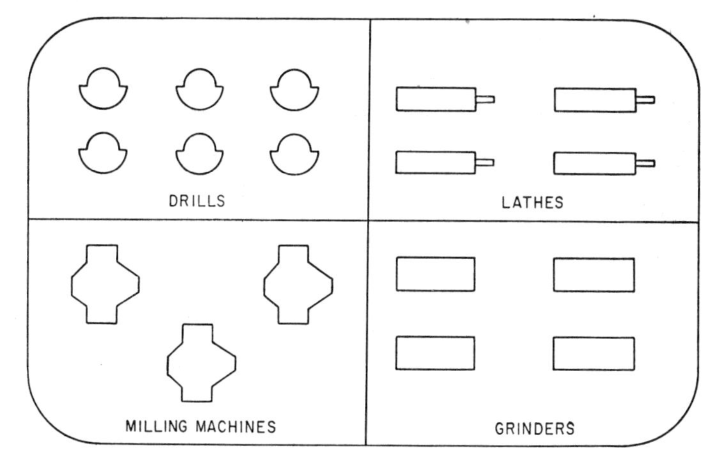

but of a much lesser degree. Process layout is developed on the basis of a team of men and machines and the variety of operations which this team is capable of performing.

There are basic man-machine operations which may be common to many, if not all, of the varied products manufactured in a given field of production. The items which the manufacturer will be asked to produce will make it necessary that his shop be equipped with at least the basic tools and machines necessary for his field of production.

Process layout involves the partition of the plant into several areas, each of which is occupied by a particular type of machine or operation.

In each of the figures, 8–6 and 8–7, areas are devoted either to machines or operations which are necessary in the line of business. In either case any particular order received need not make use of the complete variety of machines or operations. The process of manufacture would be established for each order as the order was received. Since the nature of the products may vary continuously, it is necessary that the layout be as flexible as possible.

FIGURE 8–7

PROCESS LAYOUT—PHOTO PROCESSING

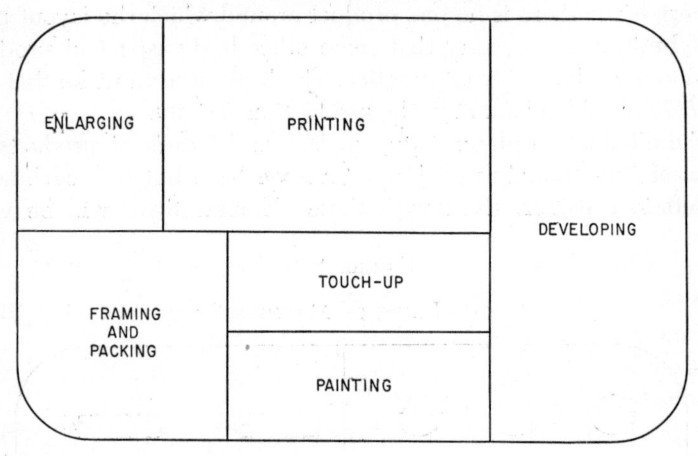

A Combination Approach to Layout Pattern

If sufficient volume of production is maintained for certain product(s) of the nonvolume manufacturer, a product-line layout may be warranted. Layout planning for the firm which has some high-volume products and, in addition, a need for flexibility in layout so as to cater to customers who seek variety may be accomplished by combining features of each of the basic forms of layout pattern. Whenever possible, the attempt should be made to apply volume-production principles even as a part of an over-all production process, for there is no law which says that a process must be either of the "line" or "process" type exclusively. Quite to the contrary, many business firms find it to their economic advantage to apply both approaches as a solution to their production problems. Line layout is the basic approach when volume of production is the prime requisite, while product-equipment relationships will be the key to layout when the basic concern of the plant is to provide variety of output.

THE PROCESS AND ITS INFLUENCE ON LAYOUT

Variations in the type of processes carried on in different industries make necessary differences in plant layout. The processing of liquid and granular products preferably seeks multistory layouts in order to make use of gravity-flow principles. A foundry, an airplane assembly line, and a great number of our modern plants find, for various reasons, that single-story layout is to their greatest advantage. In addition to the building as influenced by the production process, we find that the basic process nature adapts itself to a particular pattern of layout because of the inherent advantages of that form.

Continuous and Repetitive Process

Both these processes (see Chapter 5) involve long-term setup of productive facilities which are devoted to the production of a large volume of a limited variety of products. Since these facilities are by design economical only under conditions of quantity production, it is most natural that a line layout be employed. Certainly there is no alternative in the case of a continuous-process industry, for the sequence of operations once fixed, and as long as there are no major changes in the process, the line is fixed and layout is a dormant function. This same feature holds for the layout for repetitive manufacture, for herein we also find justification for the production-facilities investment in the form of high-production volume. Since the need for high volume is best and continuously catered to by the line form of layout, it serves most adequately the need of the continuous processing and repetitive industries.

Intermittent Process

Intermittent production cannot make full use of specialized layout. The variety of items manufactured and their respective quantities of production at any time do not usually warrant the establishment of production equipment in one fixed order of arrangement or spatial relationships. The company which offers a variety of products applies the basic rules of good layout procedure in terms of space use, the nature of operations, and the need for providing production services rather than concern itself with the establishment of a fixed sequence of operations.

If possible, the nature of equipment layout is made to conform to the customary order of use in production. This means that if most or some of the items manufactured customarily start their respective production cycles with a common type or sequence of operations and then proceed to any other common machine or similar type of operation, the machine groups which perform these operations will be located as much as is possible in the order of sequence.

The actual work of preparing a layout under these circumstances also involves the use of templates, models, flow charts, and diagrams. The details of the routes of travel and the means and volume of traffic must be evaluated for each layout pattern considered. Because of the lesser emphasis which can be placed upon machine position in a fixed order of arrangement, greater attention must be paid to the material-handling situation. In actual practice the efficiency with which the manufacturer may handle a custom order is closely related to the efficiency of the material-handling system.

Since the emphasis in layout practice for the situation of intermittent manufacturing is placed upon space, nature of operations, services, and material handling, it therefore follows that process layout is most appropriate.

THE PRODUCT AND ITS INFLUENCE ON LAYOUT

Model and style changes of a product, even though it is produced on a quantity basis and with product line setup, necessitate layout changes. Although the line caters to quantity of production, it is now obvious that any particular line layout need not be too long-lived. The principle, however, remains intact.

The product to be manufactured must be classed as to whether it falls into a luxury or necessity category. If the product is of the luxury class, line layout would be an unreasonable approach to production, for the market for such a product would not be adequate to support such a productive setup. Normally we would expect such a product to be produced on a limited scale and preferably under conditions of process layout which minimize specialized equipment and layout. A product categorized as a necessity would provide the mass market, at the right price, to support greater volume of production if produced at a reasonable price. This situation justifies the existence of line layout.

MATERIAL HANDLING

During each day of business, many dollars are spent to move materials into, through, and out of the place of business. An important part of the indirect labor payroll and of the total cost of manufacture represents payments for material-handling activities.

There are two areas of material handling, internal and external. Internal material handling involves the receiving, storage, and movement of materials between various work stations, shipping department activities, and lastly, material handling which is done by the workers at their machines or workplaces. This phase of handling must be dealt with as one of the factors of the problem of plant layout. External material handling involves the transport of materials from their source to the receiving platform of the firm and from the shipping dock of the firm to the customers. External material handling is one of the considerations dealt with as part of the problem of plant location, which is discussed in Chapter 3.

Although handling operations do not directly add value to the product, they do add to costs and thereby represent potential sources of savings. The cost areas are significant and should be closely scrutinized by the businessman. Excessive and faulty handling activities add to production costs and delays, injuries to workmen, and damage to materials.

The equipment which is used to move materials through the plant must be considered as an integral part of the plant layout. This equipment is as important as the machines which do the actual production, for unless materials are where they must be and at the necessary time, the best of production equipment is unable to serve its purpose.

A Material-handling System and Its Objectives

A material-handling system is that plan which seeks to coordinate the use of equipment and man power so as to result in the movements of materials into, through, and out of the plant most effectively. The effectiveness of any handling system must be measured in terms of the attainment of certain objectives which are as follows:

1. Saving money
2. Handling a greater volume of materials
3. Making the handling work easier and safer
4. Maintaining the correct quantity-time relationship

Control over the Handling Activity

Control over the material-handling activity should be definitely placed. The organizational importance of a material-handling supervisor will vary considerably depending upon the extent of handling and its significance to successful plant operations. In every case, however, material handling must be considered as an activity which creates cost and detracts from profits.

Equipment use may be controlled by a central authority. This presupposes adequate consideration of the coordinated use of equipment in many different plant areas so as to get the best rate of use and thereby the most economical service in view of diverse areas which must be provided with service.

Material-handling authority may, on the other hand, be decentralized, thus restricting the area of control and possibly the use of equipment to a particular department. This may be desirable because of specialized handling situations within one department which are not common to other departments. This form of control may, by virtue of the restriction imposed upon the area of use, contribute to increased material-handling costs.

The need for real control is expressed most adequately whenever the production lines are restricted in performance because of lack of ready availability of materials and parts. If material-handling equipment is idle in one department while another department can make use of it, we have an indication of ineffective control which adds to production costs. These additions to cost come about because of the idle equipment capacity and because of the handicap placed on the productive efficiency of the department which is in need of additional handling equipment.

Planning the Material-handling System

In order to establish the material-handling system, management must consider as a first step the basic methods of material handling and types of equipment which it will or can use to do the handling job. The nature of the product, light or heavy, bulky or small, granular or fluid; the nature of the building, its construction features, ceiling heights, floor-bearing loads, obstructions on floor areas, such as columns; and the nature of the production layout, line, process, or a combination form, are the principal factors involved in the selection of material-handling methods and equipment.

There are many varieties of equipment which may be suitable for a given job. As a further analysis of the handling problem is carried out, better alternatives may come to light.

The second step in establishing the handling system is to determine the work volume that can be handled by the type of installation being considered. A potential handling system which provides uneconomical handling volume forces management to seek alternatives.

The third step, assuming a final selection has been made, is to determine where the equipment is to be located in reference to the materials which are to be handled and the area where the work is to be done. This step is actually a part of the plant-layout procedure, for even as the production equipment is being considered in terms of layout location, so must the connecting links, handling equipment, be considered.

It is difficult to say which should come first in emphasis, the layout of machines or the choice of handling methods and equipment. Management may build the plant activity around a handling system. Warehousing activity is primarily concerned with the movement and storage of materials; therefore, it is natural that the greatest emphasis is placed on the methods and means of handling which will, in turn, then have an effect on the nature of the layout. On the other hand, management may build the handling system into the plant activity. A mass producer emphasizes the volume aspect of his production line. However, the desire to maintain a satisfactory flow of raw materials into, through, and out of the plant affects the nature of the handling equipment which is selected.

An alternative approach may be had to the material-handling situation. In some cases the size and/or weight of the product introduces the possibility of moving men and machines to the product rather than vice versa. Material handling is now concerned with the movement of men and their production equipment. In the construction of ships, locomotives, and giant turbines this method has been successfully used. The reasons should be apparent.

The decision as to whether the product is to be moved or the men and machines are to be moved to the product is usually governed by the respective over-all costs which are involved.

The fourth step is to establish a control over the handling system which will provide management with some assurance that the handling facilities will provide the extent of service that is deemed practical and necessary and that constant attention will be devoted to the improvement of the service and the reduction of unit-handling costs. Such assurances can be had only if in the original consideration of plant layout and organization the management placed due emphasis upon the role of the material-handling activity and, in turn, recognized its importance as a service which contributes to the over-all effectiveness of the production areas.

The form of control which is established may be that exercised by a material-handling supervisor whose concern it is to plan and coordinate the use of handling facilities. On the other hand, the control may be mechanical in that the equipment may function automatically or at a rate controllable within narrow limits. Equipment which is fixed in position and thereby is in reality an integral part of the production line is controlled along with the production activity rather than as a separate service function.

Basic Principles of Material Handling

Many principles have been formulated as a guide in establishing a satisfactory and economical material-handling setup. The following list, although not complete, is adequate for a preliminary study.

1. Handle as little as possible.
2. Use handling equipment whenever feasible in preference to manual handling. This eliminates fatigue, accidents, and damage.
3. Eliminate or reduce handling by production workers. Their time is too costly.
4. Use standard equipment whenever possible. This will facilitate repair, training, and interchangeability.

5. Use gravity flow if possible.
6. Select equipment on the basis of unit-handling cost, not initial cost.
7. Recognize the effect of the nature of handling equipment in one department on that in another department. Seek to integrate so as to maintain a smooth flow of materials throughout the plant.
8. Combine handling with processing whenever possible, thus killing two birds with one stone.
9. Plan straight-line routes and continuous flow if possible.
10. Schedule and supervise the use of equipment.
11. Consider the extent to which the equipment will serve company needs at varying rates of plant activity.
12. Check building features which may affect choice of handling methods—such as poor floor surfaces and low ceilings.
13. Take safety precautions in terms of handling equipment and its use.
14. Train personnel in the correct use of the equipment.
15. Establish a maintenance program.

Costs to be Considered

The businessman is constantly making payments to personnel and for equipment used to move materials. In the search for more economical operations there is but one valid approach to the making of a decision. An adequate knowledge of what an activity currently costs or will cost is the only basis upon which a decision regarding changes or improvements can be rendered. A material-handling situation, whether it exists now or is being contemplated, should be evaluated on the basis of the following:

1. Cost to carry the investment in handling equipment. This involves interest on the investment, insurance, taxes, depreciation, and obsolescence.
2. Cost to operate the material-handling activity. These operating costs include wages paid to operators of equipment and to personnel who do manual handling, the costs of maintenance and repair of equipment, and power charges.
3. Costs arising from administrative and supervisory activities concerned with material handling. The training of operators, supervision of handling operations, clerical activities necessary to record and schedule data, must be reckoned in dollars and cents.
4. Initial purchase price and installation costs. The dollar outlay necessary to secure equipment and set it up in working condition may appear prohibitive to management. This feature may bar further consideration by management of equipment installation or improvement. If such is the case, the possibility of large future savings which would come as a result of the investment is probably not be-

ing adequately considered. From these potential savings management may be able to finance the purchase.

The final decision as to whether change should or should not take place is determined on the basis of the unit-handling cost of the respective alternate solutions to the handling problem.

Material-handling Equipment

There are many varieties of handling equipment available. They fall generally into two broad categories, fixed-path and variable-path equipment.

Several types of material-handling equipment and situations are presented in Figures 8–8 and 8–9.

A production line which manufactures a large volume, long-lived product uses fixed-path equipment since there is no variation in the route which materials will travel. The system is usually conveyorized. A process layout must use equipment which can travel a variety of routes depending upon which of the several items in production is being moved. Some form of industrialized truck would be used in this case.

Material Handling at the Workplace

Attention to the material handling which the worker does at his workbench or in the course of operating his machine has been intentionally neglected in the development of the foregoing material. Our prime concern has been with the movement that occurs between departments and work stations. The importance of workplace handling will be considered in a later chapter dealing with the workplace layout and methods study.

SUMMARY

Once a layout plan is put into effect it depends upon people for its correct functioning. As many of these people as possible should have the opportunity to participate in the planning of the layout. The usual plant-layout problem deals with the revision of an existing layout rather than with a new layout. These revisions are caused by changes in process, product design, change in departmental size, introduction of new products or facilities, and variation in facilities.

Preliminary to any layout program, managerial objectives must be clearly stated, for only then is there a clear view of the desired accomplishments which the layout helps to achieve. We recognize the line layout as catering to volume and standard products. The process layout is most suitable to the manufacture of those products which are demanded in limited quantity but of infinite variety. Naturally a compromise layout

The Need for Effective Handling

The need for effective handling becomes quite apparent when you recognize many of the following conditions existing in your business.

The largest portion of an indirect labor payroll is spent for handling operations. Unnecessary indirect labor increases the cost of your product.

If workers manually handle large volumes of the same material daily and it weighs twenty-five to fifty pounds or more per unit, then mechanical aids should be provided.

In the year 1948, hernias, back injuries and other strains accounted for one-fifth of all accidents reported. Thousands of dollars are spent each year for lost-time accident cases due to lifting and shifting of materials. The only sure way to reduce the high cost of lifting is to mechanical handle instead of man handle.

Training in proper use of equipment and methods of handling will pay dividends in lower operation and maintenance cost, less idle man and machine time in processing, better utilization of all storage space and less damage to materials from handling.

Are you aware of the total cost of handling in your company? Handling costs are hidden in overhead, indirect labor, damaged materials, freight car demurrage, idle machine time, productive workers performing handling task, poor scheduling and inventory, excessive maintenance, poor space utilization, rehandling of material, bottleneck to production and a great many more. Take nothing for granted. Look at your plant critically, get the facts and improve your handling facilities.

SOURCE: The Material Handling Institute, Inc.

FIGURE 8–8

...Throughout an Entire Operation

MAN HANDLE OR MECHANICAL HANDLE

RECEIVING
Loose Pieces or Unit Loads
Congestion or Orderly Area
Idle Manhours or Efficient Operation
← THIS OR THIS →

STORAGE
Raw and Finished Materials
Waste Space or Full Utilization
2-Man Lifting or Mechanical Lifting
← THIS OR THIS →

TO PROCESSING
Intermittent or Continuous Flow
Bottleneck or Integrated System
Can operation be performed in transit?
← THIS OR THIS →

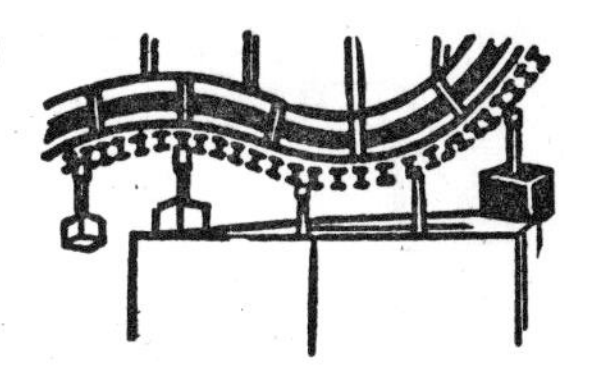

PROCESSING
Are parts damaged in handling?
Fetch material or positioned material?
Gravity or Powered Conveyors?
← THIS OR THIS →

SHIPPING
Boxes & Crates or Expendable Pallets
Haphazard or Planned Storage
Special or Standard Equipment

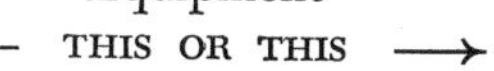

Figure 8–9

Types of Material-Handling Equipment.

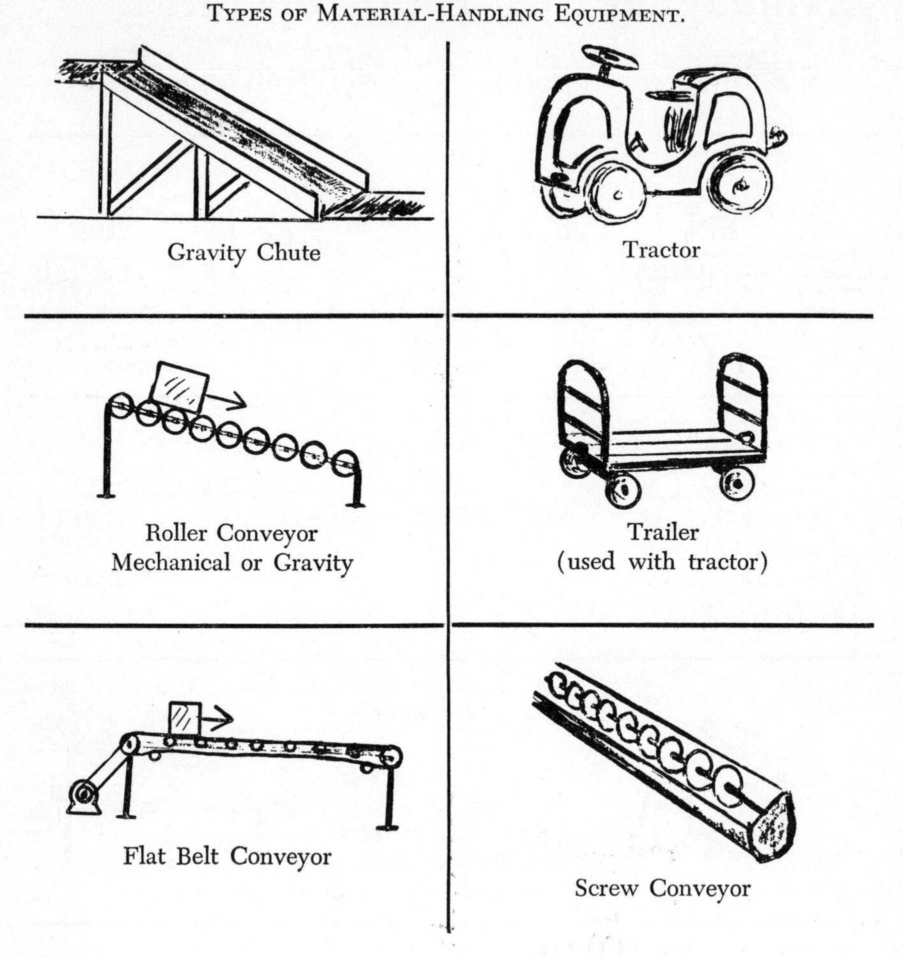

plan is available with which management seeks to gain the advantages available in each basic form of layout in so far as they are applicable.

Material handling is a function of plant layout. In some cases, the opposite may be true, as in the case of warehousing. Nevertheless, layout and the handling system must be integrated, for material movement is vital to the plan and the schedule of operations. It must be remembered that the greatest operating efficiency is reached only when materials used in the plant are moved through the necessary process steps in the shortest practical time. The longer the time cycle for the conversion of raw materials into a finished product, the higher will be the cost of production and the greater are the restrictions placed upon the use of working capital.

Fork-lift Truck

Overhead Monorail
Chain Conveyor

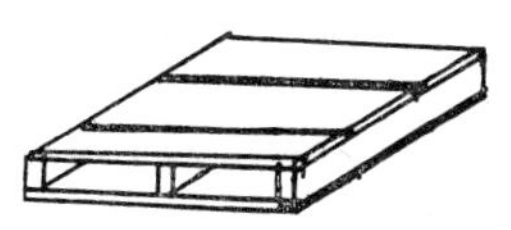

Pallet
(used with fork truck)

Overhead Traveling Crane

Skid Platform

Hand Truck

QUESTIONS

1. What does good layout involve?
2. What advantages accrue to good layout practice?
3. What does management mean by efficient production?
4. What are the basic goals of a producing unit?
5. Define process analysis. What information is derived from the procedure of process analysis?
6. What is the nature of a flow-process chart? What information appears on this chart?
7. Certain questions are raised as part of process analysis. What are these questions?

8. What are the two basic layout patterns? What is the basic characteristic of each pattern?

9. What relationship exists between the basic process of manufacture and the form of layout?

10. What are the four steps involved in the planning of the material-handling system?

11. What are the costs of a material-handling system?

12. Under what circumstances is it advisable to use fixed-path handling equipment? Variable-path?

CHAPTER 9

Layout: Criteria and Evaluation

It is impossible to enter upon the study of any phase of business management without at some point raising the question of cost as a criterion. In its final analysis the effectiveness of a layout pattern is reducible to terms of unit cost of production. Each activity carried on by the firm adds to the cost of providing a product or service. At the same time, this cost may be better or worse than it might otherwise be. Here is where equipment and layout practice may make some contribution towards minimizing these costs.

THREE SOURCES OF COST

The basic approach to cost involves consideration of three sources, or causes, of cost. These are direct labor, direct materials, and plant overhead, or burden.

Direct Labor

The cost of the time and effort which workers put into the creation of the product varies in its relative significance as a part of total unit cost. In some industries, such as the manufacture of cigarettes, flour milling, and petroleum refining, the wages paid to labor represent a low percentage of the value of the product. Paper, automobile, baking, woolen and worsted, glass, and others are industries wherein labor accounts for a medium percentage of cost. The shoe, aircraft, machine-tool, foundry, pottery, and other industries fall into the category of high-percentage labor cost.

Data such as these are the clue to the area wherein the greatest possible savings may be made through effective layout practice. By the introduction of laborsaving devices, increased mechanization, and greater efficiency in the use of workers' time because of better layout, it may be possible to reduce the direct labor cost per unit.

Direct Material Cost

Usually those industries which have high-labor-cost characteristics are found to have low material costs per unit, and those with low labor costs customarily have high material cost. In these latter cases effort is more effectively placed in the study of better means of materials utilization, inspection, and quality control, and in developing substitute materials. The layout function enters into this situation, for any revision involves reconsideration of the layout and its new potential.

Overhead Costs

The overhead or burden costs associated with the productive process may come into the picture even before a specific layout plan has been devised. The building which management may select to house the firm has inherent cost features which to an extent have already established themselves as a part of the overhead. How well management makes use of the building and of the facilities and equipment which are set up within it is a derivative of layout planning. If the plan is well executed, certainly the various overhead costs, such as heat, light, power, maintenance, insurance, etc., would each have already been considered even as the plant and the various alternative layout plans were being considered.

In those areas of industry which experience high cost in plant and processing facilities in relation to the cost of materials and labor which go into the product, layout practice is at the outset very significant. These industries may involve continuous processing and investment in long-term facilities, as in the cement and brick-and-tile industries; or extensive investment in equipment and space, as in the aircraft industry. In cases such as these the layout function looms large and important in the original design of the facilities and processing equipment. Such industries as these involve volume production, fixity of process, and immobility of equipment; therefore, it is quite necessary that the layout plan be well conceived and carried out so that the cost of overhead does not overshadow the entire production cost. Since in these cases the overhead cost is such a significant part of total costs, it is necessary that the productive facilities be capable of rendering such quantities of production as will reduce the unit cost of overhead to a desirable level. It is also necessary that the finally adopted layout plan be the correct one, for flexibility of arrangement is not provided and if desired can be had only at excessive and maybe prohibitive cost.

Cost of a Unit

In those plants which produce many products it is desirable that each production line be evaluated in terms of the cost per unit of product. This cost should be broken down into prime costs, materials and labor, and the overhead cost for each unit. In this manner management may by comparison with predetermined standards check upon the relative efficiency with which each production line is performing. By the same token, management is afforded an indication of those lines which may best be in need of reevaluation of layout and process.

CRITERIA OF LAYOUT

If each approach to layout practice were entered into after consideration of the goals and criteria of layout planning, there would doubtless be fewer occasions of layout revision which resulted from avoidable inadequacies.

The over-all activity of layout planning can reasonably be reduced to three categories, each of which may be established in terms of some respective criteria. Thus, as a given layout situation is being established, there will be guideposts which serve to keep the planning effort on course. These three categories are (1) use of space, (2) need for service facilities, (3) arrangement of machinery and equipment.

It would not be wise to restrict our consideration of layout to the industrial scene. The office, the retail store, and the facilities of the purveyor of professional services also require layout planning. Therefore, some criteria pertinent to work areas of these types will be included within this chapter.

Use of Space

Space is used for work area, storage purposes, or for traffic of materials and personnel. In view of these uses several criteria may be established as the basis for consideration of the effectiveness with which space is utilized.

1. How much work space has been allotted to the individual worker or work station? Is there adequate space for accessibility, for maintenance purposes, for accessories, equipment, and for the storage of materials which are awaiting processing or transfer to another work station?
2. In the assignment of space has adequate consideration been given to possible rearrangements and the desirability of minimizing the disturbance to other work stations in the event that rearrangement becomes necessary?

3. Has adequate provision been made for the worker's safety by allowing ample clearances of aisles, moving equipment, and conveyor systems?
4. Are storage areas convenient? The location of these areas must involve consideration of the location of the receiving and shipping departments as well as the location of the area wherein the materials will be used.
5. Are storage areas adequate in terms of special facilities for the handling, protection, inspection, and storage of materials, some of which may be dangerous, such as explosives and flammables?
6. Is the layout of the storage area conducive to a marking or identification system which may facilitate the location of items in storage?
7. How adequate is the storage area in terms of capacity? Does it meet peak needs? Is full use made of vertical stacking?
8. How well do the locations of the storage and working areas lend themselves to efficient material handling?

Need for Service Facilities

Service facilities are provided for two purposes—first, for the sake of the production process, which has need of services such as electricity, gas, steam, material handling, etc.; second, for the use of the employees, who have need for service facilities in the form of rest rooms, locker rooms, cafeterias, etc. The employees also have need of the services of a heating plant, ventilation and lighting equipment, noise abatement, and plant maintenance activity directed toward cleanliness. In view of these two areas the following criteria may be considered:

1. How flexible is the installation of the service facilities for the production process? Is electricity easily available anywhere within the production area? Would layout rearrangement involve expensive relocation of service lines? Are facilities adequate for expansion?
2. Is ample space allotted to the material-handling activity? Have aisles been established with due consideration for the nature, volume, and type of traffic flow which occurs in each area of the plant? What attempt has been made to establish fixed traffic patterns by such devices as the marking of aisles or traffic lanes and the direction of travel?
3. Do the services provided for the plant cater to worker comfort as well as to production needs? Is there an attempt to maintain pleasant working conditions? Appearance? Ventilation? Lighting?
4. What is the relation between number of workers and the capacity of such service areas as eating spaces or cafeteria facilities? Are facilities adequate in view of local sanitary codes?
5. What is the location of employee service areas in relation to the

work area of the plant? Are sanitary facilities centrally located to the disadvantage of those workers who are remotely located in the plant? Is the locker room located near the time clock, or must the employee travel unnecessary distances each time he reports to work or leaves for the day? Has ample consideration been given to multiple locations of various employee service areas and devices?

6. Do layout and location of personnel service facilities provide for ease in maintenance? Are these services so located that negligent maintenance may sometimes go unnoticed?

Arrangement of Machinery and Equipment

The final phase of layout planning involves the fixing of the position which each machine and piece of equipment is to occupy within the area assigned.

1. Has maximum use of space been made? Have odd-angle as well as right-angle positioning been considered to make material and worker movements more effective?
2. How well have natural and artificial lighting facilities been utilized? Are other services available and used to provide comfort and safety in the operating areas?
3. Is there too much space allowed? This may add to the time and cost of operations, for the worker may be covering more distance to perform his work than is necessary.
4. What is the position of the machine in relation to material-handling devices? Is it convenient enough for efficient handling but not so close as to create a hazard? Is it too close to the aisles? Do overhead conveyors pass directly over and very close to the machine operators? This is not a desirable situation.
5. How adequate are the safety provisions? Are dangerous operations segregated or screened? Are moving parts, switches, belt drives, etc., located or provided with devices to minimize or eliminate their inherent dangers?
6. How well does the location of machinery and equipment conform to the sequence of operations as established by process analysis?

OFFICE LAYOUT

The office is not without its plan and flow of work. Although the office routine does not create a product in the same sense as does the shop, it does provide a flow of information as its end result. This flow, in whatever form it finally evolves, is the product of the office. Even as the layout of the plant revolves about the process flow, so does the layout of the office revolve about its basic flow—the communications flow.

To some, communications means direct contact of person with person. To us, communications means the transferring of information, new or old, by any means available. These means may be spoken, written, graphic indications, sign language, sounds, or any other means which inventive mind may create.

The procedure involved in establishing the office layout consists of the following considerations:

1. Determination of office locations and space needs
2. Determination of equipment needs and placement within the offices
3. Determination of all the above pursuant to an examination of the company's organizational structure, pattern of communications, flow of work, and the personal and personnel considerations which are involved

Some standards have been established for determining space needs. The nature of the operation, the organizational level of the people involved, and the need or lack of need for privacy are bases for establishing the amount of space which will be allocated. A general standard for space allocation for various office activities is as follows:[1]

Workplace	*Area* (sq ft)
Private executive office	300
Private office for department head	250
Space for department head (open office)	150
Space for division head (open office)	75
Space for stenographer-secretary	50
Space for one clerical worker	40–50

In the planning of office locations it is advisable that the offices be considered in terms of the function of the occupants. In a plant of any size it is common to find a differentiation of offices in terms of the general offices and the plant offices. The general offices are those set up for executives and department heads. These are best located near each other for ease of communications. The plant offices, such as those for production control, engineering, and timekeeping are best set up in the plant area itself so as to be readily accessible from and to the plant.

Each office can be identified with its particular functional area and also in terms of those other offices and departments with which it is primarily concerned and with which it must maintain close contact and coordination of work. It seems logical, therefore, that the location of such offices be made in view of the departmental organization and the need for communication. The general offices are usually located near the main en-

[1] American Management Association, "Allocation of Office Space," *Management Review*, May, 1950, p. 179.

trance to the plant. The office of the personnel department is preferably available to the work area and also to the street in order that applicants may have direct access.

Within each office the flow of work becomes the basis for layout. The work consists of a paper-work flow which can be analyzed in much the same manner as it is possible to analyze a production process. In this case the flow of paper work can be reduced to a paper-work–procedure-flow chart and the problem of layout planning may be thereby implemented.

The considerations which accompany office layout planning are similar to those which we discussed in conjunction with the plant layout. Due consideration must be had for aisle space which is necessary to handle the flow of traffic. In this case the arrangement of equipment such as desks and files has much to do with the extent to which the working area must be cut up by traffic aisles. Along these same lines, the greater the volume of traffic in any given area, the greater the distraction of work force. Therefore, the traffic flow must be analyzed and so directed as to minimize the distraction in those areas where concentration is most necessary for effective work output.

The scheme of placement of desks varies, but in general it is recommended that all desks face in the same direction unless there is need for constant collaboration between workers. The placement of filing equipment offers great opportunity for erroneous layout. Files are primarily designed to be the recipients of records which are to be either actively or inactively used. If files are active, they should be located convenient to those who use them. Inactive files are best stored away from the work area. Files are not originally intended to serve as boundaries to aisles nor to create a dividing wall between office sections.

The provision of personnel services is important to office layout. Accommodations which are adequate, preferably adjacent to the working areas, and in keeping with the white-collar atmosphere must be planned for. In addition, all other service features and facilities which make for a better and more comfortable workplace enter into the planning of the office layout.

RETAIL STORE LAYOUT

There is no such thing as a standardized store layout. Each one is personalized and caters to the basic philosophy of the management and the policy which it develops. Today's stores run from the extreme of the exclusive shop which displays little except as the customer sees fit to ask to the opposite extreme of the self-service store which shows everything whether or not the customer had any original desire to see the merchandise. The in-between retail outlet approaches self-service in that it makes most effective use of display space but does maintain immediately available customer service.

The layout of a retail establishment caters to the plan of selling. The fundamental factors involved in establishing this layout are:

1. Sales-volume potentials
2. Appearance of the store
3. Cost of operations
4. Customer convenience
5. Provisions for safeguarding goods

Although these factors were not listed intentionally in order of importance, we cannot overlook the factor of sales-volume potentials as being paramount.

In planning the physical layout, the general approach of the nonexclusive shop is to surround the customer with goods in such a manner as to still allow him room to escape to another counter. The whole arrangement of counters and aisles should cater to the comfort and convenience of the buyer but at the same time should lead him into the area of display and provide him with as unobstructed a view as possible of the selection of goods.

A goal of retail layout is flexibility rather than fixed display units. Many firms make use of mobile units of walls, counters, and shelves. Such flexible features of layout allow easier adjustment of space allocations for seasonal needs.

Since appearance is so vital in attracting the customer, the entrance to the store must be planned to look inviting, to present a view of the store which is representative of its nature, and at the same time to allow for an orderly traffic flow of customers into and out of the store.

Customarily, the nature of the goods being sold determines the relative locations of the various departments of the store. Demand goods or staples are usually assigned an area in the rear of the store. Impulse, or pickup, items usually command a front-and-center location from which the product can virtually force itself upon the passing customer. Related items should occupy adjacent areas. Try-on items and others which involve special facilities should be located away from the heavy traffic areas.

The layout pattern of the retail establishment is designed to provide easy access to the customer who comes to the store in search of a specific product and at the same time must provide him with a view of additional items which may bring about an additional sale. The layout is a selling device.

The store personnel facilities are as necessary as in any other working area. In addition, the great volume of customers of the larger stores makes demands upon rest-room and other sanitary facilities.

EVALUATION OF LAYOUT PATTERNS

Our consideration of the layout topic has up to this point been concerned with the plant, the office, and the retail store. The criteria and considerations in each area overlap in principle and, therefore, provide the basis for restricting this final section on layout evaluation to a much narrower area.

In order to evaluate layout, it is necessary that specific situations be indicated and subjected to scrutiny. Our best opportunity exists in the evaluation of the layout forms which are applicable to manufacturing activities, namely, the line layout and the process layout. We have seen that these two forms represent extremes in terms of the basic purpose which each primarily serves. The line layout caters to quantity or repetitive production; and the process layout caters to variety of production. Each of the layout forms will be evaluated in turn.

When management is attempting to set up or revise a layout, it must evaluate the proposed plan from several points of view. The following listing is intended to serve as an indication of the checks to which any layout pattern should be subjected.

1. The equation of machine capacities
2. The effect of layout on the utilization of machine and labor skills
3. The cost of a unit of production
4. The extent and nature of material handling
5. The element of production time
6. The amount of finished goods potential

EVALUATION OF LINE LAYOUT

The Equation of Machine Capacities

In order to keep production moving efficiently, each operation should have an output potential equal to that of the succeeding operation. This principle is most efficiently demonstrated by the single machine which takes a raw-material input, automatically carries out several operations on this material, and turns out a finished product. An essential feature in this case would be the coordination of time and quantity factors involved in each of the operations which were performed within the machine.

Because of the technical or cost problems involved in acquiring a single machine so highly integrated, the manufacturer must usually equate each operational step of the process in terms of several machines. (See Figure 9–1.) The principle which must be applied is that of balancing output. The variable feature is found in the nature of the equipment used and its technical specifications, such as rate of output and reliability.

FIGURE 9–1

EQUATED PRODUCTION LINE

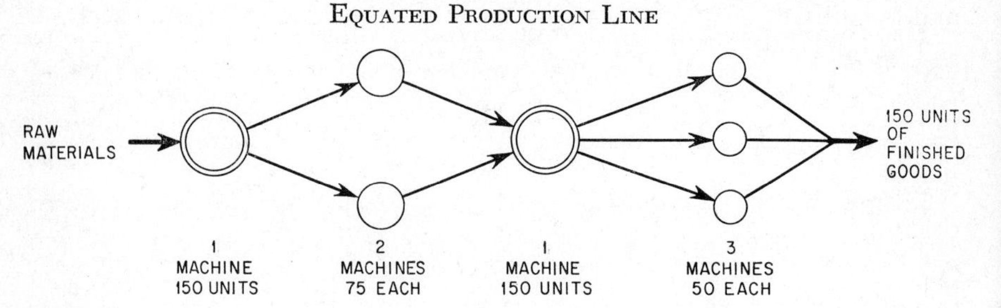

The restriction of the worker and the machine in their respective performances is justified by the knowledge that it is usually easier and cheaper to break down the over-all process into many basic operations. These operations are such that machines may be readily capable of performing them, and they will require only minor skills or training in order that the worker can adequately do his job. A task, repetitively done, usually results in a greater volume of output.

The Cost of a Unit of Production

A manufacturing plant generally will pay for itself in relation to the rate at which it produces goods for profitable sale. Therefore, any device which allows for more efficient use of machines, men, or space will provide management with either a better than average rate of profits or at least an improved competitive position. A layout which is not balanced in terms of capacity or which does not lend itself to efficient utilization of machine and manpower skills represents waste and thus higher than necessary costs. The worker must produce or lose his job. Likewise, the machine must be capable of performing certain desirable operations or management would not invest in it. However, once management has both the worker and the machine, it, too, is responsible for the volume of output achieved. By proper planning and usage of facilities management may avoid unnecessarily high costs.

Line layout, by its design, achieves high volume through efficient use of facilities. In this manner the product is produced at a lower unit cost.

The Extent and Nature of Material Handling

The handling of materials by men and machines is necessary in order to move production from one operation to the next. The businessman, in most cases, views handling as a necessary evil. The costs involved are preferably avoided, for handling, per se, does nothing to the material in the way of changing its form or enhancing its value. Material handling involves not only the direct costs of the labor and equipment used, but also the indirect costs, such as the damages to materials and equipment, and possibly to personnel, and the costs of delayed production which result from faulty or excessive handling activity.

Line layout has as one feature the location of machines and equipment in related sequence and in proximity to each other. This arrangement of order and position is fixed as long as the product produced by the line does not vary or become obsolete. In order to assist in achieving the desirable production rate from the line, the links between operations or machines must be effectively established. Conveyors, chutes, and other handling devices may be installed as an integral part of the production line.

The benefits which may be had from the use of mechanical handling devices are as follows:

1. The product can travel only through the prescribed sequence of operations. There is little likelihood that it will be lost or sidetracked.
2. Goods are always either being processed at a work station or are on the move to the next. Therefore, there is a minimum of time during which the product is not being worked upon.
3. The line may serve to pace production, thereby allowing management a close control over the quantity of output.
4. Since the human element in material handling is eliminated or lessened, there is less likelihood of personnel injury or property damage resulting from improper handling methods.
5. The total distance of the production line is fixed. Since distance means time and time means money, management uses mechanical handling devices to eliminate variances from the established time and distance features of a particular layout.
6. The conveyor or handling system may serve a dual role. It is both a storage area and a transportation device for the goods which are in process.

The Element of Production Time

The line type of layout allows management to exercise much closer control and achieve greater coordination amongst the many factors which determine the over-all time spent in the manufacture of a product. The machines and personnel, the number and sequence of operations, the distance and time involved in production, are in theory, ideally integrated. Production does not involve "stop and go" features which delay operations and thus increase the total time required to produce a unit. The continuous and orderly flow of production is the key to the successful use of time.

The Amount of Finished Goods Potential

Line layout will provide the largest output of a particular good. If the market for the product is subject to variation, how may line layout meet this problem of volume?

Reduction in output in order to meet market requirements may be achieved by slowing down the production pace or by working the production line for fewer hours each workday or with fewer personnel. In any case, higher unit costs usually result, for the line is not being used at the rate for which it was designed and at which it is most efficient.

If, on the other hand, the market demands a greater volume of goods than can be had from operating the line at its full capacity, there is one way by which greater volume can be achieved by the plant. A second line must be set up. This involves additional capital expenditure.

The line layout provides a degree of flexibility within its production capacity, but its finished goods potential beyond this capacity may be restricted.

Regardless of the level of capacity at which the line may be operating, management knows what amount of finished goods will be turned out in each hour of each day. This knowledge allows management to schedule more accurately its delivery dates to customers.

The Amount of Investment Involved

The line layout may involve a greater investment in machinery and equipment than the process layout. One reason for this is that machines are duplicated along the production line. (See Figure 8–5.) The added investment in duplicate facilities is made in order to eliminate backtracking. The product does not double back on the line, for this would necessarily involve a stop-and-go sequence.

Greater machine investment may also be caused by the nature of the equipment used. Specialized equipment, designed to perform a task with little, if any, skill necessary on the part of the operator, or designed to perform a series of operations, thus resembling several machines in one, is high in cost. As line layout approaches more and more the aspect of completely automatic production, the machine investment becomes greater. The compensating feature for this greater investment must be found in terms of a lower unit cost of production, a greater quantity, or better quality. If there is any question as to whether the item to be produced will have a limited life as a marketable product, there must be a considered evaluation as to whether the salable volume from the production line will pay for the investment made in machinery and equipment. Specialized equipment may have little or no resale value because of its restricted performance.

The materials used in production also represent an investment. Materials will vary in importance as a cost and investment factor depending on the item being produced.

Management, however, recognizes the importance of turnover of investment. The quicker a dollar invested in raw materials can be put through the production line and sold to a customer, the sooner the original dollar can be reused in the same manner. If ten dollars' worth of material can be made into a finished good, a profitable sale made, and cash collected every month, the turnover for the ten dollars is at the rate of twelve times each year. The same ten dollars helps earn a profit a dozen times during the year. Compare this to the case where ten dollars returns with a profit every two months or where twenty dollars' worth of materials is kept on hand each month, and only ten dollars' worth is processed and finds way into a profitable sales outlet each month. In both these comparisons, there is a less favorable investment in materials. Material investment must be considered from three viewpoints: the time, quantity, and dollar factors.

With line layout, the output is known and likewise the necessary material input is known. Since this relationship is established, management is able, if it wishes, to operate with virtually no raw-material investment other than daily delivery which will be enough to supply the line for the day. This would be an extreme minimization of raw-material investment. Many firms have no choice but to maintain a quantity of raw material on hand because of seasonal supply or difficulty of procurement.

The extreme minimization of finished-goods investment is possible if goods are shipped immediately upon completion to waiting customers. The fact that the production rate of the line is known to management may allow for close scheduling and coordination of delivery dates to customers and due dates from production. If the product has a seasonal market, the firm must stock the finished items pending their sale. Such a situation, therefore, adds to the material investment and cost of production.

The investment in materials which are in process may also be minimized with line layout since there is the absence of stockpiling of partly finished goods at any point along the production route. All units are kept moving.

Reliability of Line Layout

A chain is as strong as its weakest link. Such is the case with line layout. If one operation in the process should go askew or a machine break down, the whole line may be halted, for the broken link causes the production flow to stop. Such an occurence must be anticipated. Management provides for potential breakdown by setting up reserve machines at suspected or known trouble spots; by setting up more than one line to produce a given product so that in the event that one line is down, the other(s) can maintain a flow of finished goods; by planning secondary production lines which involve other machines and plant areas which can do the required emergency work until the primary production line is repaired; by establishing subcontractor relationships and letting out the work during the emergency; and by setting up "floats" of in-process work at key points in the line to keep the operation going during temporary repairs.

An added weakness is found in the nature of the equipment which may be used in line layout. The specialized machines may need the attention of specially trained service personnel or custom-made parts, either of which may not be immediately available to the firm. These needs may add to the vulnerability and potential down time of the line layout.

The Versatility of Production

The line layout is not expected to turn out a variety of products. It serves a basic goal of volume of production which can only be had by devoting all the features of the line to specialized operations. Minor variations in production are usually possible, but the basic nature and form of the goods produced cannot be changed without changing the operations performed along the line.

The Psychic Value of Line Layout

The production line layout should present a picture of orderly activity to the viewer. A well-designed layout will mesh operations as if they represented a set of gears. To the layman, line layout will depict his preconceived notion of mass production and in this respect may be satisfying for the activity is in many cases monotonous, without end, and meaningless to those who perform what seem to be insignificant tasks.

The businessmen attempt to modify the "strictly business" nature of line layout by dressing up the production area with color; by rotating personnel on jobs; and many other devices which diminish the attention given by the workers to the undesirable features of the production line.

EVALUATION OF PROCESS LAYOUT

The Equation of Capacity

Beyond establishing the basic machine set-up, an equating of capacity in process layout will be approached to some extent as the volume and variety of work make it necessary to add or eliminate equipment. With every change in product manufactured, there is a corresponding change in the rate of output for every machine or operation involved. This fact makes it impossible to establish a perfectly balanced machine set-up.

The problem of equating capacity may be approached in reverse. Rather than attempting to equate machines, management may seek sufficient customer orders so as to maintain the highest practical level of use of all machines and equipment.

The Effect of Process Layout on the Use of Men and Machines

Process layout involves the use of general-purpose machines. The successful use of a machine of this type depends upon the ability of the man who is operating it. An ordinary wood saw in the hands of an inexperienced person usually results in a crooked cut in a piece of wood. The carpenter, however, because of his skill, is capable of making a variety of accurate cuts. The general-purpose machine must have a skilled operator.

Since both the men and machines combine their efforts in the production of a great variety of work, the result is a greater utilization of both than would be had if the machine possessed the skill and the man was merely a feeder of materials.

The Cost of a Unit of Production

No clear statement of cost can be made which will apply with equal validity to each product manufactured. Each costing situation would be an individual case. However, there are certain features of production which affect cost. The labor cost increases as greater skills are demanded of the workman. Space use is less efficient when each machine is established as a center of production with its individual servicing area rather than as a link or small part of a fixed production line. If a variety of products is manufactured, additional attentions and costs are involved in controlling production and the handling of materials. Since process layout involves the above features, the cost of a unit produced is correspondingly affected.

The Extent and Nature of Material Handling in Process Layout

The quantity produced of any given item is usually not large enough to warrant the use of fixed mechanical-handling systems. Production moves to and from work stations in batches or lots. The procedure necessitates greater attention to the material-handling phase since each of the many orders being processed follows its individual route through the plant, and each order may at the same time consist of several batches in various stages of completion and at various plant locations.

The picture created is one of excessive handling activity. Handling equipment such as mechanical trucks, hand trucks, tractor-trailer units, and portable conveyors may be used.

The Element of Production Time

More time may be required to make a particular product with process layout than with line layout because of the following features which add to production time:

1. Greater amount of material handling
2. Stop-and-go movement through the plant
3. Difficulties involved in scheduling the job because of the many other products involving the use of the same facilities
4. The nonstandardized nature of the product which may require special attentions and control over production in order to meet specifications
5. "Bugs" that may show up during production thus slowing down the production rate

The Amount of Finished-goods Potential

Process layout is primarily concerned with variety rather than volume of production. However, a great range of volume of any particular item is possible. The production facilities, because of their nature, may easily be diverted from the manufacture of one product to the manufacture of another. It is, therefore, possible that all facilities could be applied to one or more production purposes. Thus a variable production rate and volume is possible for each product being manufactured.

The Amount of Investment Involved in Process Layout

Machine investment in process layout may be less than that required with an equivalent line layout. This is so because of the better potential utilization of equipment in terms of a variety of production. The desired volume of production may be achieved without the need for duplication of machines. The general-purpose nature of the equipment usually provides a good resale value and has a lower obsolescence rate than has specialized equipment. These features add to the attractiveness of the investment. However, since every machine cannot do every job, a given product-mix set by sales will probably cause some machinery to be idle. Good scheduling can minimize this.

Material investment in custom manufacture is relatively higher than in a line-production situation because the manufacturer must maintain a higher investment in raw materials and in goods which are in process. The greater investment in raw materials is necessary in order that the manufacturer may gain the advantage of time which he would otherwise lose if he had to wait for delivery of materials for a particular order.

There may be no other choice but to stock quantities of materials because of difficulties involved in procurement. An order is many times placed with a manufacturer because he has the necessary materials available. The goods-in-process investment may also be relatively high because the movement of these materials through production is slow and intermittent. Many times materials are sitting idle in storage aisles awaiting transport to the next operation.

The investment in finished-goods inventory is most likely minimized since each unit produced has already been committed to a particular sale and usually will be shipped to the customer as quickly as possible.

Reliability of the Layout

In the event that a machine breaks down in process layout, it is unlikely that there will be a cessation of production. This system of production consists of several links which are interchangeable. Therefore, a machine deficiency in terms of output of one particular product can usually be made up by diverting other facilities to the troubled area.

Since the machines are general purpose and usually of a standard design, repair and replacement parts are more readily available. This saves both time and costs which are involved in putting the machine back into operating condition.

An exception to the reliability of process layout exists where only one machine is available for a particular type of operation, and there are no alternative machines available. In this case, breakdown of the machine will stop the flow of products which involve its use. Management is herein confronted with the alternatives of a delay in production or subcontracting the work, if possible.

The Versatility of Production

Process layout may handle a variety of products. Machines are not restricted in performance, and workmen provide management with a variety and range of skills.

The Psychic Value of Process Layout

In general, process layout is not an orderly picture to view. In operation it may appear confusing and resemble a chaotic pattern of production flow.

The worker in this environment must be primarily concerned with his task and performance. He may be bothered by his surroundings if they detract from the attention he wishes to give to his work. The general nature of process layout is its own worst enemy. Because there is no orderly pattern of activity, workers are likely to become disorderly and clutter work areas and aisles with materials and tools of production. This may eventually have its effects on the worker and be evidenced by a reduction in his attention to work output or performance.

The task of management is to more closely control and regulate the use and abuse of areas in the hopes of promoting a better work environment.

SUMMARY

The significance of a particular layout pattern may be finally measured in terms of the cost per unit of production; for the layout itself has direct influence upon the efficiency with which materials, labor, and overhead costs are applied to the product. The relative importance of any one factor of production as an element of cost of production is indicative of that area wherein management places greatest emphasis upon improvement via layout practice. Thus a relatively high labor cost causes management to seek means of reducing labor effort via more efficient layout of the work area or workplace.

The over-all activity of layout planning may be reasonably reduced to three categories: (1) space; (2) service facilities; (3) arrangement of machinery and equipment. The evaluation of layout practice in the light of the several criteria in each of these areas leads management closer to the realization of the goal of effective layout.

Within the office and the retail store, the layout function is alive and very significant as a tool in the accomplishment of the purpose of the activity. Layout practice in the office may serve to enhance the communications channels. In the retail outlet, layout may be the best salesman on the floor.

The evaluation of the line and process types of layout patterns indicates the manner in which different purposes may be catered to by variation in layout. This significantly adds to the argument that layout is an expression of the goals or purposes which management establishes for the enterprise.

QUESTIONS

1. What is meant by "labor represents a low percentage of the value of the product"? What connection does this have with plant layout?
2. Overhead costs may exist before layout. Explain.
3. In what respects is layout more significant in a continuous-process industry than it is in a repetitive industry?
4. List some criteria of layout planning which are related to: (*a*) space; (*b*) services; (*c*) arrangement of machinery.
5. What is the "product" of the office?
6. What considerations are involved in establishing the office layout?
7. Is there a "standardized store layout"? Why or why not?

8. What are the fundamental factors involved in retail-store layout?

9. What relationship exists between the nature of goods sold and the location of various departments in a store?

10. Define: line layout, process layout.

11. List three of the checks to which a layout pattern should be subjected. What is the significance of these checks?

12. What is meant by the following statement? "The criteria and considerations in each area (of layout planning) overlap in principle. . . ."

PART THREE

Management of Manpower

Men in industry have made gigantic strides in the past decade toward harnessing the great wonders of nature and in developing mechanical devices. It is equally true, however, that they have not made the same advances in creating a better understanding between management and labor.

Part Three deals with manpower problems, but it in no way presents a cure for the ills of human relations. Rather, this part attempts to point out the essential ingredients of sound labor-management relations—a humanistic philosophy or policy toward the worker, procedures and techniques designed for a fair and uniform consideration of the worker as he seeks employment and as he works for the company, and an acceptance of the role of unions and the law in modern personnel relations. Proper consideration of these essentials must improve the total work environment.

Success or failure in business is often governed by the worker. Management cannot afford to neglect this vitally important aspect of its everyday affairs. The gains possible through harmonious relations are immense and must not be overlooked. These chapters are designed to present the entire manpower problem openly and clearly.

CHAPTER 10

Personnel Management

The personnel function exists in any business organization where people are hired. Generally the magnitude of the personnel problem is determined by the number of workers in the company's employ. In a small business where it is possible to gather a group of workers with like interests and tastes about an employer who understands these interests and tastes the personnel problem practically solves itself.

As a business grows, both owners and managers are likely to drift away from the worker and his problems to devote their time to seemingly more pressing matters. The resulting neglect of the worker can cause unrest and an ultimate reduction in worker efficiency. It is impossible to run a large business in the same way as a small one, yet it may be highly desirable to retain the close relationships and feelings between management and the worker even as the business grows.

Since the Great Depression of the 1930s management has given more and more attention to matters involving the work force. Management has found that it has much to gain through the establishment of a progressive personnel program. Too, businessmen have been compelled to devote an ever-increasing amount of time and energy to the problems of human relations. There are several forces that have led to this relatively new relationship between management and worker. Among the more significant is the National Labor Relations Act of 1935 in which the Federal government recognized the worker's right to collective bargaining. Management was required by this law to listen to worker grievances and demands; and through unionization the worker could effectuate his demands. This law opened the door to mass unionization of workers and enabled the rank-and-file worker to gain more concessions than ever from his employer.

Management's attitude toward the work force has also been conditioned by several structural changes in our society. Notable among these changes is the reduction of the number of immigrants who are entering our labor market. Immigrants, because of their different culture and, in many instances, their inability to speak English, were unable to make concerted demands on their employer. Labor today is much better educated than ever before, and as a result expects to be treated with dignity and respect and will not tolerate employer abuses so common in the past.

Today the industrial worker earns income equal to or greater than that of many white-collar workers or semiprofessional workers, and he lives in commensurate circumstances. Because of higher income and better education the industrial worker today feels that he is more the equal of others regardless of their job status. Management must recognize these changes in worker status and adjust its personnel activities accordingly.

PERSONNEL MANAGEMENT DEFINED

Personnel management can be divided into three distinct parts. The first relates to procedures and routines, the mechanics of personnel. Uniform procedures are needed for hiring, firing, setting wage rates, and a host of additional functions. The second part includes various personnel tools or techniques such as job evaluation, selection techniques, merit rating, and wage-payment plans. These two parts of personnel management will be discussed in some detail in later chapters. The third part concerns personnel philosophy and personnel policy; just what is management's attitude toward its workers? How does management rate the importance of its workers? Are they considered more or less important than machines, facilities, and the like? Management's personnel philosophy may be found in its statement of policy or the lack thereof.

Perhaps a clearer picture of what personnel management involves can be obtained by a statement of the functions that commonly fall within the jurisdiction of a personnel department.

1. *The Employment Function.* This includes recruiting workers, testing, interviewing, selection, placement, and orientation.

2. *Employee Relations Regarding Wage Increases, Etc.* These include promotion, transfer, layoff, downgrading, and vacations. The personnel department does not actually perform these functions, yet it falls within its province to establish policy which will govern them. Personnel administration is a staff function but a line responsibility. That is, the personnel department prepares and recommends policy to top management; and after top management adopts the policy, it becomes the responsibility of the line organization—supervisors, foremen, etc.—to apply and enforce it.

3. *Job Analysis and Evaluation.* These, as the words imply, are tools used to determine just what each job in the organization is and what its requirements are and what each job is worth in relation to other jobs in the organization. These tools are vital for proper selection, promotion, and payment of workers.

4. *Employee Rating or Merit Rating.* This is a technique used to determine how well each person in the organization is doing his assigned job. It too is an aid in selecting employees for promotion and, if properly designed and used, will give management a good indication of the value of each worker to the company.

5. *Employee Counseling.* Such counseling keeps the worker informed about his progress within the company and of company plans which will have a direct bearing on his future employment.

6. *Health and Safety Programs.* These programs frequently come within the jurisdiction of the personnel department since they are directly related to training, job evaluation, merit rating, and general working conditions.

7. *Recreational Activity.* Such activity is usually run by the workers with the helping hand and supervision of personnel management.

8. *Personnel Record Keeping.* This is vital to any personnel program. Records should be available to reveal facts and avoid the need for opinions as far as possible. A complete record showing length of service, commendations, accomplishments, disciplinary action, accident record, absenteeism, and tardiness will provide a sound basis for future dealing with the worker.

PERSONNEL POLICY

Effective personnel management requires the development of reasonable and consistent policies written so that they can be easily understood by all parties involved—worker, management, and the union. Whatever the function of personnel administration, whether it be extensive or not, it cannot operate satisfactorily for the workers until well-defined rules of conduct are approved by top management.

Policies are essential because they delineate the course of action to be taken as situations arise and prescribe the areas over which personnel administration has jurisdiction. Definite policies covering the more common employer-employee relations make management's attitude a matter of record which should reduce the uncertainty that often permeates personnel relations. Top management and top management alone must be responsible for creating personnel policy, albeit management enlists the aid of specialists to help solve this complex problem.

Essential Parts of Personnel Policy

Since a policy is designed to establish set procedures and to outline areas of jurisdiction, it is best that policies be put in writing; otherwise a good portion of their value may be lost. For a personnel policy to be complete and easily understood it should contain three parts.

1. The Objectives of Personnel Policy. Management should first state the objectives of its personnel policy in general terms and then follow with a more elaborate description of specific goals. A statement of general objectives should indicate management's basic philosophy or attitude toward personnel. The Studebaker Corporation's attitude toward its workers was expressed for years as "*Labor omnia vincit,*" or "Labor conquers all." Such statements of policy will indicate management's interpretation of the worker's position in the organization. Is the worker a commodity to be bought, used, and disposed of at management's discretion, or is he to be considered an emotional creature who is motivated by the same forces that resulted in the members of the management team becoming what they are?

Specific aspects of personnel management, such as selection, promotion, employee benefits, and the like, can have little meaning until management's general objectives are known. So often it is not what is done but how it is done that is the true indicator of just what a personnel policy means; the true meaning of a personnel policy rests with the attitude of top management toward the work force.

2. Personnel Techniques and Procedures. Personnel policy relates to the manner of guiding personnel relations within an organization. Policy in addition reflects management's philosophy toward the worker. However, something more than a philosophy and a policy is needed to effectuate a sound personnel program. Personnel techniques and procedures are needed to transform philosophy, which is broad and theoretical, and policy, which is the application of philosophy, into everyday applications which are usable by the personnel department and understandable to the worker. The techniques and procedures referred to may cover hiring, promotion, wage payment systems, employee rating, and the like.

3. Setting the Responsibility for Personnel Management. Policies are of little value unless someone is charged with the responsibility for their application. Initially the responsibility rests with top management which, in turn, is given to members of the line organization; that is, foremen, supervisors, plant manager, and the like. All along the line employees from the lowest worker upward look to their boss or superior for a statement of company policy. Line management has the authority to deal directly with the workers; whereas the personnel administrator, a staff officer, has no jurisdiction over them.

Management Objectives through Personnel Management

Management policies, personnel or other, are usually set with the profit motive in mind. Management's attitude toward personnel and personnel policy normally would be determined by the profit that would result from one policy as opposed to another. We realize that management does not set its policy solely on the profit that will result, but we must realize too that the element of profit must enter into the establishment of policy. Today, management's personnel policy and personnel techniques are governed in a large measure by two bodies operating apart from the business organization. Both our governments and our labor unions exercise a high degree of control over personnel philosophy and personnel administration. It is quite possible that at any given time management's goals will differ from union goals and objectives and from the government's stated policy on industrial relations.

The economist and the sociologist might profess that the goals of management and the union must coincide over the long run, else one or the other is doomed. This may or may not be true; not enough time has elapsed under contemporary union-management relations to draw a satisfactory conclusion. However, we do know that there is considerable difference in the manner through which these goals are sought. We also know that in terms of immediate goals there is considerable difference between these two groups.

Within the limitations imposed by the government and the union, management seeks three basic goals or objectives through its personnel program.

1. Maximum Individual Development. In *The Principles of Scientific Management,*[1] Frederick W. Taylor stated that to fully utilize the forces available under scientific management, "it is an inflexible rule to talk to and deal with one man at a time . . . to develop each individual man to his highest state of efficiency and prosperity." In opposition to the theory that management should treat all workers alike there is strong feeling among many personnel men today that better results can be obtained by treating all workers differently; that no two men are alike, so why should they be treated alike. Rather than deal with workers as a group and rather than deal with them on the basis of seniority, management may prefer to single out individual workers and one by one, if necessary, develop them into more valuable workers. Such an objective is vital to the achievement of the most effective operating plan. Through a policy of individual development management may create a healthy feeling of competition between workers wherein each worker tries to be a more valuable employee than his coworker. This may result in a more productive and better-paid group of workers. Accurate records of worker performance and progress on the job are a vital part of individual development.

2. Maximizing the Use of Human Resources. Closely related to the goal of maximum individual development is the desire of management to

[1] F. W. Taylor, *The Principles of Scientific Management,* Harper & Brothers, New York, 1923, p. 43.

utilize a worker's abilities as fully and as continuously as possible. In the long run, maximum utilization of human resources and individual development may amount to the same thing. At any given time, however, the best use of a worker's talents, from management's point of view, at least, may not coincide with the long-run objective of maximum individual development. It is quite conceivable, for example, that for the time being the best use of an engineer's talents may be as a draftsman; a foreman's as a production worker; or an office manager's as a bookkeeper. In the long run, management should determine the type of work each employee does best and develop each worker to "his highest state of efficiency and prosperity." In the short run, an alternative use of worker abilities may be in order. To maximize the use of human resources, management must be permitted to move workers from job to job or from department to department as conditions dictate. Few positions in an organization are static. As company policies and goals change, it is often necessary to shift responsibilities, to do away with some jobs and to create others. Company policy can be enforced and goals met only if management is free to use human abilities where they are most productive.

3. *Good Employer-Employee Relations.* To reach the first two objectives requires a relationship between employer and employee wherein both parties respect and trust each other. Good relationships do not imply paternalism, for too frequently workers resent such an attitude by management. Rather, management through its written policies and its interpretation of policy must lead the way in instilling a feeling of interdependence and an *esprit de corps.* Without harmonious relationships it will be difficult to gain the first two objectives.

Characteristics of Personnel Policy

Personnel policy should not be made on the basis of unilateral decisions by management. To be most effective and acceptable, policies should be made with the advice and approval of all parties concerned—labor, management, and the union. Certainly some policies must evolve from a unilateral decision by management, but these instances should be the exception and not the rule. Frequently one businessman will try to adopt in his organization a complete personnel policy that has been successful in another establishment. Generally this is not feasible since personnel policies are developed for a particular set of surroundings, and unless this setting can be duplicated in another establishment, which is quite unlikely, the plan is apt to backfire. It is extremely difficult to duplicate the personality of another personnel policy. In certain industries low wages are characteristic; in others poor working conditions are inherent; and in others irregular employment prevails. As mentioned earlier, each businessman seeks to be different from all others in some respect; it may be his key to success. Because of this and other unlikenesses of business organizations personnel policy must be tailor-made to fit one specific organization.

Regardless of the fact that personnel policy must be designed to fit a particular application, there are certain specific qualities that should be incorporated in any personnel policy.

1. It should give the worker a feeling of belonging to a group.
2. It should give the worker a feeling of importance to the company no matter how insignificant his job may appear to be.
3. It should incorporate as far as possible the feeling of security.
4. It should allow for the development of each worker as an individual.
5. It should provide for recognizing individual accomplishment.
6. It should be specific enough so that its meaning is clear, yet flexible enough to meet the exceptional situation.
7. It should allow for change as conditions change.
8. It should provide for two-way communication between management and the worker.
9. It should be consistent with the general policies of the organization.

All too frequently management's statement of personnel policy is limited to a listing of rules and regulations, "Do's and Don'ts," that govern worker conduct on the job and in no way reveal management's attitude. The reader might wonder if the above list of qualities is Utopian or actually followed. There are many companies, primarily small- and medium-sized, that have shown a willingness and desire to make their attitude toward personnel a matter for public consumption. Such policy statements are well-planned, reasonable, and indicate what the worker can expect from his employer. An overt statement of policy invariably creates worker and public confidence in the company and promotes sound business relations. Such is the case of the Eastman Kodak Company whose current-day philosophy of human relations has been handed down from generation to generation. In their employee handbook, *A Handbook for Kodak Men and Women,* there is published their personnel policy which is perhaps the finest statement of personnel policy yet to come to the authors' attention. The following statement is taken from the Kodak handbook.[1]

[1] Material in this section taken with permission from *A Handbook for Kodak Men and Women,* Eastman Kodak Company, Rochester, N.Y., 1955.

EASTMAN KODAK COMPANY—CODE OF INDUSTRIAL RELATIONS

The following policies and principles governing relationships with the Company comprise the Code of Industrial Relations of the Eastman Kodak Company.

Wages. Wage rates are established on the basis of fairness to the individual for the work he is doing. It is the Company's intention:

1. To maintain uniform wage standards which will insure equitable wage payments throughout all divisions of the Company and, consistent with this,
2. To pay wages equal to or above those generally prevailing in the community for similar work performed under comparable conditions and requiring like responsibility, experience, effort, and skill.

Constant attention is required, and is being given, to developing and maintaining this policy.

Hours of Work and Special Payments. The company makes a continuous effort to maintain fair procedures covering both normal work hours and payment for overtime, shift work, and work under special conditions. The interests of Kodak people and general industry practice are given careful consideration in establishing these procedures.

Holidays. Allowances are paid for time away from work in the observance of recognized holidays, and special rates are paid for work on such holidays.

Stability of Employment. There are wide seasonal variations in the demand for many of the Company's products. In order to avoid, so far as possible, the effect of these seasonal variations upon stability of employment, the Company for many years has given constant attention to the planning of its production schedules. As a result, a marked stability of employment has been achieved.

This planning program cannot, of course, prevent lessened employment when business in general is bad and the demand for the products of the Company is greatly reduced.

Vacations. All Kodak people employed on a regular basis have an annual vacation with pay to provide a period of rest and relaxation.

Wage Dividend. For many years, Kodak people have received an annual lump-sum payment in addition to their wages, which is called the Wage Dividend. The Wage Dividend is not taken into account by the Company in establishing wage rates. It is paid in recognition of the contribution made by the loyal, steady, and effective efforts of Kodak people to the Company's success. Payment of the Wage Dividend in any year is dependent upon the cash dividends declared on the Company's common stock and upon special action by the directors.

Pensions. The Company provides for retirement annuities, payable each month for life after retirement, to all those who are qualified by their age and service.

Group Life Insurance. Group Life Insurance is made available upon employment—the Company sharing the cost with the individual.

Disability Benefits. In case of total-and-permanent disability, the individual receives monthly payments for a period and in amounts determined by the individual's earnings and length of service. The Company pays the full cost of disability benefits after the individual has had 15 years of service, having shared the cost of these benefits with him up to that point.

Sickness Allowance. Under an established plan, Kodak people absent on account of illness are paid definite allowances based on their length of service and their earnings.

Medical Insurance. The Company makes available on a group basis, and shares the cost of, insurance plans which help to pay medical, surgical, and hospital expenses incurred by the individual and his or her dependents.

Freedom of Discussion with Management. The Company cannot emphasize too strongly its desire that all Kodak people shall feel free to seek information and advice from members of management on any matter which is troubling them, or to call attention to any condition which may appear to them to be operating to their disadvantage. No individual need hesitate to do this, and his standing with the Company will not thereby be prejudiced in any way. He will find his foreman or Supervisor or the plant industrial relations department (Personnel Department if at Kodak Office) ready to talk over any of these matters and to give any assistance they can. The Company believes that most difficulties will be satisfactorily adjusted between the individual and the foremen or supervisor; but, if for any reason a person is not satisfied with such adjustment, he or she is and should feel completely at liberty to bring the matter to the attention of any one in the management. A definite and formal procedure for getting assistance in handling personal problems and complaints is available to anyone who may wish to use it.

Improvements in Methods and Processes. The continual development and the introduction of new and improved methods and processes are necessary to the successful conduct of the business; and only by utilizing such improvements can the Company continue to provide stable employment at adequate wages. Nevertheless, before such improvements are made, careful attention is given to any possible effect upon the individuals concerned. Through this policy, the Company adopts improved methods essential to its growth and at the same time endeavors to avoid any considerable hardship to the individual.

Safety. The Company has endeavored for many years to lessen the accident hazards in its plants by the installation of safety devices and by systematic safety instruction and supervision. Constant study is carried on at all Company locations to discover possible sources of accidents and to plan means of avoiding them. As a result of this intensive work and the cooperation of Kodak people, both the number and the severity of accidents in the Company's plants have been kept at a very low rate.

Working Conditions. The Company makes every reasonable effort to provide and maintain sanitary working conditions. Protective clothing is supplied by the Company whenever it is deemed necessary for safety and health reasons.

Hiring Ages. The Company has not established any arbitrary age limit beyond which applicants will not be employed, provided they are physically and mentally able to perform the work.

Particular care is given to the placement of people under age 21, and no one under age 16 is employed for any job.

Promotion. The Company aims to provide channels of promotion and to advance Kodak people to more responsible work on the basis of their record of workmanship, competence, and general ability. Insofar as practicable, promotions are made from within the organization.

Reduction in Force and Re-employment. In the event of business conditions requiring reduction in the force, consideration will be given to the length of service, individual ability, workmanship, general record, and financial and family circumstances. The same factors will determine the rehiring of any who may have been laid off.

Medical Service. Adequate medical personnel and equipment are available in case of accident or illness at work. Special attention is given to the avoidance of health hazards and to the placement of Kodak men and women in work for which they are physically adapted.

Savings Facilities. A plan for systematic savings (and in Rochester for financing the purchase of homes) is available through the Eastman Savings and Loan Association, a corporation organized independently of the Eastman Kodak Company and operated under the Banking Law of the State of New York.

Training and Education. The interests of both the individual and the organization depend largely on adequate training and the full development of the individual's abilities.

It is intended that everyone shall benefit from sound and adequate training for both his present work and any future responsibilities which he may undertake. Thorough on-the-job training is provided in all cases. In the manufacturing establishments, training in certain skill trades is also provided. Outside studies of value to the individual and his work are encouraged.

Suggestion System. The Company welcomes constructive suggestions from Kodak people on all matters in connection with the business. All suggestions are impartially considered, and cash awards are made for original ideas adopted and put into operation.

Employee Co-operation. The success of any company depends on satisfying the fair interests of customers, employees, and stockholders. The wholehearted co-operation needed to do this is expected of everyone in the organization.

The foregoing statement of principles will remain in effect unless changes are considered necessary because of general economic conditions or because of conditions pertaining particularly to the industry. No changes will be made except after due consideration of the mutual advantages, benefits, and responsibilities of the Company and Kodak people.

At times and in some cases, application of the principles may be affected by government regulations.

It should be noted that in this statement of general policy no reference has been made to absolute wages, hours, or other conditions of employment. Rather, the company has stated its philosophy or attitude toward the worker. Specific policies relating to wages, hours, and employee benefits which stem from a sound basic policy are bound to be in the best interests of the worker.

The policy of the company toward personnel is summed up very well in a paragraph on page 34 of the handbook entitled *The Square Deal,* which states:

> Everyone wants to feel that his work is important, and that his efforts are appreciated. All of us want the people we work with to treat us with respect and consideration. We quite properly want and expect to get a square deal.
>
> Eastman Kodak tries in many ways to make sure that you do get a square deal. In all matters affecting the interests of the individual, actions and decisions are expected to conform to the Company's Square Deal Policy.
>
> . . . if you feel that you are not getting a square deal, Kodak wants you to call attention to the matter right away. There are a number of ways (to) . . . get immediate action. (These are explained to the worker.)

One could expect that personnel relations founded on such a code would be highly desirable from both the employer's and the employee's viewpoints.

SUMMARY

During the past century American business management has made tremendous strides in improving production methods, lowering production costs, and in providing the consuming public with more and better goods. This progress, it can be seen, results largely from an ability to perform mechanical feats. The problem of dealing with people, on the other hand, is far more involved and complex than the problems of production and distribution. Few people will question the fact that the greatest weakness in personnel management lies in the attempt to deal with people as if they were machines.

Perhaps businessmen fail to realize that the American worker is a human being, not a machine as they often wish he were. Fifty years ago management could look upon the worker as a commodity or a human machine because little resistance could be offered by the worker to counteract this thinking. Today's educated and financially successful worker will not tolerate such treatment, and he can back up his position through collective bargaining. Intervention on behalf of the worker by both unions and the government has created an entirely different atmosphere for labor-management relations.

Shall management continue to live in the past and fight the progress made by the worker, or shall management accept this newer philosophy? If for no other reason than the fact that forces operating against the older philosophy are gaining momentum and strength, management should accept the newer approach. Management has much to gain through recognizing the worker as an integral part of the organization. Increased production, cost reduction, and improved public relations are but a few of the gains available to management through a personnel policy dedicated to the interests of the worker. It seems safe to say that in the future workers will demand more and more from their employer. If management does not provide for worker advancement in its policy, the worker through collective bargaining will force the issue.

QUESTIONS

1. Why, in recent years, has management given greater attention to problems involving the worker?
2. What effect have the "structural changes in our society" had on labor-management relations?
3. Personnel management can be divided into three parts. What are they and what does each involve?
4. Specifically, what functions usually come under the jurisdiction of personnel management?
5. What are the essential parts of a policy—a personnel policy, to be specific?
6. What qualities should be incorporated in any personnel policy?
7. Evaluate the Eastman Kodak "Code of Industrial Relations." What does it accomplish?
8. What are management's objectives through personnel management?
9. Distinguish between maximum individual development and maximum utilization of human resources.
10. What is meant by the newer philosophy of labor-management relations?

CHAPTER 11

Personnel: Selection and Training

A well-managed personnel department helps management to acquire and maintain an efficient work force. To facilitate the operation of this department certain techniques and procedures must be adopted and applied. By applying specific techniques and procedures, management can greatly reduce the possibility of poor selection of workers and avoid many of the common personnel problems. These techniques and procedures, which will be discussed in this chapter and the one following, relate to selecting and training workers and to dealing with them as established employees.

SOURCES OF LABOR SUPPLY

The need for new personnel is a continuous one in most business organizations. There are several reasons why this is true. First, most business organizations grow, and growth creates new jobs. Second, there is a natural turnover of labor caused by the retirement of workers. Third, nearly all businesses are faced with labor turnover which results from the worker's dissatisfaction with his job or place of work or from the employer's dissatisfaction with the employee. The constant movement of workers and the growth of manpower requirements create the need for frequent additions to the work force.

At times management can plan its future manpower requirements, but there are also times when it cannot. Regardless, an organization that has developed sources from which it can draw to satisfy manpower requirements is in a much better position to obtain qualified personnel than the employer who waits until the need for a worker arises. The quality of worker obtained by management is determined initially by the caliber of its labor pool.

The importance of a labor pool to management will be determined by the type of worker needed or the job that is to be filled. If the labor requirements are basically for unskilled workers who can be trained and made into efficient workers in a matter of hours, then there is little need for a highly specialized labor pool. When highly skilled or key workers are needed, the selection process becomes more difficult, fewer applicants will meet the company standards, and a larger pool of workers should be available. When management hires a new worker, it is imperative that he reach the required level of productivity in as short a period of time as possible; good selection enhances the possibility of early worker productivity. A good labor pool greatly facilitates the selection process.

The type of labor pool needed by an employer is determined also by the company's promotion policy. If the company policy is to promote from within and vacancies are filled mainly by raising workers up a notch on the job scale, then only the lower-rated jobs will need to be filled when vacancies arise. As noted above, management need not be so selective in choosing workers for low-rated jobs, and a limited labor pool may suffice. Even with this policy, workers selected for employment must have sufficient growth potential to warrant their being elevated to a higher-rated job.

Sooner or later, however, in most establishments vacancies will occur that cannot be filled from within the organization, and management will be forced to go into the labor market, perhaps for key personnel. It is in this situation that management stands to lose because of an inadequate labor pool.

There are several sources available to any employer, through which a manpower pool can be established and new employees obtained. For many employers the best source of manpower is within the company. If management follows a policy of observing and rating its workers, the results thus obtained can be used to earmark individuals to fill the new jobs which arise. Frequently fellow employees are more receptive to changes involving existing personnel than they are when someone is brought in from the outside. While perhaps not completely ethical, it is the practice of many employers to observe the progress of employees in other establishments and secure those who are desirable through a process of weaning or pirating. Usually promises of greater opportunity or enhanced security are offered as bait to get the person wanted. Employment agencies, both public and private, perform a valuable service for the businessman. These agencies act as a clearinghouse for people seeking employment, and they are able to screen out many undesirables who might otherwise approach the prospective employer. Colleges, universities, technical schools, and labor unions are frequently used to create a labor pool. These are valuable sources of personnel since the basic abilities and training of individuals in each of these groups are known in advance. A union bricklayer or carpenter is a known quantity of skill and ability, else he would not be a member of the union. Likewise, a person who has earned his B.S. in Mechanical Engineering is a known, within limitations, quantity. The cost of hiring and training new employees can amount to a significant annual expenditure. Many employers have found that money spent in recruiting or in cultivating a labor pool is a wise investment.

SELECTION PROCEDURE

There is no one procedure for selecting new personnel that is applicable to all business establishments. Each business must plan a selection procedure that will produce the desired quantity and quality of manpower at the least possible cost. Initially the selection or employment procedure will be governed by a general management policy regarding the centralization or decentralization of the selection function. The current trend is toward centralizing this function in a single office rather than having each department act as an employment office. Under such a plan, all applicants for employment will be governed by the same basic rules and regulations. The gains possible through centralized selection and employment procedures are many. Among them are the following:

1. It reduces the administrative cost associated with selection by consolidating all activity in a single office.
2. It relieves line officers of the detail involved in hiring workers, which is common under a decentralized plan.
3. It tends to make selection of workers scientific. The personnel involved in the selection process can become selection specialists equipped with all the latest approved selection tools.
4. It permits the development of a centralized manpower pool within the company.
5. It permits a wider range of possibility in placing an applicant in the several departments of the company. An applicant for a job in Department A may be more useful in a job in Department C, etc.
6. It tends to reduce favoritism as a basis for selection.

The selection process usually begins when someone in authority finds it necessary to fill a vacancy or expected vacancy caused by the creation of a new job or because a worker has left a job. Some sort of hiring requisition will be issued stating the title of the job to be filled and any special considerations that would help in selecting a desirable candidate for the job.

Next, the employment office will survey those individuals who comprise the labor pool, workers who are presently employed, or who have been laid off, in search of the most desirable applicant. The task becomes one of determining just what type of person is needed for the job and then finding the person who can fulfill the job requirements. The first step is to obtain a complete description of the job and an indication of the human qualities essential for effective job performance. This information can be obtained from a formal job description and job analysis. (See Figure 11–1.) The second step is to determine the aptitudes, abilities,

FIGURE 11–1

JOB DESCRIPTION FORM

PILGRIM ENGINEERING COMPANY

Job Description

Job Title Hand-Screw Machine Operator Job No. 400

Department Machine Shop Date October 7, 19—

General Description of Job

The purpose of this job is to perform a number of machining operations on a wide variety of metals and synthetic materials. Materials may be bored, reamed, turned, cut off; or they may be threaded, tapped, or knurled. Generally this is the first operation performed on raw stock. To do this job, operator:

1. Receives material from stock room or cut-off department.
2. Has screw machine set up by setup man.
3. Inserts materials to be machined; operates turret by hand at correct speed. Receives instructions from the setup man relative to machine speeds.
4. Removes finished part from machine.
5. Inspects his work with gages provided according to the instructions of the setup man.

Job Requirements

1. Eyesight corrected to 20/40.
2. Average to good strength.
3. Ability to read simple blueprints.
4. Ability to use micrometers and other simple inspection devices.
5. Good manual dexterity.
6. No previous machine shop experience required.

Job Surroundings

1. Standing required for the majority of the time worked.
2. Job may be dirty at times when coolants, cutting oil, and lubricants are used.
3. Accidents are rare, seldom serious.

Remuneration

Job pays $1.30 for inexperienced beginner to a maximum of $1.65 per hour. Normal work week 44 hours.

Promotion

Promotion may be to lathe operator, milling machine operator, or setup man.

Additional Qualifications

Age: 20–50 years Sex: Male Height: 5′4″ to 6′2″

and skill of the applicant to see if they match the job requirements. The closer men and jobs can be matched the better.

The Job Description

A job description is a written record of the duties, responsibilities, and requirements of a particular job. The job description is concerned with the job itself and not with the person who performs the job. The job description is used to establish a mutual understanding between the personnel department which assists in selecting the worker and the foreman or department head who will actually use him. In addition the job description is helpful in acquainting the worker with the job and as a part of the process of job evaluation which is discussed in a later chapter.

Specifically, the job description may include the following:

1. Name or title of the occupation and the names of departments in the organization that have need for the occupation. Names of all allied occupations should be indicated, for they may be the best source of manpower.
2. An indication of the duties performed by the employee should be given—an indication of the machines, tools, and materials used and the responsibility of the worker for property, money, and the like.
3. Conditions surrounding the job such as:
   a. Skill requirements necessary
   b. Degree of accuracy required in work
   c. Type and degree of supervision
   d. General working conditions, factory or office
   e. Job hazards
   f. Nature of the work—routine or analytical, standing or sitting, light or heavy, etc.
   g. Pay, rates, bonuses, paid holidays, vacations, etc.
   h. Training required to reach normal productivity
   i. Sex, age, physical qualifications
   j. Personal characteristics
   k. Mental ability

There is no single list of the components to a job description; rather, the components will vary from occupation to occupation depending on the difficulty of establishing the exact nature of the occupation. Figure 11–1 illustrates a job description for a hand-screw machine operator. A good job description provides adequate information for the reader to appreciate the nature of the occupation.

Securing the Job Description. Some aspects of the job description (see Figure 11–1) can be compiled from records in the personnel office; others cannot. For office and clerical operations the job description may be obtained by asking workers to fill out a questionnaire about their jobs.

Office and clerical workers generally have a greater appreciation of the questionnaire approach to a situation than do factory workers. The information thus obtained from the workers should be verified through comparisons of questionnaire results and through interviews with the workers and their supervisors before the job description is formalized.

Factory job descriptions on the other hand are best obtained by having qualified persons visit the work area and prepare a description based on their observations of workers in action. Verification of the results of the observation should be made through consultation with superiors, checking instructions given the workers, and checking blueprints from which the worker operates. From the information thus obtained, the job description is prepared.

The Application Blank

When the job to be filled is fully described, the personnel department next examines job applicants in search of the person who most fully meets the requirements of the job. The objective is to match worker abilities and job requirements as closely as possible.

Most of us are familiar with the application blank, for it has nearly universal usage in the hiring function. The purpose of the application blank is to record information concerning the abilities, background, and interests of the applicant. The applicant is afforded an opportunity to tell his prospective employer who he is and what he can do. The application blank should furnish enough information to provide a basis for an intelligent interview. (See Figure 11–2.) Many times the information given in the application blank is sufficient to rule out certain applicants from further consideration, thereby saving valuable time for the employment office.

The Preliminary Interview

The preliminary interview is an essential part of the selection process; it should be planned to obtain information from the applicant and to give the applicant information about the company and the job. Management cannot obtain the type of worker it needs without an interview, nor can prospective employees know whether the job offered and the company policy will be to their liking.

Valuable time of department heads can be saved through the use of a preliminary interview conducted by the employment office. The preliminary interview is designed to weed out those applicants in whom, for the time being at least, the company has no further interest and to channel the desirable applicants for further processing at higher levels. The interview is of great importance to both the prospective employee and the company; for if an applicant should fail to impress, it is quite

FIGURE 11–2

JOB APPLICATION FORM

APPLICATION FOR EMPLOYMENT
PILGRIM ENGINEERING COMPANY

Personal

Name ______________________________ S. S. No. ______________
Address ____________________________ Date of Birth ____________
Married _____ Single _____ Children _____ Citizen _____ Height _____ Wt. _____

Education

	Location	Years attended	Date graduated	Major
Grammar School				
High School				
College				
Other				

Work Experience

	Date	Employer	Salary	Position	Reason for leaving
From *To*					
From *To*					
From *To*					

References

	Name	*Address*	*Business*	*Years Acquainted*
1.				
2.				
3.				

Do not write below line.

Interviewed by ______________________ Date ______________

Remarks

Neatness ______________ Character ______________
Personality ______________ Ability ______________

unlikely that he will be given any additional consideration for employment. It is important that a clear picture of the applicant be developed at this point.

Tests As an Employment Tool

In addition to the information obtained through the application blank and the interview many companies use various types of tests as an aid in the selection process. Preemployment tests should not be used as the sole criteria of measuring the aptitudes and capabilities of a job applicant. While such tests have been developed and refined over the years, they are best used as indicators of aptitude or capabilities rather than exact measures. Often such tests are used to tell the employment officer whom not to hire rather than whom to hire. To illustrate, during World War II the Army administered a General Classification Test to all personnel, generally at the beginning of their service. The purpose of the test was to get an indication of the capabilities of personnel before assigning them to jobs. Various grades were established for test scores; those with test scores of 130 and higher were classed as Grade I; those with scores 110 through 129 were classed Grade II; and so on down the line. In addition, standards for jobs were also established; for example, to be eligible for officer training, a minimum score of 110 was needed. This does not mean that all personnel having test scores of 110 or more would make good officers; rather, experience showed that "as a rule" those men whose test scores were Grade I or II were better officer potential than those whose test scores were Grade III or IV.

There are several different types of tests available to help in the selection process, but the more common tests fall into one of three categories described below.

General Intelligence Tests. It would be helpful to employers to have some means of measuring the degree of intelligence possessed by an applicant. One might infer an answer from the worker's performance record but still not know whether he has applied himself to the full extent of his abilities. The intelligence test is designed to give an indication of the applicant's ability to understand, learn, and use ideas. There may be some doubt as to just what these tests measure, but correlations secured through the application of these tests seem to offer definite proof of the subject's ability to learn or his speed of learning. Such data, if accurate, are an invaluable aid in assigning workers to jobs.

Ability or Achievement Tests. Frequently applicants will claim certain skills which they have developed during previous work experience. Management would be foolish to accept these claims at face value. A worker who was rated a skilled welder in one plant may not possess the abilities required to do welding work in another plant. Trial on the job offers an answer to the question of skill, but this could be a costly and time-consuming check. Tests have been developed to measure the level of skill possessed by workers in a variety of occupations. These tests can be administered and graded and an answer given in a matter of a few hours. The Air Force used such tests during World War II in an effort to locate usable skills, to shorten training periods, and to reduce the number of training units necessary to supply the needed manpower skills. Often the test score may indicate that a person is not skilled but has a basic understanding of the trade. Such results will indicate the amount of additional training needed to build a worker's skill to the desired level. Such tests, like others, are not foolproof; but if a person passes the machinist's achievement test for the XYZ Company, it is reasonable to assume that he will meet the requirements for a machinist at that Company.

Aptitude Tests. Many applicants for employment do not possess any specific skills, but all applicants do have some latent potential. This is especially true of young people just out of school, seeking their first job. These applicants should be trained and developed to a point where they will be of greatest value to their employer. Through the application form, the interview, and the intelligence tests a general guide is at hand; but still there is no indication of the natural bent of the applicant.

Aptitude tests have been successfully used to determine that area of work for which a person has natural leaning. It is assumed that if a person has a high mechanical aptitude, for example, he will do better at mechanical jobs than at clerical work. A person who has a high clerical aptitude is not apt to do well in mechanical work, and so on. Aptitude tests are used to determine if an applicant leans toward sales work, detailed work, routine work, or any of several other categories.

The value of the aptitude test lies in its use with other tests. A person who has the mental capacity to learn a job combined with an aptitude for the job is a most desirable type of applicant.

Other Tests. Closely allied to the aptitude tests is the dexterity test which is often used to determine whether a person can work effectively with his hands and fingers. One such test requires the applicant to position loosely piled brass pegs into drilled holes on a board. The speed with which the task is performed is used as a measure of dexterity. Many jobs require that a person be specially adept at using his arms, legs, hands, or fingers; dexterity tests reduce the possibility of putting the person who is "all thumbs" in a job that requires a particular dexterity.

Interest tests, while newer than some of the tests mentioned above, have also been used with success. Such tests might be used to determine if an applicant for an accounting job really has an interest in accounting work or to determine if the electrical engineering major in college actually has an interest in this field or elected this major because his grandfather had been a successful electrical engineer forty years before. A person who works at a job in which he has little or no interest usually will quit after a short period of time or will be a mediocre performer.

Personality tests designed to measure certain emotional characteristics of people have been used with some success. Personality is a difficult thing to measure by testing, much more so than intelligence or aptitude. However, this type of testing has helped in the development of work teams, especially among office workers, and is being studied constantly in an effort to make the results more valid.

To indicate the wide range of possibilities in preemployment tests, the Revere Copper and Brass Company has developed an accident proneness test. This test is designed to locate those workers or applicants who have a faculty for being involved in accidents. Experience has shown that a relatively small portion of workers are responsible for a large portion of accidents in industry; the same workers are involved over and over again. Through this test accident-prone workers can be detected and assigned to work that offers little opportunity for injury.

Many elements of the human complex cannot be measured by these tests, notably those actions in human behavior due to emotions. Tests, for example, do not measure reliability, loyalty, courage, and many other indicators of a person's character that contribute to human efficiency. Within these limitations, tests serve a real purpose and make their contribution to greater certainty in the selection process. Tests should not be called upon to make fine differentiations between applicants; but they will clearly indicate high or low ability to learn, great or little aptitude, interest, or dexterity.

The Hiring Interview

If an applicant has passed his preliminary interview and the results of the tests given indicate that he has the necessary qualifications, it is customary to conduct another interview which would include the applicant and the department head or other line officer who made the request for additional manpower. In theory, all applicants who have come this far in the selection process have the necessary qualifications to fill the vacancy. The department head or line officer explores the applicant's background, likes, and dislikes more thoroughly as they apply to the specific job in question. If, during this interview, it is decided to hire the applicant, it is important that the exact terms of the job be defined. There should be a definite understanding with a new employee whereby he accepts his new job with a complete knowledge of the terms under which he will have to work. He should have definite information, written if possible, as to the hours he will work, the amount of overtime he can expect, the wages he will receive, and when he will be paid. He should be fully informed as to the rules of conduct governing workers in the company in general and in his work area specifically. The worker should go to his job knowing what management expects of him and what he can expect from management.

TRAINING THE WORKERS

All new employees should be trained before they are allowed to work by themselves on their new jobs. For the experienced skilled worker who has just joined the work force this training may be limited to company policies and procedures. No matter, training is a vital aspect of managerial control. The modern establishment conducts studies designed to determine the best operating procedures, the best ways to do the various jobs, and the best manner for dealing with particular situations. Unless new workers are told of the meaning and purpose of these methods, their advantage will never be fully realized. When workers are transferred or promoted within the organization, they should be fully oriented to their new jobs through some form of training program.

TRAINING METHODS

As implied above, training methods can be quite extensive or formal or they may simply involve a few minutes' discussion of company policy before the worker takes over his job. Some of the common training methods are described below.

On-the-job Training

The most common method of worker training today is on-the-job training where the worker is put into the situation where he will remain after the training period is over. Such training lasts until the worker has demonstrated that he can perform the job with only normal supervision. It is assumed that the new worker has the capacity to learn the job, interest in the job, and an aptitude for the type of work involved. If the above assumptions are correct, it can be expected that the worker will respond satisfactorily when placed in the job environment. The success of this or any other type of training depends upon the proper selection of workers as noted above and the caliber of instruction the new worker receives. Management wants the new worker to learn to do the job effectively, but if his instructor does not possess training know-how, the worker will not grasp the details of the job as quickly or as accurately as management intends. There are many sources of instructors for on-the-job training: experienced workers, supervisory staff, or specially trained instructors. If the experienced worker has the ability and desire to instruct, the proper work habits, and a knowledge of what the trainee needs to learn, then he could be a very satisfactory instructor. When this method of instruction or training is used, suitable adjustments should be made in the experienced worker's work load and earnings so that he will not be penalized for slowing down while instructing the new worker. Rather, there should be some incentive so that good workers will want to train the newcomers.

Much the same precaution should be taken when using supervisory personnel in training. The supervisory staff generally has a considerable amount of responsibility and often must interrupt one task in favor of another. If training is considered a function of a foreman or a supervisor, it should be considered when mapping out his over-all job in order that there will be enough time for satisfactory training. Generally this class of worker is more highly paid than production workers. Management should consider this fact before finally deciding whom to use as instructors.

If there is a considerable amount of training to be done and there will be a continuing demand for instruction, it might be to management's advantage to employ a full-time training staff. The professional instructor has the necessary time and ability to train workers as they should be trained.

Apprentice Training

The apprentice system continues to exist today in many of the trades. It has persisted in spite of specialization owing, in large measure, to the desire of the craft unions to keep trades or crafts intact. The apprentice system can be quite economical for the employer, for it may provide him with a skilled worker at the end of the training period, although the worker is not obliged to remain indefinitely with the training establishment.

Today many young workers are participating in apprentice training through the Veterans' Administration, labor unions, and state agencies. The following illustrates how the apprentice program operated in connection with Public Law 550 and is indicative of many apprentice training programs: A Korean veteran approached a counselor at his local Veterans' Administration office, indicating that he wanted to learn the machinist's trade, preferably in a small shop near his home. A small ten-man shop was located by the V.A. that was willing to participate in the program. The worker and the shop owner signed an agreement covering forty-eight months, whereby the apprentice agreed to apply himself to the job and the shop agreed to give him a specific amount of training under the supervision of journeymen machinists. As a trainee, the apprentice was paid $1 per hour to start, with semiannual increases at such a rate that he would be earning journeyman rates when he completed the training program. At the same time he received a subsistence allowance from the Veterans' Administration amounting to about $70 per month at the start and decreasing as his rate of pay increased. Thus the apprentice could afford the schooling, and the employer could afford the training.

The Vestibule School

Frequently on-the-job training is desirable but not feasible because of the nature of the production processes. As an alternative, simulated production areas are set up apart from the production area for the purpose of training. In this situation the advantages of on-the-job training and trained instructors are available to the worker. Since the goal of the vestibule school is training, not production, more time can be spent in planned and thorough training.

Formal Schooling

Company schools, colleges, universities, and technical schools are commonly used in worker training. The purpose of formal schooling extends well beyond job training. Such training programs are usually designed to groom employees for greater responsibilities either in their own job or different jobs. The courses of study offered resemble a program of academic education more than technical training.

SUPERVISORY TRAINING

In the past a vast majority of supervisory personnel has come up through the ranks with no special training for their supervisory duties. Training for them was largely a matter of trial and error or copying what others about them had done. Supervisory jobs are important jobs to management and labor; they are a vital link between the work area and top management. It is essential, therefore, that supervisors know their jobs well. Training for supervisors is often aimed at leadership development, informing supervisors on company policy and the importance of policy. Such training brings all supervisory personnel together for a discussion of their common problems. Much of this training can be conducted through lectures, group discussions, and conferences. To obtain the maximum value from a supervisory training program, it should represent a continuous effort carefully designed to improve the quality of supervision.

Many of our larger corporations are going to colleges and universities for supervisory trainees rather than following the older practice of bringing men up through the ranks. Trainees are put through a comprehensive training program which requires from six to thirty-six months. It is felt that supervisory help enlisted from outside the firm will have no preconceived ideas of what should be done or how it should be done, and will, therefore, be more receptive to the training program.

SUMMARY

The personnel department is charged with the responsibility of obtaining qualified personnel for the many openings that arise in a business organization. To accomplish this, the personnel department must have a complete description of each job to be filled so that it can determine the type of person needed. A search is then made within the company or outside to find a person who possesses the desired characteristics and capabilities and who is interested in getting the job in question.

A screening process is used for all applicants for the job to weed out those who are deficient in any respect, leaving a small and potentially qualified group for final consideration. Application blanks, screening interviews, preemployment tests, and interviews with foremen and supervisors all play an important part in the selection process. Workers thus selected, when given proper orientation and training, should become satisfied and productive employees in the minimum span of time.

QUESTIONS

1. Why is the need for new personnel a continuous one in most business organizations?
2. What is the advantage of maintaining a labor pool?
3. What factors determine the size and type of labor pool needed by an employer?
4. What sources are available to satisfy an employer's manpower requirements?
5. What is meant by centralized employment?
6. What gains are possible through centralizing the employment function?
7. What steps are involved in the selection procedure?
8. What is the function of the job description?
9. What elements are included in the job description?
10. What is the function of the application blank?
11. How does the securing of the job description for office jobs differ from that for factory jobs? Why?
12. What should be accomplished in the first interview with a job applicant?
13. In general, what is the function of employment tests?
14. Distinguish between an ability test and an aptitude test.
15. What is the general intelligence test designed to measure?
16. What is the function of the hiring interview?
17. Discuss: "Training is a vital aspect of managerial control."
18. Distinguish between on-the-job training and apprentice training.
19. What are the advantages of bringing in supervisory trainees "green" from the outside?
20. How does an apprentice-training program operate?

CHAPTER 12

Personnel: Evaluation Techniques

Selection, training, and placement of workers are vital personnel functions; yet they do not describe the real nature of personnel relations. In fact, these functions are considered more or less routine for most personnel departments. Management is interested in building a satisfied and productive work crew; personnel administration must aid in accomplishing this end. To do this, the personnel department needs certain tools to insure that the best interests of management and the worker will be served. This chapter is devoted to a discussion of some of the tools, techniques, and policies that are applied primarily after the worker has been placed on the job.

JOB EVALUATION

It would be difficult, if not impossible, for management to determine an appropriate rate of pay for any job or to determine what constitutes a promotion for a worker unless it knew the relative value of each job being performed within the organization. Job evaluation is a procedure that is used to rate jobs so that management will know the relative value of each job to the company. Jobs are studied or evaluated, and a numerical value or an appropriate classification is assigned to each job. Thus a job might be given a numerical value of 140 and be considered worth twice as much as a job which has a rating of 70. In no way can job evaluation by itself determine wage rates. Job evaluation does allow for equitable pay rates within the organization after management sets the level of wages that will apply. It should be remembered that job evaluation rates only the job, not the worker who performs the job. It states the value of the job to the company when it is filled by someone who meets the minimum requirements for the job. An additional reward should be given to those workers who contribute more than the minimum requirements. The more common methods of job evaluation discussed below present a clearer picture of what job evaluation is and does.

The Point Method

All job evaluation methods will differ in some respects, but they all operate on the same basic principle. When an employer pays a worker $2 per hour, actually the worker is being paid a few cents each for the physical effort he exerts, the responsibility he assumes, the mental and physical skill required to perform the job, the conditions under which he works, and so on. Job evaluation seeks to determine the extent to which each of these factors is present in each job to establish its relative value. To obtain an accurate measurement of jobs, they must each be compared to a standard of some sort. The standard is the rating chart. (See Figure 12–1.)

FIGURE 12–1

POINT-METHOD RATING CHART

Factor	*Max. pts.*	*1st deg.*	*2d deg.*	*3d deg.*	*4th deg.*	*5th deg.*
Skill:						
Mental	100	30	50	70	90	100
Physical	60	20	30	40	50	60
Physical effort	70	25	35	45	55	70
Responsibility	80	10	30	45	60	80
Education	40	5	15	25	35	40
Working conditions	50	10	20	30	40	50

The point-method rating chart contains two major considerations—a list of the factors to be considered in the evaluation and a description of the various degrees to which a factor may be present in a job. Each of these factors is assigned a maximum point value, and each degree of the factors is assigned a point value. The maximum points represent management's best judgment of the relative value of each factor to the total. The "degree" points are allotted on the basis of the varying importance of each degree. In this manner the rating chart is constructed.

The rating chart shown is for illustrative purposes only and is not designed to show the proper relationship between the various factors. To illustrate, working conditions may warrant more or less consideration in different plants than physical effort, depending on the nature of jobs being performed and the general working conditions that exist. Each of the degrees indicated for each factor should be described so that the job rater will be able to associate the individual job requirements with a degree of each factor.

Before any job is rated or evaluated, a complete analysis of each job should be made. This involves three steps: collecting all the facts about each job, preferably in some standard form; writing descriptions based on the facts collected; and preparing job specifications which are brief definitions of job requirements. With this as a background for rating, the following illustrates how Job A and Job B would be evaluated:

Factor	Job A		Job B	
	Degree	Points	Degree	Points
Skill:				
Mental	3	70	5	100
Physical	5	60	2	30
Physical effort	5	70	2	35
Responsibility	1	10	5	80
Education	1	5	4	35
Working conditions	3	30	1	10
Total points	.....	245	.....	290

Job A is worth 245 points while Job B is worth 290 points. Therefore, *if* Job A is worth $2.45 per hour to the company based on the general level of wages, then Job B would be worth $2.90 per hour because the rating tells what one job is worth in relation to other jobs. However, we should not conclude that point scores indicate rates of pay; they indicate relative job values.

Factor-comparison Method

The factor-comparison method differs from the point method primarily in the structure of the rating chart. This method begins with the selection of several key jobs, 10 to 15 in practice. A key job is a job whose money rate is not in dispute and whose component elements are known and agreed upon. It is, in effect, a preevaluated job. A rating chart is prepared from the knowledge of key jobs, and all other jobs are rated against the chart as in the point method. (See Figure 12–2.) The rating of each job denotes its value; therefore, *if* a machinist's job is worth $1.70 per hour, then a janitor is worth 90 cents per hour and a toolmaker, $2.40 per hour, and so on. The nature of job evaluation by this method is indicated below. The point rating given Job A indicates that it is worth 150 points because the mental skill is similar to that required of a machinist and is worth 40 points; the physical skill is similar to that of an inspector and worth 30 points; the responsibility is like that of a welder and worth 30 points; and so on.

The factor comparison method is flexible inasmuch as there are no maximum points, but it is limited to the number of key jobs in existence.

It also has the advantage of comparing jobs to existing jobs rather than to a point-rating scale.

FIGURE 12–2

FACTOR-COMPARISON RATING CHART

KEY JOBS

Factor	*Machinist*	*Toolmaker*	*Janitor*	*Lathe Oper.*	*Inspector*	*Welder*
Skill:						
Mental	40	50	10	20	30	25
Physical	40	50	10	30	30	30
Physical effort	20	20	30	30	10	30
Responsibility	40	80	15	20	100	30
Education	20	30	5	10	30	15
Working conditions	10	10	20	15	5	25
Total	170	240	90	125	205	155

Factor	Job A	
	Type	Points
Skill:		
Mental	Machinist	40
Physical	Inspector	30
Physical effort	Toolmaker	20
Responsibility	Welder	30
Education	Lathe Operator	10
Working conditions	Janitor	20
Total	....	150

Ranking Method

This method, sometimes called the "card shuffling" method, ranks each job above or below one another based on the factors included in the methods discussed above. It does not involve a rating scale as such, but those who rate the jobs must consider the factors that would normally be included in a rating scale. After jobs are placed in proper relation to one another, classifications or groups are established and jobs take on the rating of Grade I, Grade II, Grade III, and so on. Civil service jobs are evaluated by a method which embodies these principles. The ranking of jobs may be done by an individual, several individuals, or a rating committee. When jobs are rated in approximately the same relation by several qualified raters, it is reasonable to assume that the evaluation is accurate and fair. This plan is simple and requires less time than the two mentioned above. It is not at all scientific and merely tells whether one job is higher than another, not how much higher.

Advantages of Job Evaluation

When a complete evaluation of all jobs in an organization is made, there are several advantages that may accrue both to management and the worker. First, management will have better control over labor costs since pay for each job is consistent with its value to the company. Second, workers doing a similar type of work will receive similar pay. This too aids in controlling labor costs and can improve worker morale. Third, since job evaluation shows the relative worth of jobs, it provides a sound basis for establishing a sequence for promotion. Fourth, job evaluation aids in the selection, placement, and training of workers by indicating the extent to which each of the various factors is present in a job. Fifth, it provides a means for justifying different rates of pay on different jobs. And finally, it provides a basis for setting rates of pay on new jobs.

Limitations to Job Evaluation

To avoid any misconceptions of the role played by job evaluation in setting rates of pay, we must understand that there are times when wages are influenced by several forces operating outside the realm of job evaluation, albeit management would generally prefer to premise wages on this basis.

One of the reasons why wage rates may deviate from the amount determined through job evaluation is that management may find labor supply ample and be able to satisfy its manpower requirements by paying less than the job calls for. Conversely, management may be unable to hire workers at job-evaluation rates and may be forced by conditions in the labor market to pay more. Frequently unions have their own ideas on the general level of wages, the relative worth of jobs, and the rate of pay for any job. In the past unions have narrowed the differential in wages between the skilled and unskilled worker, an action which tends to destroy the effect of job evaluation.

Some jobs by their very nature offer little certainty of continued employment, a factor seldom considered in job evaluation. Many feel that if there is little certainty of continued employment, the job in question warrants a higher rate of pay than a steady job even though both jobs are rated equally through job evaluation. Similarly, two jobs may be rated the same, yet one job may offer a better promotional opportunity than the other. Again, there is a feeling that the job that offers little chance for advancement warrants the higher rate of pay.

The factors mentioned above apply to a very large percentage of jobs. One might wonder just where job evaluation fits into the scheme of wage determination and what is its over-all value to management. Despite the limitations on job evaluation as a device for setting wages, it is an important personnel tool. First, job evaluation tells management what jobs are worth in relation to each other, even though actual rates paid may not be in this relation. Rates determined through job evaluation may be considered as standards and actual rates of pay, which may be affected by outside influences, deviations from standard. It is desirable to know how much higher or lower rates of pay are than they "should be." Second, job evaluation does establish a basis for pay rates in a wide area of office and clerical jobs; jobs in the executive, administrative, and professional category; or in any other situation where the establishment of wage rates is a management prerogative. Quite frequently it is in these areas that job evaluation is more vitally needed.

EMPLOYEE RATING

How much should management pay an employee? Management should consider two factors in determining the amount paid to any worker. First, how much is his job worth? This can be answered through job evaluation, as outlined above. The second factor considers how well the worker does his job. In the discussion above, it was mentioned that job evaluation seeks to determine what a person should be paid when he meets the minimum requirements of the job. The question that now arises is how much more should a person be paid who gives the job something over and above the minimum requirements. Obviously some form of employee rating is needed to answer this question.

A worker's pay may be based on his output—piece rate for example. There are, however, worker attributes other than output that management should consider in evaluating its employees. What is the worker's attitude toward his job, the company, and those with whom he works? Is the worker dependable, is he cooperative, is he the type of person that brings credit to his employer? These and other considerations are important to management and should become a part of any employee-rating program.

Uses of Employee Rating

Determining differentials in pay is but one instance where employee rating is used to advantage. Some of the other uses are indicated below.

1. *As a Basis for Promotion.* We realize that management should, with few exceptions, promote the most qualified worker. The problem is that management many times does not know who is best qualified. A well-organized and well-conducted employee-rating program will go a long way toward providing the answer. Since formal employee rating is often a continuous function, management can build a file on each worker and

will have concrete evidence upon which to base its decision. Unions frequently seek to promote the worker with the greatest seniority; therefore, it is vital that management have positive proof that one person is more worthy of a promotion than another, seniority notwithstanding. A program of employee rating may give management a greater degree of control over promotions in a union shop. Employee ratings also provide a basis for downgrading workers and for deciding which workers should be laid off.

2. *To Locate Individual Worker Weaknesses.* Employee ratings will show individual weaknesses. They will show whether the weakness lies in the quality of work done, unit output, reliability, ability to get along with fellow workers, or in some other area. It becomes an effective means for diagnosing a worker's weaknesses—diagnosis which must precede the cure.

3. *To Locate Worker Talents.* Similarly, as weak points are uncovered, so are strong points uncovered. Management can then concentrate on the strong points in its plan of worker development.

4. *To Stimulate Competition between Workers.* Just as examinations provide a means for college students to show how good they are, employee rating provides a means for workers to show how valuable they are to their employer. The program also indicates the factors that management feels are important and the relative value it attaches to each.

Employee Rating Illustrated

The most widely used method of formal employee rating utilizes a procedure similar to the point method of job evaluation. Figure 12–3 shows in very simple form the general principle of employee rating. A series of personal characteristics is selected, and a numerical maximum and minimum assigned, which show the importance of each characteristic. Workers are awarded a number of points for each characteristic based on the rater's appraisal of the worker. In this manner workers can be compared with one another, and a basis for distinction is established. A worker who accumulates 160 merit points is obviously more valuable to his employer than the worker who earns, say, 130 points. If the two workers were both qualified for a promotion based on experience, the one who earned 160 merit points would be entitled to the promotion. It must be remembered that employee rating rates the worker, not the job he is doing.

The major objection to employee-rating plans stems from the fact that judgment must be used in rating certain characteristics and that judgment can often be wrong. The "quantity" and "quality" ratings can be made quite accurately by referring to production records. The other

FIGURE 12–3

EMPLOYEE RATING FORM

EMPLOYEE RATING
PILGRIM ENGINEERING COMPANY

WORKER JOB TITLE DATE

CHARACTERISTIC	MAXIMUM POINTS	EXCEPTIONAL	ABOVE AVERAGE	AVERAGE	BELOW AVERAGE	POOR	RATE
QUANTITY	20	20	16	12	8	4	
QUALITY	20	20	16	12	8	4	
COOPERATIVENESS	30	30	24	18	12	6	
INITIATIVE	40	40	32	24	16	8	
DEPENDABILITY	20	20	16	12	8	4	
JOB KNOWLEDGE	25	25	20	15	10	5	
CAPACITY TO DEVELOP	35	35	28	21	14	7	
ATTITUDE TOWARD WORK	20	20	16	12	8	4	
ATTITUDE TOWARD OTHERS	30	30	24	18	12	6	
RATED BY:						TOTAL POINTS	

REMARKS:

characteristics are much more abstract and should be judged only by a person who knows how to rate and who understands the purpose of employee rating.

Ratings are most frequently made by the worker's superior, his foreman or supervisor. All raters should receive training in the art of rating to insure a uniform application of the program. The factors considered in rating should be meticulously defined and described to the raters. If this is done, there is greater assurance that all raters will interpret all factors in the same way and hence produce ratings that are based on the same standards. Raters should be cautioned to include in their ratings only those characteristics incorporated into the rating program; they should not be influenced in their ratings by extraneous factors. Raters should be instructed to guard against using the single instance, favorable or unfavorable, as a basis for rating; rather, the rating should consider the over-all performance of the worker during the period for which he is rated. This suggests that several ratings for each worker gathered over a period of time will be much more valuable and valid than a single rating.

Ratings will be unacceptable to the worker and useless to management unless they can be validated. Unless management can prove that a highly cooperative employee is more valuable to the company than a moderately cooperative employee, the rating is meaningless. Unless management can show that worker A is more or less cooperative than worker B, the rating is not valid. Rating factors therefore must be both significant and measurable on an acceptable basis.

Seniority Rating

Because of the inadequacies of formal employee-rating plans, stemming primarily from their subjective nature, many nonunion as well as unionized establishments rate workers on the basis of their seniority rather than on the so-called "ability" basis. Frequently seniority ratings will be combined with ability ratings to arrive at a final evaluation of the worker.

Before discussing and evaluating seniority as a basis for rating workers, a clear understanding is needed of what seniority means. A senior employee is an older employee, of course, but the question arises, older on what basis. Seniority relates to time, but it may be the time a worker has been employed by the company, in a particular plant of the company, in a department within the plant, in a particular job classification, or the length of time he has been in the union. We then have several different bases for measuring seniority, each of which could give a worker a different seniority rating. A worker may top the seniority list in terms of time with the company and conceivably rank at the bottom of the list when seniority is measured by length of time on a specific job. Seniority must be clearly defined before it is used as a basis for rating workers.

When defining seniority, provisions should be made for a number of interruptions that might affect a worker's seniority rating. What effect will sick leave have on seniority? Will extended sick leave interrupt or terminate a worker's seniority? What effect will layoffs or absenteeism have on the accumulation of seniority? These aspects of seniority maintenance will cause difficulty unless they are specifically provided for in the union contract or in the company rules and regulations.

As indicated above, employee ratings establish which workers are entitled to certain employment privileges, promotion, bonus pay, etc. Whether seniority is a desirable or undesirable basis for rating employees depends initially, after seniority has been defined, on the employment privilege affected. The following is an enumeration of several of the areas wherein seniority provisions may be invoked: layoffs, rehiring, transfer, promotions, distribution of overtime, shift preference, vacation preference, length of vacation, severance pay, sick leave, and pensions.

Seniority appears to have its most common application to situations involving layoffs and rehiring with less application to the other employment privileges. This is quite normal since it guarantees the older worker a degree of job security; security may have been promised or inferred by both management and the union.

Unions generally favor seniority, as opposed to ability ratings, as the basis for distinguishing between workers. There are two major reasons for this attitude: first, seniority can be completely objective in its application once terms have been defined; second, it rewards the long and faithful union member. Management's attitude toward seniority varies, based on the type of seniority under consideration and the employment privilege involved. Some employers approve of seniority as a basis for rating on the ground that it is quick, simple, certain, and reduces the possibility of grievances. On the other hand, employers have argued that it is unsound; it encourages inefficiency; it offers a false sense of security to the worker; it stifles incentive, especially for the younger worker; and it is too restrictive on management when decisions need to be made. Regardless of one's views, it appears that seniority will continue for some time as a basic means of differentiating between workers.

PROMOTIONS, TRANSFERS, AND LAYOFFS

As indicated earlier, there is considerable movement of personnel within a business organization. New machines, new processes, new products, and varying levels of activity cause constant changes in manpower requirements. Promotions, transfers, and layoffs are needed to balance the ever-changing manpower requirements. In many establishments the union contract governs these aspects of personnel administration; in others it may be a management prerogative. Regardless, they are significant enough to warrant some analysis.

Promotions

A promotion, from management's point of view at least, is a transfer to a position that requires "more" from the worker. "More," of course, can be measured through job evaluation. A promotion ordinarily involves an increase in responsibility and is a change which commonly results in higher earnings. Promotions sometimes do not result in increased earnings; such promotions are referred to as "dry" promotions. Since a promotion may carry with it an increase in responsibility, prestige, and earnings, and since workers have differing attitudes toward accepting additional responsibility, it may well be that what management considers a promotion is to a particular worker a demotion. Unless the worker feels that his job change is a bona fide promotion, much of the incentive potential of promotion is lost.

Reasons for Promotions. Management promotes workers for several reasons; some of these satisfy management and others satisfy workers. Management often promotes workers to put them in positions where they will be of greater value to the company, thereby seeking to develop the best in a worker. As a foreman the value of a given worker to management is limited to the foreman's role. As a supervisor the same worker would be in a position to assume additional responsibility and therefore be of greater value to his employer. Promotions are given all too often to remove workers from their jobs as an alternative to the embarrassment of firing and demotion. This, of course, is not usually a promotion in the true sense of the word and is a policy that cannot be defended except as a temporary expedient. Promotions "upstairs" such as these denote definite weaknesses in personnel techniques. Promotions should be given in recognition of individual performance and to create an incentive for workers to get ahead. In this way promotion policy tends to strengthen the working organization. Management may feel with some justification that it has an obligation to promote the long-time and faithful employee. This is in effect a seniority promotion which by itself cannot be defended on sound grounds. Finally, management may utilize its promotion policy to systematically develop members of the top-management team.

Bases for Promotion. The reasons for promoting a worker should be quite clear, but there remains the problem of deciding which worker should be promoted. Some reference to the selection of employees for promotion has been made above. Now we will consider as a separate topic the more conventional bases for promotion. If management wishes to promote the most qualified man, if it desires to recognize individual performance, or if it desires to create an incentive for workers to get ahead, then promotion should be based on the worker's ability. If management wishes to recognize and reward the senior employee or is unable to distinguish between the ability of employees under consideration, then promotion can logically be based on seniority.

The most widely used basis for promotion combines both ability and seniority. Such a policy tends to satisfy management, which prefers ability, and the union, which prefers seniority. A major problem, of course, is deciding the relative weight of the two factors. Frequently this issue is decided by the rule that if two men have about the same ability, then the senior man will receive the promotion. Systematic promotions are quite common, especially with jobs at the management level. Here promotions are based on a long-range program of providing for future manpower requirements. Under this plan of promotion definite routes of advancement are established which lead to positions of increased responsibility. Workers are then able to see beyond the next step of promotion and may have a greater appreciation of the promotional opportunity.

Transfers

Frequently it is necessary and desirable that management transfer workers within the organization to aid in building a more effective work crew. An indication of the need for transferring individual employees may clarify this statement. The following conditions give rise to the need for transfers:

1. The worker may have little interest in his present job, yet he may have considerable ability that management can utilize. The lack of interest may result from improper placement, or the nature of the work may have changed, or the worker may be just "fed up" with his present job.
2. A reduction or reallocation in the work force may require the transfer of workers.
3. A worker may have many desirable qualities yet fail to fit in with the personalities in a particular department. While it may be undesirable to give in to a worker in such cases, a transfer may work to the benefit of all.

Layoffs

Management seeks to avoid layoffs because they tend to break up an effective work team; they destroy worker morale; and they, of course, increase the costs of unemployment insurance. Layoffs are something that management usually cannot control since most frequently they are the result of external factors. It is difficult to say what policy management should adopt when a reduction of the work force is dictated. In some situations the best policy is to reduce the work-week of all employees and avoid layoffs. If layoffs are required in only a portion of the plant, transfers may be preferred to layoffs. When layoffs are dictated, generally a policy of laying off the junior workers is followed. This may result in losing desirable employees, but it has the advantage of maintaining the morale of the older employees.

SUMMARY

To deal effectively with its work team, management needs to know who the workers are and what jobs they are doing. Job evaluation tells management what each job involves; employee rating provides information about the worker and how well he does his job. This information, coupled with seniority ratings, provides a basis for dealing with workers in matters relating to promotion, transfer, and layoff.

QUESTIONS

1. What is the purpose of job evaluation?
2. Describe the operation of the point method of job evaluation.
3. How does the factor comparison method of job evaluation differ from the point method?
4. What is a key job?
5. What advantages are claimed for a job-evaluation program?
6. What forces cause wages to deviate from the norm as determined through job evaluation?
7. Why is job evaluation a vital personnel tool?
8. How much should management pay a worker? Discuss.
9. What are the uses of an employee-rating plan?
10. How can employee rating stimulate competition between workers?
11. How might an employee-rating program operate?
12. What factors should be considered in training raters?
13. What is meant by validating the ratings?
14. What is a promotion?
15. What is a "dry" promotion?
16. Why does management promote workers?
17. On what bases is seniority measured?
18. When would you expect transfers to be made?
19. What are the different bases for promotion?
20. Discuss the union's attitude toward seniority.

CHAPTER 13

Manpower Costs

A study of manpower costs should rightly include all expenditures involved in obtaining and maintaining a work force. By considering together in a single discussion the costs associated with manpower the reader will be enabled, it is felt, to develop a greater appreciation of this area of management activity.

WAGES

Salaries and wages are by far the largest of the manpower costs and warrant primary consideration. Wages may account for less than 15 per cent of the costs of operation for some business organizations—self-service food retailers, for example—or more than 60 per cent of the costs of operating a job-order machine shop. Wages are always a significant cost item, but it can be easily seen that they are of greater importance to some businessmen than others. Likewise, savings in labor cost are of more importance to some businessmen than they are to others. An increase or decrease of 10 per cent in wages may alter the food retailer's operating costs only 1½ per cent, yet alter the operating costs of a machine shop more than 6 per cent. Through an analysis of wage-payment methods management may find the means of both controlling and reducing its labor costs.

The general wage level in a business organization and the wage policy itself must be determined by top levels of management. These in turn will be set, in part at least, by management's basic philosophy of wages and work. To many people work is something that is basically unpleasant, an activity that takes something out of the worker. When this philosophy prevails, and it frequently does, higher wage rates, shorter hours of work, and improved working conditions are the only answers to the wage question. At the other extreme there is a school of thought that looks at work as being rewarding in itself; it can be a way of life. This group will not put the same emphasis on hours of work and rates of pay because they receive considerable satisfaction from their jobs. Some bank employees, social workers, authors, teachers, and many administrative and professional workers view their work as a way of life. Production workers, especially in the unskilled and semiskilled occupations, will normally adopt the former philosophy. It is obvious, then, that wages in some instances will be considered primarily in terms of money; and in others the psychic value of the job will be considered a part of the reward for a worker's efforts.

Bases for Wage Payment

There are only two bases for determining a worker's earnings, albeit there are innumerable wage-payment plans in operation today. Wages are based either on the passage of time or upon worker output. A worker who is paid a salary or an hourly rate is paid on the time basis. A worker who is paid a piece rate is paid on the basis of his output. There are instances, of course, when workers are paid partly on time and partly on output, such as the salesman who is paid a salary plus a commission. Workers may be paid according to group output rather than individual output. In any instance, however, time and/or output must be the basis for determining wages.

Of the two bases, payment on time is more widely used. It has as its primary advantage simplicity. When pay is based on time—hour, day, week, or month—the payroll function is facilitated, and each worker can easily compute his gross earnings. The major weakness lies in the inability of management to maintain close control over its labor costs. Two workers may each receive $16 for working an eight-hour day under time wages, yet one worker may produce 80 units and the other, 100 units. In one instance the unit labor cost is 20 cents and in the other, 16 cents. Unless workers produce a given amount of work for each dollar received in wages, management does not have control over its labor costs. Payment on a time basis may be preferred, however, where high-quality standards of work are required, for under time rates there is less pressure on the worker to produce than under incentive wages. Time wages may be preferred when it is difficult to measure worker output, where there are frequent delays in the work schedule, or where worker pace is set by a machine. In the latter instance workers, on an automobile assembly line, for example, are paid an hourly rate, but since their output is regulated by the speed of a conveyor, management has control over its labor cost.

Another criticism of the time rate is that it by itself offers no special incentive for employees to put forth their best efforts. As indicated above, a worker earns $16 whether he produces 80 or 100 units per day. Many workers see no reason for producing more than 80 units in a day, for there is no direct incentive to produce more. It is felt by many businessmen that unless the superior worker is given some direct reward for his extra contribution he soon will relax into a level of average performance. For these reasons employee rating, discussed above, and incentive wage plans have been adopted.

Incentive Wages

One of the earliest contributions of the scientific management movement consisted of special methods of wage payment wherein an attempt was made to associate earnings with output. An almost endless variety of such plans has appeared in the past fifty years. Incentive wages have been used extensively in the past and continue to be popular in many phases of manufacturing. They have a very wide application in the field of distribution where employees are paid in whole or in part on a commission basis. Incentive wages can be justified in that they allow management to control its labor cost, and they may reward a worker in proportion to his contribution to the company's endeavors. The discussion of incentive wage plans below explains how this is possible. Incentive wages have been frowned upon by labor unions because unions feel that incentive wage plans tend to exploit the worker and create undesirable relationships between workers. If an incentive wage plan is properly conceived and management is willing to abide by the essentials of a good incentive-wage plan, both management and the worker stand to gain.

Essentials for a Sound Incentive-wage Plan

The following are suggested as the requirements for a sound incentive-wage plan:

1. A plan should meet the approval of management, the worker, and the union.
2. A plan should be simple and easily understood.
3. A standard procedure must be established for every job so that each worker performing the job will be held to the same standards.
4. The job must be repetitive, and the worker should be allowed to set his pace.
5. A competent time study of each job should be made to establish standard output.
6. Time standards should not be changed unless methods of doing the job are changed.
7. There should be a standard base rate of pay for each job developed through job evaluation. The worker should be paid a reasonable minimum regardless of his output.
8. The incentive pay earned by the worker should be in direct proportion to his output above standard.

9. The incentive plan should cover the largest portion of workers possible.
10. Workers should be allowed to present their complaints, which are almost certain to arise, to someone in authority according to a predetermined grievance procedure.

Very few incentive-wage plans incorporate all the features listed above, especially the requirement that wages should be in direct proportion to output. Fewer objections will be raised if the wage plan adheres to sound principles.

Incentive-wage Plans

The following is a description of several incentive-wage plans. For our purposes these plans are merely indicative of the details that are involved in the structure of incentive systems. The plans as used in industry will vary greatly in detail and purpose.

The Piece-rate Plan. One of the oldest and most widely used incentive wages is the piece-rate plan. It retains its popularity because it is simple and easily understood, and because it rewards the worker in direct proportion to his output. The piece-rate plan could meet all the essentials of a sound incentive-wage plan. A piece rate is no more than a time standard converted into dollar value. For example, if as a result of time study it was determined that 60 units per hour was the standard rate of production and if through job evaluation or some other acceptable method it was determined that $1.20 was a satisfactory hourly rate, then the piece rate would be 2 cents per unit. Once a piece rate is put into operation, the $1.20 rate disappears and the worker's pay is determined by the units produced times 2 cents. A person who produces more than 60 units per hour will earn in excess of $1.20, while the worker who produces less than 60 units per hour will earn less. The labor cost remains at 2 cents per unit irrespective of the number of units a worker produces. Piece-rate plans generally guarantee a basic hourly rate to those workers who produce less than the standard rate.

Share-the-gain Plans. There are many incentive-wage plans that do not reward the worker in direct proportion to his output. Share-the-gain plans, as the title suggests, fall into this category. Under these plans a definite time is established for doing each job, and any saving resulting from above-standard performance is shared by the worker and his employer in some predetermined ratio. The Halsey Premium Plan is based on the share-the-gain principle, but guarantees the worker his hourly rate. The following illustrates how the Halsey plan operates. Suppose the time allowed to do a particular job is 10 hours, the hourly rate is $1.80, and the gain is to be shared 50–50 between worker and employer. If a worker takes 12 hours to do the job, he will be paid $21.60 because his rate is guaranteed. If he does the job in 10 hours, he will be paid $18 because there is no saving of time. If the worker does the job in 8 hours, he will earn $16.20 calculated as follows:

8 hours worked × $1.80	=	$14.40
2 hours saved × 1.80 × 50%	=	1.80
Pay for the job		$16.20

It should be noted that the faster a worker does this job, the less he earns for the job. This is characteristic of share-the-gain plans. However, there is an incentive to increase output because when the job is done in 8 hours the worker earns over $2 per hour rather than the guaranteed rate of $1.80. The incentive comes from the increased hourly earnings, not the pay for doing the job. Labor costs are controlled to the extent that all workers who do the job in less than 10 hours earn under $18. Workers who take more than 10 hours can be singled out for special training and supervision.

Other Incentive-wage Plans. A brief description of several other incentive-wage plans is presented below to indicate the variety of considerations that may enter into the determination of incentive wages.

1. *The Taylor Differential Piece-rate Plan.* This plan incorporates two piece rates, a higher rate used when the worker exceeds or equals the standard rate and a lower rate that applies when output is below the standard rate.

2. *The Gantt Plan.* This plan guarantees the hourly rate. When a worker exceeds the standard rate, he receives a bonus which is a percentage of his base pay. If the standard for a job is ten hours at $1.80 per hour and a worker does the job in nine hours, he receives $18 plus a predetermined percentage of the $18. When a worker does the job in eight hours, he receives the same pay for the job as the worker who took nine hours. The average hourly earnings of course are not the same. Thus the Gantt Plan becomes a piece rate for all workers who exceed the standard.

3. *The Emerson Plan.* The Emerson Plan rewards the workers who do not reach the standard rate of output. A sliding scale of bonuses ranging from zero to 20 per cent are paid for performance between 66⅔ per cent of standard and standard. This plan amounts to a high piece-rate plan with wages computed on a time basis. This type of plan provides incentive for beginners and does away with the pressure developed by a plan which provides a premium only when the standard of performance is achieved.

4. *The Group Piece Rate.* A group of workers earn a piece rate as de-

scribed above. Payment of the piece rate is made to the workers on a predetermined basis. Group piece rates are used when workers must perform as a team rather than as individuals.

Profit Sharing As an Incentive

For more than a century profit-sharing plans of various descriptions have been used to promote efficiency and to reward those who have contributed to profits. There is no complete agreement on the value of profit sharing as an incentive. Those who have used it successfully support it and advocate greater usage. Others claim that it has no value to management or the worker. Those who favor profit sharing maintain that workers who share directly in the earnings of the company will redouble their productive efforts, reduce waste, and contribute in any way possible to higher company profits. Those who disapprove of profit sharing do so on the grounds that workers themselves cannot make for profitable operations. Unfavorable economic conditions and the exercise of poor judgment by management can easily turn the tide against workers who are doing their utmost to produce company profit. They also feel that it is impossible to determine the extent to which individual workers contribute to profits if they are earned. For these reasons it is felt that a share of profits is a poor incentive.

An evaluation of the worth of profit sharing is difficult because there is no absolute criterion of a successful or unsuccessful profit-sharing venture. However, several large organizations and countless smaller ones are convinced that profit sharing brings rewards to workers, management, and owners that could be achieved in no other way. More than 100,000 employees of the Sears, Roebuck Company participate in a profit-sharing fund worth over ½ billion dollars; the employees are together a major stockholder in the company. The employees of the Lincoln Electric Company in Cleveland have benefited tremendously through profit sharing for more than twenty years. Frequently Lincoln employees receive a share of profits each year that exceeds their normal annual earnings. For several years the average share of profits has exceeded $4,000 per employee. Certainly in view of experiences such as these profit sharing deserves some consideration as a means toward more efficient operations.

PAYROLL TAXES

Most employers in the United States are required by law, state and/or Federal, to pay certain taxes based on worker earnings. In all states there are three taxes or payments that employers must make in behalf of the workers. First are payments required under the Social Security Act passed in 1935 and amended several times since. Virtually all workers engaged in industrial or commercial activity are covered by the act. Self-employed persons, domestic help, and employees of nonprofit institutions are to a large extent covered by the act.

The act requires that employer and employee contribute equal amounts on behalf of the employee. The tax rates amended in 1950 and applicable to both employer and employee vary progressively from 1½ per cent in 1951 to 3¼ per cent in 1970 and thereafter. Congress may from time to time alter the tax, as it did in 1956. Effective January 1, 1957, the rate was increased to 2¼ per cent, an increase of ¼ of 1 per cent over the rate planned in 1950.

The act as amended specifies that the tax will be levied only on the first $4,200 paid by any employer. In 1958, for example, a worker may contribute up to $94.50; and his employer, an additional $94.50. The fund thus created will provide a pension for the worker when he retires at age 65 or later.

Second, the Social Security Act provides for unemployment insurance to be paid by the employer. The Federal law provides for the allocation of funds to individual states to cover the administration of state unemployment acts. The details of coverage, benefits, and administration vary from state to state but have great similarity arising out of the provision in the Social Security Act requiring approval by the Social Security Board of the state law before Federal funds will be made available for administering the state act.

The Federal tax is 3 per cent with a provision of rebating to the states 90 per cent of this amount. The Massachusetts law is quite typical of unemployment compensation laws, and will be used to describe the tax burden on the employer. Unless an employer is specifically exempt from the act,[1] he must pay to the state's Division of Employment Security as much as 2.7 per cent of his payroll. The law covers employers of one or more individuals and specifies that earnings by any employee in excess of $3,000 in any calendar year shall be exempt from the tax. Thus an employer may pay up to $81 per employee to the state for unemployment insurance. The Federal portion of the tax is .3 per cent of taxable payroll. The Massachusetts law incorporates a merit-rating provision which allows employers who have good layoff records to reduce their state employment tax to a minimum rate of .5 per cent.

The third payroll "tax" results from workmen's compensation laws which are more fully discussed elsewhere in this text. Actually, the payment for workmen's compensation may not constitute a true tax, for in many states employers buy insurance coverage from commercial insur-

[1] Agricultural labor, government employees, domestic help, casual labor, and employees of charitable, religious, and educational organizations are, in general, exempt from the law.

ance companies. Some states allow employers to be self-insured. However, workmen's compensation laws impose an additional burden on employers. The cost of workmen's compensation varies from state to state. In general the cost is determined by the size of the payroll of an employer and the degree of hazard present in the jobs performed. The greater the degree of risk involved in the job, the higher the premium charged. In the long run the cost of workmen's compensation insurance for an employer should at least equal the payments made by the insurance company to injured workers. The actual cost may vary from a few cents to many dollars per hundred dollars of payroll.

EMPLOYEE BENEFITS AND SERVICES

Not too long ago when an employer agreed to pay a worker $35 for working a 48-hour week, he would hand the worker $35 on Saturday night and know that the payment constituted virtually his entire labor cost. Today a large variety of payments are made to or on behalf of the worker in addition to his wages. These fringe benefits mentioned below became popular during World War II when legislation prevented the increase of wage rates. It was a way of giving the worker more for his services without increasing his take-home pay. The vast majority of these benefits and services are highly desirable despite the fact that they may add 20 per cent or more to an employer's labor cost. Old-age and survivors insurance, workmen's compensation, and unemployment compensation are considered fringe benefits although they antedate World War II. Through choice or through collective bargaining employers have granted additional benefits. These include pension plans financed wholly or in part by the employer and frequently linked with Social Security benefits, employer-financed insurance and medical assistance programs, welfare funds, paid vacations, holidays and rest periods, recreational programs, company lunchrooms, stock purchase plans, educational aid, and in some instances a "guaranteed annual wage." The current tendency, which undoubtedly will continue, is for employers to be more liberal with fringe benefits even as wages continue to rise.

GUARANTEED ANNUAL WAGES

American businessmen have had a long though very limited experience with plans designed to provide workers with an income throughout the year. Actually, "guaranteed annual wage" is a misnomer for the dozens of plans that recognize the problem of unequal weekly earnings by workers. Few, if any, companies actually guarantee their workers a specified annual wage. The three most publicized guaranteed-annual-wage plans are the Proctor and Gamble plan (Ivory soap), the Nunn-Bush Shoe Company plan, and the George A. Hormel Company plan (Spam and other meat products). The Proctor and Gamble plan guarantees 48 weeks of work each year to workers with 24 or more consecutive months of employment. At the discretion of management a week's work may be adjusted to 75 per cent of the normal work week. Workers may be shifted from job to job as conditions warrant, and their rate of pay is determined by the job performed; there is no guaranteed rate. The Nunn-Bush plan does not guarantee full-time employment; rather it guarantees workers 52 pay checks each year. Nunn-Bush establishes a salary fund prior to the start of each year. The fund is a percentage of the volume of business the company anticipates during the following 12 months. Workers are paid from this fund based on a predetermined breakdown. Payments to workers are reduced if the level of activity falls below the estimate; surpluses in the fund are distributed to the workers at year's end. The Hormel plan budgets work for the year by departments and allocates the number of men required for it based on a 40-hour week. If at the end of the year a department has produced less than the planned volume, the workers in that department are indebted to the company to make up the deficit at the first opportunity. If production exceeds the budgeted amount, then the workers are paid a bonus.

Since the early 1950s, unions have presented demands to several major employers for what they called a guaranteed annual wage. The first of these annual-wage agreements, incorporated into union contracts in June, 1955, bears little relationship to the three plans described above. The intent of these three plans is to guarantee work, not wages. The union plans are designed to guarantee income for the workers irrespective of work. In essence they provide for supplemental unemployment benefits (S.U.B.). The United Auto Workers (CIO) was the first union to win a "guaranteed annual wage" from a major industry. In 1955 the UAW plan covered more than one million workers employed in some 232 companies—auto, aircraft, farm equipment, etc. The principle of the plan has spread to the glass industry, the electrical industry, can manufacturing, and a scattering of plants in other industries involving upwards of 100,000 workers. The UAW plan ties in with state unemployment-insurance programs and guarantees only a portion of normal earnings for a specified number of weeks. To illustrate, an unemployed Ford worker may collect up to 65 per cent of his average weekly earnings less taxes for four weeks; then 60 per cent of his average weekly earnings less taxes for the next 22 weeks. Workers receive part of this compensation from the state unemployment insurance fund and the balance from a fund created by the employer. State law regulates the amount received from the state; the balance due the unemployed worker is paid from his employer's fund, but cannot exceed $25 per week. The agreement signed by Ford in 1955 requires the payment of 5 cents for each hour a worker is employed to create the employer's fund. The maximum size of the fund is established at about 55 million dollars. The employer's liability to unemployed workers is limited to the amount in the fund.

Thus there are two separate approaches to the "guaranteed annual wage": one tries to guarantee work; the other attempts to guarantee income. It seems quite certain that the latter approach will receive considerable attention in the years ahead because of the determined labor push for income guarantees.

LABOR TURNOVER

As management decides to make or sell a particular product using certain methods and machines and as it develops a layout for its operations in a certain type of building located in a particular area and as it develops policies for dealing with workers, an atmosphere emerges that determines employer-employee relations. If the atmosphere is conducive to good employer relations, the movement of personnel into and out of the company employment ranks can be held to a desirable minimum.

Labor turnover is a term used to describe the shifting of workers into and out of a company. It may be expressed numerically by dividing the number of replacements hired during a specific period by the average number of workers on the payroll for the same period. A certain amount of labor turnover should be expected and may be quite desirable for it allows old blood to leave the company and new blood to enter. However, labor turnover can be quite costly and needs to be watched and controlled. Before labor turnover can be controlled, a standard of "normal" turnover should be set and a study made of the causes of labor turnover.

Causes of Labor Turnover

The following list indicates the more common causes of labor turnover:

1. Death of a worker
2. Pensioning of workers
3. Accidents and illness
4. Marriage
5. Layoffs
6. Growth
7. Discharges
8. Voluntary quits

Labor turnover caused by growth presents a different type of problem from the other causes. Growth causes additions to the employee group, additions that can be planned well in advance. The other causes require replacements simply to maintain normal personnel requirements. Accessions to the employee ranks are a necessary part of growth; replacements are often a necessary evil. Of the causes listed, the last two warrant primary consideration because separations are most frequent in these categories and they represent areas over which management can exercise considerable control.

Frequently when workers are fired both the employer and the worker may be at fault. Why did the worker have to be fired? The problem of such involuntary separations may be traced to poor selection techniques which resulted in hiring an undesirable person, training and job orientation may have been inadequate, or supervision on the job may have failed to discipline and correct the worker. Management can reduce this type of labor turnover through well planned selection, training, and supervisory techniques.

Voluntary quits are more difficult to analyze since the impetus for the separation comes from the worker rather than the employer. Some quits are of greater significance to an employer than others. If young workers or workers who have been employed for a short period of time are leaving, there is less cause for concern than when long-service and highly skilled workers are involved. It is known that young workers often seek short-term employment as they search out the most desirable type of job; thus a higher amount of turnover should be expected from this category of worker. The cost of labor turnover from this group should not be high since few young workers hold responsible positions. However, if older workers, thirty to fifty years of age, who generally have family responsibilities and who possess specific skills, are leaving, it may signify a serious weakness in employer-employee relations and the entire work environment. The following factors are often considered by the mature worker in deciding whether or not to remain with an employer:

1. Steadiness of employment
2. Opportunity for advancement
3. Quality of supervision
4. Wages
5. Employee benefits
6. Fairness of treatment
7. Job interest
8. Job environment

Management has some control over each of these factors which prompt workers to seek employment elsewhere. Before workers sever their connection, the employer should determine why workers are leaving and if possible take steps to reduce the loss of more valuable personnel.

Costs of Labor Turnover

It is not always possible to determine the cost of labor turnover for the impact of losing a single worker will vary, depending on existing conditions. Some indications of the cost of labor turnover can be gained by examining the specific areas of cost that are involved when workers are replaced.

1. The administrative cost of hiring a new worker.
2. The loss of production caused by the absence of a worker during the replacement period.
3. The cost of training the new worker.
4. The loss of production while the new worker is being trained. This includes production by teacher as well as learner.
5. The increased waste and spoilage due to the new worker's inexperience.
6. The impairments to production in dependent or related areas.
7. The loss of morale caused by labor instability.

It has been estimated that the actual cost of replacing a worker ranges from a low of about $10, administrative costs only, to a high of thousands of dollars. Labor turnover that can be avoided represents an area of great savings to an employer.

SUMMARY

Since the turn of the century there has been a steady, though frequently interrupted, increase in the obligations of an employer to his employees. In the past, wages have constituted the largest of the manpower costs, and this trend undoubtedly will continue well into the future. Because of many outside pressures, including the improved social status of the worker and the rapid growth of organized labor, workers today can demand additional benefits from their employer. There appears to be virtually no limit to the number of benefits that will accrue to the worker in the future, for each new benefit won becomes a steppingstone to additional benefits.

Few employers can avoid paying for the more common fringe benefits —paid vacations, paid holidays, coffee breaks, insurance, and the like— because they are firmly implanted as a part of labor-management relations. The granting of additional benefits is a device used to attract and hold employees. This all adds up to the fact that manpower costs are high and will continue to rise in the future. Alert management will offset this increased cost by more effective use of manpower.

QUESTIONS

1. Why are savings in labor costs of more significance to some businessmen than others? Explain.
2. Explain the different philosophies of work. What is the significance of each in respect to wages? What types of workers are likely to accept each philosophy?
3. Describe the two bases for wage payment.
4. Evaluate time as a basis for wage payment.
5. When are time wages preferred over incentive wages?
6. Justify the use of incentive wages.
7. What are the requirements for a sound incentive-wage plan?
8. What is meant by the statement that "incentive pay earned by the worker should be in direct proportion to his output above standard"?
9. What is a piece rate?
10. Describe the operation of the piece-rate plan of wage payment.
11. Describe the operation of the share-the-gain plan of wage payment.
12. In what ways do share-the-gain plans violate the essentials of a sound incentive-wage plan?
13. Why do many businessmen favor profit sharing as an incentive?
14. Why is profit sharing opposed as an incentive to increased worker productivity?
15. How much does the Social Security Act cost an employer? Discuss.
16. What are fringe benefits? How did they gain their popularity?
17. Does the Proctor and Gamble plan guarantee workers an annual wage? The Nunn-Bush plan? The Hormel plan? Discuss.
18. How does the UAW plan to guarantee income operate?
19. Compare the two different approaches to the "guaranteed annual wage."
20. Define "labor turnover."
21. Is labor turnover caused by growth more or less of a problem than labor turnover caused by voluntary quits? Explain.
22. How is labor turnover measured?
23. Are some "quits" more significant than others? Explain.
24. Why do workers quit their jobs?
25. What items make up the cost of labor turnover?

CHAPTER 14

Union-Management Relations

Management's attitude toward personnel and personnel policy normally would be determined by the profit that would result from one policy as opposed to another. This is a logical situation since management's goals are defined largely through profits. Today, management's personnel policy and personnel techniques are governed in large measure by two bodies operating apart from the business. Both our governments and the labor unions exercise a high degree of control over personnel philosophy and personnel techniques. The role that our governments play in the life of a businessman is discussed in Chapter 15. Here we are interested in the effect that unions have on labor-management relations.

No one can foresee just what will happen when a union enters a business to represent a group of workers who previously had not been organized. Under certain circumstances the entry of a union may have little or no effect on employer-employee relations, while in other instances a completely new relationship may be established. To be sure, the goals of all unions are similar in many respects, but one should not conclude that a particular new order of relations will exist because of the presence of a union. Initially, union-management relations are determined to a great extent by the events that transpired during the union's organizing campaign. Union demands and attitudes are governed in part by the nature and extent of the resistance of management to the entry of the union. In general it will exert as much pressure on management as is necessary to achieve its goals.

UNION DEVELOPMENT

Prior to the early 1930s the growth of unions in the United States was quite slow. Union activity was centered in the trades, and the great mass of American workers was not affiliated with any union. There were four primary causes for the lack of union growth. First was the yellow-dog contract, an agreement between employer and employee whereby as a condition of employment the worker forfeited his right to union membership. In many instances workers could not find employment unless they promised not to join a union or engage in any prounion activity. Thus the employer had an effective device to prevent unionism. The second deterrent to the union movement was a legal procedure called an "injunction." An injunction, according to Black's Law Dictionary, is "a prohibitive writ issued by a court of equity . . . directed at a party . . . forbidding (the party) to do some act . . . which he is threatening or attempting to commit. . . ." In the case of a labor dispute, an employer could obtain an injunction against the union to prevent picketing, for example, and thereby render a strike ineffective. It was a device which made it virtually impossible for a union to make concerted demands on an employer. Both of these obstacles to union growth were removed in 1932 with the passage of the Norris–La Guardia Act. The third reason for the slow growth of unions was the fact that an employer was not obliged to recognize a particular union; in fact he could organize a company union to compete with outside unions. Of course, he would not seek yellow-dog contracts if his union was involved, nor was there any need for injunctive processes against company unions for these unions were frequently employer dominated. Not until the Norris–La Guardia Act of 1932 and the Wagner Act of 1935 did the employer lose the freedom of dealing with the union of his choice. These laws allowed workers to select their union without management interference and forced management to bargain with the union on issues pertaining to employment. Fourth, the employer was able to fire a worker summarily for engaging in union activity. This form of discrimination was outlawed by the Wagner Act of 1935.

Goals of Unions

As mentioned above, the goals of any two unions will probably differ in specific content and in the manner through which the goals will be sought. Union objectives spring from the dynamic nature of American industry and as a result are constantly evolving. However, experience has made it clear that there are several issues on which there is common agreement among most unions. These issues invariably become a part of union-management negotiations. In general, union objectives are aimed at limiting management's personnel activity.

Group Development. Management is interested in individual development; the union, in group development. We should not conclude that one objective opposes the other because one party is the union and the other management. Rather, the union has a sound reason for its position just, as explained above, does management. Unions are made up of groups of workers; their demands are made on a group basis; and a spirit of "all for one and one for all" prevails. A union would violate its basic purpose if it put individual development ahead of group development. The union distinguishes individuals by the length of time they have been in the union (seniority), not by their individual accomplishments on their jobs.

Minimum Human Sacrifice. The union has as an objective the smallest human sacrifice possible for a worker to make a living. The unions feel that since, with technological improvements, the individual worker's productivity rises, he should receive a higher wage for his efforts or get the same pay for working a smaller number of hours.

This objective is not limited to the physical aspect mentioned above. As labor, management, and the union become more mature, there should be less conflict and mixed feelings between the parties. The union puts forth the idea that management should recognize the unions, consider that the unions will constantly try to exercise control over management prerogatives, and, since they all must live together, bury the hatchet.

Worker Security. When a union is organizing a group of workers, one of its strongest arguments for union membership is the element of security. Most workers will react favorably to anything that will make their jobs or income more secure, especially if they lose nothing in the bargain. By "security" is meant the protection of seniority as it applies to promotion or layoff, recognition of a worker's job classification so that he cannot be arbitrarily downgraded or overlooked on a promotion, and financial security through insurance, pensions, separation pay, and possibly a guaranteed annual wage. Opposed to this theory of security by force, management professes the logical theory that security has its place in a standard of values, but to put too much emphasis on security means that something else will be lost. The price for security often runs high. To have security one must live by the terms set up by the groups "guaranteeing" security; the individual loses his individuality since the rules of the security game require workers to stand by until it is their turn to advance. Many workers seek to obtain a degree of security by performing a service for management in such a satisfactory manner that continued employment will follow. Whether one avenue toward security is better than another depends upon the individual, his job, and the importance of his job to management.

Industrial Citizenship. For many decades in American industry a worker was a pawn that management moved about, in and out, as it saw fit. Management did not have to answer to the worker for its actions. Today the situation is quite different. It is the exception rather than the rule that management can unilaterally decide what will be done with a particular worker. Nearly all union contracts provide for a mechanism whereby the worker can be heard. According to law (National Labor Relations Act, Section 7A), management must bargain with the union;

the union, in turn, allows a worker to state his case and takes it up with management. Through the grievance procedure the worker is guaranteed a measure of industrial citizenship.

Growth of the Union. By its very nature the union is a body that must continue to grow. It must grow in terms of membership; because as a union represents larger and larger groups of workers in a plant, in an industry, or even in a craft, its bargaining power grows. The more control a union exercises over a group of workers, the more it can demand and receive from the employer. As an outgrowth of this, the union seeks to grow by increasing the areas of business relations over which it has control. It has been said that the goal of any union can be defined in a single word—"more." This is of course true. Worker loyalty toward a union is based on what the union can do for the workers. By demanding more, year in and year out, the union strengthens its hold over the work group. When a union feels that it has won as much as it can for the workers regarding wages, hours, and working conditions, it strikes out into new areas of demands, such as sick leave, pensions, or guaranteed annual wages. There is no telling how much the union will grow in terms of the amount of control it exercises over business management. The only logical conclusion is that more and more control will be sought rather than less. Few unions are satisfied to rest on their laurels for any length of time.

Nature of General Goals. Management usually makes its goals in terms of a long-range plan that is quite definite. This plan must be flexible enough to allow adjustment for change but not so flexible that the basic goals can be undermined. The union, on the other hand, has a long-range plan that is not definite in its objective. We know that the union will continue to demand more from management as long as it continues to function. However, since a union does not deal with factories, machinery, and inventories, it is flexible and can alter the immediate objectives overnight with no impairment of any long-range plan or of its current bargaining power. While management is more or less committed to a long-range plan that offers little opportunity for variation, the union is free to change its goals in terms of those factors that will naturally bolster its bargaining position. In general, the union thinks about the immediate future, feeling sure that it will be able to handle long-range problems as they present themselves since the union's strength is constantly increasing.

THE UNION ENTERS

We now have an indication of the nature of management's objectives through personnel administration (see Chapter 10) and the basic goals of unions. Management might well ask this question: "What difference will it make in personnel administration when the union enters?" Changes will be noticed in several areas. Some of the basic changes are discussed below.

Let us make it clear at this point that no clear-thinking person will say that unions are undesirable and bad. The most antiunion person must agree that workers have made rapid and immense gains through unionism —gains that undoubtedly would not have been made at all without the constant pressure of the union. We are not interested here in the issue of unionism, whether it is good or bad, or who is at fault in particular issues. We are interested in union tactics and goals, for all management policy today must be attuned to the goals of the union.

The Social Change

Prior to the entry of a union in a nonunion situation, worker loyalty, if any, must be toward management. As the union conducts its organizing campaign, one of its first objectives is to win worker loyalty away from management. It must weaken or destroy whatever bonds already exist with management and establish new ones with the union. The devices and techniques employed in reaching this objective will vary in each situation and depend solely on the measures needed to reach the goal. If milder techniques will not win over the worker, then stronger measures will be taken; the goal cannot be lost, or the campaign will fail. If name-calling, enemies, and fighting are necessary devices to capture this fundamental goal, they will be employed. The nature of a particular management often determines what techniques will be employed by the union as it sets up its organizing campaign. The stronger management's defenses against the entry of the union are, the more potent will be the union's offenses. The union seeks to drive a wedge between management and the worker and build a fence between them. The union wants workers to continue to communicate with their employer, but not directly, as in the past; rather, through the union.

The alienation of employer and employee that takes place when the union enters appears to be an undesirable feature of union relations, and of course it is. However, it is a basic requisite of a strong and healthy union. Frequently, after the new order of relationships, which will include the union, has been established and the parties become more mature in their thinking, much less attention is given to the techniques originally employed in obtaining bargaining rights. Under a going order of relationships, most frequently the primary loyalty of workers is toward the union, but there is and must be some loyalty to management.

Absence of Unilateral Policy

Since the very purpose of unionism is to exercise control over management's personnel administration, one must expect that management's area of unilateral decisions will grow smaller and smaller. The effect of the union will be felt not only in those areas that affect the worker in his day-to-day activity, such as hours of work, rates of pay, working conditions, and the like, but also in the much wider areas of production scheduling, retirement pay, movement of production facilities, and the ever-present demand for greater security.

Management must adjust its policy of dealing with workers to stay within the meaning of the union contract. Since the union's basic goal is always "more," management must be ever mindful that poor policy on existing prerogatives will open the door for the union in its drive toward greater control over all policies that affect the worker.

Disruptions of Production

Here we are not concerned with work stoppages that may result through disagreement over the meaning of the union contract or the strike that may be called to enforce the union's demands in a particular issue. Rather, we are concerned with the work stoppages that result because of the nature of national or international unions. Workers in a particular plant may be members of a local union that is a part of an international union. Longshoremen in Boston belong to a particular local; in New York they belong to another local. However, both locals are a part of an international union. Therefore, work stoppages in New York can have a bearing on the Boston employer, even though relations with Boston workers may be satisfactory. Apart from work stoppages caused by the interrelations of unions, there exists the impact of labor unrest caused by the interdependence of one business organization on another. Work stoppage in supplier plants or in the transportation industry can have the same effect on plant operations as that described above. Thus the complex nature of unions and business results in a chain reaction whenever labor unrest exists.

Compulsory Bargaining

It is an unfair labor practice if management refuses to bargain with the union (National Labor Relations Act, Section 7A). This means that when the union has an issue that it wants discussed, management must listen, talk it over, and reach an agreement. Workers who have a complaint are asked to take it to their union representative, usually the shop steward. The shop steward, in turn, may take this complaint, which when formally presented becomes a grievance, to a representative of management for settlement. The foreman generally is the member of management who first hears the grievance. If the grievance is not settled at this level, it becomes the responsibility of higher levels of both the union and management to reach a settlement. Thus top management can be drawn into a worker grievance no matter how insignificant it may appear to be. Most union contracts specify a particular grievance procedure that must be followed with specific time intervals between successive levels. A common type of grievance procedure follows:

ARBITRATION OR STRIKE

Company president	President of international
Personnel relations director	President of the local
Plant superintendent	Union business agent
Foreman	Shop steward

Aggrieved worker

Since all levels of management can be drawn into a labor dispute, it rests with management to make every effort to have worker complaints settled between worker and steward, or at least at the lowest level possible in the grievance procedure. As grievances rise in this ladder of procedure, costly time of major executives is lost. Also, the farther the grievance gets away from the party involved, the less significant are the real issues and the greater the importance of personalities who are handling the dispute.

However, this procedure is an essential part of any worker-management agreement since it affords the worker an opportunity to be heard whenever he feels that someone has discriminated against him. Through the grievance procedure the worker has one of his few opportunities to be a part of collective bargaining.

THE UNION CONTRACT

The union's organizing campaign, if successful, will have won the workers away from management. Then follows the election to formally recognize the union as the sole bargaining agent for the workers. According to law,[1] "employers must not interfere with their employees in the exercise of their right to self-organization," nor can they dominate or interfere with the formation of the union or encourage or discourage union membership through discrimination. Accordingly, the existence of the union is a matter that is decided by the workers in a manner supervised by law.

Most union contracts cover about the same area, although some are more elaborate than others. The common provisions of a work agreement are described below. The purpose of this discussion is to outline more clearly the exact manner in which the union limits management's per-

[1] National Labor Relations Act, sec. 101, subsec. 8(*a*).

sonnel administration. The sequence of topics makes little difference except that the first point is commonly considered first in all work agreements.

1. Union Recognition. The purpose of this provision is to assure the union that management will recognize this union and no other as the sole bargaining agent for all workers covered under the contract.

2. Check-off. Collecting dues can be a troublesome and costly task for any union. To simplify the collecting of dues, a clause is usually inserted whereby management agrees to deduct union dues from the worker's pay and forward them to the union. Under law a worker must first agree to allow management to take dues from his pay.

3. Working Conditions. Usually the contract contains a rather broad statement whereby management agrees to provide suitable working conditions and in general protect the worker from injury on his job.

4. Hours of Work. This section defines a workday or a work week for all employees covered. It also considers shift differentials, overtime provisions, and the like.

5. Rates of Pay. This provision, which must be directly related to hours of work, indicates the rate for all types of work, transfer rates, bonuses, call-in pay, holiday-pay provisions, and any other matters that affect a worker's rate of pay.

6. Seniority. Basic to the union's theme of security is the seniority provision. Since seniority can be by job classification, time in the company, or time in a department, or perhaps on some other basis, it must be clearly defined.

7. Vacations. Who will get vacations, for how long, and at what rate of pay? This clause covers these items.

8. Promotions, Transfers, and Layoffs. The union contract usually indicates the importance of seniority in promotion, transfers, and layoffs. This is another indication of the importance of seniority to the union.

9. Distribution of Work Load. Workers want to know what will happen to them when production levels change. When the level of production is reduced, will all workers work a shorter week or will a portion of the workers be employed full time and the balance laid off? Some contracts provide for a reduction of the work week to a minimum of thirty-two hours per week for all workers before there are any layoffs. Others are so worded that those with highest seniority will work a full week, with those having less seniority laid off.

10. Wage Reopening. Frequently both management and the union want the privilege of reopening the question of wages and wage rates after the contract has been agreed upon. Typical wording for this provision might be: "On or after February 15, 19— the Union may reopen collective bargaining negotiations by written notice to the Company, solely for bargaining concerning adjustment of wages for all employees covered by this agreement. Similarly, management may also request negotiation."

11. Grievance Procedure. As described above.

While this is not intended to be a full description of the matters that might come within a union contract, it does indicate the general areas of coverage. The length and breadth of the contract are often determined by the trust that the parties have for one another.

THE SHOP STEWARD

A union contract would be of little value to the worker or to the union if its provisions were not enforced. The difference between a strong and a weak union is often shown by the ability of a union to make the parties involved adhere to the contract. Contracts that can be readily violated or ignored in essence are not contracts at all.

The shop steward is a union official who is elected by the workers he represents. He may be the only union official in a plant, store, or office; or he may be one of several stewards each with his own particular group. In addition to his duties with the union, representing the workers and enforcing contract provisions, the steward is also a worker in the employ of management. Thus the steward may be a production worker part of the day and a union official handling worker grievances during the same day. The amount of time this worker spends on union business in any day will depend on the provisions of the work agreement and the volume of grievances that arise. It is quite conceivable that the steward will spend his time solely as a representative of the union, performing no production work at all. How the steward will be paid in such a situation is a matter for the union and management to decide.

Since the shop steward is frequently at the lowest level of union management and since he is usually involved with the foreman in the handling of worker complaints, it behooves management to insist that desirable working relations between them be cultivated. If foreman and steward are at odds, then it appears obvious that few issues will be settled by them and that the responsibility for ultimate settlement will rest with higher levels in the grievance procedure. Because the steward is beneath the foreman when he is a worker and on a par with him when a union representative, it would be quite natural for a steward to use any opportunity he had to get even with the foreman. Good foreman-steward relations are essential, for they keep disputes from reaching higher levels of management. When foreman and steward settle issues, often in the presence of the aggrieved worker, more satisfactory results can be obtained.

SUMMARY

The impact of unionism is felt in virtually all areas of business activity. The manager of a union shop feels the impact many times each day in matters concerning the workers and in an ever-increasing area of activity formerly considered a management prerogative. The manager of a nonunion shop feels the effects of unionism too. Improved hours of work, rates of pay, fringe benefits, and the like gained in the union shop soon become part of the labor-management picture in the nonunion shop.

The character of union-management relations is determined in large measure by the attitude of management toward unions. If in the past and during the union's organizing campaign, management has used all possible means to prevent unionization, it should be expected that the union will use fighting tactics, if necessary, in its dealings with management. We must remember that the union has its objectives just as does management, and that to continue as a dominating force in labor-management relations it must reach these objectives.

Management should appraise the potential benefits to itself and to the worker of union affiliations. To say the least, unions will be a permanent part of our economic life and a powerful stimulant to better management.

QUESTIONS

1. What determines management's attitude toward personnel policy? Discuss.
2. What underlying bases determine the character of union-management relations?
3. Discuss the reasons for the slow growth of unions prior to the mid-1930s.
4. Of what significance was the Norris–La Guardia Act to unionism?
5. Why are unions interested in group development rather than individual development?
6. What are the implications in the idea of minimum human sacrifice?
7. What is meant by "worker security"?
8. What is meant by "industrial citizenship"?
9. In what different ways does the union grow?
10. Compare the nature of the long-term goals of the union and management.
11. What difference does it make to personnel administration when the union enters? Discuss.
12. Discuss the application of a grievance procedure.
13. What topics would you expect to find in a union contract?
14. What is the function of a shop steward?
15. Discuss the significance of the shop steward's position.

CHAPTER 15

Government Regulation in Personnel Administration

In both the union shop and the nonunion shop management's personnel administration is limited by law, both state and Federal. Regulation of labor relations by the Federal government is based primarily on its power to regulate interstate commerce. The power of the states to regulate in this field has been much broader in that it comes within the recognized police power through which states have the power to create laws to protect the health, welfare, and morals of the people.

There have been various devices employed by the government in its regulation of labor relations, and they cover many years in time. The important changes in the regulation of employer-employee relations stemming from law have occurred in the last half century. During the past three decades there has been more labor legislation enacted than in any other like period in our history. As a result, the effect of law is felt in many everyday personnel experiences. It seems rather unlikely that the government will reverse the current trend and adopt a hands-off policy in this field. Rather, it appears that government policy will continue to be to act as a referee in this important phase of our economic and social life. Some of the more important laws and phases of law regulating management in its dealings with workers are considered below.

HEALTH AND SAFETY

Laws governing the health and safety of employees in industry are as old as the factory system itself. To be sure, in the early days protection was often inadequate and unsatisfactory. However, many of our current worker safeguards over health and safety had their origin in these earlier laws.

Workmen's Compensation Laws

Workers today are protected against the hazards of their employment by workmen's compensation laws and various safety codes enforced by state agencies. To date, the Federal government has been content to let the state governments handle this issue with a minimum of interference. Under English common law it was held that the employer was much better able to stand the costs of accidents than was the injured worker. As a result, workers enjoyed a degree of protection against occupational hazards. Employers were made liable for the costs of industrial accidents if the employee could prove in court that his employer was responsible for the injury through negligence. Workers had to sue their employer to collect damages under this law, and frequently were at a disadvantage in trying to cope with management's superior legal talent. Under this law the employer was able to limit his liability through the common-law defenses which became a part of this law. The three common-law defenses were (1) the fellow-servant doctrine, (2) the doctrine of contributory negligence, and (3) the assumption-of-risk doctrine. Thus if a fellow servant was at all responsible for the accident, then he, not management, was responsible, and the injured worker should seek recourse from him. If the worker himself committed some act which caused the accident, then he, not the employer, was responsible and he had no recourse. Finally, in any job there is a certain inherent risk. Thus if a worker was injured owing to risk inherent in the job, then the job, not the employer, was responsible for the accident, and of course the worker had no recourse.

These provisions may seem antiquated, but surprisingly, they have some application today. In some states an employer who does not carry workmen's compensation insurance, and according to law is not required to do so, waives his right to use the common-law defenses. Some occupations are not insurable because of the hazard involved, and the worker assumes the risk of injury when he takes the job. In Massachusetts an employee injured because of his serious or willful misconduct cannot receive compensation. Thus the common-law doctrines are, to some extent, still employed today.

English common law left much to be desired in terms of protection for the worker, and the undesirable features of this law were remedied to a great extent with the passage of workmen's compensation laws early in the twentieth century. The first workmen's compensation laws in this country were declared unconstitutional by state courts; but later similar laws were upheld by the Supreme Court of the United States, and one by one the states adopted these laws until 1948 when Mississippi at last joined the fold. Since workmen's compensation laws are state laws, with the exception of certain groups coming under Federal jurisdiction, their provisions will vary considerably. (See below.) However, all state laws have certain features in common. First, the philosophy of the law. Under common law the worker had to sue his employer, obtain a judgment, and then collect. Under workmen's compensation laws the philosophy of "liability without fault" prevails. Thus the employer is responsible in the great majority of cases for the cost of accidents unless the worker is guilty of a flagrant violation of safety regulations as noted above or is intoxicated. All a worker need do is to notify his superior of the accident. A report will be forwarded to the insurance company, or similar agency, which will take over from there. Second, employers are liable for the medical costs of an accident plus weekly payments to the injured employee if and when he is unable to work because of the injury.

It is the intent of most laws to pay the injured worker's entire medical costs arising from an accident. There is no intention that a worker be allowed to receive as much income while injured and not working as when he is fully employed. Such a provision would place a potential premium on being injured. Disability benefits vary greatly from state to state. It is of interest to note that maximum payments to those workers who are totally disabled for a temporary period range from a low of $20 a week in the state of Idaho to a high of $150 a week in Arizona. However, the Arizona worker cannot receive over 65 per cent of his normal wages. In Rhode Island a person can collect benefits for as many as 1,000 weeks, while in West Virginia he is limited to 156 weeks. In addition to these specific benefits most states have a special agency set up to administer the law and to look after the welfare of the injured worker. While protection under existing laws may appear inadequate to some, it is a definite improvement over previous law.

In many states the law requires that the employer buy insurance to cover the costs of accidents or else set up a reserve fund from which the costs of accidents to workers can be paid. The cost of this insurance or the size of the reserve is determined by the size of the employer's payroll, the hazards present in the work area, and the employer's experience with industrial accidents. Since the law is designed to penalize the employer with a poor record through higher premium or reserve costs and to reward the employer with a good record, there is an incentive for management to make its plant a better place in which to work. Insurance company regulations and state safety codes are important elements in the gradual reduction of accidents in industry. Preventive measures are always more desirable than punitive measures.

Child and Female Labor

Closely allied to workmen's compensation laws are laws which govern the employment of child and female labor. Such laws are generally designed to limit the hours of work per day and/or per week, and the length of work shift; to regulate lunch periods, quitting times, and types of work performed; and to specify what facilities must be provided by the employer to protect the health and safety of these workers.

HOURS OF WORK

Many states limit the hours per day or per week that child and female labor may work. With few exceptions there are no legal limits placed on the number of hours an adult male worker can work per day or per week. This is a matter for the employer and the employee to iron out unless there is a union contract which specifically covers this situation. Attempts were made to regulate hours of work under the National Industrial Recovery Act of 1933, but this law was declared unconstitutional by the Supreme Court of the United States. However, there are laws that indirectly limit the use of manpower.

Fair Labor Standards Act

The Fair Labor Standards Act of 1938, commonly called the Wages and Hours Law, was enacted by Congress to spread employment and reduce the number of hours a worker would work in any week. This latter purpose was achieved by requiring the payment of a penalty wage of time and one-half the normal rate for all work performed in excess of 40 hours in any work week. While an employer can work an employee over 40 hours in any week, under this law the increased rate often acts as a deterrent and results in work being given to other workers. This "time and one-half" provision has been continued during periods when there was a shortage of manpower in industry, which indicates that the law had the ultimate purpose of raising wage levels as well as providing employment for more workers.

This law applies, of course, only to businesses engaged in interstate commerce or that produce goods that enter interstate commerce. In defining interstate commerce, the courts are inclined to say that any business is interstate unless its activity is strictly intrastate. The law excludes from the provisions of the law certain employers such as service establishments, store employees, and seasonal workers. It is suggested that the reader obtain a copy of this law if he is interested in the exact exemptions, for there are so many different situations and interpretations to consider.

Walsh-Healy Act

The Walsh-Healy Act of 1936 is another important law which pertains to regulating hours of work. This law provides that any agency of the United States contracting for the manufacture or furnishing of materials, supplies, or equipment above $10,000 must require that no employee be permitted to work more than eight hours in any one day or forty hours in any week unless paid overtime at the rate of time and one-half the normal rate. This law often reaches beyond the prime contractor to include subcontractors and does not consider the intrastate nature of an employer's activity.

MINIMUM WAGES

Both state and Federal governments have enacted legislation designed to restrict the payment of wage rates below a basic minimum. State laws, of course, relate to intrastate commerce as indicated above; and Federal laws, to interstate commerce. Certain groups of employers are exempt from the provisions of these laws.

Fair Labor Standards Act

The Fair Labor Standards Act referred to above is the basic Federal law governing minimum wages. The original minimum wage under this law was 25 cents per hour in 1938. Thereafter the minimum wage gradually rose to $1 per hour as of 1957. There has always been some pressure on Congress to increase this minimum wage. The goal of labor groups is to make the basic minimum as high as possible. This goal is, of course, opposed by employers since it reduces their flexibility in setting wage rates and places a minimum price on labor. Under this law it is illegal for an employer to pay an employee less than $1 per hour if he is covered by the law.

Walsh-Healy Act

The Walsh-Healy Act sets a minimum-wage rate for all employees in work on government contracts in an amount exceeding $10,000. Section 41 of this law provides that "all persons employed by the contractor will be paid not less than the prevailing minimum wage for such work in the community as established by the Secretary of Labor." The minimum wage on government contracts is much more flexible than it is under the Wages and Hours Law since congressional approval is not required for changing minimum rates under the Government Contracts Act. Through the minimum-wage provisions of this law the administration can exert considerable influence on the general wage level.

State Laws

In addition to these Federal minimum-wage provisions, more than thirty states currently have minimum-wage laws. Provisions of these laws vary greatly, but in general they set the minimum wage at a level lower than that set by the Federal statute. There may be some attempt on the part of state governments to set a low minimum wage for the purpose of attracting certain types of business in which low wage levels generally prevail.

COLLECTIVE BARGAINING

Since most union contracts have provisions in them relating to hours of work, wage rates, and conditions of employment at equal or more favorable levels than the law requires, the area of collective bargaining takes on special significance.

While laws governing the relationship between employer and employee are known to have existed as early as colonial times, the first notable legislative recognition of the field of labor relations occurred with the passage of the Clayton Act of 1914. The Clayton Act specifically excluded labor unions from the provisions of the Sherman Act dealing with unlawful monopolies and activities operating in an "unreasonable restraint of trade." The protection actually afforded under this law was rendered less broad than that originally intended by judicial interpretations placed upon it by the courts. It was not until after the great "crash" of 1929 that there was any significant change in the attitude of the Federal government toward collective bargaining.

Norris–La Guardia Act

The change in government attitude toward collective bargaining became noticeable in 1932 with the passage of the Norris–La Guardia Anti-injunction Act which set forth the right of workers to bargain collectively "free from the interference, restraint, and coercion of employers of labor or their agents." To make this policy effective, the courts refused to enforce the yellow-dog contract whereby the worker forfeited his right to union membership and union activity as a condition of employment. In other situations the courts were forbidden to issue injunctions for employers involved in a labor dispute until after an open hearing and an opportunity for labor to cross-examine in open court. Where unusual circumstance surrounded the dispute, the courts could issue five-day restraining orders if sufficient evidence could be presented to warrant such action.

NIRA Policy

The trend started in 1932 continued in 1933 with the new administration through the National Industrial Recovery Act. Section 7(a) of this act provided that: "Employees shall have the right to organize and bargain collectively through representatives of their own choosing and shall be free from the interference, restraint, or coercion of employers or their agents in the designation of such representatives." Thus this law was a bit more specific than the Norris–La Guardia Act of 1932. Two years later the NIRA was declared unconstitutional by the Supreme Court of the United States, but one month later to the day Congress passed the National Labor Relations (Wagner) Act whose constitutionality was upheld by a more cooperative Supreme Court on April 12, 1937.

This law was consistent with the underlying philosophy of preceding legislation; it gave employees the rights expressed in Section 7(a) of the NIRA and, in addition, required that the employer bargain with the duly elected representatives of the worker. The act permitted the closed-shop agreement and curtailed management's freedom of speech when the union was involved; yet it afforded no right at all, for all intents and purposes, for the nonunion worker. No single piece of legislation has done more to promote union growth in this country than the Wagner Act. Total union membership was under 3 million in 1933 but it exceeded 7 million in 1937.

Labor Management Relations Act

The Wagner Act was amended in 1947 by the Labor Management Relations (Taft-Hartley) Act which is still the fundamental law governing labor-management relations. The significant parts of this law, and many which have been carried over from the Wagner Act, are related to certain unfair labor practices. Under the Wagner Act unfair labor practices on the part of the employer were emphasized, but under the amended law the union is restricted through statement of unfair labor practices. Section 8(a) of the current law mentions the following unfair labor practices aimed at the employer:

1. To interfere with, restrain, or coerce employees in their exercise of rights guaranteed in Section 7.
2. To dominate or interfere with the formation or administration of any labor organization or contribute financially or otherwise to its support.
3. To discriminate in regard to hire and tenure of employment or any term or condition of employment to encourage or discourage membership in any labor organization.
4. To discharge or otherwise discriminate against an employee because he has filed charge or given testimony under the act.
5. To refuse to bargain collectively with the representatives of his employees.

To curb the great power of the union that existed under the Wagner Act, Congress considered certain unfair labor practices which apply to the conduct of the union. Section 8(b) of the law mentions the following unfair labor practices governing unions:

1. To restrain or coerce employees in the exercise of their guaranteed rights or to restrain or coerce the employer in the selection of his representatives for the purpose of collective bargaining or in the adjustment of grievances.
2. To cause an employer to discriminate against an employee with respect to whom membership in such organization has been denied or terminated on some ground other than his failure to pay dues or initiation fees.
3. To refuse to bargain collectively with an employer.
4. To engage in, or to induce or encourage the employees of any employer to engage in, a strike or concerted refusal to work with or on goods where the object is:
   A. Forcing an employer to join any labor or employer organization or to cease doing business with any other person.
   B. Forcing any other employer to bargain with an unauthorized labor organization.
   C. Forcing an employer to give work to one particular group of workers rather than another where no agreement on assignment of work has been made.
5. To require employees to pay excessive initiation fees.
6. To cause an employer to pay money or other thing of value in the nature of an exaction for services which are not performed or not to be performed.

The Labor Management Relations Act is supervised and directed by the National Labor Relations Board which is composed of five members appointed by the President with the consent of the United States Senate. This board is actually a judicial body, or a labor court, that investigates disputes or grievances arising under the law and after investigation hands down a ruling. The board is assisted in its work by a general counsel, an appointed officer, who is responsible for investigating charges of unfair labor practices and issuing complaints if he feels there is a violation. In many instances the general counsel settles issues in the field on behalf of the board. In addition to the board mentioned above, there are regional offices of the board which hear and decide cases. The general counsel is extremely powerful in the administration of this law since in the majority of cases the judicial power of the board is inoperative until the general counsel has filed complaints.

When the board finds that there has been a violation of the law, it can order the offender to correct the conditions that exist. The board order, however, is in itself ineffective and without legal compulsion. The board cannot fine or penalize anyone for violations. The board must petition to a circuit court of appeals in the circuit where the unfair practice took place, asking them to enforce the order. Violations of the court order are subject to fines, penalties, and perhaps imprisonment, since they amount to a contempt of court.

State Laws

Many state legislatures have enacted laws designed to control or regulate certain aspects of collective bargaining. Many of these laws reaffirm Federal law, while others reach into areas not covered by Federal law. State laws perhaps are more specific than Federal laws since they are designed for application in a limited area.

The role of the state in labor legislation is often governed by the presence or absence of Federal law and the attitude of the Federal government toward the role of the state in national affairs. Under the Eisenhower administration there has been a definite attempt to put labor-policy making back with the states. Labor unions eye this trend as the biggest threat to organized labor. Organized labor is much more vulnerable at the state level than at the Federal level. Unions are quite naturally against any return of labor-law formation to the state, since they have prospered under Federal law. With states making laws, unions will have to watch forty-eight lawmaking bodies rather than one, and it appears that some state legislatures have neutral or negative attitudes toward the union.

As long as Federal laws were blazing new trails on behalf of labor, state laws didn't matter so much, but now the climate has changed. Significant in current state legislation is the trend toward "right to work" laws. At the present time some fifteen states have laws of this type. A right-to-work law bans the union shop and all other forms of compulsory unionism. Under these laws a person cannot be required to join a union as a condition of employment. In the absence of such laws union membership can be a condition of continued employment; it is generally accepted that most workers will join a union if there is one present. The union, of course, wants all workers to join.

Mediation and Conciliation

Both state and Federal governments have enacted legislation to encourage the peaceful settlement of labor disputes. Since both state and Federal laws have the same purpose, though operating in different areas, only the Federal law will be considered here.

Title II of the Labor Management Relations Act covers conciliation of labor disputes in industries affecting commerce and national emergencies. Section 201 states: "That it is the policy of the United States that (*a*) sound and stable industrial peace . . . can most satisfactorily be secured by the settlement of issues between employers and employees through the process of conference and collective bargaining . . . (*b*) the settlement of issues . . . may be advanced by making available full and adequate government facilities for conciliation, mediation, and voluntary arbitration. . . ."

Section 202 provides for the Federal Mediation and Conciliation Service, an independent agency, which absorbed all mediation and conciliation functions of the Federal government. While the service has no legal power, it does carry the prestige of the government and has aided in the settlement of many major disputes. In the event of a labor dispute where a strike could imperil national health, safety, or welfare, the President may, after full investigation and report, direct the Attorney-General to petition any district court in the United States having jurisdiction over the parties to enjoin the proposed strike. Such restraining orders as may be issued by the court are limited to eighty days, during which period the service will attempt to arrange for a settlement by bringing the parties together and helping them to bargain in good faith. A worker's right to strike is not denied as a result of this provision; it is merely postponed by a "cooling off period."

FAIR EMPLOYMENT PRACTICES ACT

There has been a continuous attempt, dating back several generations, to reduce discrimination in employment. Such attempts are designed to give all people equal opportunity for the occupation of their choice, progress on the job, and job security. Attempts have been made, though not with complete success, to equalize pay for male and female employees performing like work under like conditions, and to eliminate discrimination because of race, color, creed, or ancestry. On several occasions the Federal government has attempted to pass legislation to reduce discrimination as described above. Each time there has been sufficient opposition, primarily from "states rightist" states, to defeat enactment of such laws. Many people believe that such laws, if passed, should be at the state rather than at the Federal level.

Since there are no broad Federal laws covering discrimination in employment, such laws exist only in certain states. Several states today have Fair Employment Practice Acts. Massachusetts passed such a law in 1946, and its purpose and provisions will be used as a guide to describe the general nature of such laws.

The Massachusetts law is designed to prevent discrimination with respect to employment or union membership on account of race, color, religious creed, national origin, ancestry, or age. This law applies to employers who are engaged in interstate commerce as well as those engaged in intrastate commerce. The law does not apply to the employer of less than six persons, to social, fraternal, religious, or educational organizations.

Under this law it is declared an unlawful practice to—

1. Refuse to hire a person because of race, color, religious creed, national origin, ancestry, or age, or to discharge from employment or otherwise discriminate for these reasons unless they be true occupational qualifications.
2. Exclude a person from union membership for the reasons stated above unless based on true occupational qualifications. This principle, which is included in several state laws, was upheld by the Supreme Court of Connecticut in April, 1954, and may become a key ruling in this field. Most unions admit Negroes as members, but some have membership color bars. A union refused membership to a Negro and ultimately was fined $2,000 for violating the law plus a penalty of $500 per week for every week in which it failed to stop practicing racial discrimination. Since union membership is often a condition of employment, a union that can practice discrimination in terms of membership actually dictates who will and who will not work in a given plant.
3. Print or circulate material that would lead to discrimination.
4. Aid, compel, or coerce anyone to do any of the above forbidden acts.

If a person feels that he has been the victim of discrimination, he may file a complaint with the commission which administers the law, which, in turn, will investigate the charges. If it is found that there has been discrimination, the commission will try to arrange a peaceful settlement. If necessary, the commission may resort to legal compulsion for the enforcement of its orders.

SUMMARY

Personnel relations are governed by the union contract as indicated in Chapter 14; they are also regulated by several state and Federal laws. An attempt is made to protect the health and safety of the worker through workmen's compensation laws. These laws are designed to take the burden of injury from the worker and make it a management responsibility. Provisions for overtime pay and minimum wages have been in existence since the mid-1930s. Our Federal government has set up a procedure for the formal recognition of unions and the protection of the worker's right to collective bargaining. Considerable time generally elapses between the enactment of labor laws, indicating that it is the philosophy of the government not to enact regulatory measures unless the need for them is vital.

QUESTIONS

1. In the future what probably will be the role of our Federal government in labor-management relations?
2. Discuss English common-law protection afforded workers injured at their jobs.
3. What common-law defenses were available to an employer?
4. Do these defenses have any application today? Discuss.
5. What is the basic philosophy of our workmen's compensation laws?
6. Describe the worker's protection under workmen's compensation laws.
7. What restrictions are there on the number of hours a man can work a week? Discuss.
8. How does the minimum-wage provision of the FLSA differ from the minimum wage set by the Walsh-Healy Act?
9. What did the Clayton Act do for unionism?
10. Of what significance was the NIRA to current collective bargaining regulations?
11. What is an unfair labor practice?
12. What are the unfair labor practices mentioned in the Labor Management Relations Act?
13. Do unfair labor practices apply to both union and management? Discuss.
14. What is a right-to-work law? Discuss.
15. Discuss the function of the Federal mediation and conciliation service.
16. What is the purpose of a Fair Employment Practices Act?
17. What are the unlawful acts under the FEPA in Massachusetts?

PART FOUR

Production

Part Four of this text deals with the problems and functions involved in the actual planning for production. It is assumed that at this point in the evolution of the business the physical plant and manpower requirements have been satisfied and that product requirements have been established. The major problem is now one of providing materials and production know-how.

Efficient production requires having the right materials at the right place at the right time. This is accomplished through the establishment and exercise of purchasing and inventory-control procedures. It also requires the optimum utilization of men and machines. Standards of performance are needed to measure the capacity of men and machines and provide a basis upon which production may be planned.

In Part Four the great emphasis should be on the need for coordinating the operating plan with the facilities of the organization. It is in this stage of company development that management proves the wisdom of all of its earlier decisions.

CHAPTER 16

Purchasing

In virtually all business organizations—manufacturing, wholesaling, or retailing—large sums of money are invested in either trading goods or raw materials, parts, supplies, machinery or equipment. Since large portions of a company's funds may be invested in various classes of purchased goods, it follows that the profitability of a business venture may be determined to a great extent by the efficiency with which management carries out the purchasing function. Through the establishment of sound purchasing procedures management can minimize the cost of its investment in purchased goods, reduce shortages, obsolescence, and pilferage, and maximize its return from this portion of the firm's resources. In any business organization, large or small, the purchasing department performs a function which can contribute significantly to its success.

Purchasing may be defined as the securing of goods and services from sources outside the company. The objectives of the purchasing function are to secure materials, parts, supplies, and services in the right quantity, of the right quality, for delivery at the right time, and at the best price to the company.

ORGANIZING FOR PURCHASING

These objectives of purchasing can be achieved only if management has created a sound organization for purchasing. Good organization is essential to the effective performance of all management functions. The most effective purchasing programs are found in those companies that have well-organized purchasing departments which are located in the organization structure at a level of authority commensurate with the responsibility delegated to the department. The position of the purchasing function in the scheme of organization varies from company to company depending on the size of the business and the importance of this function in management's over-all plan. Management often appraises the value of the purchasing function in terms of the importance of materials as an element in the cost of doing business.

In wholesale and retail activity between 50 and 80 cents of each sales dollar might well go for purchased goods. In an experimental machine shop, at the other extreme, as little as 4 or 5 cents of the sales dollar goes for purchased materials. Naturally, the importance of the purchasing function would differ significantly between these organizations. Figure 16–1 shows the breakdown of the sales dollars of a large steel producer.

FIGURE 16–1

UNITED STATES STEEL CORPORATION—SALES, COSTS, AND INCOME, 1954

	Millions of Dollars	*Per cent of Total*
Receipts from customers	3,250.4	100.0
Employment costs	1,387.0	42.7
Products and services bought	1,134.3	34.9
Wear and exhaustion	261.8	8.0
Taxes	266.7	8.2
Interest	5.2	0.2
Dividends	110.7	3.4
Income reinvested	84.7	2.6
Totals	3,250.4	100.0

SOURCE: Paul V. Farrell and Dean S. Ammer, "Buying at U. S. Steel," *Purchasing*, May, 1955.

In one year the United States Steel Corporation bought some 40,000 different commodities from about 50,000 suppliers involving more than a billion dollars.

> Today the purchasing department is regarded as a vital part of overall management, a qualified balance wheel on business expenditure. Management should never let itself, consciously or otherwise, minimize the profound influence on the success of the company's operation which is exerted by the purchasing department. This is apparent immediately to anyone who realizes that the purchase of materials and services represents more than one-half of the manufacturing dollar.[1]

Figure 16–2 presents an organization chart of the Purchasing Division of United States Steel Corporation. A brief study of this chart even by the novice will quickly reveal the complexity and importance of purchasing in a large organization.

Decentralized Purchasing

In many business organizations the purchasing function is decentralized; that is, each department in the organization is responsible for its

[1] Clifford F. Hood, "Buying at U.S. Steel," *Purchasing*, May, 1955.

own procurement problems and requirements. Such a system is, of course, very flexible; and under this plan, each department can create a purchasing section designed to fit the specific departmental needs. This plan also relieves upper levels of management from the responsibility of purchasing. However, as desirable as this plan may appear to be on the surface, it has at least one major defect. Under decentralized purchasing management cannot have control over its physical property—inventories and equipment, for example—and consequently cannot make the most effective use of its resources. Good management practices invariably provide for adequate control over all business functions. For this reason such a system is basically weak and undesirable.

Too frequently, it has been found, management tolerates decentralized purchasing because the system worked satisfactorily when the business was small; rather than interrupt a going order of relationships, it has allowed the system to remain even as the business grew. Management also condones the practice of decentralized purchasing to avoid a perhaps minor personnel problem that could easily arise if purchasing activity were centralized. Department heads, supervisors, or foremen would be virtually relieved of an important function over which they previously had had complete control. It is quite possible that they would rebel at the thought that their domain was to be diminished.

Centralized Purchasing

To provide for better control and to make purchasing more scientific, management assigns to one person in the organization the responsibility for all purchases, large or small and of any nature; i.e., the vice-president in charge of purchases. (See Figure 16–2.) A business need not be large to operate a plan of centralized purchasing; in fact, the smallest organization can enjoy the same relative advantages available to the largest industrial giant.

Although, under a plan of centralized purchasing, one individual is made responsible for all purchases, we should not conclude that all decisions relating to purchases are made by him alone. Figure 16–2 indicates that the vice-president in charge of purchasing receives assistance from several sources in the organization. In practice the purchasing department is a service unit, which buys only when someone in the organization requests that a purchase be made. While the final decision on a specific purchase, i.e., source, price, and terms, is usually made by the purchasing agent, good management requires that the purchasing department should not dictate to the departments it serves.

To illustrate the intent of the purchasing department under centralized purchasing, suppose that the foreman in the shop needs a new air compressor. The foreman will prepare a purchase requisition (see Figure

Figure 16–2

Organization of Purchasing Division
United States Steel Corporation

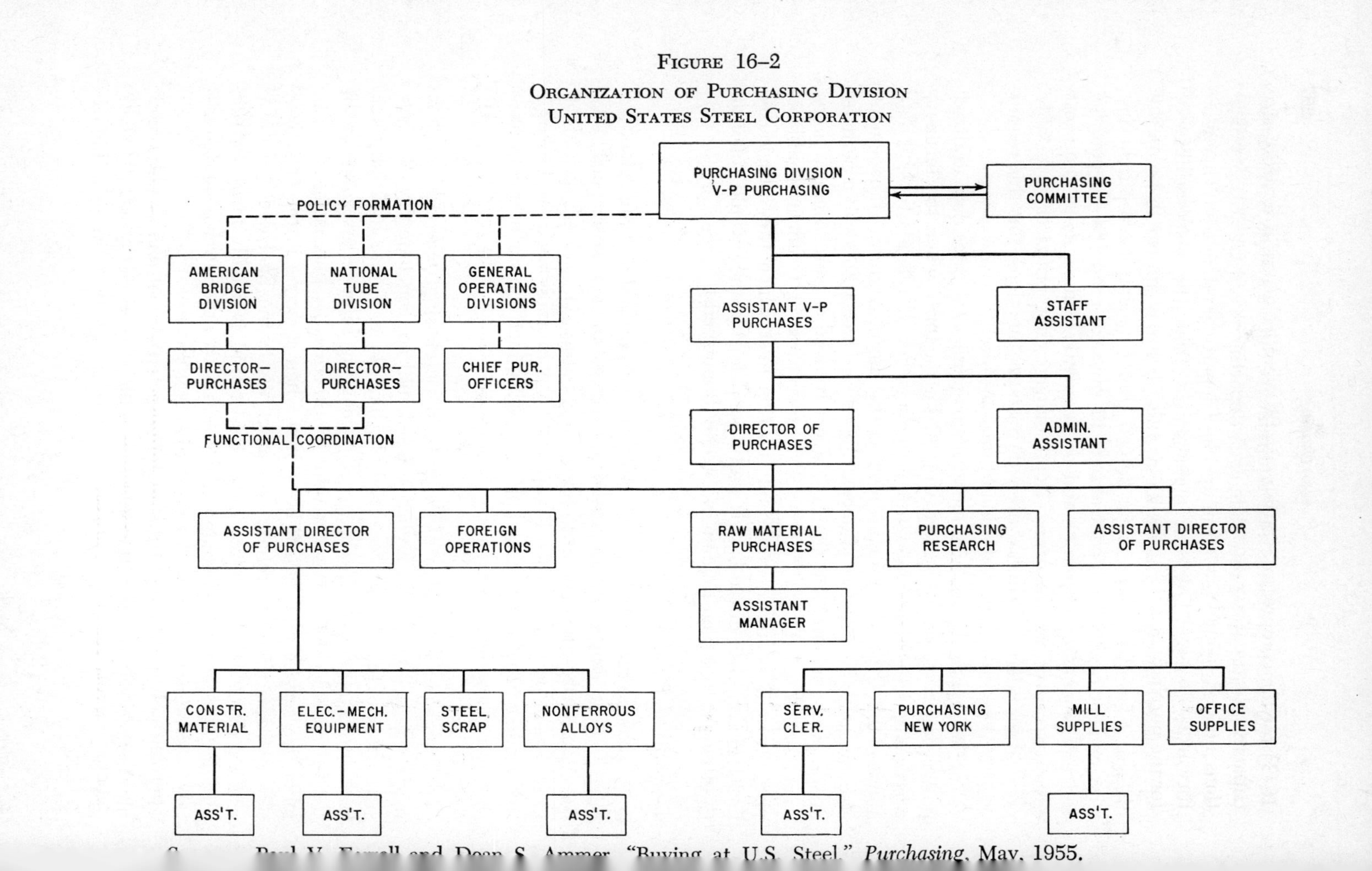

Source: Paul V. Farrell and Dean S. Ammer, "Buying at U.S. Steel," *Purchasing*, May, 1955.

16–3) for the compressor, stating exactly what he needs in terms of size, capacity, electrical requirements, delivery date, and any other considerations needed to make an intelligent purchase. This requisition will be forwarded to higher levels of management who will appraise the need for the purchase and who will approve the purchase if the need is evident

FIGURE 16–3
PURCHASE REQUISITION

ABC COMPANY
PURCHASE REQUISITION

TO PURCHASING AGENT: REQUISITION # ________

PLEASE ORDER THE FOLLOWING DATE ________

FOR DEPARTMENT ________ REQUISITIONED BY:

DATE WANTED ________ ________

SHIP VIA ________ APPROVED BY: ________

QUANTITY	DESCRIPTION	LAST PRICE	REMARKS

THIS SPACE FOR PURCHASING OFFICE

DATE ORDERED ________ PURCHASE ORDER # ________

VENDOR ________ APPROVED BY ________

CHARGE TO ACCOUNT # ________

REMARKS

and funds are available or will be available to pay for it. After approval by management, the purchasing agent will check various sources of supply and make a purchase to the best advantage of the company. Thus the purchasing agent does not determine what items will be bought; he buys only what he has been asked to buy. Similar routines apply to the purchase of materials, parts, and supplies. When purchasing many basic or stock items, the initial requisition may start automatically when inventory levels reach the lowest desirable level. In large organizations there undoubtedly will be several purchasing agents, each a specialist in his line, who are responsible to the chief of the purchasing department.

From the discussion above it should be quite apparent that there are several advantages to the businessman who employs a centralized purchasing technique. Centralized purchasing reduces the number of people who can make purchase commitments, thereby reducing the possibility of creating unwarranted liability. (A purchase order may result in an enforcible contract.) In addition, centralized purchasing may allow for the most economic use of purchasing specialists. A foreman may be quite certain of what materials or equipment he needs to get a particular job done, yet he may be completely ignorant of the market wherein the purchases are to be made. A purchasing agent must know the markets—it is a part of his job—and he is in a better position to acquire material to the best advantage of the company.

Because centralized purchasing introduces a centralized control over all physical property, it can reduce the waste of duplicate inventory which is common when purchasing activity is decentralized. Central control also facilitates standardization of machines, parts, and supplies. This is possible because the purchasing office is a clearing house for all information relating to purchases. Earlier discussions have pointed out the gains possible through a program of standardization.

Centralized purchasing brings about many purchasing economies. It reduces the administrative costs of purchasing by making it a specialized function. At U.S. Steel about 600 people operating at 24 major points are needed to carry out U.S. Steel's buying. This represents only a fraction of 1 per cent of the company payroll. Centralized purchasing implies buying in relatively large quantities with resulting savings in terms of discounts and transportation costs. Last but certainly not least, centralized purchasing brings professional status to the buying function. Because of their professional status purchasing men develop a greater interest in their work and seek to improve their over-all value to management by engaging in purchasing research activity, exchanging ideas with other purchasing agents, and by the establishment of a code of ethics for all men in the field.

PURCHASING RESEARCH

We are aware that good purchasing can add to company profits. We also know that market conditions are constantly changing; prices fluctuate continuously, and new and better products appear on the scene day by day. Because of the dynamic nature of the American economy it is imperative that the purchasing department be in constant contact with the markets in which it should operate. Purchasing research is a relatively new field of management, designed to coordinate and direct activities of the purchasing department concerned with increasing efficiency of purchasing operations and obtaining the maximum potential effect of each dollar expended for purchased goods and services. This is accomplished through planning and program development, commercial and product research, and value analysis of purchased acquisitions. It is the focal point for ideas that will get the maximum value from purchases, either through cost reduction or increased efficiency.

To indicate the scope of purchasing research the following outline of duties of the Manager of Purchasing Research at U.S. Steel is presented.[2]

Planning and Program Development

1. Designs and institutes programs for the evaluation of the performance of procurement ideas.
2. Analyzes operations of the Purchasing Division and prepares studies of improved techniques, systems, and controls.
3. Contacts purchasing agents of other companies to ascertain methods employed in executing purchasing responsibilities and determines applicability of such methods.
4. Develops methods of performing operations incidental to actual procurement for the purpose of increased efficiency and reduction in administrative expenses.
5. Reviews, interprets, and controls development of statistical reports and information required by the Purchasing Division.
6. Is responsible for the coordination of information on the acquisition and delivery of major purchase requirements with consumption rate and standard inventory levels to maintain proper balance of procurement with availability of requirements.
7. Represents the Purchasing Division in development of programs concerned with disposal of surplus and waste purchased materials, including salvage activities.
8. Provides staff services to Chief Procurement Officers of other operating divisions.

Commercial Research

9. By direct contact with suppliers and visitations to their plants, evaluates sources of supply of purchased goods and services in terms of vendor performance, facilities and capacity to produce, financial standing. Also assists in the development of new sources of supply for purchased commodities.
10. Ascertains and investigates new products and materials introduced on the market and determines the possibility of satisfying procurement needs more effectively or more efficiently with such products or materials.
11. Analyzes and interprets trends of business in general and supply-demand relationships of specific purchased commodities.

[2] Extracted from "Buying at U.S. Steel," *Purchasing*, May, 1955.

12. Analyzes price of purchased commodities in terms of market conditions and cost of production.
13. Prepares long-range economic studies concerning major purchased commodities to assist in resolution of procurement policy.

Value Analysis

14. Designs, establishes, and develops, on behalf of the Purchasing Division, programs and projects concerned with evaluating the quality of purchased commodities, including consideration of standardization, specifications, substitution, inspection, and testing of such commodities.
15. Is responsible for development and execution of projects in the Purchasing Division concerned with obtaining greater value in purchased goods and services through analysis of product design, packaging, transportation, manufacturing methods, and material handling.

THE PURCHASING FUNCTION

It was mentioned above that there were four specific objectives of the purchasing function: quality, quantity, price, and delivery. Each of these factors must be considered prior to any purchase for they represent the standards for purchasing.

Quality

Quality of the product is of primary importance in purchasing, for unless goods are of satisfactory quality, they will not meet the requirements for which the purchase was made. Quality is an attribute that is built into a product, and the cost of a good increases as more quality is added. While too little quality in an item is generally a greater mistake than too much quality, it must be remembered that quality in excess of actual requirements represents a waste of material and money. Since nearly all commodities are produced in varying degrees of quality, someone in the organization must establish the degree of quality needed in a purchased item. Top management would undoubtedly answer the quality question when new products are being developed and when major equipment purchases are contemplated. In other instances the office manager, the foreman, or the storeskeeper in consultation with the purchasing agent will make the quality decision. Fine judgment is needed to ensure that just the right amount of quality is present in purchased materials.

Quantity

While it is generally considered better to have too much rather than too little of any inventory item, goods on hand which are not needed may represent poor utilization of company resources. A major purchasing problem is determining how much to buy, (1) in terms of economic lot sizes and (2) in terms of production or use requirements. This problem will be discussed in detail below. In determining how much to buy, the purchasing agent must weigh the cost of carrying excess inventory with the gains to be had from purchasing in quantity.

Price

Invoice price is too often the sole factor considered in planning a purchase. Only when all other factors are equal among vendors should price alone govern the purchase. More often than not there are other factors to consider when a vendor is selected. Will the vendor skimp on quality because of his low price; will the vendor be able to provide the service that should go with the product; and can the vendor be counted on to deliver according to the purchase agreement? These are some of the factors that should be considered in addition to price. The successful purchasing agent has a large number of sources that he can call upon as the need arises. Continuous and mutually profitable relationships are necessary in the establishment of reliable sources of supply. Few reputable suppliers want to deal continuously with a buyer who thinks solely in terms of price. Most businessmen build their reputations on standards of quality and service rather than price. In the long run it is impossible for a supplier to maintain high standards of quality and service unless he charges for them. Suppliers who stand behind their products and services cannot afford to do business with the buyer who thinks solely in terms of price.

Delivery

A dependable source of supply is more desirable than a cheap source. Goods may be purchased at the lowest possible price, but they will be of absolutely no value to the buyer until he receives them. Some suppliers are able to operate on low margins of profit by carrying little or no inventory and, therefore, can offer little service. The supplier who carries a varied inventory, one who anticipates the demands of his customers, is a far better person to deal with.

THE PURCHASING ROUTINE

The purchasing routine begins with a request for purchases from someone in the organization who has been designated to participate in the purchasing function. The formal request for a purchase is made on a purchase requisition (Figure 16–3). The purchase may be made to replace inventory of materials, parts, and supplies; or it may be for the acquisition of machinery and equipment. All purchases should be made through the same routine so that maximum control may be achieved.

Anyone in authority can initiate a purchase requisition since it in itself has no significance until it has been approved by the proper authority. Approval is usually given by the department head if the purchase is to be charged to the departmental budget. Routine purchases made to replenish inventory generally may not need approval since such purchases are often based on predetermined inventory levels.

After the purchase requisition has been completed and approved, it is forwarded to the purchasing department. The purchase requisition should

FIGURE 16–4

PURCHASE ORDER

ABC COMPANY
PURCHASE ORDER

TO:__________ PURCHASE ORDER NO.__________

__________ DATE__________

PLEASE FURNISH US WITH THE FOLLOWING, AT THE PRICES AND ON THE TERMS AND CONDITIONS SPECIFIED BELOW:

SHIP VIA__________ TERMS__________

QUANTITY	DESCRIPTION	UNIT	TOTAL

REQUISITION NUMBER__________ SIGNED__________

CHARGE TO ACCOUNT NO. __________ TITLE__________

CONDITIONS:

now contain all the information that is needed to make the desired purchase. The purchasing department then locates the most desirable source of supply available. There are several devices used by the purchasing agent for locating good sources of supply. Among them are the following:

1. Company records acquired through the years
2. Trade journals
3. Manufacturers' associations
4. Visits to prospective vendor plants
5. Requesting quotations publicly

Since nearly all vendors advertise in some manner, it is not difficult to locate potential sources of supply. A greater problem is to evaluate them once they have been located. Location and evaluation of vendors is a regular function of the purchasing agent.

After the supplier is located and price, quality, delivery, and other terms have been agreed upon, a purchase order (Figure 16–4) is completed by the purchasing agent; when confirmed by the vendor it results in a contract to which both parties, buyer and seller, can be bound. Whenever the buyer deems it necessary, he may check upon the progress of his order to ascertain that the vendor is complying with the agreement.

The purchasing cycle is completed when the goods are delivered and "received" (Figure 16–5). All receipts of goods should be checked as to quality, quantity, and other specifications indicated in the purchase order. After it has been ascertained that the goods meet the conditions of the purchase contract, they are formally added to inventory or equipment

FIGURE 16–5
RECEIVING SLIP

ABC COMPANY
RECEIVING SLIP

RECEIVED FROM ______________ PURCH. ORDER # ______
DATE ______________ PURCH. REQ. # ______

QUANTITY	DESCRIPTION

FOR DEP'T. ______________
FOR STORES ______ CLASSIFICATION ______ CODE ______
REC'D. BY ______________

accounts through the receiving record. The receiving record ultimately informs all parties concerned that the goods requested have been received.

PURCHASING POLICIES

The purchasing policy adopted by any establishment must be designed to make the purchasing function most effective. For this reason there is a wide variety of policies in use. Several of the basic policies are discussed below, and it should be remembered that management will alter these basic plans when it is in its interest to do so.

Hand-to-mouth Purchasing

This policy involves purchasing in relatively small quantities for immediate use rather than purchasing for stockpiles. Many organizations can justify this policy, for it keeps inventories at low levels and may make working capital available for other uses. As a result of low inventories, storage costs are kept to a minimum, the possibility of creating stocks of obsolete materials is minimized, and the possibility of inventory value losses due to price changes is for all practical purposes eliminated. This policy also has the great advantage of flexibility since it implies that long-range commitments will not be made. Design changes involving materials can be instituted as management desires since there are no large inventories on hand that must be used. There may be an advantage in the fact that buyers will have more frequent contact with the market. This frequent contact with the market may also put buyers in a position where they can take advantage of favorable market changes.

Hand-to-mouth buying is not without its faults, however. Because of smaller purchases discounts are generally lower, and transportation and administrative costs are higher. More serious is the fact that production may become overdependent on the supplier and his ability to meet immediate delivery requirements. Suppliers do not particularly like a hand-to-mouth purchasing policy, for it is difficult to anticipate their customers' demands.

Hand-to-mouth buying is often the only logical purchasing policy when future sales cannot be estimated. For those who can estimate their needs there are more satisfactory purchasing policies.

Purchasing by Requirement

This type of purchasing differs from hand-to-mouth buying in that it is used primarily with goods that are not regularly purchased, such as a special piece of material or a special part for a particular production order. It is used when items are purchased so infrequently that the only feasible plan is to buy as needed.

Market Purchasing

Some buyers try to plan their purchases so that all purchases will be made when the market is "right." The buyer studies the market, estimates the course of commodity prices, and places his orders when he feels prices will be the lowest. When buying is based on price levels, it is impossible to plan purchases that will conform exactly to production needs. Also, prices may not take their expected courses, and losses rather than gains may result. When this policy works, it is fine, but production may suffer while waiting for a favorable market. This type of purchasing can be best applied to the purchase of goods that are subject to major seasonal changes in price.

Speculative Purchasing

This policy involves some of the principles of market purchasing but includes a greater element of risk. Under this policy the buyer seeks to make a profit by buying and selling in anticipation of price changes. This type of buying is common in the purchase of agricultural and other basic commodities and is carried on with the consent of higher management. It cannot be defended as a desirable policy from the point of view of scientific management because of its uncertainty and the fact that this type of purchasing is not concerned with a program of use, such as production.

Scheduled Purchasing

This is perhaps the most widely used and scientific purchasing policy for here an earnest attempt is made to schedule purchases that coincide with present and future production requirements. This plan does away with most of the drawbacks of other policies and still retains the bulk of their strong points.

Since the basic purpose of all purchasing is to facilitate production, directly or indirectly, it quite naturally follows that if production can be scheduled into the future, purchases too can be scheduled, or planned, for a like period. Scheduled purchasing assures management that there will be adequate supplies of all material needed and offers a safeguard over excessive inventories. However, such a plan could not exist unless a buyer were able to locate reliable sources that could be counted on to make future deliveries. Likewise, the supplier must be sure that he will have customers for his goods in the future. This plan requires that both the buyer and seller act in good faith since each becomes more dependent on the other; it requires a cooperative agreement between the parties. Since this plan works to the benefit of both buyer and seller, purchases can often be made under the most satisfactory terms. Under this plan a buyer might place an order for a year's supply of a commodity to be delivered as needed and subject to limited changes in the buyer's requirements. The buyer is assured of his supply of goods, and the seller is assured of a market. Generally the most satisfactory prices and service result when this arrangement is utilized.

PURCHASING PROBLEMS

Two of the more basic problems that confront the purchasing agent are (1) determining when to buy and (2) determining how much to buy. If the rate of consumption of a particular item is fairly stable and if the price of the item is not subject to rapid change, it is possible to set quantitative standards for purchased items. The standard will indicate how much should be purchased at a time and when the order should be placed. It must be remembered that these standards are valid only if the rate of use does not vary to any great extent and the price of the item is not subject to drastic changes. A purchasing agent who buys to varying levels of production or in a market where prices change rapidly must plan his purchases in view of these varying circumstances.

Quantitative Standards

The situation presented below shows the information needed to answer the "when" and "how much" of purchasing when purchasing is based on production requirements. It should be noted that several other purchasing considerations come to light as a result of the same examination. Later in this chapter an illustration will be presented which includes the price factor. Suppose that the following data were available concerning a particular inventory item:

a. Units on hand.......................................800
b. Delivery time required.............................. 3 weeks
c. Cushion stock needed for emergency.................. 4 weeks
d. Average monthly consumption.........................400 units
e. Maximum supply to have on hand...................... 17 weeks

Units on Hand: Amount in inventory at the time the problem is studied.

Delivery Time: Time required to receive material after the purchase order has been confirmed.

Cushion Stock: Amount deemed necessary to hold in reserve to be used when delivery time exceeds the estimate or when other factors limit deliveries.

Average Monthly Consumption: Consumption as determined from past and future schedules of production. Adjustments should be made when average consumption is much higher or lower than actual.

Maximum Supply: Based on storage facilities, usage, and market factors, a ceiling is placed on the size of inventory at any time.

Since any of these values are subject to change at any time, the schedule of purchases must also be revised in light of these changes.

From the figures given above the following questions about purchases can be answered:

1. *How much is there on hand now?*
   $800 \div 400 = 2$ months' supply
   $2 \times 4.33 = 8.66$ or 9 weeks' supply
   (4.33 weeks per month)
2. *How soon should this item be reordered?* (When)
   4 weeks' cushion plus 3 weeks' delivery or 7 weeks' supply in reserve is needed.

9 weeks (time on hand) − 7 weeks = 2 weeks
Order in 2 weeks.

3. *What is the ordering point in terms of units?*
7 weeks' supply times weekly consumption rate of 92 units or 644. This item should be reordered when the amount on hand drops to 644 units. This becomes the low limit for this item.
4. *How much should be ordered at a time?*
Based solely on the information given, the following calculation shows the amount to order:

Maximum quantity.....	17 weeks
Cushion stock.........	4 weeks
Amount to order.......	13 weeks or 3 months

Three months' supply is 1,200 units.
5. *How frequently should we reorder?*
Every three months, or four times per year. This assumes that the given facts remain unchanged.
6. *What is the minimum balance we should ever have in inventory?*
Four weeks' supply, or 368 units.

It bears repeating that these relations exist solely in the light of given values. As any of the values change, the relationships too will change. Such estimates of inventory values may be followed carefully or they may simply serve as a guide to purchasing.

When to Buy

For sake of illustration, purchases can be classified as specific purchases or planned purchases. When the purchasing agent receives a specific request to buy goods and an immediate delivery is called for, there is no problem in determining when to buy; the order should be placed immediately if possible. In many instances, however, purchasing agents plan their purchases of basic or stock items, at least, based on anticipated need and the expected variation in price levels. By planning in advance, it is often possible to take advantage of lower prices offered during a vendor's off season. Commodity price indexes are prepared by government agencies that will indicate at what times during the year prices of a commodity will be higher than average and when they will be lower than average. Buying during slack periods instead of peak periods has proved to be a tremendous money-saver for many organizations. When a purchasing agent buys or refrains from buying in anticipation of a change in the price level of a particular commodity, he naturally takes a chance. He may buy heavy today because he feels that the price will rise tomorrow, or he may refrain from buying today in anticipation of a price reduction tomorrow. In either event he does not know what will actually happen; all that he can do is gather all possible information, analyze it, and draw the soundest conclusion possible.

How Much to Buy

While purchases may be planned into the future under scheduled purchasing (see below), there still remains the problem of determining how much to buy when factors other than production requirements are considered.

Generally, the starting point in determining the amount to buy is governed by three factors: (1) the rate of consumption as dictated by production, (2) the time required to replenish inventory, and (3) the size of the current inventory. The greater the rate of consumption, the larger the volume of purchases, the longer the time required to replenish inventory, the greater the amount that must be held in reserve pending delivery; and the greater the amounts currently in inventory, depending on rate of use, the greater or the less the time before repurchasing.

A buyer might feel that he should buy more than the amounts dictated by the above factors. How much more than normal requirements should he purchase? The answer is determined by comparing the savings resulting from larger purchases (discounts and transportation savings) with the increased costs of carrying inventory in excess of normal requirements. It has been estimated that the cost of carrying an item in inventory amounts to about 25 per cent of its value when measured as an annual cost. This figure may appear to be high; but when all the costs of carrying an item in inventory are considered, it seems quite reasonable. Some of the costs of carrying inventory are as follows: interest, usually figured at 6 per cent; insurance against fire, theft, and damage; taxes, since inventories are property and are subject to tax either as personal property or as corporate property; depreciation; obsolescence; occupancy charge for extra space required; and extra handling required for good inventory management. The excess inventory requiring extra space and handling should not be so large that it will cost more to keep than can be saved by buying in quantity. Of course, this principle can and should be violated when extenuating factors are present, such as impending shortages caused by labor disturbances or government controls, or when relations with foreign powers might change and thus cut off foreign sources of supply.

Under what conditions should the purchasing agent increase the size of his purchase over and above normal requirements dictated by the use factor? Unless there are other considerations, the answer is: when savings to be had are greater than the additional costs incurred.

In reference to the following illustration, suppose that the buyer could buy a carload of 4,800 units at a price of 80 cents per unit or the normal requirement of 1,200 units at a cost of 90 cents per unit. By buying 4,800 units there will be a saving of 10 cents per unit or $480 total, but the inventory will be increased by 3,600 units over the normal purchasing quantity, requiring an additional investment of $2,880. This amounts to 9 months' extra supply. If inventory carrying charges are 25 per cent per annum as mentioned above and there is a constant rate of consumption, a saving of $140 will result from purchasing the larger quantity. (See below.)

Calculation

The $140 saving was calculated by applying the average value concept wherein average value equals ½ value $\times \frac{N+1}{N}$. N refers, in this case, to the number of months inventory is held.

Cost of carrying a three-month inventory:

$$\text{A.V.} = \tfrac{1}{2}(\$1080) \times \tfrac{4}{3} \text{ or } \$720$$

Carrying charges on $720 for three months at the 25 per cent rate amount to $45. Annual charge for carrying three-month inventories is $180.

Cost of carrying a twelve-month inventory:

$$\text{A.V.} = \tfrac{1}{2}(\$3840) \times \tfrac{13}{12} \text{ or } \$2080$$

Carrying charges on $2080 for twelve months at the 25 per cent rate amount to $520.

Inventory carrying charges are $340 higher with a twelve-month inventory. However, there is a saving of $480 on the purchase price, resulting in a net saving of $140.

SUMMARY

The purchasing function may be of vital importance to many organizations. Some businesses have larger purchases than others, and naturally the purchasing function is more important to them. Effective purchasing requires an effective organization whereby responsibility for the purchasing function is centered in one man. This principle holds whether the organization is large or small. An effective purchasing department will provide operating divisions with a steady flow of information regarding market conditions, new products, and the like.

Purchasing must be coordinated with production. The more accurate the estimates of future production, the easier it will be to have the desired amounts of material in inventory. Purchasing causes inventories to increase; inventories by themselves are not productive. A close working relationship must exist between the purchasing department and the production departments to prevent a needless investment in inventory.

QUESTIONS

1. Describe a plan of decentralized purchasing. What advantages does it have?
2. Describe a plan of centralized purchasing. What advantages does it have?
3. Can centralized purchasing principles be applied in the small establishment? Discuss.
4. Discuss the function of purchasing research.
5. What are the four specific objectives of the purchasing function?
6. Which would you rate as being most important? Least important?
7. Describe a formal purchasing routine.
8. Distinguish between a purchase order and a purchase requisition.
9. How does a buyer determine when to buy?
10. How does a buyer determine how much to buy?
11. How does hand-to-mouth buying operate? Under what conditions would it be a good policy?
12. What is meant by "purchasing by requirement"?
13. What is market purchasing?
14. Describe scheduled purchasing.
15. What advantages does scheduled purchasing have over the other methods?

CHAPTER 17

Inventory Control

To ensure adequate control over materials, parts, supplies, and other items that are purchased, management must apply certain inventory-control devices, or else the gains made through effective purchasing may be lost. Management needs to know many things about the state of its inventory. This information can be obtained through the application of control devices.

To facilitate the establishment of effective control devices management usually breaks its inventory down into several manageable parts and treats each one separately.

1. Raw-material inventory which is made up of materials that will be fabricated in the process of production and ultimately will become a finished product. Sheets of steel that are used to make body panels in the manufacture of automobiles or crude rubber used in production of tires are illustrations of raw materials.
2. Purchased parts which are finished products of another manufacturing process that are added to other parts and raw materials in the process of manufacture. Spark plugs used in automobile engines are purchased parts.
3. Supplies which are comprised of numerous products that are not a major part of the product manufactured but are necessary for efficient production, such as lubricating oils, abrasives, tools, or sweeping compounds.
4. Work-in-process inventory which is made up of raw materials and/or parts that have had some work performed on them. Management is interested in the value of work-in-process because it affects its periodic financial statements; profits cannot be accurately determined until all inventories have been given dollar values; and the quantity of work-in-process is needed to gage productive activity.
5. Finished goods inventory which is made up of items that have been completely manufactured and presumably are available for sale or shipment.

Each of these inventories will be of more or less importance from company to company. In the job-order shop finished goods inventory is of little or no consequence since work is generally performed to order. However, other inventories mentioned above are of significance to the job-order shop. In a company where a product is manufactured for stock, each of these inventories is of great importance and must be carefully controlled.

Purpose of Inventory Control

From the discussion of purchasing policies, in Chapter 16, it appears that the inventory problem of a businessman is directly related to purchasing. The businessman who resorts to hand-to-mouth buying generally has no inventory-control problem. The businessman who tries to anticipate future material needs and buys in advance to satisfy them faces a more significant problem. However, as long as inventory exists, inventory management of some sort is essential. Management needs to know the size of its inventory, its value, its age, and whether or not there are any inventory shortages. Management needs to know the size of its inventory on a day-to-day basis so that no productive process will have to wait because of lack of materials and to make sure that the investment in inventory does not become too large. Financial data on inventories, such as unit cost and issuing price, must also be available on a day-to-day basis to properly charge inventory to production and to serve as a basis for valuing inventories for use in preparing financial statements. Inventories can spoil or become obsolete; the older an inventory becomes, the greater are the chances of its decreasing in value. Management needs to keep accurate records to avoid the losses that arise when inventories are improperly managed. By the use of both physical and book inventory procedures management can locate shortages. This function is explained below.

Inventory-control Devices

Basic to any system of inventory control is the perpetual inventory. The perpetual inventory is a book record of inventory transactions kept item by item and in total, if desired. After the opening inventory balance has been verified through a physical count, the entire inventory record is kept apart from the storage area by simply recording all transactions that affect the inventory item on perpetual-inventory sheets. (See Figure 17–1.) All additions to inventory are recorded based on information contained on receiving slips, which should be made out every time goods are received, and on any other records that indicate additions to inventory. Similarly, all deductions from inventory are recorded based on information given on the material requisition or any other form that is used

FIGURE 17–1

PERPETUAL-INVENTORY RECORD

ABC COMPANY
PERPETUAL INVENTORY RECORD

ITEM CONDENSER STAN. ORDER. QUAN. 1200

ITEM NO. 456J MAXIMUM 1600 REORDER POINT 300

ON ORDER			ON HAND				RESERVED			AVAILABLE	
DATE	QUANTITY	UNIT COST	DATE	QUANTITY	UNIT COST	VALUE	DATE	REQ. NO.	QUANTITY	DATE	QUANTITY
			3/1	1000	.50	$ 500.–				3/1	1000
							3/6	496	600	3/6	400
							3/9	499	200	3/9	200
3/10	1200	.52									
			3/16	400	.50	200.–					
			3/24	400 1200	.50 .52	200 624				3/24	1400
			3/27	200 1200	.50 .52	100 624					

when materials leave the inventory. The figure thus obtained, additions minus withdrawals, indicates the amount that should be in inventory. If a physical count reveals that there is a different amount from what the record shows, then there is a shortage or overage of that inventory item. The only effective way to uncover shortages is the use of a book inventory in conjunction with the physical inventory count.

The perpetual inventory, if properly used, has the following strong points in its favor. It is a quick method of determining operating results; that is, inventory values obtained from perpetual-inventory records can be used in the determination of periodic profits. In addition, it provides the information necessary to keep inventories in proper balance and to help locate shortages. It also provides an accurate estimate of inventory values for insurance purposes. All in all, it does away with the need for frequent physical inventories since purchases can be based on the perpetual record rather than actual count.

The major weakness in any system of perpetual inventory control is that it requires an accurate flow and recording of all information that affects the inventory. If any transactions that affect inventory are overlooked, then the perpetual inventory will not reveal the true state of inventory. It is difficult to operate a perpetual-inventory control where inventory items are used frequently and in small quantities, as in a retail store. Nevertheless, this system is widely used and is an invaluable tool of management.

Perpetual Inventory Control Illustrated

Figure 17–1, upon which the following transactions have been recorded, illustrates the use of the perpetual-inventory system:

Balance on hand, March 1, 195–, 1000 units valued at 50¢, none of which has been reserved.
March 6, reserved 600 units on Req. #496.
March 9, reserved 200 units on Req. #499.
March 10, ordered 1,200 units at 52¢.
March 16, issued 600 units for Req. #496.
March 24, received order of March 10.
March 27, issued 200 units for Req. #499.

From this record the complete status of the inventory is immediately available and easily obtained. On March 27, for example, there were 1,400 units on hand and available for future production. These units had a value of $724 based on a first-in, first-out, valuation.

The "maximum" refers to the largest quantity that should be in inventory at any time. This quantity is determined by such factors as storage space available, spoilage, probability of price change, and the factor of need. Ordinarily this high limit to inventory is of little concern because if goods are ordered as planned and in the quantity planned, then the high limit cannot be exceeded. It serves as a stop-look-and-listen signal so that too large an order will not be placed and excessive inventory accumulated.

The "reorder point" indicates the level of inventory at which additional inventory should be ordered. This quantity should be based on the rate of use for the item and the time required to replenish this item after ordering.

The "standard ordering quantity" is the amount that normally will be purchased at one time. This quantity represents the most economical lot for management to purchase at a time, all factors being considered.

When the above information is available, the task of buying can become a simple and routine one. Many staple items are purchased in this manner. The decision on how much to buy and when to buy is preplanned. The remaining questions regarding the purchase are from what source and at what price. In many instances these two questions also are answered in advance. The values that determine the nature of the reorder point and the standard ordering quantity are subject to change and should be audited periodically to keep them from becoming outdated.

The "on order" section indicates that an order has been placed and normally should be based on the "available" column. When the amount available falls to 300 units, then an order for 1,200 units should be placed. The "reserved" section indicates what portion of the "on hand" has been set aside for future production requirements. If a physical inventory taken on March 31 indicated that there were actually less than 1,400 units on hand, then the difference is a shortage.

The Retail Method

The perpetual inventory illustrated is widely used and can be depended upon to provide management with up-to-the-minute inventory data. Manufacturers, wholesalers, and retail-store warehouses rely on this method of inventory control. Because of the frequency of transactions involving inventory in a retail store, perpetual inventory systems may not be practical. The retail method of inventory described below is used by retailers to provide management with inventory data without frequent physical count.

To produce reliable results through the retail method an accurate record of the following items must be kept:

1. Cost and retail value of the opening inventory for the period involved.
2. Cost and retail value of all purchases or shipments from warehouse.

3. Additional markups taken.
4. Freight charges for goods received.
5. Markdowns taken.
6. Employee discounts, spoilage, theft allowances.
7. Sales for the period.

To illustrate how an inventory value is obtained via the retail method, let us assume the following for the month of March; inventory, March 1, cost $78,000, retail value, $100,000; merchandise received during the month, cost $237,000, retail value, $300,000; freight charges, $3,000; additional markups, $20,000; markdowns, $10,000; employee discounts, etc., $10,000; and sales of $340,000. The cost value of inventory as of March 31 is determined by the following calculation:

	Cost value	*Retail value*
Inventory, March 1	$ 78,000	$100,000
Received during March	237,000	300,000
Freight charges	3,000	
Additional markups	....	20,000
Total to account for	$318,000	$420,000

The store manager must account for $420,000 of retail value which cost $318,000. The accounting is accomplished in the following manner.

Sales for March	$340,000
Markdowns	10,000
Employee discounts	10,000
Total accounted for	360,000
Inventory at retail	60,000
Total	$420,000

Since management is interested primarily in the cost value of inventory, the retail value shown above must be reduced to a cost basis. The reduction is accomplished by applying the average cost complement of the month's activity. The reasoning is that if the total cost value of goods handled during March is $318,000 and the total retail value of goods handled during March is $420,000, then on an average the goods handled cost 76 per cent of their retail value ($318,000 ÷ $420,000). Therefore, the cost value of the ending inventory is 76 per cent of its retail value, or $45,600. If a physical inventory revealed that the actual value of inventory was only $45,000, then a shortage of $600 exists.

Physical Inventory

There is no substitute for the physical inventory. Regardless of the size of an inventory it should be audited periodically through a physical count. This is the only way to determine the exact number of units in inventory. The perpetual inventory and the retail method simply help to keep inventory data up to date between physical inventory counts.

Inventory Valuation

There have been many techniques devised to determine the value of items issued from inventory and, of course, the value of inventory at any time. Some techniques have been developed to simplify the task of inventory pricing, while others are designed to value inventory to the advantage of management. Inventories often are not valued at the price paid for them, and the price at which items are issued from inventory often does not reflect their actual cost. Various theories of inventory pricing have been developed, giving rise to a difference in opinion as to their actual worth for accounting purposes. Since low values on ending inventories will result in a lower profit than a high value, there can be a tax advantage in adopting a plan that will tend to show low inventory values. Even though different methods of inventory valuation will result in different profit levels, all of the methods described below are accepted and commonly used.

First in, First out. This method, which applies the oldest price first, consistently values inventory items at their actual cost, provided physical movement of inventory is also first in, first out; and for this reason it is widely used.

Last in, First out. Under this method the most current price paid is applied to goods as they leave inventory regardless of the actual cost of the goods. As a result, in periods of rising prices goods leaving inventory tend to be overpriced, and the units remaining in inventory carry a value less than their actual worth. Many businessmen have adopted this technique since World War II to show lower inventory values, lower profits, and of course, lower taxes. However, when a period of falling prices sets in, inventories tend to be overvalued resulting in the showing of higher profits than are actually earned. When goods sold are priced according to "last in, first out," management is in a good position to charge prices that will be consistent with the cost of replenishing inventory. If an item purchased three months ago at 20 cents now costs 25 cents, it could be priced for sale at 20 cents under "first in, first out" and at 25 cents under "last in, last out."

Standard Cost. Under this method all goods are priced out of inventory at a predetermined standard price. The standard price is determined in advance and is based on management's best estimate of what the price will be based on past experience and future expectations.

Average Cost. To smooth out the fluctuations in prices an average cost might be employed. The danger in using an average cost is that often the average cost is not kept up to date and in essence is not a true average cost.

Management should exercise great care in determining its policy for inventory valuation. While it may appear that there is a method to meet every situation, management cannot change its method as it sees fit; because inventory values affect profits and profits affect taxes, the Bureau of Internal Revenue will not allow management to suit its own purposes by arbitrarily changing valuation methods. Generally, once a method is adopted, it must be followed from year to year.

Storeskeeping

In addition to the inventory recording and pricing devices mentioned above, systematic inventory control requires an adequate stockroom, a system of material identification, and intelligent stockroom management. These three elements comprise storeskeeping.

Storage areas should be provided and arranged so that a minimum of productive time will be lost in obtaining tools, materials, or parts and supplies needed on the job. At the same time storeroom arrangements should allow for the necessary control of all inventory items. In some shops there will be a single storeroom from which all items will be drawn. In other plants conditions may warrant the location of several storerooms at strategic points throughout the plant. The decision to have one or several storage rooms will be determined by the size of the plant, material-handling facilities, protection required, and the bulk of the materials stored.

The layout of the storeroom must also be given consideration. A well-laid-out storeroom will provide facilities for receiving and disbursing materials and for the immediate location of any item in inventory. All items in inventory should be classified and given a number or symbol that will make their location easy. Good layout will decrease the possibility of spoilage, breakage, and theft and thereby strengthen control devices.

The finest system for material control will fail unless it is properly managed. The storeroom area should be "off limits" to all but the storeskeeper and his crew. No materials should be taken into inventory unless authorized, and nothing should be drawn from inventory unless it has been duly authorized. It is hopeless to expect that there will be good storeskeeping unless these basic rules are adhered to.

SUMMARY

Inventory control is a tedious yet vital aspect of good management. Poor inventory management needlessly ties up working capital, jeopardizes the financial status of the company, and interferes with the entire operational plan. It is not a question, then, of whether inventory control methods be used; rather, of what methods will, at least cost, provide management with the knowledge of inventory necessary to make sound decisions.

QUESTIONS

1. Distinguish between a raw-material inventory and a parts inventory.
2. What bearing has purchasing policy on inventory control?
3. What are the advantages of the perpetual inventory?
4. What are the disadvantages of the perpetual inventory?
5. What is a standard ordering quantity?
6. Describe the operation of the retail method of inventory.
7. Describe last-in, first-out as an inventory valuing method.
8. What elements comprise storeskeeping?
9. What effect does inventory value have on profits?

CHAPTER 18

Bases for Production Planning

The cycle of business activity may be said to involve three phases: first, adequate facilities must be established; second, the work must be done; and third, the product or the results of endeavor must be distributed. In each of these phases management must engage in considerable planning activity by means of which it seeks to predetermine the nature and extent of the activities which are to be carried out. In addition, management is concerned with establishing bases for this planning which at the same time will serve as yardsticks for control.

Thus, we recognize that plant location, plant layout, material handling, and job analysis and evaluation each represent areas which must be planned for and established prior to the performance of work. The amount of preliminary planning in these areas varies greatly in the various types of industry. A repetitive or continuous-process industry needs a great deal of planning for facilities, for as has been indicated previously, such facilities are intended for long-term use and must be established primarily for economical high-rate production. However, such industries usually involve less endeavor in the second phase, getting the work done, for the limited or singular line of product once established as to production requirements and process demands less effort in the subsequent work. The reverse usually holds true for the intermittent-process industries. Not that the planning for facilities is of little importance, but rather that in getting the work done the great variety of work and products demands continuing and original efforts in the establishment of bases for the planning and control of the work.

Although we have endeavored to establish three phases of the activity of the firm, it is not possible completely to separate any one from the others, nor can we establish the relative importance of each phase. Each must be coordinated with the others and planned simultaneously. In any event it is most desirable that as much as possible of the preparatory work and bases for planning be established as early as possible in the cycle of business activity.

Production Standards

As management proceeds with the planning of activity, it finds that it must reckon with the problem of doing the best job possible with the facilities available at the time. Catering to this purpose, it is necessary that management engage in the planning of work and the development of standards of performance. These standards are representative of what management believes to be the most desirable level and nature of activity as determined by means of scientific analysis.

The procedure of developing standards stems from the raising of basic questions pertinent to an area of activity. Of the many questions raised in the search for standards and of the many techniques employed by management as means of providing the answers, the following are illustrative:

The Questions Raised	*The Answer Source*
How is the job best done?	Process and operation analysis Motion study
How long should it take a man or a machine to do a job?	Time study
How and by what system should work be inspected or checked?	Quality standards
Can we economically produce a given size of order?	Economic manufacturing-lot size
How can we most efficiently provide our material requirements?	Material standards
What should the cost be to produce a given volume?	Cost standards

MOTION STUDY

Every action or movement by man or machine dissipates energy. Some movements are inefficient in the usage of both time and energy. Motion study is the attempt to establish the best series of motions with which to accomplish a particular task. The over-all process of work or a particular operation involving the machine and/or worker may be the object of motion analysis.

Planning the Process

A manufacturing process or a flow of paper work such as an office procedure can be broken down into its basic elements of work and movement in order that a detailed study and attempt at improvement of the job may be made. (See Figures 8–1 and 8–2.) If management is able to establish a particular form and sequence of process steps, it is therefore able to most clearly visualize the operational needs and the potential output rate of the process. In theory, if not in fact, the sequence of operations which management sets up for a particular process or procedure represents the best manner and order of utilizing equipment, space, men, materials, and time as elements of production. However, analysis from a process viewpoint provides only an over-all view. It is necessary to examine the nature of the specific operations which are being performed by the workers and machines.

Planning the Operations

The analysis of the way in which a worker does his job and the attempt to establish the "best" way in which an operation should be performed involves application of the principles of motion economy.

Most of us have at one time or another observed a friend or fellow worker who, as we would say, was doing a task "the hard way." Whether it was the manner in which the person was using a hand tool, the way in which he stooped to pick up an object, or the fact that each time he used a particular tool he first had to hunt for it, we recognized that something was being done incorrectly and there must be an "easier and better way."

Each worker's task may be planned as to the details of performance. If the worker follows the procedure of work which has been developed as the standard method, there is assurance that the job will be done as desired and within the time period allowed. Planning the operation involves, as one aspect, motion analysis.

In determining the most efficient way of doing a manual operation, it is necessary to consider the worker who is to perform the task. The development of an efficient method does not necessarily mean that the desired goal is one of speed in doing work. The speediest method may be more tiring for the worker, thus defeating its own purpose. The real goal is the establishment of a pattern of routine performance on a particular job which will do three things: make the job easier to perform, fix the method of doing the job, and thereby reduce time and cost per unit of production.

The objections which are raised to the establishment of a standardized method of doing a task revolve around the perennial attitude that standards of any sort stifle imagination and improvement because they restrict performance to a rigidly defined manner. The counterargument to this attitude considers standards of any sort as steppingstones to further improvement. The setting of standards involves detailed insight and appreciation of whatever factors are under consideration. The knowledge of details is an essential preliminary to improvements. Standards provide this knowledge.

Classifications of Motion

Studies of the movements of manual workers have resulted in the recognition of five basic classifications of motion.

1. Finger movements
2. Finger and hand movements
3. Finger, hand, and lower-arm movements
4. Finger, hand, lower- and upper-arm movements
5. Finger, hand, lower- and upper-arm, and shoulder movements

When setting up the specific motions which a worker is to use in doing his job, there is the attempt to restrict each motion to the lowest possible classification. The lower the classification, the less is the energy output necessary to accomplish the desired movement. Fatigue is lessened. Time is saved.

Principles of Motion Economy

Motion analysis and study does not conform to the idea of "the right hand not knowing what the left hand is doing." Preferably both hands of a worker should be active and working together. One of the cardinal principles of motion economy is that idle time on the part of the worker's hands should be eliminated to whatever extent is practical. To apply this principle it is necessary to consider the worker in conjunction with the tools, materials, machines, and his workplace in order to involve all the factors which govern or restrict the extent to which the worker may efficiently use his body and limbs to do his job. The following principles of motion economy are applied by the motion analyst in the attempt to make work easier, safer, and more economical.

Principles applied to the worker:

1. Both hands should start and finish their work together.
2. Both hands should not be simultaneously idle except at rest periods.
3. Arm motion should be in symmetrical and usually opposite directions and should be made simultaneously.
4. Motions should be confined to the lowest possible classifications.
5. Momentum should be used to assist in doing the work and should be minimized if it has to be overcome by muscular effort.

6. Continuous and curved motions are preferable to straight-line motions which involve sharp changes in direction.
7. Ballistic movements are faster, easier, and more accurate than restricted movements.
8. A motion sequence should be established which has a rhythm and thereby develops automaticity in the operation.

FIGURE 18–1

CHECK POINTS OF MOTION ECONOMY AT THE WORKPLACE

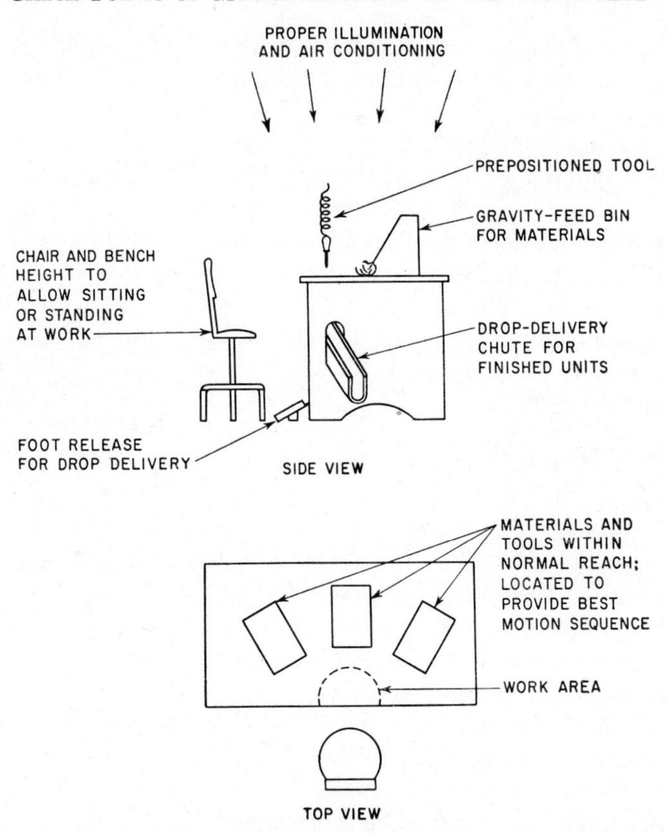

9. The feet or other parts of the body should be used to do work whenever possible, thereby relieving the hands.

Principles applied to the workplace:

1. Color scheme of workplace should assist in visual perception and reduce eye fatigue.
2. There should be no lifting of materials to point of use.
3. There should be no changes in direction of motion in the transport of materials or tools to the point of use.
4. Other principles are indicated in Figure 18–1.

Principles applied to the tools and equipment:

1. Two or more tools should be combined into one tool wherever possible.
2. Machines which are finger-operated, such as typewriters, should be designed to make use of the individual fingers according to their respective inherent capacities.
3. Tool handles should be of correspondingly larger surface area as the leverage to be exerted increases. This allows a greater palm area to come into contact with the handle.
4. Levers, cranks, and handwheels which are to be manipulated by an operator should be located so that the least change in body position and the best mechanical effort are made by the operator.

The above principles of motion economy form the bases upon which a standard method of doing a task is formulated.

The Analysis of Motion

Graphic devices are used to assist in depicting and analyzing the variety and efficiency of the motions performed by a worker. Among these devices are therbligs (symbols depicting motion classifications, developed by Frank Gilbreth), left-hand–right-hand charts, and man-machine charts.

Therbligs are a series of symbols, each of which depicts either a motion, a mental activity, or idleness. These symbols are a shorthand device. Some of the therbligs and their meanings are as follows:

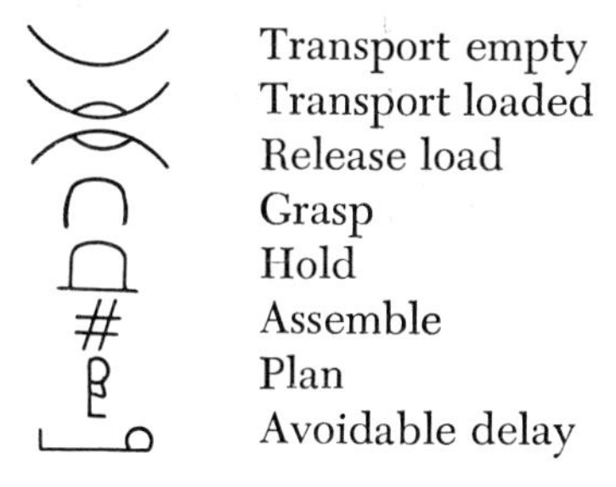

The motions involved when one hand of a worker reaches out and picks up an object are indicated by the following series of therbligs:

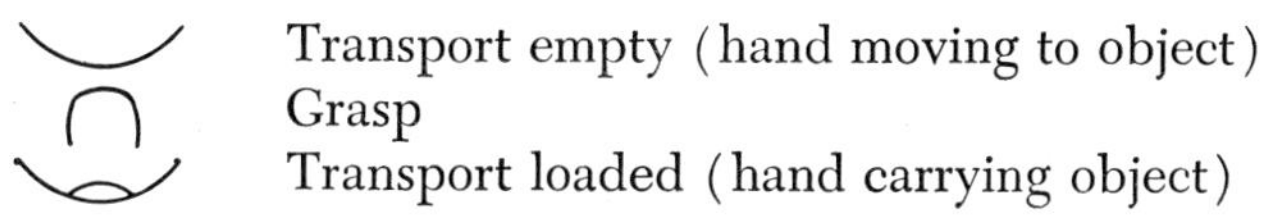

The motions of both hands must be considered, for a basic desire of motion-economy practice is that the hands be made to work together and that idleness on the part of either hand be eliminated if practical.

Left-hand–right-hand charts may involve the use of therbligs or other devices to portray the motions of both hands of a worker as he performs his task. If we assume the same series of motions as are involved in the preceding illustration, the LH–RH chart would appear as in Figure 18–2.

Other features which are recorded as a part of motion-study work are the time, distance, frequency, and nature of motion (or lack of motion).

FIGURE 18–2

LEFT-HAND–RIGHT-HAND CHART

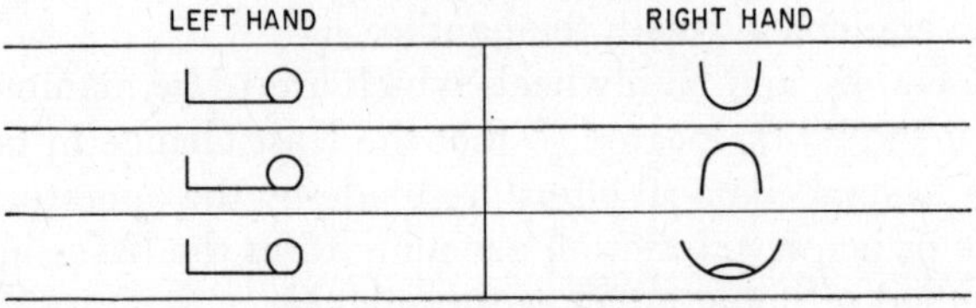

LEFT HAND	RIGHT HAND

The distance over which each movement is made is questioned by the analyst as to the extent that a revised workplace arrangement or a new method of performing the work may lessen the total distance of movement. Excessive idle time, delay, or holding is indicated by the frequency with which each respective symbol occurs. The addition of a time scale to the chart will show the amount of time which is lost or nonproductive because of a particular series of motions. The time scale will also allow a relative comparison of each motion as to its use or misuse of time.

FIGURE 18–3

MAN-MACHINE CHART

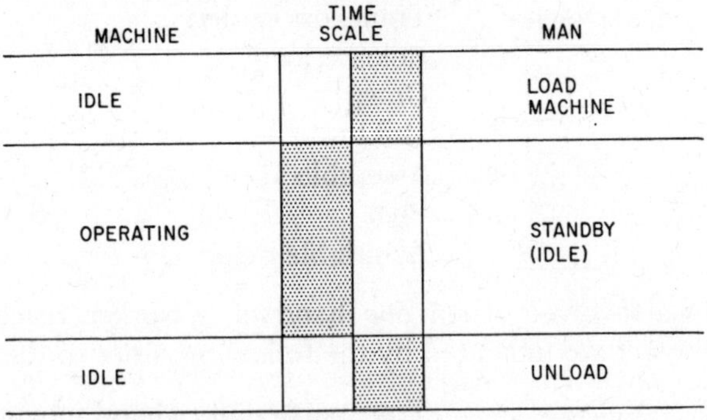

MACHINE	TIME SCALE	MAN
IDLE		LOAD MACHINE
OPERATING		STANDBY (IDLE)
IDLE		UNLOAD

Motion analysis attempts to reduce the present or proposed method of doing a job to a clear and detailed statement of facts which will allow an objective approach toward improvement.

Much of the work done in business involves the use of a machine by a worker. The man–machine chart may be used to depict the effectiveness with which the man and machine are used as a production team.

A worker who tends a machine which automatically performs an operation usually must attend only to loading and unloading it. The first illustration of the man–machine chart, Figure 18–3, shows that both the worker and the machine are idle a great deal of the time. Can better use be made of machine time? Can better use be made of man time?

In the search for answers to these questions, management has come upon automatic loading and unloading devices which replace the worker

FIGURE 18–4

MAN-MACHINE CHART

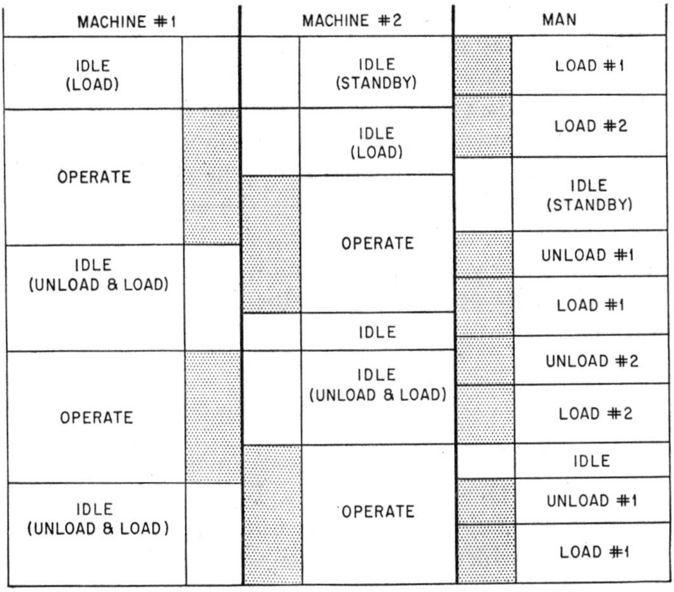

MACHINE #1
IDLE (LOAD)
OPERATE
IDLE (UNLOAD & LOAD)
OPERATE
IDLE (UNLOAD & LOAD)

MACHINE #2
IDLE (STANDBY)
IDLE (LOAD)
OPERATE
IDLE
IDLE (UNLOAD & LOAD)
OPERATE

MAN
LOAD #1
LOAD #2
IDLE (STANDBY)
UNLOAD #1
LOAD #1
UNLOAD #2
LOAD #2
IDLE
UNLOAD #1
LOAD #1

or the assignment of multiple machines to a worker in order to make more effective use of his time. If the worker activity as illustrated in the man–machine chart in Figure 18–3 were modified to involve his attendance to two machines, the chart depicting this new setup would appear as shown by Figure 18–4.

It is apparent in the second chart that much better use is being made of the worker's time. His idleness is almost eliminated.

The analysis and improvement of motion is a constant activity in industry. The material presented in this chapter presents an insight into the formal approach of motion analysis and improvement. However, every worker or supervisor is constantly seeking better and easier ways of accomplishing work. A gain is had whenever a task can be accomplished more easily, with greater speed, or with less cost as long as there is no sacrifice of the quality requirements of the work.

The improvements in methods of work are many times fostered and developed by the workers themselves. This would seem to indicate, and rightly so, that methods improvement need not be viewed as a highly specialized field of activity. The prevalence of suggestion systems which are used by firms to provide employees with a means of presenting their ideas for improvements is testimony to the fact that better methods need not originate solely in the methods department.

Often in the pursuit of methods improvement too much attention is given to one particular phase of work without recognizing it for its own worth and also for its relative importance as a part of a process. What consequences will result in the working of an over-all process must be considered before an attack is made upon any specific work area as the target for improvement.

As a result of motion analysis and adherence to the principles of motion economy, management is able to set the standard of "how" to do the job. This standard method forms the backbone of the training program for new workers. The instructions given to the new worker as to how he is to use machines, tools, his body, etc., are the direct results of the program of motion analysis, formal or informal. The standard method of performance is usually established concurrently with the standard time for performance.

TIME STANDARDS

Management seeks to achieve two goals in the use of time: first, to plan its use; second, to use it efficiently. Before planning the usage of time, there must be made available the information which will indicate the amount of time which each phase of work should take. If each aspect of production can be reduced to a statement of the respective amounts of time involved, the summation of these time periods provides the over-all time for the completion of the process.

Time study is a procedure whereby a job is subjected to observation and recording of the time which is taken to do the job. This information is then used in the development of a time standard, which is a statement of the average period of time that should be taken to do the job studied.

Management applies the time study procedure to a particular job, a machine operation, an over-all process, or any aspect of work for which some representative knowledge of the time factor is desired. Different methods of doing the same work may each be timed in the attempt to determine which method affords the best use of time.

The steps involved in preparing and taking a time study are as follows:

1. Establishing the method, equipment, and workplace conditions under which the job is to be done in the production area

2. Selecting and indoctrinating the worker who is to be studied as he performs the task
3. Breakdown of the job into elements suitable for timing purposes
4. Recording time
5. Grading the study
6. Applying allowances
7. Determining the time standard

The Method, Equipment, and Job Environment

A job which is to be studied must first be standardized as to the method of performance (motion study), the equipment, and the environment in which the job is to be performed. The areas of motion study and time study cannot actually be considered separately, for even as the best method is being devised, it is necessary to associate a time factor with each method under consideration.

The environment in which the job is to be performed has its influence upon the worker. A time study taken under conditions which are not representative of actual working conditions can give incorrect results.

Selection of the Worker

The worker who is selected for observation should be informed as to the purpose of the time study. There still exists on the part of some workers an attitude of fear and distrust towards time study. This attitude stems from the abuses of time study during the early years of its use. Even today it may be a common worker reaction that time study is a managerial device which seeks only to get more work out of a man for the same or a lesser amount of wages. The purpose of time study should be to establish as soundly as possible the time period which the average worker should take to do a specific task. Once established, the time standard may be used as a basis for setting wage rates, production quotas, and cost estimates. These standards also provide the basis on which the production planners establish the time schedule of work which is to be done in the plant.

Many have the opinion that the worker studied by the time-study man has a pronounced effect upon the final time standard which is calculated. The thought persists that an above-average worker will do work more quickly than an average worker, and that time-study results therefore depend upon and are biased by the particular subject studied. The significance of the worker who is studied and the means by which the time-study procedure attempts to eliminate such bias is discussed in later sections of this chapter.

The worker who is selected for observation should be sufficiently trained in the job method so as to provide a reasonable work performance for time-study purposes. This feature is of particular significance when the job to be studied is a new one. If a job of long standing is being studied for the first time or is being restudied, the need for training the worker is eliminated. An old job is classified as new if the job itself or any single feature of the job, such as the tools and materials used, the method, the workplace arrangement, the environment, or any other pertinent feature differs from that of the original job setup.

The Job Elements

A job which is to be subjected to timing is customarily broken up into its elements, or component parts. The performance of a complete unit of work comprises a cycle. Each cycle of work consists of elements which are the series of motions comprising the job. An athlete who runs a mile race finishes his unit of work when he has completed the mile. Thus the mile is the job, or cycle. However, the total race distance is readily broken down into laps, or fractions of the mile, for timing purposes. These laps or fractions comprise the elements of the cycle. Each element should be recognizable, capable of description, and of sufficient time duration to allow a recording of time. The stop watch may be used to time elements of as little as .03 to .04 min duration. A time-study machine, the Marstochron, will record elements of .01 min duration. Micromotion analysis involves the taking of motion pictures of the job which not only allow time readings to .001 min or better, but also provide the most detailed motion analysis.

Recording Time

The actual timing of the job as done by a time-study man involves close attention to the worker's performance and the recording of the actual time taken to accomplish each element of each cycle of work which is observed.

During the course of the study, the analyst records the occurrence of, and the time lapse due to, foreign elements which may enter into the performance of the worker. If the man being studied has to pick up material which was dropped during a work cycle or if he must adjust his machine or move materials, these interruptions to the basic operation should be noted and recorded if possible so that time lost due to causes other than the routine performance of work can be eliminated from the study.

How many cycles should be recorded in order to provide a reliable time study? The duration of the study will depend upon the time taken for each cycle. If the job consists of a relatively short time cycle, such as 1 min, a study of 15 to 30 min will provide many observations. As the work cycle becomes longer and more complex, hours or even days of time study may become necessary. More cycles must be observed if stopwatch technique is applied than if Marstochron or micromotion studies are made. The time machine and motion pictures provide much more detailed and reliable studies in shorter periods than does the stop watch.

Grading the Study

As soon as the recording of time is completed, the study should be graded. The analyst may evaluate the job on the basis of the following factors:

1. The skill displayed by the worker
2. The effort exerted on the part of the worker
3. The consistency of the performance
4. The conditions under which the job was performed

The purpose of grading is to compensate for the extent to which the particular job studied and the performance recorded deviate from "normal." This phase of time-study procedure is most often subjected to criticism and attack. The same study as graded by one analyst may differ from the grading applied by another analyst. These variations in grading are primarily the result of different concepts of "normal." The training of time-study personnel by means of motion pictures which portray normal work and variations from normal work has proved effective in narrowing the range of grading interpretations.

The time-study work up to this point has been, for the most part, scientific. We must now involve the human element, judgment, in order to grade the study. Experience in grading is probably the most important factor in the development of ability to accomplish effectively this particular aspect of time-study work.

Each of the four grading factors is stated mathematically as to the extent to which it deviates from the "norm."

The grading of skill may involve interpretation of the craftsmanship, knowledge, judgment, and accuracy which the worker displays.

The grading of effort may involve the recognition of the extent to which the worker overexerts himself or kills time, concentrates or shows lack of interest in work, works consistently or is irregular.

The consistency of a performance is indicated by the record of watch readings. The analyst reviews the time readings recorded for each element of the study. He determines the consistency grading on the basis of the extent of variations in time periods taken to perform each respective element. If each element was done in exactly the same time each time it occurred as part of a cycle, the consistency would be perfect for this element. Usually, the greater the skill of the worker, the more consistent is his performance. The grading of consistency does not depend upon the experience or judgment of the analyst. Factual data, the time recordings, are the basis for establishing this grading.

The conditions existing while the job is studied are graded in so far as they vary from the conditions standardized for the job.

The grading of the study is reduced to mathematical terms by first defining the study as being above or below average in terms of each factor. The particular evaluations are then translated into numerical equivalents by means of a grading scale. (See Figure 18–5.) The grading may be ap-

FIGURE 18–5

A TIME-STUDY GRADING SCALE

	Skill	*Effort*	*Consistency*	*Conditions*
+.15	A_1 Super			
+.13	A_2 Super	A_1 Excessive		
+.12		A_2 Excessive		
+.11	B_1 Excellent			
+.10		B_1 Excellent		
+.08	B_2 Excellent	B_2 Excellent		
+.06	C_1 Good			A Ideal
+.05		C_1 Good		
+.04			A Perfect	B Excellent
+.03	C_2 Good		B Excellent	
+.02		C_2 Good		
+.01			C Good	C Good
.00	D Average	D Average	D Average	D Average
−.02			E Fair	
−.03		E_1 Fair		E Fair
−.04			F Poor	
−.05	E_1 Fair			
−.07				F Poor
−.08		E_2 Fair		
−.10	E_2 Fair			
−.12		F_1 Poor		
−.16	F_1 Poor			
−.17		F_2 Poor		
−.22	F_2 Poor			

SOURCE: Lowry, Maynard, and Stegemerten, *Time and Motion Study,* McGraw-Hill Book Co., Inc., New York, 1940. (Adapted.)

plied to the work cycle as a whole or to the individual elements. If the analyst determines that the elements of the job are not comparable for grading purposes, he will grade each element separately. If the job cycle consists in part of elements which are automatically performed by a machine and are in no way influenced by the operator, such elements are not subjected to grading.

As an alternative grading method each element of the time study may be graded solely on the basis of the operator's speed. This is a simpler method but also relies upon personal judgment. In this case a grading table is used which gives numerical grading for the single factor, speed.

Applying Allowances

An average man is not expected to apply himself completely to his job during every working hour of the day. He is not capable of this degree of application. There will be interruptions which will force him to take his attention from the job. Allowance must be made for such interruptions before the standard time for the job is stated. The short period of time during which a man is time-studied is no real indication of the rate of production which he will be able to maintain throughout the working day.

The allowances which are made on the job are usually of three types:

1. *Personal Allowances.* These represent the time necessary for the worker to attend to his personal needs. This commonly ranges from a 3 per cent to a 5 per cent time allowance. It tends to be higher when work is heavier or more unpleasant.

2. *Fatigue Allowances.* This type of allowance recognizes that fatigue tends to limit production. It is made on the theory that it will provide a period for relaxation during the course of work, thereby eliminating or reducing the occurrence of fatigue. Fatigue allowances are usually low in plants where management has conscientiously established job methods and working conditions which serve to minimize fatigue. A common practice in light manufacturing work is to give an average allowance of 3 per cent. The severity of the individual job must be considered when establishing this allowance.

3. *Delay Allowances.* Both avoidable and unavoidable delays will occur during working hours. Avoidable delays are the interruptions to work which should not be included in job times. They are unnecessary and not assignable to the nature of the job. Unavoidable delays are the minor interruptions which will occur as part of the job, such as tool breakage, faulty materials, and the need for machine adjustment. These unavoidable delays should be minimized. The determination of how much allowance should be made for unavoidable delays involves careful study of the job routine. If possible, a study should be made over a sufficiently long period of time in order that the nature, frequency, and time duration of various delay items can be recorded. This information then serves to determine delay time as a percentage of production time.

The Determination of the Time Standard

Assume that an operation consists of nailing the tops on wooden boxes. The four elements of the cycle are as follows:

Element #1. Pick up and position wooden top on box.
" #2. Pick up hammer in right hand and nails in left.
" #3. Drive eight nails in designated places.
" #4. Push sealed box along conveyor with left hand and deposit hammer on bench with the right hand.

The following table of figures represents the actual time in seconds which was taken to perform each element for a total series of ten cycles.

CYCLES

Element	1	2	3	4	5	6	7	8	9	10
#1	5	5	5	6	5	4	5	5	5	6
#2	2	2	3	2	2	3	3	2	2	2
#3	22	24	24	21	25	27	24	25	28	24
#4	3	3	3	4	3	3	4	3	3	3

(Time is recorded in seconds.)

From the above data a representative time must be determined for each element. This is called the *selected time.* It may be determined by calculating an arithmetic average or by examining each series of element times and selecting any one figure which appears to be most representative of the group.

The determination of selected time by means of the arithmetic average is as follows:

Element	*Total Time (in sec)*	*No. of Cycles*	*Selected Time (in sec)*
#1	51	10	5.1
#2	23	10	2.3
#3	244	10	24.4
#4	32	10	3.2
Total selected time per cycle			35.0

The next step is the application of the grading factor to the selected time. The job has been graded on an over-all basis as follows:

Factor	*Grading*	*Numerical Value**
Skill	Good C_2	+.03
Effort	Good C_1	+.05
Consistency	Good C	+.01
Conditions	Fair E	−.03
	Sum of Grading	+.06

* Values are taken from the table presented as Figure 18–5.

The sum of the grading factors, +.06, indicates that the performance of the worker was above average. A negative sum would indicate a below-average performance. In this particular case, the worker did his work in less time than would have been taken for an average performance. Since the purpose of grading the study is to state time in terms of an average performance, it is evident that the total *graded time* in this case will be greater than the total selected time. To determine the graded time, multiply total selected time by the factor 1.06. Average grading is stated as 1.00 (or 100 per cent). The sum of the factors is added to 1.00 to determine the total grading factor.

Total Selected Time	×	*Total Grading Factor*	=	*Total Graded Time*
35	×	1.06	=	37.10 seconds

The allowances for this job are as follows:

	Per cent
Personal	4
Fatigue	5
Unavoidable delays	5
Total allowances	14

Total graded time is increased by 14 per cent, the sum of the allowances.

Total Graded Time	×	*Allowance %*	=	*Allowance*
37.1	×	14%	=	5.198 sec

Total graded time	37.1
Total allowances	5.198
Standard time per cycle	42.3 sec

Our illustration establishes a time standard of approximately 42 sec for each unit of production. In one hour's time an average worker should turn out almost 86 units of work.

The determination of a time standard allows management to anticipate the rate of production and plan the use of time more effectively; it also provides the basis for establishing incentive-wage plans.

Other Approaches to the Setting of Time Standards

Many time standards are set on the basis of job experience rather than by specific time study. Responsible personnel who have supervised or worked on particular types of operations may be able to estimate with reliable accuracy the time which a particular operation should take. A shop which handles a great variety of work, none of which is carried out on a volume basis, will resort to past experience with similar work as the basis on which to establish time standards for new jobs.

Another means of arriving at time standards involves the classification of time data in the form of a manual of element times. Studies of different jobs will provide much basic data for this manual. An operation for which a standard is to be set may not involve the same product or overall process as other jobs which were actually time-studied, but it may involve some elements of work which are common. Many if not all of the element times of a new job may be available in the time-data files. The procedure of establishing the time standard involves the finding of as many pieces to the puzzle as it is possible to find in the file of data and then filling in the gaps, if any, by taking time studies or by estimating times for those elements for which no previous data are available.

A third method, labeled MTM, methods-time measurement, is based upon the conclusion that all normal human activities are combinations or sequences of unvarying basic motions. MTM classifies all these basic motions and applies time values to each. With such data it is possible to take any task, regardless of product or process involved, and classify the human activities into basic motions. The motion pattern is recorded, and then by reference to time tables the time values of motions are added to equal the time standard.

QUALITY STANDARDS

The plans for production must include the definition of the quality requirements of the product. Management desires that the quality which its products possess be neither excessive nor deficient. It is possible to make too good a product as well as too poor a product. Quality standards are established to ensure that the product which is shipped conforms to the standards established by the company for manufacturing purposes and by the customer according to the use to which he is to put the product. This latter is called functional use, or the extent to which the product will do what it is designed to do.

The quality standards of production should be set in recognition of the relationship between resultant cost of production and the selling price of the product. Each of the quality features of a product helps determine the nature of materials, labor, and machines which must be used in the process. The quality standards must be stated so as to make clear to the workers the necessary characteristics of production and so as to provide some basis for determining whether a unit is acceptable or must be rejected. This involves the establishment of limits of acceptability.

Any physical attribute or the performance characteristics of a product may be subject to a defined standard of quality. Dimensions, degree of surface smoothness or finish, malleability, viscosity, and weight are examples of product attributes. Performance characteristics refer to the extent to which the product will do what it is designed to do and also to its potential life in use.

How and When to Inspect

When, in the process of manufacture, is the product to be subjected to inspection? What specific inspection procedures are to be followed, and what inspection devices are to be used? These questions are raised in connection with the establishment of quality standards. Different inspection procedures may be established.

1. *One Hundred per Cent Inspection.* Every unit is inspected.
2. *Sampling Inspection.* If it is not practical or is too costly to inspect each piece, a random sample from a batch is inspected. If the sample is satisfactory, the batch is accepted. If the sample is unsatisfactory, the entire batch may either be inspected piece by piece or rejected as a whole. Statistical methods are used to determine the portion of total quantity of the batch which will serve as a reliable sample.
3. *Destructive Testing.* This method tests the resistance or effectiveness of the product. A sample steel or wooden beam may be tested to determine the point at which it will collapse under pressure or weight. Paper samples may be tested to determine the tearing point. Thread may be tested for its breaking point. Explosives may be set off to test the explosive effects. In each test the product is destroyed.
4. *Performance Testing.* The product is used. An engine may be run on a test stand. A pen may be subjected to a writing test.

Inspection may occur during production and/or upon completion of production. The inspection may occur as a built-in feature of production. In the case of product-line layout, the machines which do the work on the product are arranged in sequence so that one check at a key point may serve as a check on preceding operations. In some cases, where the cost of the part is insignificant, specific inspection stations or procedures may not be established. It may be left to the worker who uses the part to discover that the part is defective. In assembly operations, parts may be so designed and handled in production that a defect in work becomes obvious when a worker attempts to perform a succeeding operation. If a particular operation is very critical or expensive, inspection may occur prior to and immediately after this operation. The attempt here is to prevent doing critical work on a piece which is not up to par to begin with and also to catch defective work from the critical operation before it has a chance to move on to the next stage of production.

Systems of Inspection

Two main systems of inspection are used singly or in combination.

Floor inspection occurs in the production area. The inspection may consist of a general checking of the product or a specific setup of inspection stations within the production line.

Centralized inspection is carried on in a specifically designated inspection area which is separate from the production area. The product is brought into this area where supervised inspection procedures are carried out. Since the inspection work is concentrated in an area, very effective procedures and specialized equipment can be set up. Several central inspection stations may be established at different locations in the plant. Each one will serve a particular production area.

The disadvantages involved in the use of centralized inspection are:

1. Defective work may be discovered too late to stop a large amount of spoilage.
2. There is more material handling and tie-up of product.
3. There is the need for greater work effort in coordinating the flow of materials through production and inspection.

Summary of Quality Standards

Management sets its standards for quality on the following bases:

1. What features to inspect
2. How to inspect
3. When and where to inspect
4. Why inspect

The question of "why inspect" is always raised as a means of eliminating unnecessary inspection or as a means of validating such inspection standards as may already have been set up.

Inspection procedures and quality standards are actually a means to an end. Inspection procedures in themselves do not create quality in the product. The desired end result is the control of the quality of output. Quality control will be discussed in Chapter 19, Production Planning and Control.

ECONOMIC MANUFACTURING-LOT SIZE

The planning of production, the setting up of machines, the manpower, the materials and facilities of a plant are sources of production costs. Is there a desirable production level at which it is preferable to operate? Is there any relationship between the unit cost of production and the volume of production? Management seeks to determine whether or not there is a most desirable method of using its plant facilities in order to produce a given volume of production. The calculation of the economic manufacturing-lot size will provide management with some information which may be used in answering these questions.

If a total volume of 20,000 units is to be produced for sales during the year, is it most economical to produce the total quantity all at once and carry the item in stock pending sales? Would it be preferable to produce 10,000 units or some other quantity at different times during the year as long as the total production totalled 20,000 units? If the single large-production run is made, inventory will be high, greater storage costs will be incurred, and there is greater danger of losses from obsolescence, depreciation, and deterioration of the product while it is being held in inventory pending sale. If the market for the product should fail, the company will have on hand a large quantity of an item which it may not be able to sell or dispose of except at a loss. On the other hand, the production of all the requirements on the basis of a single production run of 20,000 units provides some savings. The clerical aspects of production and the physical setup of the plant are necessary for a single occasion. If the manufacturing-lot size were smaller, the inventory risks and some costs would be lowered, but clerical and setup costs would be incurred for each production run necessary in the accumulation of the 20,000 units.

The economic manufacturing-lot size is that quantity of an item which should be manufactured at one time so as to realize the lowest possible unit cost. If the item to be manufactured is one which is regularly carried in stock, the economic lot size may serve as the stock reorder quantity.

Determining the Economic Manufacturing-lot Size

There are many formulas available which serve to identify the economic lot size. Each one is tailored to fit the needs of a particular situation. One management may consider that its costs involve factors which must be considered in a different order of importance than does another management. For our purposes a simplified version of the calculation of economic lot size will suffice. The cost factors involved are as follows:

1. Total production cost per piece
2. Total inventory carrying charges
3. Total setup costs

The total production cost per piece includes direct labor, materials, and overhead.

Inventory carrying charges, which may run as high as 25 per cent per year, represent the cost of keeping an inventory on hand. These inventory charges result from losses in inventory due to spoilage, theft, and depreciation, and the handling charges and costs incurred for storage of goods. The cost also includes an interest charge on the average dollar-investment in inventory.

The total setup cost represents the expense of preparing a production line for work, and this involves the setting up of machines to do specific operations. The cost will also include the clerical costs which are associated with production planning and control work. Setup cost may be very significant in shops where general-purpose equipment is used.

Assume the following data:

Production quantity for the year: 12,000 units
Setup cost per production run: $100

Number of runs per year:	12	6	4	3	2
Size of production run:	1000 units	2000 units	3000 units	4000 units	6000 units
Total setup cost...........	$ 1,200	600	400	300	200
Total production cost......	48,000	46,500	45,000	44,000	44,000
Inventory carrying charge...	400	800	1,200	2,000	3,000
Total cost................	$49,600	47,900	46,600	46,300	47,200
Cost per unit..............	$4.13	3.99	3.88	3.86	3.93

Area of economic manufacturing-lot size

The economic lot size is in the vicinity of 3,000 to 4,000 units, or approximately three to four production runs per year. This would appear to be the most desirable level of production, for it is the one at which unit costs are at their minimum.

If management knows the economic manufacturing-lot size, production of certain items may be postponed until a sufficient backlog of orders is available to provide the necessary manufacturing quantity. Many other factors, however, may prevent management from adhering strictly to the principle of economic lot size. The existence of idle plant capacity, the need to satisfy a rush order, or the inability of management to forecast accurately the arrival of additional orders for a product may force management to overlook the aspect of economical lot size and to produce at a volume level which does not provide the lowest unit cost of production.

If circumstances allow, it is definitely to management's advantage to consider as part of its production planning activity the extent to which unit production costs are influenced by variation in the quantity of a product which may be produced at any one time.

MATERIAL STANDARDS

Chapters 16 and 17 bring into focus those aspects of purchasing and inventory activities that are important to the planning of production. Details concerning the quantity of purchase, frequency of purchase, nature of purchase, etc., are discussed. The student should refer to the chapters indicated in order to reacquaint himself with the nature of planning for material usage. Some of the standards established for materials are the standard ordering quantity; the order point; and material specifications as to type, amount, and time of need. These and other facts such as the current inventory data are the bases upon which effective planning for material usage may be carried out. Production cannot commence or continue without an adequate and satisfactory supply of materials which must be available when and where they are needed.

Standards for materials are established to assist in maintaining the correct relationship between the types and amounts of goods which are needed for the production program and those which are available for use.

COST ESTIMATES

Cost estimates are the final development of the production-planning activity. The significance of each area of planning must be stated in terms of dollars and cents. Management does not knowingly assume the responsibility of production without knowledge of the costs with which it must contend and which it must attempt to control. Control in any area of endeavor cannot be exercised unless some basic measuring stick has been established which will serve to indicate when the situation is in or out of control.

Source of Costs

All business activity involves cost. The sources of cost are basically men, materials, machines, and facilities. Costs increase or decrease in relationship to three factors: the duration of the activity, the quantity of activity, and the quality of activity.

Throughout the planning stages of production the emphasis has primarily rested upon these three factors—time, quantity, and quality.

Derivation of Cost Estimates

The plan of production represents a preview of what management believes will occur. Necessarily, it must be subject to change, for business itself is dynamic; therefore, any business unit must recognize that the "best laid plans of mice and men . . ." However, some basis must be established as a fixed point, even if only temporary, in order that a start may be made. This start involves, among other factors, the establishment of the estimates of the costs which will be incurred if the production plan is followed.

The cost estimates may be established as follows:

1. *Material.* The quantity of specific materials to be used *times* the respective unit costs.

2. *Labor.* The quantity of each labor skill *times* the respective hours of work *times* the respective labor wage rates. If time standards have been established, the quantity of labor and the necessary hours of work may be determined as follows: Quantity of production *times* standard time per unit of production *equals* total time necessary to accomplish a quantity of production.

The total man-hours determined as necessary to do the task when related to the production schedule will indicate what number of workers must be put on the job so that the work will be done within the scheduled time period.

3. *Machines.* For each particular machine, the hours of operation *times* the hourly cost for machine time.

The hours of machine operation will depend upon the machine rate of output in relation to the desired production quantity.

The hourly cost for machine time arises from three sources: the cost to possess, to service, and to operate.

Machine possession costs are depreciation, insurance, and taxes. These costs do not usually vary with the extent to which a machine is used. Therefore, a higher cost rate per machine-hour is associated with a low rate of machine use, and vice versa.

The service charge includes repairs and maintenance, power, light, heat, supervision, setup costs, and, in general, those expenses incurred by the area or department in which the machine is in use, e.g., the power cost to operate the machine. Other costs are incurred whether the particular machine is in operation or not. They are the stand-by costs. A higher service charge per machine hour is associated with a low rate of use, and vice versa.

In the case of both service and possession costs, management in establishing the production plan must recognize that there will always be a certain fixed amount of cost which will have to be borne regardless of the level at which the plant operates.

The cost to operate the machine refers to the wages which are paid to the operator. This cost may be that referred to under the labor-cost category.

4. *Facilities.* These costs are those associated with the administration of the organization. The problem here is one of recognizing not only the extent of these costs, but also that the goods which are to be manufactured and sold represent the only source of income available for the payment of these costs. Therefore, in planning the cost of operations, some basis must be devised not only for assigning the anticipated cost of facili-

ties to production, but also for recognizing the extent to which these costs will vary with production.

There is no simple approach in expressing the relationship which should exist between the facilities' costs and the planned-production program. Experience and a scientific approach in the evaluation of the cost relationships must serve as the guide in establishing the cost standard for facilities.

Need for Cost Estimates

Although we cannot expect that cost estimates always be completely accurate, we do find that they are necessary in order that sound bids may be offered to customers and that management may have some assurance of the ability of its production scheme to provide its product within the competitive price range. Companies which manufacture to order must submit price bids before getting orders. Companies which manufacture to stock also find cost estimating of extreme importance, for product attributes are set in accordance with an anticipated selling price; and if any fluctuations occur in the cost of achieving the necessary volume and quality of production, it is quite possible that losses will occur.

Cost estimation is preferably done after all the details of the product and its production have been established, but this is not always the case. Many times the process of estimating costs results in the recognition that a more economical method is necessary. Cost estimation is a means of evaluating alternative methods which may be available for doing the job.

Requirements for Accurate Estimating

Those who are entrusted with the responsibility of cost estimating should have a thorough acquaintance with the products and processes of the company, the nature of the equipment and its potential for work; and finally they should also know something of the cost, volume, and price interrelationships which exist.

Careful estimating requires that the details of production be written out. Such information as materials lists, parts lists, operations nature and times, etc., are indicative of the details necessary.

SUMMARY

This chapter has been devoted to an exploration of the establishment of bases for production planning. These bases are those pertinent to performance in the work area, and as such are established after the work facilities have been set up. However, the consideration of these bases must be concurrent with the planning of the facilities because of their counterpart natures.

The manner in which the job is to be done and the establishment of the time which it should take to do the job provide management with the information necessary to determine and allocate men, machines, and time as needed to perform assigned tasks. Furthermore, such standards become bases for the comparison of actual performance with the theoretical or standard as a means of control.

The desired quality of materials and work must likewise be predetermined in the interests of satisfying market requirements and turning out a product which is neither too good nor certainly less than suitable.

In the interests of economical practice and enhancing the profitability of operations, it is necessary that the effect of variation in the quantity of production of an item be investigated so that the most efficient manufacturing-lot size may be determined.

Since the final measurement of business success is typically the rate of profits, it is necessary that the bases for production planning also include an estimation of the costs of production in order that some assurance be had that planned work and its cost are in line with competitive needs. This estimation of costs also provides a means of comparing actual costs as they are incurred to the estimates of cost, thereby giving indication of satisfactory or faulty cost situations.

QUESTIONS

1. The cycle of business activity may be said to involve three phases. What are these three phases? How does each fit into the over-all planning activity of management?
2. What is the nature of motion study?
3. What objection is raised to the establishment of standards? What is the counterargument to this attitude?
4. The principles of motion economy apply in three areas. What are these areas?
5. What is a therblig? Its use?
6. What features of the job would you consider important enough to be recorded on a left-hand–right-hand or a man-machine chart? For what reason(s)?
7. What are the steps involved in preparing for and taking a time study?
8. What is the significance of that part of time-study procedure which involves selection of the worker who is to be studied?
9. If the total selected time for a work cycle is 17 min, 30 sec, the sum of grading factors is −.04, and total allowances amount to 10 per cent, what is the standard time for one work cycle?
10. What is the purpose of grading a time study?

11. What are the three types of allowances made on jobs being time-studied? What is the reason for applying allowances?

12. List five reasons for the establishment of quality standards.

13. Identify four different inspection procedures.

14. What is meant by "economic manufacturing-lot size"? What cost factors are involved in its determination?

15. Where do cost estimates fit into the picture of planning for production?

16. Why are cost estimates necessary?

CHAPTER 19

Production Planning and Control

By this time it would seem that we have adequately learned the lesson that prior to activity we must have a plan. In addition, in order that there be some assurance that the plans are soundly conceived and adhered to, some sort of checking or control devices must be put to use. The creation and execution of a plan of work in the factory is generally referred to as Production Planning and Control. This title is indicative of three things:

1. Bases for planning work have been established.
2. The plan of organization of work has been established in detail and preferably has been recorded.
3. Such devices as are available and practical have been set up to serve as controls over the production process to ensure as much as is possible that the desired production plan is adhered to and to provide management with immediate information of discrepancies or inadequacies in the plan of production or its performance.

Communication As a Link

Communication is the key to successful operations. A flow of information must occur among those who are responsible for planning, controlling, and performing work. In some cases these activities may involve but one person; this fact, nevertheless, does not diminish the need for a plan, adherence to it, and some means of recognizing and correcting errors. Of course, where many people in different locations are all part of the same planning and control effort, the task of communication is more complex and costly. Verbal contacts, paper-work flow, graphs, charts, bells, flashing lights, sirens, mechanical and electrical indicators, and any other device which may serve to convey information or meaning are communicative devices. Too often we think of communication solely in terms of the spoken word.

In the ordinary business firm the details of work which must be coordinated and communicated are never few in number. It would seem at times that the flow of paper work and other communication involves more work than does the work effort itself. If the flow serves a needed purpose and its cost does not exceed the saving it accomplishes, it is warranted.

THE MASTER PLAN—ROUTING AND SCHEDULING

Regardless of the nature of the operations to be performed or the size of the company there are few variations in the basic functions of production planning. Each company will either receive orders for specific goods or services or else will produce its goods for stock awaiting orders. In either event it is necessary to break down the order into requirements for parts, raw materials, the operations which will have to be performed, and the men and machines required. This type of preliminary planning is necessary to be sure that facilities are available when they are needed. It is at this stage that we can most easily see the complete interdependence of all the company departments. The purchasing and inventory-control divisions are concerned with the provisions for raw materials and parts. The personnel department is concerned with the adequacy of labor supply and skills. The engineering divisions are needed for the work of process analysis, time study and motion study, and other information which is essential in the planning stages.

Routing

This is the determination of the sequence of operations necessary to manufacture a product or to carry out a procedure. The first step is preparing a list of the steps involved. This list should indicate the nature of each operation and the equipment necessary to perform it. From this listing the most economical and practical method of doing the particular task is determined. Often a given step in the operation may be performed by different types of equipment or by different methods. In this event the choice is finally made on the basis of availability of equipment and lowest unit cost of production.

The routing of production is much more of a task in those firms which produce a great variety of products and do not have a specialized layout. This is the case with the custom shop. Each product calls for an individual approach to production and must therefore be individually planned. At the same time, the facilities of the company must be devoted to the production requirements of many varying products. This fact complicates planning, for constant decisions must be made regarding the allocation of specific machines to one order in preference to another. Because of this it is not always possible to produce at the lowest unit cost. Management may be forced to use a higher-cost procedure because of nonavailability of equipment if it wishes to satisfy the customer by meeting the scheduled delivery date.

Once established, the route of production for repetitive process remains fixed until the product or process changes. Such changes are costly and, therefore, management strives in its initial process planning to arrive at the most effective plant layout consistent with the needs of the production process.

In addition to establishing the most desirable sequence of operations, the routing function calls for the establishment of the time element involved in each step of the process. This information comes via motion and time study. Since all production planning and control is aimed at making the most effective use of facilities consistent with customer demands, it becomes necessary that accurate statements of the need of time of both men and machines be available.

Routing is fundamental to the execution of the production plan. It provides the basis for the establishment of the production schedule and for the dispatching function which initiates actual production. It fixes the sequence of operations, the equipment and manpower need, the time element, the departmental locations in which the work is to be done, and possibly the specific workers and machines which are involved in carrying out the work order. The routing function finally evolves in the form of a route sheet which contains all the information indicated above. Once a master route sheet for a product has been prepared, it is kept on file in the event that repeat orders come in.

Scheduling

The function of routing establishes the "how" of production. Scheduling establishes the "when" of production and determines the time at which each stage of production should be started and completed in order that the desired completion date be met. On some occasions, prior to accepting an order, the management must work backward from the customer's desired completion date to determine when production must start in order to finish on schedule.

When the job calls for the manufacture and assembly of many parts into a completed unit, it is very important that the time schedule of operations be carefully planned and executed so that parts are available when needed for assembly.

Scheduling not only sets up the time when each process step should occur but also serves as a control or check device in that actual performance may be checked against the schedule.

Although it is much easier said than done, it is desirable that the scheduling function be flexible enough to include provision for the emergencies which occur in the course of normal operations and also that it make whatever provision possible for the handling of rush orders.

The scheduling function in some companies is carried out by the production control department. In other companies it is carried out on a decentralized basis wherein the foreman of each department assumes responsibility for getting the work done on schedule. In either event, centralized or decentralized scheduling needs some degree of coordination to assure management that commitment dates will be met.

Scheduling cannot be carried out unless production rates of the plant, departments, machines, and individuals are known. Time study will provide the data on the production rates of the man and machine. The combined rates of man-machine teams will give the departmental rates of production. The sum of the departmental rates will provide the plant capacity in terms of the particular product(s) being planned. The overall production schedule of the plant and the amount of each respective product scheduled to be produced are finally reduced to a time basis in the form of a master schedule. This schedule provides the time basis for work flow, shows the sales department the expected volume of work to be completed, and provides a basis for quoting delivery dates.

THE CONTROL OF PRODUCTION

Up to this point our discussion has been concerned solely with the planning of production. We have concerned ourselves with the physical needs of production and the time features involved. As yet there has been no start of production. The production activity commences once we are assured that all the planning has been taken care of. Our planning activities have been finally reduced to written schedules or statements which will provide the basis for authorizing all activities and for checking upon the adequacy of performance in the work areas.

Paper Work

As a necessary coordinating element in our system of production planning and control, paper work serves as the basic communicative device. The route and schedule of production have been reduced to written statements. In addition it is necessary to state all other necessary authorizations for work, material movement, material usage, equipment and tool utilization. These written statements are what we refer to as production-control paper work. They serve as the authorization for work and as the communicative devices which tie together the various elements of the production system in order that all effort will be coordinated in the accomplishment of the assigned task.

Some of the paper work involved in production control is as follows:

Materials: Purchase requisitions, materials reservation orders, materials move orders.

Men and Machines: Job and time tickets, work orders.

The Product: Inspection orders, rework orders, completion schedules.

The purpose of the above paper work is to provide authorization for the procurement and use of materials; instructions and authority for the use of men, machines, and facilities; instructions and authority for the movement of materials according to the established schedule; and authority to inspect and order replacements as the need may occur.

Dispatching

The time schedule of production is put into operation by means of the function called "dispatching." The dispatcher is responsible for maintaining the sequence and flow of work orders to the various production areas. These work orders are part of the production-control paper work. They are the authorizations to the departments or the workmen in the various departments to do certain tasks as instructed on the work orders. The dispatching function is actually the "go" signal for the wheels of production. Material-move orders, instructions to truckers and to the tool crib are also released on schedule so that all activities are coordinated according to plan.

As each job is handed out or completed, the central-control office is informed so that progress of actual production in comparison with planned production may be noted.

In many companies the dispatcher himself may establish the sequence of jobs and assign them to available workers. He must in this case have a basic guide of job priority in order to make logical choices of work. In some companies which are less highly organized, the foremen of the various areas may be responsible for the dispatching function.

Production Follow-up

Once the work has been dispatched to the various departments or work stations, the first stage of production control has been accomplished. How successfully depends upon whether the work was started according to the master schedule. It is at this time that follow-up procedures commence. The production follow-up function is designed to keep track of the work effort with an eye towards smoothing the way for each order, anticipating difficulties, and in general trying to keep the work on course and on schedule. This activity may be accomplished under different follow-up systems. Departmental follow-up refers to the situation wherein each department assigns personnel whose specific function it is to make sure that work assigned to the department enters, passes through, and leaves the department in accordance with both the work orders and the time schedule. A fathering system of follow-up may be used wherein a particular work order is assigned to a follow-up man and it becomes his responsibility to keep track of this particular order during its complete process. In either case, the follow-up man is attempting to facilitate the production process. Other follow-up devices involve the use of visual and graphic forms on which are posted the performance data which are called in to the production-control center from the work areas. This information is compared with the established plan for comparison and for an indication as to whether corrections or adjustments must be made in the plan or the performance of work.

Progress Chart

One of the visual devices used to portray the status of a production plan is called the "progress chart." The reports which are periodically

FIGURE 19–1

PRODUCTION-PROGRESS CHART

PLANNING SCHEDULE FOR WEEK *JULY 11–16*

MACHINE NO.	MONDAY	TUESDAY	WEDNESDAY	THURSDAY	FRIDAY	SATURDAY
B–04						
D–05						
		R				
B–11	*R* *R*	*R*				

GANTT TYPE CHART USED FOR DAY-TO-DAY SCHEDULING

R INDICATES: DOWN FOR REPAIRS ┌──┐ INDICATES: RESERVED TIME

THE PLANT IN THIS CASE WORKS A SIX-DAY WEEK, EIGHT HOURS EACH DAY. EACH BLOCK EQUALS 4 HOURS

sent to the production-control center are posted on this chart in order that a quick interpretation may be had of the progress of work in comparison with the prescribed plan. The chart will indicate where failure is occurring, thus enabling appropriate investigation and action to be taken.

The progress chart is ruled up to represent the working hours of the plant. All the machines or production benches in use are listed by name or number along the left-hand side of the sheet. (See Figure 19–1.) Each order to be processed is first analyzed as to the order in which it will make use of the machines. Commencing with the first machine to be used, the scheduling proceeds.

An angle opening to the right ┏ indicates work is scheduled to start.

An angle opening to the left ┓ indicates the scheduled completion date.

A light line connecting the angles indicates the total time schedule for the order. ┏━━━━━┓

Each machine or bench to be used for a particular order is first checked for its availability and is then scheduled for use.

The progress of work is indicated by a heavy line drawn under the light line. ┏━━━━━┓ If the work is on schedule, the end of the heavy line will coincide with the position of the date-and-time arrow V which moves along the top margin of the chart. Figure 19–1 shows additional details of the progress chart.

A graphic device such as this chart makes it possible to schedule and note the progress of work. If it becomes necessary to handle a rush order, the chart allows for a quick decision as to whether or not there is time and machine capacity available to handle the job. It will also indicate what work will have to be sidetracked or delayed in order to push the rush order through production.

This type of control chart can also be used to depict the planned activity and the actual progress in the use of men, materials, a department, a whole plant, or a particular order.

Control of Quality

The quality of production may be checked by inspection. If the check is made after production is completed, there is no real control being exercised over quality. In a case such as this, the product is either acceptable or must be rejected, and there has been no attempt to minimize or control the extent to which defective items appear. Quality control is the attempt to forestall defective production. It seeks to determine as soon as possible during production when quality is slipping so that corrective action may be taken before real loss occurs.

This infers that the product must have a quality leeway, a tolerance; and rightly so, for it is not practical to assume that there can be perfection.

When quality standards are established, a statement of the amount of quality variation which is permissible must be made. A certain machine may be working to a specification of .258″ ± .004″. A check on each unit turned out by the machine would give a quick indication of whether or not the product conformed to specifications; it would also indicate whether the machine was beginning to "wander" and thus needed adjustment. The checking of each unit produced can be very costly and in cases of volume production it may not be necessary. Statistical quality control, based on the laws of probability, is a sampling procedure. It works on the principle that if a few items out of a batch are inspected, the quality of those items will be representative of the whole batch. The number of items in the sample and the method of selecting these items from the batch will affect the results of the inspection procedure.

The application of statistical quality control to a machine operation would be as follows:

1. Establish tolerance-control limits.
2. Test sample units of the product as to the extent to which they deviate from the norm.
3. Record the inspection results on some device such as a quality-control chart. (See Figure 19–2.)

FIGURE 19–2

QUALITY-CONTROL CHART

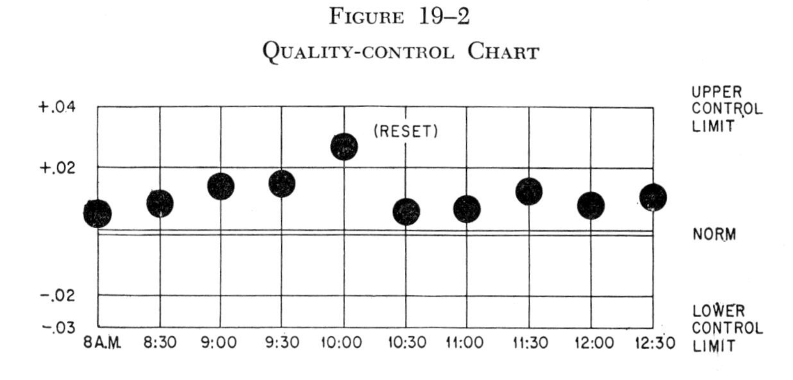

4. Interpret the quality-control chart and take corrective action when the need is indicated.

Figure 19–2 represents the recording every half hour of the measurements of several sample units. The sample is a check on the results of a machine operation. The inspection occurs directly after the operation. This proximity of location of the operation and the inspection gives quick indication of the quality of the work and also allows for an immediate indication of whether the machine is tending to wander in its accuracy. The control over quality is maintained by stopping work and making the necessary adjustments whenever the sample measurements approach tolerance limits.

The interpretation of Figure 19–2 indicates that the quality was in control at the start of the operation at 8 A.M. Each successive half-hour check shows that the measurements of the product vary in increasing amount from the norm. This variation occurs until 10 A.M. when the sample at that time seems to prove that there is a definite trend in product variation. The process is stopped at this point in order that the quality not go out of control. The machine is adjusted, and production is resumed. During the remainder of the morning the sample measurements indicate that the process is in control.

Some machines may have a mechanical control device built in. When the machine starts to wander, it will automatically shut itself off. It may also adjust itself and resume operations.

The control department should receive continuous or periodic reports concerning the quality of work being produced. The flow of information may be used to determine if it will be necessary to schedule extra production to provide the desired quantity of acceptable units. These reports will indicate the extent of difficulties involved in keeping production within tolerances and prompt a reconsideration of the process setup which may, in turn, lead to production-process revisions.

Control of Costs

The estimation of production costs serves as a basis for control. As production proceeds through its various stages, data are accumulated which indicate the amount of men, machine, and material costs actually incurred.

Actual costs are historic in that they represent the cost of an event which has already taken place. Once costs have been incurred, they are not subject to change. If cost data are not gathered until production is completed on the product, the control of cost is impossible. The anticipated cost compared with the actual cost of each stage of production provides the basis for cost control. The more frequently that actual costs are reported from the production area, the sooner may corrective action or investigation be initiated in the event that a variance between estimated and actual cost appears imminent or actually occurs.

The control of costs may be centralized or decentralized. Centralized control is better used in a situation where the production process is continuous or repetitive and little, if any, variation in process is possible because of the rigidly defined details of performance. Decentralized control of costs is better used when production is varied as to products and processes. In this case, the departmental supervisor or foreman in each area may be responsible for control over costs. The principle of control is the same in either case, for it must be based upon the extent to which there is an observed difference in the actual costs when compared with the estimated or planned cost.

Rigid cost control makes it necessary that any material or time usage beyond that which was planned for production be brought to the attention of the control department in order that authority to incur these extra costs be had. This procedure definitely brings to attention each variation in cost and helps maintain the "in control" status of the costs of production.

To be in control does not necessarily mean that actual cost must exactly coincide with planned cost. Planning is an attempt to predetermine. The future, in most respects, is difficult to anticipate. Whereas, in one case, control may be rigidly interpreted as complete adherence to a plan, it may, in another case, refer to a system which will indicate the occurrence or imminence of cost variation, thereby indicating those areas which must be subjected to consideration.

Control in the Work Area

Every process must somewhere make use of men. The machine is not capable of thinking. Individuals lay out the plans and must also serve to put the plans into operation.

Supervisors and foremen are the linkage between the plan and the action. The best plan may fail because of inadequate performance at the supervisory level. The production responsibilities must be clearly understood by supervisory personnel and must, in turn, be interpreted to the workers. The significance of the cost and quality features of work may be lost unless there is a determined effort to translate these factors into something which is meaningful to those who perform in the work area.

A serious planning defect exists when management does not carry through its planning activities to the consideration of the men who are to work the plan.

Control through Research

Production control may be considered as the attempt to do something more than control activity in accordance with a prescribed plan. It is also considered as the attempt to improve and originate upon a given situation. This involves research which is aimed at improvement in any area.

A firm must constantly strive to improve its status in order to maintain or improve its competitive position. Research activities in the areas of material usage, production processes, cost accounting, human relations, etc., provide additional knowledge which may be useful in improving or better controlling any activity.

SUMMARY

The major duties involved in the function of production planning and control are as follows:

1. Determine the volume of production necessary to conform to sales requirements.
2. Establish raw material, parts, and supplies requirements.

3. Analyze process in order to establish man and machine requirements.
4. Fix the economical sequence of operations as the route for production. This involves the assignment of time requirements.
5. Make up the production paper work which includes work orders, material orders, etc.
6. Establish the production-time schedule.
7. Dispatch work.
8. Check progress and initiate corrections.
9. Check actual costs with estimates.
10. Check quality and issue orders for rework or replacements as necessary.
11. Maintain schedule of completion and provide sales department with data concerning delivery dates.

The responsibility for these various functions may be centralized in some firms, while in others it may be assigned to various departments. Nevertheless, whether formally organized on a centralized or decentralized basis, they are the basic functions of production planning and control and exist in all industry.

The greater the number of details involved in the function of production planning and control, the greater is the value of visual aids. Charts and graphs depict most clearly the elements which must be understood and kept up to date for the use of those involved in production planning and control.

QUESTIONS

1. The title Production Planning and Control is indicative of three things. List these three.
2. Why is communication important to the work of production?
3. Preliminary production planning brings to light the interdependence of all the company departments. How?
4. What is the nature of the routing function?
5. How does the routing function differ in the case of custom versus repetitive process?
6. What is a route sheet?
7. Define scheduling.
8. Distinguish between production planning and production-control activities.
9. How does paper work serve to coordinate the work of the production planning and the control system?
10. Define the term "dispatching function."
11. What is production follow-up? Identify two methods of follow-up.
12. What is the nature of the progress chart?

13. "Quality control is the attempt to forestall defective production." Explain this statement.

14. How are costs controlled? What does it mean to be "in control"?

15. Why is supervision considered a control device?

16. What bearing does research activity have upon the scheme of production planning and control?

PART FIVE

Selling and Financing

Part Five of this book deals with two closely related areas which are of tremendous importance to any organization—selling and financing. Ideas and plans for production will never come to fruition unless funds are available to acquire the necessary factors of production. Many organizations fail early in their life because of inadequate financial planning. In fact, this has proved to be one of the more significant causes of business failure. The inadequately financed organization is often a high-cost, low-profit venture perpetually hindered in its attempt to reach prescribed goals.

The selling function is equally important, for sales are the life line of any business organization. Sales volume is the factor responsible for perpetuating the business. Adequate initial financing is prerequisite to starting the business off on the right foot. Sooner or later, however, sales dollars must flow back into the organization in sufficient volume to pay operating costs and cover the other varied expenditures.

The following four chapters will point out many of the areas requiring investigation prior to the formulation of realistic policies for the selling and financing aspects of business.

CHAPTER 20

Building the Selling Organization

With the exception of Chapters 2 and 4 the great bulk of material presented to this point has emphasized the factors involved in building an organization to produce a product, a line of products, or a service. It is not enough, however, merely to produce a product—it must be sold. For survival, products and services must be sold in sufficient quantity and at satisfactory prices. This, then, is the task of the selling organization, to obtain a market large enough to support an economical level of production and willing to pay a price satisfactory to the producer. However, it would be extremely difficult to build an effective selling organization without first considering the nature and extent of production.

The selling function involves the performance of many services and generally requires the use of individuals outside the producing organization. Selling, transportation, storage, financing, advertising, and promotion illustrate the activities that may come within the jurisdiction of the selling organization. In some instances the manufacturer may wish to perform all or most of this activity himself, while in others management may deem it best to enlist the services of others.

Initial Considerations

Selling organizations vary tremendously from company to company in terms of both size and complexity. Some large manufacturers may engage a sales agent to handle their entire sales program and therefore have no selling organization as such. In other situations the selling organization may command a dominant position in the over-all organization structure. There are several initial considerations that play an important role in the development of a selling organization for any business.

Sales Volume Needed. This is a paramount consideration in the building of a sales organization. As we have seen, some businessmen create large-scale, mass-production manufacturing methods which require a high volume of output to be economical. The selling organization in this case must be founded on mass-distribution methods; there is no alternative. We often wonder whether production determines sales or whether sales determine production. Quite often we find that the former is true. If the most economical level of production is 100,000 units a month, then a selling organization capable of moving this volume to the consumer must be created. Henry Ford II, president of the Ford Motor Company, has made a public statement to the effect that the manufacturer must decide how many automobiles will be produced in any given period and that it is up to the selling organization to dispose of them. For any manufacturing organization there is a level of production more economical than any other. Management must strive to maintain this level of production and will place the responsibility of disposing of this volume squarely on the selling organization. It has been proved over and over again that the selling organization that is pushed by the producing organization does a better job than the selling organization that sets its own goals.

Price Field of Competition. The price field of competition plays an important role in building the selling organization. If a businessman chooses to produce a low-priced product to be sold in large quantities, then, as above, mass distribution is essential. Frequently, however, a businessman prefers to engage in limited production of a high-quality prestige product. To develop and maintain a prestige product requires a high degree of control over distribution and, of course, a more elaborate selling organization. The manufacturer of one brand of golf ball will allow virtually any retailer from drugstore to department store to sell his product at whatever price the retailer desires. Another manufacturer will allow only "pro shops" at recognized golf clubs to sell them. In the latter instance the quality aspect of the product is maintained by the environment in which the balls are sold. Again, because of the environment, there is little opportunity for price cutting. Price field of competition may determine the degree of control a manufacturer needs to maintain over distribution; and it thereby sets the requirements for the selling organization.

Scope of the Market. A manufacturer in Cleveland, Ohio, produces and sells 1 million dollars' worth of goods per year. His customers are all located within a radius of ten miles. A manufacturer of industrial valve packings located in Everett, Massachusetts, produces 1 million dollars' worth of goods per year and sells them all over the United States. No explanation seems necessary to point out the differences that must exist in the selling organizations of these two firms.

Trade Practice. A manufacturer must consider trade practices and competition when establishing his selling organization. Frequently purchasers become so accustomed to buying in a particular manner that they rebel at any variation. Trade practices should be analyzed to locate any weaknesses, and from this study a more effective selling program may result.

Nature of Product. The products of industry are classified as business goods or consumer goods; this distinction was made in Chapter 2. At this point a distinction in the types of consumer goods should be made to point out the different problems associated with marketing them. Consumer goods are classified as (1) convenience goods, (2) shopping goods, and (3) specialty goods. Convenience goods, as the term implies, are goods that are frequently purchased and are relatively inexpensive. The consumer generally will buy convenience goods from the nearest or most convenient dealer. The consumer will substitute brands of convenience goods in preference to seeking out the preferred brand. Bread, milk, candy, and tobacco products are examples of convenience goods. Convenience goods require a highly concentrated type of distribution; that is, they must be offered in a wide variety of retail establishments located within easy reach of the consumer. Shopping goods involve a larger expenditure than convenience goods and are less frequently purchased. In this case the consumer desires to compare the quality and price of various offerings before making a purchase. It appears that shopping goods have their best chance of success in an established shopping center where a large portion of consumer wants can be satisfied. Specialty goods are appeal items that may not be specifically included in the consumer's shopping list. This type of good is best sold in areas where there is a large volume of pedestrian traffic seeking to buy shopping goods.

Type of Purchaser. A selling organization must be geared to deal with the prospective purchaser. An analysis of the wants and habits of various types of purchasers may throw some light on the selling problems associated with each. The Bureau of Census gives the following classifications of purchasers:

1. Industrial and commercial
2. Wholesalers and jobbers
3. Own wholesale branches
4. Retailers for resale
5. Buyers in other countries
6. Own retail stores
7. Consumers at retail
8. Export intermediaries

When a businessman must cater to several different types of purchasers, his selling problems become more involved and complex. Little or no selling effort is required in dealing with some of these purchasers, while in other cases intensive selling techniques must be employed.

Number of Customers. The number of customers to be served must be considered in building a selling organization. At one extreme a businessman may serve a large number of customers by automatic vending machines, self-service retailers, or some other highly impersonal means. At the other extreme a few customers, each requiring a high degree of personal contact, may comprise a businessman's market. In one instance advertising and promotion play an important role in selling the product, while in the other personal contacts are all-important.

Organization for Selling

The importance of an effective selling organization can be brought out by the fact that frequently more than one-half of the consumer's dollar is spent to cover costs incurred between the point of production and the point of ultimate consumption. Thus savings in selling costs can be of great significance to both the producer and the consumer. While no single form of organization for selling can be said to be best or most successful, it is significant that selling divisions are organized on one of three bases. The size and scope of the operation in question may determine which of these to use.

Organization by Product. In this case the selling organization is set up by product. A large dairy, for example, may have one selling unit responsible for selling milk and cream products, another for frozen products, and still another for allied products. The advantage of this type of organization comes from product specialization. To the extent that a line of products presents a wide variety of selling problems, this type of organization may be preferred.

Organization by Function. Here the selling organization is set up by function; one division might specialize in advertising, another in sales promotion, or sales management, etc. The advantage of this type of organization comes from specialization of function. It requires the centralization of all advertising in one division, all sales promotion in another, and so on. This type of organization may not be satisfactory if the requirements for selling a line of products are too varied to be handled from a single division.

Organization by Territory. When market characteristics vary greatly from region to region, it may be desirable to organize the selling division on a basis of territories. Foreign operations often present an entirely different sales situation from that presented by domestic operations. Within the United States variations in market characteristics may be so great that there is a need to specialize by territory rather than by function or product.

Components of Distribution

The broad function of the selling organization is to coordinate the demands of the consumer, on one hand, with the productive facilities available to satisfy those demands, on the other. The economist defines this function as the creation of time, place, and possession utility. More specifically the following functions are involved in distributing goods to the consumer:

1. Warehousing
2. Transportation
3. Financing
4. Advertising and promotion
5. Channels of distribution

Some manufacturers may perform all these functions, while others may prefer to perform none or a few. Regardless, to sell goods someone must perform each of these functions, whether it be producer, consumer, or middleman.

Warehousing. Warehousing creates time utility; that is, it holds goods until a time of greater usefulness. There is almost always a lag between production and consumption, which makes storage highly essential. Goods must be stored until consumers are ready to use them because consumption of most products is fairly even and continuous, while production is often intermittent.

Transportation. Transportation creates place utility. The transportation and warehousing functions must be closely correlated to avoid, as far as possible, a duplication of effort. The most desirable situation is to have not more than one warehousing period and a single movement of goods to create both time and place utility.

Financing. Goods produced are of little value to management until they are sold and paid for. They may be sold to the ultimate consumer or to a wholesaler. From the previous discussions the implication is that considerable time elapses between production of a good and its consumption, time during which a manufacturer may have to wait before receiving any return on the goods he has produced. The amount of financing required during the selling process depends upon the channels of distribution employed by the manufacturer. The manufacturer of shoes who maintains his own retail outlets must wait until the shoes are sold to the ultimate consumer before he gets his money. The manufacturer of shoes for a large mail-order house may receive his money immediately after production. If a businessman intends to control all phases of the distribution process, he must plan to wait a longer period of time for his money than the person who sells to jobbers or retailers.

There is an additional phase of financing in the distribution process. Today people expect to use their power of credit for an ever-increasing number of goods that they buy. When credit is extended to the purchaser, someone must wait for his money. If goods are sold on open account at any stage of the distribution process, the seller must wait for his money. Frequently the purchase of goods is financed through a bank or some loan agency, and the seller gets his money immediately. The credit transaction in this case actually involves the customer and the lending institution and presents little or no problem to the seller.

Advertising and Sales Promotion. Advertising and sales-promotion departments in cooperation with outside advertising agencies have become highly specialized businesses within themselves. Through advertising and sales promotion a businessman attempts to convince the consumer that his product will do more to satisfy the consumer's wants than any competing product. The means whereby the advertising and sales-promotion departments will disseminate information regarding the product are too involved and complicated for discussion at this point. It is safe to say that in advertising and sales promotion the businessman sees a means for widening the area of distribution for his products—and also a constant threat from more powerful competitors who may use this means to greater advantage.

Channels of Distribution. The success of any selling organization is determined by the channel of distribution utilized and the caliber of each segment of the distribution process. The problem of selecting appropriate channels of distribution is complicated by the fact that there is such a wide variety available. The following illustrates several commonly used channels of distribution.

1. Manufacturer to consumer (many custom-made goods)
2. Manufacturer to manufacturer's outlet to consumer (Thom McAn shoes)
3. Manufacturer to retailer to consumer (food products)
4. Manufacturer to franchised dealer to consumer (automobiles)
5. Manufacturer to jobber to retailer to consumer (candy)
6. Manufacturer to consumer through manufacturer's representative (electronic supplies)
7. Manufacturer to retailer (consignment) to consumer (new products such as power lawn mowers)

Selection of Channels of Distribution

There is no absolutely standard policy that must be followed in the distribution of merchandise from producer to consumer. Each company must select its own trade channels. What has proved successful for one manufacturer may not be successful for others. Before adopting any one or a combination of trade channels, the manufacturer must carefully analyze each one, and, through the process of elimination, arrive at what appears to be the best. The channels decided upon should be tested for a reasonable period of time and, if necessary, changed or modified to meet existing circumstances. New types of middlemen may appear on the scene, or changes in the demand for a product may require a change in the distribution setup.

Convenience goods and shopping goods are usually not suited for direct-to-the-consumer distribution. In many instances this channel is used by manufacturers of new and unknown products that require demonstration and intensive selling. Aluminum combination windows, vacuum cleaners, sewing machines, encyclopedias, and the like are well-known direct-sale items. After a product becomes well established, then it may be desirable to turn to retail stores as a means of distribution.

Consumers are frequently contacted through retail stores owned by manufacturers. Convenience goods are seldom sold in this manner because the products of many different manufacturers must be assembled in a single store to produce the variety of retail stock that is necessary for selling this type of good. Fanny Farmer candy stores, Thom McAn shoe stores, and Adam hat stores are examples of retail stores owned by the manufacturers themselves. The operation of retail stores by manufacturers requires a heavy investment in inventory and physical property and creates many problems not associated with the manufacture of goods.

When selling directly to retailers, the manufacturer must recruit, train, and direct a field force of salesmen and sales supervisors. This force must be large enough to make frequent calls on all retailers that can profitably handle the company's line. Catalogues, brochures, and promotional materials are all necessary tools when this channel is used. Merchandise must be available for the retailer, which means that the manufacturer may need to provide storage facilities. This is especially significant when retailers practice a policy of hand-to-mouth buying.

In many instances manufacturers strive for a degree of exclusiveness in the distribution of their products and allow only franchised dealers to handle them. Singer sewing machines, Hoover vacuum cleaners, and the various makes of automobiles fall into this category. In these cases specific agreements are reached between manufacturer and dealer which serve to maintain the quality aspect of the product.

For years the traditional method of distribution was manufacturer-to-jobber-to-retailer-to-consumer. The jobber was set up to provide many of the functions involved in distribution, such as storage, financing, and selling. In many instances today it is still considered the best policy to use jobbers. The weakness in jobbers stems from the fact that they are not pioneers and they are not the best salesmen in the world. In situations where the manufacturer himself intends to do the bulk of the selling and promotion the jobber may be adequate to his task.

Manufacturers' representatives are not widely used today except in special lines of activity. The manufacturer's representative does not provide any marketing services except selling. He gets an order for goods from a customer and turns it over to the manufacturer, who must complete the sales transaction. Manufacturers' representatives are used in the electronics-supply field where a special knowledge of products is needed.

Effect of Channels on Sales Volume and Stability

The best selling organization is one that allows management to make the best use of its productive abilities. The best use of productive abilities results when production is carried on at a rather even rate. This means that the selling organization should maintain a sales volume consistent with productive activity. We realize that this is not always possible, yet it is a goal that must be kept constantly in mind.

Certain trade channels provide management with a higher degree of control over sales activity than others. If management distributes its products through wholesalers and jobbers who are allowed to select their retail outlets, it will have little control over sales volume and sales activity. On the other hand, if a manufacturer maintains his own wholesale outlets and sells only to authorized dealers, each of which has an annual sales quota to meet, a much higher degree of control can be maintained. It boils down to this: If management wants a high degree of control over sales activity, it should control as many of the distribution facilities as possible.

Effect of Channel on Control of Distribution

If controlled distribution is a goal of management, the selling organization must have control over every phase of the distribution process. It must supervise retail outlets, jobbers, storage facilities, price policies, and the like. The best control comes from company ownership. Whenever outsiders are allowed to determine selling policy, control is lost.

Effect of Channel on Margin of Profit

Maintaining control over all phases of distribution can be an expensive proposition. Controls are used to build up the quality of a product and to maintain company price policy. The largest manufacturer of outboard motors in this country has been very successful in building and maintaining quality leadership through close control over distribution. This does not mean that all manufacturers should attempt to engage in closely controlled distribution. A manufacturer of low-priced ready-to-wear apparel has little to gain through controlled distribution for generally quality is not important in his product, and most likely he has no brand name to promote. The cost of one trade channel as opposed to another should be compared with the gain that results. It is difficult to justify a trade channel that over the long run will not produce the greatest possible profit.

A successful trade channel must provide a satisfactory profit for all members of the trade as well as the manufacturer. If the retailer is expected to store, advertise, and sell a product, he must be paid accordingly. If a retailer merely displays goods on self-service shelves, leaving the selling and promotion to the manufacturer, his reward should be proportionately smaller. In all instances management should define the function to be performed at each step in the trade channel and work out a system of discounts that will make handling the product profitable.

The Sales Organization

The organization of the sales division will vary from company to company depending on the size of the operation, the channels of distribution employed, and the availability of personnel. It is also conditioned by the basic policy of organization according to product, function, or territory discussed earlier in this chapter. Many of the earlier comments on trade channels are brought into clearer focus through a discussion of the organizational structures involved.

1. Organization for Direct Selling. (Figure 20–1.) This type of organization is most easily controlled, for all elements of distribution come

FIGURE 20–1

ORGANIZATION FOR DIRECT SELLING

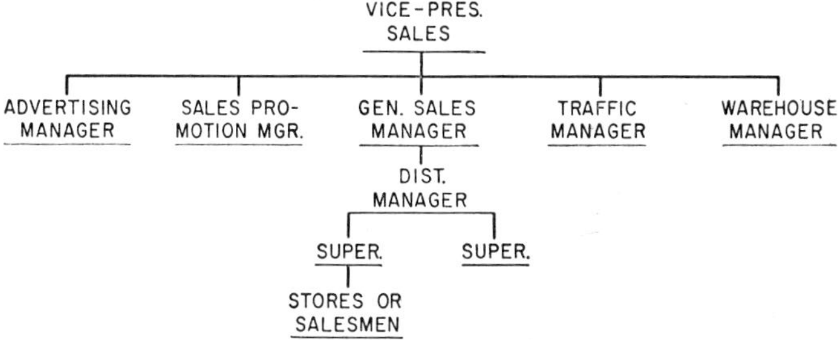

within a single management. Here there is a clear-cut organizational setup from the top down. There should be no question as to authority and responsibility. Salesmen or retail store managers receive their orders from supervisors, who in turn receive their orders from the district sales manager, and so on all the way up to the top.

2. Organization Involving Middlemen. (Figure 20–2.) In this situation there can be many variations in the organizational setup because of the different middlemen who may be involved and because of the difference in relationships that may exist between the manufacturer and his middlemen. Figure 20–2 illustrates how easily absolute control may be lost when

FIGURE 20–2

SALES ORGANIZATION INVOLVING MIDDLEMEN

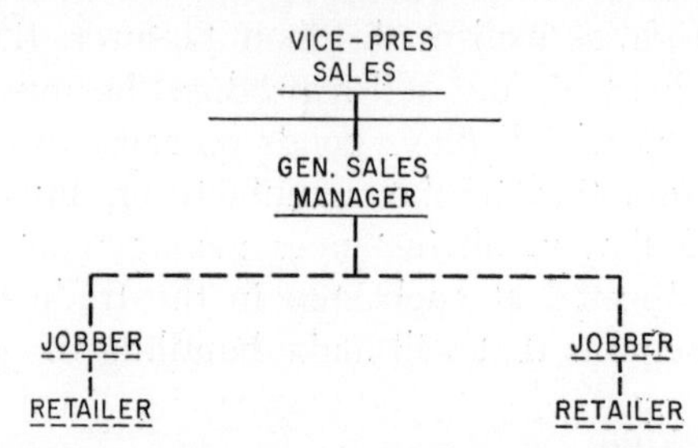

distribution involves outsiders. The illustration includes only the line aspect of organization. The staff functions shown in Figure 20–1 should be included in this organization plan also. The broken lines used below the district-manager level indicate that there is no direct control over these areas.

SUMMARY

The selling function involves the performance of many services. Selling, transportation, storage, financing, advertising, and promotion are involved in selling goods and indicate the scope of the selling function. The selling organization developed by a business organization must perform or supervise the performance of all of these functions. The scope of the selling function may be determined by the nature of production. If mass-production techniques are used in making a product, then mass-distribution techniques must be employed in selling them. If the company deals in custom-made goods, then an entirely different sales approach must be made.

Initially, management must determine the degree of control that is needed over selling operations. If there is a definite advantage in building product prestige and in maintaining established prices, then management should closely control selling activity. If the object is to sell as many units as possible through all types of retailers, then close control over selling may not be the answer. Frequent study of the functions performed by the sales division should be made to ascertain that they are necessary. As consumer wants change, the selling function should be altered to meet the changes in consumer demand.

QUESTIONS

1. What is the task of the selling organization?
2. What functions are involved in selling a product?

3. What effect does sales volume needed have on the selling organization?
4. What effect does the price field of competition have on the selling organization?
5. Distinguish between convenience goods and shopping goods.
6. How does the distribution of convenience goods differ from the distribution of shopping goods?
7. What are the different classifications of purchasers made by the Bureau of Census?
8. How does the number of customers involved affect the selling organization?
9. What is meant by "organization by product"?
10. What is meant by "organization by function"?
11. Under what conditions should management consider organization of its selling division by territories?
12. How does the economist define the selling function?
13. What utility does transportation create? Storage?
14. Discuss the effect that channels of distribution have on a manufacturer's financing problem.
15. What is a channel of distribution? Give four illustrations of distribution channels.
16. What types of goods are suited to direct-to-the-consumer distribution?
17. What effect do channels of distribution have on sales volume and sales stability?
18. What effect do channels of distribution have on profits?
19. What problems are involved in dealing directly with the retailer?
20. Discuss the statement that certain trade channels provide management with a higher degree of control over sales activity than do others.

CHAPTER 21

Prices and Terms of Sales

The prices charged for goods and services are significant to businessmen and consumers in many respects. Prices influence the distribution of personal income and the size of national output. They are among the determinants of the choice of goods which the market will offer and which the customers will buy. Prices, if they exceed costs, are the source of profits and thereby provide the means of satisfying those who have invested their funds and time in business enterprise. In addition, these profits influence established firms to increase their size and new firms to enter business.

Even though prices are readily recognized for their importance in each of the areas indicated above, it is the rare businessman who actually spends his time thinking about all these complex relationships which the price of his product has with the other elements of the economic scene. Primarily the businessman finds greater need for his attention in the other areas of business, production, personnel, finance, etc. However, he never loses sight of the need for profit. His approach to profit, in the usual case, permits limited price manipulation, for the competitive situation or market environment in which the firm operates may quite clearly indicate the general price range within which the product must be sold.

It would not be very practical for us to assume that competition is some force apart from the people who make up the competitive scene. When we speak of prices set by competition, we actually mean to say that people have set the price. Different people *ask* different prices for their products, while customers *offer* varying prices for the goods. Each group has its own peculiar motivations. The conglomeration of *asks* and *offers* establishes the competitive price range. Hence, the usual businessman finds that he is partly responsible for the competitive environment within which he must operate.

The range of prices charged for identical or closely related goods may vary widely in the case of consumer goods, such as gasoline and food products; or but slightly in the case of standardized producer goods, such as industrial supplies and tools. A greater price range usually exists when customers are ignorant of the availability or source of alternative products, or when they prefer convenience and service in procurement and for such reasons are willing to pay a higher purchase price.

The businessman seeks to improve his profit position by reducing costs and creating a greater profit spread or by stimulating the market to a greater sales response, thereby seeking a greater amount of profit through volume sales.

Price policy is a very important consideration in the determination of profits. It is quite variable in both nature and intent for the policy is not always aimed at a maximization of profits. In some cases, as will be noted later, profits may not be considered as an essential part of the immediate pricing situation.

Variable Nature of Price Policy

The freedom which businessmen have in establishing price policy varies considerably. The small firms which make identical or similar products that are sold in a common market have little, if any, control over the prices for their products. The single producer of a unique product, the monopolist, has complete price control. Most firms find themselves somewhere between these two extremes—with neither complete control nor certainly complete lack of control over the prices which may be set. The degree of control available to the firm has its bearing upon the price policy and may serve to restrict or allow great leeway to management in its decision as to the nature of its basic pricing policy. This statement of price policy, regardless of the environmental or competitive handicaps and advantages which may be available, is founded upon the basic need(s) of the firm. These needs are the expression of the basic business goals in so far as they may be stated in the light of price-policy significance. The variable nature of price policy is influenced by the following:

1. The need to cover costs
2. The need to earn a profit
3. The desire to gain entry into a market
4. The attempt to dispose of merchandise

Each of the above needs cannot be considered significant without some prior understanding of other factors which influence price policy, such as the product and its characteristics, the market, and the position of the individual firm within its industry. Although it is practical to assume that immediate profits may or may not be one of the considerations involved in setting a price, it is impossible to conceive of any industrial or commercial situation wherein the long-run goal is not one of optimum profits. Optimum profits may mean the maximization of profits or the accumulation of a return which management feels is adequate for continued operations. Needless to say, the firm without some profit prospect is destined for the junk heap.

In essence, the price policy of the firm, depending upon the factors which influence it, falls somewhere between the extremes of a rigid price as dictated by the business environment and a negotiable price policy which allows management to seek the advantage of its position and ability to wrest the best possible price from the market.

FACTORS AFFECTING PRICES

The Product

The reputation, distinctiveness, utility and convenience which the product brings to the customer have a direct effect upon the price which may be asked. Many times the visual impression which the product makes does more to add to its price potential than do its operating characteristics. This is more likely to be true with consumer goods which are so often purchased on the basis of eye appeal or psychological motivations rather than on rational or economic bases. The product which is sold to industrial purchasers must carry its own weight, and there must be an intelligent relationship between the price of such producer goods and their quality and operational characteristics.

If the product meets with direct competition, its price must be established in consideration of those goods with which it competes. The product may be priced above, below, or at the competitive level. If it is priced above the competitive level, there is the risk of losing some, if not all, sales. In a competitive market consumer preference may gravitate to the lower price levels. If the product is priced below the competitive level, sales volume may increase because of the lower price, but this is no assurance of greater profits. If production costs are lowered because of greater volume or if sales increase or if both facts come to pass, then we may anticipate an increase in the amount of profits. Pricing below the market may either stimulate or depress competition. Some firms will attempt to meet competition on a price basis. Others will fall by the wayside because their higher costs prevent them from taking part in price competition for too long a period of time.

Pricing at the competitive level is the third alternative. This is an advantageous policy in that it does not encourage price cutting, and yet customers are neither confused nor driven away by higher prices. Of course, this policy of following the price lead is not a very stimulating one; and it does not offer the individuality and benefits to be derived from active pricing.

A product which does not meet with direct competition may find itself in a world of its own with the "sky's the limit" as the restriction on price possibilities. A product which is truly unique or is made to appear so can be priced at whatever level the traffic will bear. In many cases the approach to pricing is applied in reverse. First, find out how high a price the market will support. Second, peg the product price at that level and promote the product so as to substantiate the price. Ordinarily we would suspect that the product is evaluated and priced on its inherent merits. This need not be so.

A product which is in distress, losing its style life, running the risk of deteriorating, or running the limit of storage and other inventory costs presents another case where the price is a negotiable thing and is customarily set with the hope of minimizing losses rather than maximizing profits.

In each of these cases the price setter is motivated differently and will practice differing pricing approaches.

The Contribution to Profits

The selling price is normally expected to cover costs and help provide a profit. Whether it does these things and how well is very important. The extent of accomplishment is measured in terms of the "contribution" which the selling price makes toward a coverage of costs and a provision for profits. Selling price in its aggregate sense, total income, is first considered as applied to the payment of the variable costs of business, such as materials and labor. The income in excess of this amount is then considered as contributing to the coverage of the overhead costs of the business. Lastly, whatever amount of income remains represents the contribution to profits of the firm. The amount of this contribution to both overhead and profits enters into our discussion of pricing methods. At this point we are primarily concerned with the extent to which the sales income is capable of covering all costs and contributing to profits.

The profit margin which the seller desires is the most important determinant of price policy and price level. This margin represents the contribution which income makes to the owners for their investment and risk taking. How great a contribution is necessary to provide an adequate return depends upon each situation. With products of minimum risk a small contribution may be considered reasonable. The satisfactory contribution in any situation depends upon the particular product and the risks, uncertainties, and labor associated with it. During the preliminary planning of production, when selling price enters into the discussion, it is important that the necessary or desirable profit margin be a major topic. It is not necessary that management set its sights upon a large contribution to profits. For that matter, it is just as practical to assume that management considers no profit as a necessary short-term operating situation. What is important is that the requirement of profits, how much and when, and the influence of that requirement upon selling-price policy and market activities be considered.

The determination of a satisfactory contribution to profit is much more the problem of the manufacturer than of the wholesaler or retailer. The latter usually have a much simpler pricing problem. Retailers and wholesalers may adhere to a one-price policy for all comparable purchasers or may apply a markup formula in determining selling prices. In many cases the prices of some products are fixed by the manufacturer under fair-trade laws.

Position of the Firm within the Industry

The position of the individual firm within its industry raises the question of two potential influences upon the pricing policy. Either we may anticipate some degree of rivalry, or on the other hand we may find that agreements on the price situation are entered into.

The number of firms and their respective sizes have a bearing upon what may be anticipated. Many times the pricing activities of small firms may go unnoticed because of the very small share of the market which is involved. Sometimes the smaller firm may introduce price variations to its own advantage without fear of retaliation on the part of larger operators. This is possible when the larger operator is handicapped by his costs and by his inability to act as quickly as the smaller operator.

Often the large firm acts as a price leader to the smaller firms. Among the larger firms there may be little independence in price activity, for each realizes that price rivalry can result in benefits to none. The larger firms are more concerned than the small ones with the problems of price variations. They seek to establish a stable price level which will allow them to make future commitments with some assurance of income prospects. Customers, large buyers particularly, prefer stable prices.

If the firm enjoys a position of leadership within its industry, it must keep in mind the extent to which its price policy adds to or stifles competition. High price maintenance by the leader may create a "price umbrella." This is feared by businessmen since it adds to competition by allowing the less efficient operator to continue in business and still cover his higher costs. The price unbrella also attracts competition because it provides the attraction of a large contribution to profits.

On the other hand, the maintenance of low price levels in industry will discourage new entry and may also stifle creativity in the industry. The low contribution is not considered adequate to newcomers. Of course, such a price policy must be accompanied by a sales volume which assures management of a satisfactory return. Low price maintenance may be initiated to restrict entry of competition into the field or to provide the customer with exceptional value for his money, thereby promoting the position of the company and the acceptance of the product line.

Although we have raised several considerations in these last paragraphs, it is quite impossible to predict just what the response of any one company, the members of the industry, or the customers will be under any particular circumstances. A high price may attract customers who feel that high price means quality, and it may also attract competition which seeks the large profit contribution. The high price may also discourage customers who question the value of the item. This may provide an opportunity for a newcomer with a lower price level. Even in this case we may find the customer wary of the new entry and the different price policy. A low price maintenance policy may discourage competition, confuse the customers, or cause the industry to seek means of product improvement which will justify a higher price level. These are but a few of the potential occurrences.

There is no question that price agreements do exist among the members of industry. These agreements are aimed at preservation of the status of competition (or noncompetition) by stifling the entry of new firms. Usually the agreement is such that a new firm is forced to use the device of lower prices as a means of market entry. This, of course, increases the possibility of failure. How prevalent price agreements are, how bad the pricing situation is in this respect, and how one establishes proof of price agreements, are all difficult questions to answer. There is no need for agreements in the case of price leadership, for in each area there is a leader who may or may not be followed by others.

The major effect of price agreements and price leadership is to stabilize prices by eliminating price cutting. Where, however, do prices stabilize? Are they high, low, or at a moderate level? With price agreements in effect it is necessary that firms compete on nonprice bases, such as quality of the product or sales promotion activities.

Government Influences on Price

The government influences prices in many ways. In some cases it sets the prices for some services such as local government, the cost of services offered by government corporations, and postal rates. In other cases the government influences prices by legislation. The legislation may pertain directly to the establishment of a price or may indirectly influence industrial prices.

Excise tax rates have an influence upon the prices set for items subject to the tax. Labor legislation influences union security and thereby wages which are a part of the price of goods. Of importance to us at this time is the influence upon prices brought about through the enactment of antitrust legislation. These laws were originally passed to prevent abuses that arose out of agreements entered into by large firms. These agreements were aimed at the destruction and elimination of competition. The antitrust legislation is currently being applied to ensure that prices are determined in markets which are relatively free of any devices which substantially lessen competition or tend to create a monopoly.

Although the meaning of the law and its interpretation by different courts has varied, it encompasses consideration of the following areas:

1. The expressed or implied agreement among rivals as to prices and output, or practices even indirectly having an effect upon price, are illegal.
2. In general it is bad to be big. Large size offers the opportunity of abuse. A firm is large relative to its share of its industry's market.
3. Practices such as exclusive dealerships, price discrimination, tying clauses, etc., are not clearly considered illegal. Each is subject to examination. Agreement among rival firms is, however, without question illegal.

The antitrust laws do not set prices. They influence them. The individual businessman sets his own prices. The law is applied to correct or eliminate objectionable practices which arise out of a situation of excess market power in the hands of one business firm or a group of business firms.

The Nature of Demand

In Chapter 2 a discussion of the nature of goods and the elasticity of demand was entered into. These topics are now raised again since they are vitally involved in a consideration of prices.

A price cannot be set without consideration of what it means in terms of demand and how it compares with the prices of substitutes and directly competing products. The price charged for a product, when varied, may have extreme effects upon its sales. Some products have what is called an "elastic demand." This means that if the price of the product is raised, sales will be curtailed. If the product price is lowered, sales will be increased. Other products possess inelastic demand, and we find that the sales of such products are little affected by either increases or decreases in price. The real results which come about after price changes can only be known once the fact is accomplished. However, the businessman has at his disposal a few means of discerning the nature of the demand for his product and thereby is able to establish his pricing policy more intelligently.

If many substitutes are available for a product, it usually has an elastic demand. If the price of the product is too high in the buyer's estimation, the substitutes will be purchased. How close a substitute must be and how great a range of price differential must exist before the customer switches his preferences is difficult to state. Substitution involves consideration not only of the immediate attributes of the product but also of other features of the market which attach themselves to the purchase situation. Such things as geographic availability and services provided enter into the list of considerations which help shape the final decision as to which product to accept at what price.

If a product is without close substitutes, a price reduction would possibly attract new customers; while a price increase, depending upon whether the product is classified as a necessity or luxury, might have no effect upon demand, might stimulate it, or might reduce it.

It is significantly difficult to make a clear statement of implications in the area of pricing and the results of price variations. However, our discussion would not be valid if this topic were excluded from consideration.

The demand for some products is found to be dependent upon the sales of other products. For instance, the golf ball has little value without the gold club. Razors and razor blades, lumber and nails, automobile tires and the auto, each duo represents items that exist in combination. In situations such as these, we raise the question of price interrelationship. If the price of golf balls were increased 10 per cent, what would happen to the demand? If the prices of razor blades and nails were increased, would fewer blades be used? Would fewer nails be used? In cases such as these we find that there is leeway for price variation which would not alter the demand for the product since it represents a relatively small investment in view of the product or service into which each enters.

These products do not compete with their mate products, but they must be priced in recognition of the effect that their prices and any changes therein will have upon the final situation of which they are a part. The less significant the cost of the product as part of the whole, the less the effect of price variation upon the demand for the product.

PRICING METHODS

The actual procedures employed to arrive at a selling price for a specific situation involve all the considerations thus far mentioned in this chapter. In addition, several methods of pricing are used by the businessman. Let us consider the nature of pricing based upon two approaches, cost plus and less-than-cost.

Cost-plus Pricing

In the ordinary layman's understanding of pricing practice, the businessman is in complete possession of all cost data pertinent to production and he then adds to this cost whatever margin he deems desirable and necessary to reward him for his efforts. The result of this procedure is a selling price.

Two areas herein deserve investigation. First, the existence of cost data—which in many cases are neither available nor significantly accurate. Second, the addition of a desirable margin to costs—which involves some concept of what amount is correct. It would seem that determining the margin was an easy task. Yet studies have disclosed that there is no clear-cut explanation for the margin applied to cost other than some concept that the margin is "fair" or simply the fact that it has been historically established as the margin to apply.

A great deal of individuality is applied in this type of pricing situation, and although the layman has an approach to the procedure of establishing a cost-plus price, he certainly oversimplifies the whole matter. Although we may start at the level of cost and build up to the selling price, in view of all the other considerations which enter into price determination it would be better to state that price setting starts by stating prices and then determining whether or not the costs of the product are consistent with the prices which the market can support.

A manufacturer of a competitive product will probably be involved with considerations in his price setting different from those of his competitors. His product distributors, however, all have the same cost bases. Pricing for the manufacturer and distributor, therefore, differs. All the distributors for the firm will find that their costs vary at the same time; thus their selling prices will probably vary simultaneously. The individual manufacturer's costs are not so related to those of his competitor; therefore, his costs vary by different amounts and at different times.

If the margin applied to the cost base is consistently uniform, we have fixed markup pricing. If the margin is varied, we have variable markup pricing. This latter procedure may be considered as an approach to charging "what the market will bear." On the other hand, it may reflect an accurate estimation of the market situation and be a statement of the "right price" for the particular time.

The persistence of a fixed markup practice is evidence of the mechanical nature of pricing as practiced by some businessmen. Retailers many times, regardless of pertinent market situations, do not alter prices established on a fixed markup basis until the stock has been sold and replaced at a different price level.

Less-than-cost Pricing

The price should preferably cover all costs associated with the product and in addition provide a return above this amount. In some cases, however, the market will not support such a price level and the businessman is too concerned with moving goods or salvaging what he can to become too involved in the profit function of the selling price. This leads us to a situation wherein a selling price may be established at less than cost.

In any event, we prefer to lose as little as is possible. Our pricing approach does not involve a concession to the customer.

In order to carry out effectively a less-than-cost pricing procedure, knowledge of costs is necessary. Preferably we should have a breakdown in terms of variable and fixed costs. Since fixed costs are assumed to exist regardless of the level of business activity, it therefore follows that the maximum loss that is desirable is one which does not exceed the amount of fixed costs. The selling price established by this method should be one which is capable of covering the total of the variable costs associated with the business activity. Here again we refer to the contribution which the price makes to costs and profits. In the less-than-cost pricing situation it is desirable that our price contribute as a minimum enough to cover variable cost. Any excess is applied to cover the fixed costs.

Less-than-cost pricing is a short-term, emergency type of pricing procedure. It is used when necessary to stimulate sales, to move merchandise or to make use of plant capacity which would otherwise be idle and incapable of supporting the work force. This method provides no profits, although it provides other advantages as indicated.

Loss-leader pricing is another situation wherein costs are not fully covered. In this case merchandise of known value is offered at what are recognized as below-cost prices. The merchant makes no profit on such merchandise; what he seeks to do is attract customers in the hope of making additional sales of items which contribute to profits.

Miscellaneous Pricing Methods

Other pricing methods are used, such as intuitive pricing. This method involves the guess, or hunch, as to what the correct, or best, price is. Trial-and-error pricing involves sales of the product for different prices in various areas and the evaluation of the market response to these different prices. Out of this evaluation comes the "best" price.

Price lines, a method which represents a combination of cost-plus and fixed markup, start with the selling price and work backward to the cost necessary to allow the desired profit margin. In this case the quality of the product is varied to conform to the necessary cost level, while the selling price provides the desired margin of profit.

TERMS OF SALES

One of the basic sales decisions to be made is whether to sell for cash or to extend credit. In either case the terms of the sales transaction must be spelled out in specific terms. These terms relate to the cash-and-credit situation. If credit is to be extended, terms to be offered should be established. Whether consideration should be given to the quantity of purchase by the extension of quantity discounts and whether classes of customers should be recognized in terms of trade discounts necessitate the establishment of a scale of discounts and the establishment of different classes of customers.

The decisions made in these areas have their bearings upon the amount of profits to be realized. If the desired profit is to be realized, careful consideration must be involved.

Trade Discounts

If the firm has but one class of customers, there is no problem of establishing trade discounts. If, however, the scheme of distribution involves selling to wholesalers, jobbers, and directly to consumer, each of these and other channels of distribution (see Chapter 20) make demands for the establishment of a specific system of prices. Each channel wishes to be recognized for the quantity of purchases and the level at which the distribution function is being performed. Therefore, the wholesaler expects a lower price than the retailer, and so forth.

Quantity Discounts

Related to, if not part of, the trade discount is the discount given in recognition of the quantity purchased. These quantity discounts are founded upon the fact that there are certain cost savings involved in the large sale. Paper work and other clerical and administrative matters are reduced relative to the amount of sales, thereby affording the merchant some leeway for price concession as a reward to the large-scale buyer.

Cash Price Concessions

As a sort of reward for a cash purchase, cash-price concession terms are sometimes offered the buyer. These terms are justified as a reward for the savings or gain which the seller has as a result of being immediately provided with cash availability. The cash concessions are deducted from price once trade and quantity discounts have been taken care of. They are not to be confused with cash discounts which are credit terms.

Advertising Allowances

The price concession many times is cloaked in the guise of an advertising allowance. This allowance is a discount which the seller makes in return for which the buyer promises to promote the product. Such advertising allowances are many times shams and add up to nothing more than additional cash discounts. In other cases terms are explicitly spelled out and such allowances as are made are actually spent in advertising the product. The seller uses this method of promotion with the knowledge that the buyer has a better understanding of the final market area and may be able to promote more effectively the sales of the product to the ultimate consumer.

Credit Terms

Credit terms refer to the statement of the terms of the buyer's obligation to pay for goods within a certain specified period of time. These terms in some business circles are rigidly defined and adhered to. Very often they are not strictly applied and are used as a competitive device, for the extension of credit beyond normal terms may be just as much a concession to one buyer as a price concession may be to some other buyer.

The nature of the product being sold, the financial position of the seller, and the position and reputation of the buyer are determinants of the credit terms. Goods classified as raw materials and those which have a quick turnover, such as perishables, usually have the shortest credit terms. Items of equipment which represent long-term investment are extended long-term credit. The credit terms of the seller must often be established in cognizance of the seasonal nature of the buyer's business. There seems to be good reason for not pressing for payments when the seller is in the middle of a normal seasonal slump.

The poorer the risk associated with the buyer, the shorter are the credit terms. These terms recognize the extremely poor risk by demanding prepayment or deposits on the order. The buyer who purchases in small quantity is usually provided with shorter terms than the quantity buyer. Credit terms are usually varied in the case of the good customer who is temporarily embarrassed.

The weaker the financial position of the seller, the tighter he tries to make his credit terms. If the seller finds his competitive position difficult, he may use easy credit terms as a lure. This amounts to selling credit.

Cash Terms

If goods are sold on cash terms, this customarily means that the seller desires payment within ten days. Sometimes the terms are expressed as "bill-to-bill or drop delivery," which means that the outstanding bill must be paid at the time of the new delivery.

Prepayment Terms

Payment before receipt of goods is customarily expressed as COD or CBD or SD-BL. COD means "cash on delivery." CBD means "cash before delivery." SD-BL means "sight draft, bill of lading attached." These prepayment terms are used with poor risks, overdue accounts, when the buyer is in receivership or process of reorganization, or when goods are made to special order and have no other market. In this case a deposit is frequently asked of the buyer before production commences on his order.

Individual-order Terms

The customer who buys occasionally is extended credit terms for each individual order. These terms commence with the invoice date. For example, credit terms of 2/15/30 or 2/15 net 30 mean that 2 per cent discount is allowed if the invoice is paid within 15 days of billing; otherwise the full amount must be paid within 30 days. These terms, it is evident, contain two features—the discount rate and period and the length of the credit period.

If the customer is located at some distance from the seller, time is lost during the transportation of goods, and in order to compensate for this, terms such as ROG or AOG are extended. These terms, "receipt of goods" and "arrival of goods," indicate that the discount and credit terms are to commence upon the date that the goods are received by the buyer.

Lumped-order Terms

For the customer who purchases many times during the month the seller may lump together the various purchases and bill them as of one or two dates. The discount and credit terms begin with the lumped billing date. The terms used in this case are EOM, MOM, and prox. EOM means "end of month"; and in the event that the terms are 2/10/30 EOM this allows the buyer to discount until the tenth day of the month following and extends credit to him up to the thirtieth day of that month. MOM terms involve two separate billing dates, one at the fifteenth of the month, the other at the end of the month. All goods purchased from the first to the fifteenth of the month are billed as of the fifteenth, and the discount and credit terms for these goods start the fifteenth. The goods purchased during the latter half of the month are billed as of the end of the month at which time the credit period starts for this batch of orders. Terms expressed as "5/10 prox net 20" indicate that a 5 per cent discount is allowed if the invoice is paid by the tenth of the following month. In any event full payment must be tendered by the 20th of the following month. The abbreviation prox (proximo) is understood to refer to some specific date in the month following billing.

Lumped-order terms may be used by the buyer to gain very favorable credit terms. If purchases are made early in the month and credit terms are EOM net 30, it is possible for the buyer to enjoy 60-day credit.

Consignment Terms

If the buyer does not wish to commit himself to a purchase, or where the risk is too great for the seller, consignment terms may be used. Consignment terms usually require the consignee to segregate both the goods which he is consigned and the income which he receives as he sells these goods. The consignee is required to make periodic reports and accounting for cash to the consignor. Through the term of the consignment, the title to the goods remains with the consignor; the seller acts as a sales agent.

Season Dating

A manufacturer confronted with a seasonal problem may, in order to stabilize his production level during the year, offer credit terms to customers which are intended to induce them to purchase well ahead of their seasonal needs. If the customer takes advantage of the terms, he does so in full recognition of the extra storage and handling costs which will be incurred by acquiring inventory prior to the need for it. By the same token, the manufacturer minimizes his accumulation of finished-goods inventory and can therefore afford to make some concession to his customers. This concession takes the form of an extra period of time added to the regular credit terms. For example, "net 30, 60 ex." would mean that the regular terms involve net payment within 30 days but in this case an additional sixty days are allowed.

Our interest in credit terms involves their significance as part of the pricing problem and as a competitive device, as well as their influence upon the flow of cash funds into and out of the business.

SUMMARY

The methods used to price goods vary greatly. The prices charged for goods depend upon such factors as the product and its attributes, competition, desired profits, and the position of the firm within its industry.

All prices stem from an initial recognition of a pricing policy. Whether this policy is to provide a product at a sound price which provides a "fair" return or whether the intent is to maximize profits or minimize losses, all prices must be set with competition and government in mind.

The terms of sales, credit, and discount are additional devices used by the businessman to make his offer more attractive. Although many such terms have been established as standard trade practice, the variation from such standard terms is the means whereby additional inducement is offered the prospective purchaser. Many times these terms are used by the seller as security measures in the event of less than desirable credit risks.

There can be no minimization of the significance of the role which pricing and prices play in the economic well-being of the firm. The coverage of costs in the long run and the need for funds to meet current working capital needs are requirements for successful operation which are intimately involved with the pricing and sales situation.

QUESTIONS

1. In what areas of business and economic activity are prices important?
2. Basic business goals influence price policy. What are these goals?
3. Price policy may fall between two extremes. What are these extremes and what are the factors which determine where a particular firm's price policy may be set?
4. How does the government enter into the pricing situation for the firm?
5. What is the significance of demand elasticity?
6. Describe cost-plus pricing and its variations.
7. Less-than-cost pricing may be used under what circumstances? What is the maximum desirable loss associated with less-than-cost pricing policy?
8. Price lines are a backward approach to establishing a selling price. Explain.
9. List the various sales terms. Why does each exist?
10. Sales terms are a competitive device. Explain.
11. Define the following credit terms: EOM, COD, SD-BL, prox.
12. Explain season dating.

CHAPTER 22

Costs and Budgets

The business manager is concerned with costs for many reasons. Costs represent an objective measurement of performance which states all activities on the basis of a standard yardstick, the dollar. The accumulation of the cost data of the firm is one form of written history of the business. This cost history is a means of evaluating performance and establishing standards for future accomplishments. The record of various cost-income relationships provides management with a means of comparing the company financial position and operating results with those of other members of their industrial group.

Figures, cost-and-income data, are very much a part of the language of business. Just as the shop or the trade has its vernacular, so does each area of professional management. The businessman speaks of cost, its nature and variability, cost-income relationships, break-even points, spreading fixed costs; and he uses many other expressions which are part of the language of cost.

The reputation in which the firm is held by others is determined more on the basis of financial evaluation than on any other basis. Certainly social value and institutional standing are significant; but when the firm is gaged by other business enterprises, the yardstick applied is almost invariably that of dollar-and-cents standards. Costs, the understanding and control of them, play a very important role in establishing the financial portrait of the firm.

Because of the significance of costs and the purposes which cost accumulation and analysis may serve, there are many who place excessive trust in the results of such analysis. Needless to say, the validity of the results of cost studies may vary. The fundamental shortcomings in the analysis and understanding of costs are inaccuracy and the lack of details. The barrier to greater effort in improving cost data is the expense involved.

Areas for Cost Improvement

Cost improvement is possible in any area in which money is spent. If every firm were to make it a matter of policy that each person responsible for incurring or controlling costs should on a daily basis make intelligent reference to the operating statement of the firm, it is certain that a better understanding of the various areas of cost, their interrelationships, and the need for cost cognizance and control would be impressed upon this personnel to the advantage of the operation of the business.

The areas of purchasing, production, distribution, and administration all take a portion of the income dollar for the payment of their respective operational costs. Each of these areas offers multiple opportunities for improvement in techniques and reduction of costs which will add to the profitability of the company operations.

In order to create a better cost situation in any area, it is first necessary that the area itself be fully understood in terms of operations, relationship to other divisions of the firm, and its own cost structure. For example, the purchasing function is basic to the operation of the manufacturer or retailer. It is a primary function. As such, the complete operational cycle of the firm may get off to either a fine or a poor start as a result of the efficiency with which the function is performed. The cost of the materials procured and the cost of operating the department may in some cases amount to but a very small percentage of the total cost of the plant's operations. On the other hand, such costs may be very significant and may be the prime determinant of whether the firm is to operate at a profit or loss. The manufacturing or operating division of the firm must also be measured in terms of its relative cost significance and the degree to which variations in the operations may serve to improve the company profits or otherwise. With each department of the enterprise, the same approach may be followed to an understanding of relative cost position and importance. This is preliminary to actual cost analysis and the attempt to improve the cost situation.

If the role of each cost-creating function is thus understood, management is in a better position to determine the starting point for analysis. The analysis is fundamental to improvement.

INVESTIGATION OF COSTS

Cost is the accumulation of all expenses incurred in the manufacture of a product or the performance of a service.

What are the areas of business cost?

The services rendered to the company, the materials, the facilities, and the manpower used by the business are the general areas in which costs are incurred.

What is the significance of costs?

Every dollar spent by the firm represents cost incurred because of long-term or short-term activity. It is desired that the spending of business funds bring about the return to the firm of every dollar spent and an additional return in excess of this cost.

Every dollar spent by the firm should eventually return via the sales routine. This is necessary so that the company can at least maintain its dollar status quo. The incentive to continue in business, to grow, and to provide greater amounts of goods and services for the consumer is usually present only if the businessman recovers more than his costs. The search for profits is the strongest motivating force in industry. It leads the businessman into an examination of all the features of business management so that he may be better able to recognize the significance of his decisions and efforts in terms of their effects upon profits. This examination cannot be expected to be fruitful unless there is first an appreciation of what costs are and how they may vary and thereby change the profitability of any venture.

It is erroneous to think that each sale made by the firm adds to profits simply because the selling price of the unit sold was greater than the costs associated with it. A businessman must recognize that the operation of a business involves some expense which must be paid even if no sales are made and that many units have to be sold before any profit results.

It is possible to place too much importance on figures which represent the cost of doing business. The figures are not infallible, yet it is necessary that some approach to costing be followed by every business concern. There exist in industry continual efforts to improve not only the methods of accumulating cost data but also the interpretation of these data. Some firms for years continue costing procedures which later are proved to be inadequate or incorrect in the light of better techniques and understanding.

Short- and Long-term Costs

We cannot specifically designate what periods of time are to be considered as short-term or long-term, for time is of varying importance and meaning in each peculiar circumstance. A man who has spent his total available money supply in preparing an article for sale would consider time to be of the essence, for a quick sale and collection of money are necessary in order that he be able to continue to operate his business. In this case a short period of time may be too long. Another individual who is supplied with money in excess of immediate needs feels less the pressure of time. A delay between the sale and the cash collection may be of little significance in this case. These two situations are not meant to give the impression that the nature of one man's cost situation differs from that of the other. The point of importance here is that the situations simply demonstrate the relativity of time.

In every case, regardless of the cash availability of a particular company, we must recognize that the costs of doing business fall into the category of those which are of current or short-term origination and those which are associated with long-term periods of activity.

The payments which are made to workers, to suppliers of raw materials, to utility companies, and to others who supply everyday services or needs usually fall into the category of short-term activity costs and are usually met periodically in the form of full cash payment.

On the other hand, if the firm invests in a new machine or building or other physical asset, this cost is usually of long-term nature and is, therefore, prorated over the life of the particular asset.

Physical assets are customarily used for long periods of time. During this lifetime they continue to serve the purpose for which they were acquired; therefore, the total cost of any one of these assets cannot be rightfully charged to any indiscriminate period of time or volume of production.

If a machine costs $20,000 and is expected to serve a useful life of eight years, the total cost should be charged off during the time period estimated. In this case, the annual machine cost, which we recognize as the depreciation expense, would amount to $2,500 per year. If at any time the original estimate of life seems erroneous, an adjusted depreciation basis may be established. The depreciation basis represents management's best estimation of the situation.

The fact that the $20,000 purchase price of the machine may have to be paid all at once or over a period of time which does not coincide with the period of life is important in so far as it represents the need for cash outlay. However, the manner in which the machine purchase price is financed should not be confused with the method by which the total cost of the machine is to be charged to production activities.

EXPENSE ANALYSIS

In addition to recognizing the extent and purpose of incurring cost, it is also necessary to understand what happens costwise when the firm's volume of activity varies.

We expect costs to vary with activity, but to what extent? The nature of the particular cost determines the extent of cost variation associated with activity variation. There are three types of costs.

1. Variable costs—vary in total amount in direct proportion to the volume of activity.
2. Semivariable costs—increase in total amount as the volume of activity increases, but not in direct proportion to the volume of activity.

3. Fixed costs—are constant in total amount regardless of the volume of activity.

Depending upon which category a particular cost falls into, it is possible to anticipate the variation in the cost which will occur with a change in the volume of activity.

If every unit of product contains 50 cents' worth of materials, two units involve the use of one dollar's worth, and three involve a cost of $1.50, etc. This is the expression of a variable expense. The relationship between the number of units and the total cost of the materials is in direct proportion.

Units produced	1	2	3
Total material cost	.50	1.00	1.50
Nature of expense	VARIABLE		

If a salesman is paid a basic salary plus a percentage commission on sales, the salary expense is semivariable. It consists of a fixed portion, the basic salary, which theoretically would be paid even if no sales were made, and a variable portion, the commission, which increases in total amount in direct relationship to the dollar amount of sales.

Dollars of sales	$100	$200	$300	
Basic salary	40	40	40	Fixed portion
Commission 10%	10	20	30	Variable portion
Nature of expense	SEMIVARIABLE			

The salary increases as sales increase, but not in direct proportion. The expense must be broken down, as above, into its fixed and variable portions.

A night watchman in the plant may get the same salary regardless of the volume of daytime plant activity. This salary would be a fixed expense since the total remains constant.

Level of plant activity	Low	High
Watchman's salary	$3,500	$3,500
Nature of expense	FIXED	

All expenses, regardless of which of the three categories each may fall into, are finally stated in terms of their respective variable and fixed portions. Such analysis of expenses leads to a greater understanding of costs and the way in which they react when the level of activity is varied and is a prerequisite to any plan of variation in company activity.

Illustration of Expense Analysis and Estimation

The purpose of analyzing expenses is to provide a basis for the estimation of what costs will be incurred at various production levels. The procedure of expense analysis and estimation is as follows:

1. State the costs associated with the extremes of the normal production range.
2. Determine the nature of each expense.
3. Determine the characteristics of each expense in terms of variable and fixed portions.
4. Calculate the estimated costs for a particular production level.

The extremes of the normal production range may be stated as the low and high production levels. The costs associated with each level must be ascertained by management either through experience or by estimation. In either case they must be sufficiently valid to allow straight-line interpolation of the costs between the two production levels.

The estimated costs for a production volume of 1,800 units would be determined in the following manner:

1. The Expenses and Their Amount at the Low and High Production Levels.

Expense	*Low level 1000 units*	*High level 3000 units*
Labor	$ 10,000	$ 30,000
Materials	40,000	120,000
Manufacturing Expenses	35,000	45,000
Administrative Expenses	15,000	15,000
Selling Expenses	11,000	29,000
Total	$111,000	$239,000

2. The Nature of Each Expense. Once the cost situation has been stated in terms of the various expenses and their respective amounts, the next step in analysis is the determination of the nature of each expense. Expenses fall into three categories as discussed previously; and although we customarily expect that certain expenses have a particular nature, such as materials or labor being variable expenses, we may find that in some cases this is not so.

The illustrations provided below are not intended to indicate that labor is always a variable expense, nor that materials are always variable, nor that any of the other listed expenses are always of the nature indicated in the illustrations. Each situation must be treated individually. In some cost situations we may find that labor is a fixed expense, etc.

Labor in the illustration provided above is a variable expense, for it increases in direct relationship to the production level. The labor cost represents the payment to those who actually perform work on the product.

Materials are also a variable expense in this illustration. This cost represents the expense involved in the use of materials which directly enter into the manufacture of the product.

Manufacturing expenses meet the test of a semivariable expense and represent the cost of machines, indirect labor and materials, power, insurance, supervision, and other expenses associated with the production area.

Administrative expenses are a fixed expense and represent the payments made to personnel and for materials, equipment, and the services which are necessary for the administration of the organization as a whole.

Selling expenses are a semivariable expense and represent payments made to the sales force, for advertising, shipping costs, and other expenses which are incurred in behalf of the sales effort of the firm.

3. *The Characteristics of Each Expense.* (*a*) *Variable expenses* have but a single characteristic, a variable portion. This is determined by dividing the total amount of the expense at either low or high level by the respective number of units of production to determine the variable cost per unit.

Expense	*Cost*	÷ *Production*	= *Variable Portion*
Labor	$10,000	÷ 1,000 units	= $10 per unit
Materials	$40,000	÷ 1,000 units	= $40 per unit

(*b*) *Fixed expenses* also have but a single characteristic, a constant total amount regardless of number of units of production.

Expense	*Fixed Portion*
Administrative	$15,000 regardless of volume

It must be noted at this point that a very significant difference exists between our determination of the characteristics of the variable and the fixed expenses. In the first case, our variable expense was stated in terms of an amount per unit while our fixed expense was stated in total amount. The reason for this lies in the fact that we wish to state the characteristics of an expense in terms of a constancy.

A variable expense is not constant in its total amount, for as we have seen, it increases in proportion to the level of activity. It is, however, constant in terms of the amount of increase in expense for each unit increase in production.

A fixed expense, we have noted, is constant in total regardless of variation in production volume. If we were to divide the quantity of production into the fixed expense total, we would have a different unit fixed cost at each production level. Our need for a constant expression of this type of expense is found in terms of its total.

Our expenses must be stated in terms of some constant relationship, for if we are to establish the cost of production at various levels, it is necessary to hold one factor constant. To have both production variations and cost factors which were not constant would be an incalculable situation for our purposes.

(*c*) *Semivariable expenses* must be analyzed in two stages. First, the variable portion per unit must be calculated; and second, the fixed portion is determined. The variable portion is arrived at by dividing the increase in the total amount of cost between low and high levels by the increase in total number of units produced between these levels.

First Stage of Analysis

Expense	*Increase in cost*	÷	*Increase in production*	=	*Variable portion*
Mfg. Expense	\$10,000	÷	2,000 units	=	\$5 per unit
Selling Expense	\$18,000	÷	2,000 units	=	\$9 per unit

Since the total cost of each semivariable expense consists of the two portions, variable and fixed, the difference between the total cost at a particular level of operations and the total variable portion of this cost will equal the total fixed portion.

Second Stage of Analysis

Expense	*Total cost*	—	*Total variable portion*	=	*Fixed portion*
Mfg. Expense	\$35,000	—	1,000 × \$5 or \$5,000	=	\$30,000
Selling Expense	11,000	—	1,000 × \$9 or \$9,000	=	2,000

The characteristics of each expense as determined above are to be considered valid only through the range of 1,000 to 3,000 units. Any production level above or below this range must have its respective costs analyzed before estimations can be prepared. The tabulation of the expense characteristics would appear as follows:

Expense Characteristics

Expense	*Variable portion per unit*	*Fixed portion*
Labor	\$10	
Materials	40	
Manufacturing Expenses	5	\$30,000
Administrative Expenses		15,000
Selling Expenses	9	2,000

4. *The Estimated Costs for a Production Level of 1,800 Units.* The estimated volume *times* the variable portion per unit *plus* the fixed portion *equals* the estimated cost.

Expense	*Volume*	×	*Variable*	+	*Fixed*	=	*Estimate*
Labor	1,800	×	$10	+	0	=	$ 18,000
Materials	1,800	×	40	+	0	=	72,000
Mfg. Expenses	1,800	×	5	+	30,000	=	39,000
Admin. Expenses	1,800	×	0	+	15,000	=	15,000
Selling Expenses	1,800	×	9	+	2,000	=	18,200
TOTAL ESTIMATED COST FOR 1,800 UNITS							$162,200

Need for Expense Estimation

The procedure of expense analysis and estimation is used by management in the evaluation of prospective production levels. This predetermination of costs provides a basis on which decisions regarding the acceptance of orders may be made. Such estimation also indicates the feasibility of higher production levels on a cost-income basis.

Knowledge of expense characteristics provides a means of investigating the activity of each department in order to determine its best operating level and its best level of cost relationship within the firm. Certainly no valid extrapolation of costs may be done without the knowledge of expense characteristics. And no businessman would enter into a new area of operations or a new level of production without some preview of the potential costs involved.

Expense analysis provides management with some knowledge of how the variations in levels of activity are reflected costwise. It also provides data on the interrelationship of the various costs. If the question of more manpower versus more machine time should be raised, estimation of the costs involved in each consideration is possible only if expense-variation data are available.

Spreading of Fixed Costs

A plant represents a cost burden to its owners even when the plant is idle. This burden consists of the fixed costs of doing business and involves such expense items as depreciation, insurance, taxes, and other expenses which are incurred even though production is not being carried on. Management must recognize that the greater the volume of output achieved from a given production unit, such as a machine or a factory or the firm as a whole, the less is the per-unit fixed cost. This fixed cost may be of great significance to many companies which make heavy investment in plant and facilities. In these cases the volume of production must be high so that there are many units over which the fixed costs may be spread. This provides a low-unit fixed cost and helps in providing a total cost per unit which assists the firm's competitive efforts. There are many companies which have heavy fixed costs yet do not need a great volume of production to support the plant. These firms make and sell fewer units, but each unit provides a large contribution toward the coverage of the total fixed costs.

The following illustration demonstrates the spreading of fixed costs. It will be noted that although fixed costs remain constant in total, the fixed cost per unit decreases with each increase in number of units produced. It must be remembered that a firm does not necessarily produce a single product, and if such is the case, the total fixed cost of the plant must be apportioned as a burden of cost for each product.

SPREADING FIXED COSTS

Production Volume Potential of the XYZ Company

	0 units	*100 units*	*200 units*	*300 units*
Total fixed costs	$1,000	$1,000	$1,000	$1,000
Fixed cost per unit	....	$ 10	$ 5	$ 3.33

It is necessary for the management of the firm to consider both the technical and cost efficiencies of operations. A point may be reached where additional production volume is possible only if the plant is increased in size, if additional equipment or facilities are acquired, or if operating time is increased by additional shifts or overtime work. Any one of these possibilities may cause an increase in total and unit fixed costs. The decision as to whether or not to increase plant size or level of production is affected by the influence which fixed costs have upon the unit cost of production, for changes in the cost structure will alter the break-even point.

Break-even Analysis

The relationship between cost and sales income is investigated in order to determine the effect of various sales volumes upon the firm's profit. Total income must certainly exceed total costs in order to provide an element of profit. The question, however, is when does the firm start making profit? When does total income finally exceed total costs? Does the firm make profit at any or all levels of production and sales? Break-even analysis is a tool used by management to answer these questions.

The production costs used in the preceding illustration will also be used for the break-even analysis which follows. We will also assume that each unit of the product can be sold for $100. Therefore, the total income and the total cost at each of the two production levels are as follows:

Level of production	1,000 units	3,000 units
Total income ($100 per unit)	$100,000	$300,000
Total cost	111,000	239,000
Net result	(11,000) LOSS	61,000 PROFIT

It is apparent that the lower production level provides no profit; the upper does. We wish to determine what production (and sales) level the firm should seek to achieve in order to at least break even. This level is indicated on the break-even chart, Figure 22–1.

The firm will break even at about 1,300 units of production and sales. A lower level will result in losses; higher levels provide increasing amounts of profit.

The break-even chart is useful in depicting the effect upon the cost-income relationship which will result from any variations in the company activity. Therefore, any managerial program may be tested for its influence on profits by means of break-even analysis.

The break-even chart, like many of the other tools which management

FIGURE 22–1

BREAK-EVEN CHART

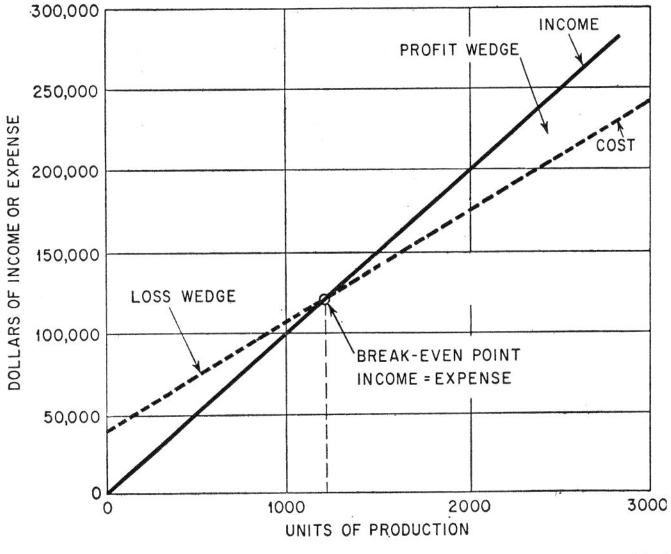

applies, is only as good as the person using it. The chart itself does not give the answer to a problem; it merely interprets information in a manner which may assist management in the making of business decisions.

EXPENSE ALLOCATION

One of our primary concerns with the cost of operating is recognizing the reasons why each cost has come into being and the purposes which are served by its incurrence. The objective is that of tracing each element of cost to the department or product which benefited. The direct cost of materials and labor which are used is identified by means of material and labor tickets which are prepared with the production orders. The many indirect costs, commonly called overhead, or burden, are determinable in total amounts but not always in terms of what portion of the total should be charged against a particular operating division or as part of the cost of each product being manufactured.

If the firm creates a single product, all costs, direct and indirect, are assigned to this product. Thereby the cost of a unit is easily available. If the firm operates many divisions, each of which is responsible for some part of the manufacture or servicing of multiple products, the task of expense allocation becomes more involved. If material and time tickets are available for each of the products, these direct costs can be applied directly to the total cost of the product. The overhead costs, however, must first be assigned to the various operating and service departments. These costs may be allocated on the following bases:

Cost	*Distribution*
Indirect Materials	Actual usage
Indirect Labor	Actual payroll
Depreciation	Value and life of assets
Heating	Space
Lighting	Wattage
Power	Horsepower
Maintenance	Space
Insurance	Valuation
Rent	Space
Advertising	Volume of sales

Since the service departments—power, heat and light, maintenance, general office, etc.—have no direct participation in the manufacture of

SCHEDULE OF EXPENSE ALLOCATION

Expense	*Total*	*Operating departments* #1	*Operating departments* #2	*Service depts.* Heat, light, power	*Service depts.* Maintenance
Depreciation	$4,000	1,500	1,000	1,000	500
Indirect labor	3,000	200	400	1,400	1,000
Indirect materials	1,500	300	500	200	500
Insurance	1,000	400	200	300	100
	9,500	2,400	2,100	2,900	2,100
Service Depts.					
Heat, light, power	2,900	1,160	1,740		
Maintenance	2,100	630	1,470		
Total		4,190	5,310		

the products, the total cost of each of these service departments is first charged to the service department itself and then must be reallocated to the operating departments. This allocation is made in proportion to the services rendered each of the operating departments. The illustration above shows the method of allocating costs to the various operating and service departments and the final distribution of the service-department costs to the operating departments. It is not intended to portray a complete listing of the costs and the bases for allocation.

The percentage breakdown of each total expense is as follows:

Expense	*Operating departments* #1	#2	*Service depts.* *Heat, light, power*	*Maintenance*
Depreciation	37½%	25%	25%	12½%
Indirect labor	Record of actual costs incurred			
Indirect materials	Record of actual costs incurred			
Insurance	40%	20%	30%	10%

The depreciation and insurance expense distribution percentages were determined as follows:

Depreciation

Department	*Equipment value*	*Life (in yr)*	*Per cent*	*Depreciation charge*
Operating #1	$15,000	10	37½	$1,500
Operating #2	20,000	20	25	1,000
Heat, light, and power	30,000	30	25	1,000
Maintenance	2,500	5	12½	500
		TOTAL	100	$4,000

Insurance

Department	*Department valuation*	*Per cent of Total*	*Insurance charge*
Operating #1	$48,000	40	$ 400
Operating #2	24,000	20	200
Heat, light, and power	36,000	30	300
Maintenance	12,000	10	100
		100	$1,000

As we have indicated above, certain departments are not directly involved in the production of goods, and therefore the expenses which are associated with their operations must be reallocated to the operating departments. Such is the case with the heat, light, and power and the maintenance departments. The expenses incurred by each of these two departments in respect to depreciation, insurance, indirect materials, and labor have been determined, and we are now in a position to establish the total expense which must be allocated to Operating #1 and #2. We find this accomplished in the Schedule of Expense Allocation above. It will be noted that the total expense amounts—$2,900 and $2,100—have been distributed percentagewise in accordance with the proportion of services provided each operating department. The percentage distribution is as follows:

Service Department	*Percentage Allocation* Operating #1	Operating #2
Heat, light, and power	40	60
Maintenance	30	70

By means of these procedures the businessman attempts to isolate the cost of producing a unit of product. If his production consists of varied products, the procedure of cost allocation becomes more involved, for the costs must first be charged to the various operating divisions and then assigned to the various products which may be produced by each operating division. If a single product is prepared by each division, the total cost per unit is determined by dividing total costs by the total number of units produced. If varied products are handled, the total costs of the division must be prorated according to the amount of production of each unit or on some other equitable basis, such as direct labor hours or machine hours applied to each product.

DETERMINATION OF DEPARTMENTAL COST PER UNIT

Single-product Division

Total costs	$115,000
Number of units produced	10,000
Cost per unit	$11.50

Multiple-product Division

Total costs	$200,000
Number of units produced	
X	7,000
Y	4,000
Number of direct labor hours	
X	1,400
Y	2,100
Total costs in ratio of direct labor hours	
X	$ 80,000
Y	120,000
Cost per unit	
X	$11.43
Y	30.00

SYSTEMS OF ACCOUNTING FOR COST

There are three principal cost accounting systems in use today: job-order, process-cost, and standard cost accounting. Cost accounting systems are applied by the manufacturer to determine the cost of a unit of production. General accounting is concerned with the recording of over-all financial activity. The difference is primarily one of emphasis.

Job-order cost accounting seeks to accumulate all costs incurred in producing the units called for in each order. The costs fall into one of three categories—direct labor, direct materials, and overhead. To the direct, or prime costs—materials and labor—is added a portion of the factory overhead according to some basis of expense allocation. This total cost divided by the number of units produced provides the finished-goods unit cost. This system identifies specific costs with each order.

JOB-ORDER COSTING

Materials..................	Applied to the order	=	Total Cost	÷	No. of Units	=	Unit Cost
Labor.....................							
Overhead..................							

The process-cost system identifies all costs first with a manufacturing process and second with the product. With some products, such as soap, food, chemicals, and others, it is not possible to break up the materials or labor cost on an order basis. The materials and labor are applied to the process without recognition of a particular order. All materials, labor, and orders are homogeneous and therefore not readily segregated by orders. For example, the cost of a pound of a chemical product, regardless of the particular order, is the average cost per pound resulting from the over-all process costs.

PROCESS COSTING

Materials.............	Process #1	Additional) Materials)......	Process #2
Labor.................		....Transfer....................	
Overhead.............		Additional Labor...........	
		Overhead..................	
	Orders #334 #337 #338		Orders #335 #336

Standard costs represent the costs which should be incurred if production is planned and executed efficiently. These standard costs are predetermined. They are estimates established as standards of performance and thus provide a means of measuring and controlling the efficiency of the manufacturing processes.

Predetermined rates may be calculated for all the elements of cost. These rates are established on the basis of past performance records plus the concept of what comprises efficient performance. They represent a somewhat subjective evaluation inasmuch as they do involve the concept of efficiency which is subject to varying interpretation.

BUDGETS

The budget represents a consolidated estimate of what a firm plans to do and how it plans to do it. It is a forecast of business activity which is set up to serve as a guide to actual performance. This forecast is an attempt to set up in advance the details of cost and operation in each of several areas of business. It is established on a dollar, time, and quantity basis in order that the aspects of dollars, hours, and volume of work may be clearly depicted. The budget forecasts the following:

1. Sales—how much, at what price, when will they be made.
2. Production volume—how much and when.
3. Costs—how much, when they must be paid.
4. Income—how much, when received.
5. Capital expenditures—how much, when necessary, and when the debt can be liquidated.
6. Profits—how much.

Purpose of the Budget

The budget provides the basis for a controlled relationship between cost and income. Since it specifically states money, time, and quantity relationships, it pin-points the specific responsibilities of all who are charged with the operation of the budget. Many times the budget actually promotes an internal competitive spirit, and each budgetary department attempts to make the best showing budgetwise.

An additional purpose served by the budget is that it forces the various departments of the company to fully recognize the significance of each area of operations beyond their immediate area. The interrelationship and the need for close cooperation in the attainments of the singularly stated final business goal, profit, is brought into the clearest focus possible by means of budgetary procedures.

Often the budget is described as a predetermined profit and loss statement. It establishes the cost and income factors which should lead to the desired profit objective. In addition the budget procedure provides each department concerned with creating cost with an insight into its specific function from the profit-making viewpoint.

Prerequisites to Sound Budgeting

1. The budget must not be set up hastily.
2. It is necessary that adequate statistics and cost data be available.
3. It is presupposed that an adequate cost accounting system is set up in the company.
4. It is necessary that those who are to work the budget are people capable of accepting responsibility.
5. The budget is a goal; this goal must be translated to the work force in terms which have significance to them.
6. Provision should be made for quick reporting of actual performance in order to allow for comparison with the budget plan and the early discovery of any discrepancies.
7. A system should be established for the improvement of budgetary procedures and for the investigation of any discrepancies.
8. Management should not expect the budget to do the work. The budget has to be worked.

The plan of budgetary control cannot operate by itself. To have real assurance of successful operation the company must be organized in such a manner that the operation of control measures may be feasible. This means that the scope of authority and responsibility must be clearly stated and understood by each member of the organizational structure. Confusion of responsibility and overlapping authority reduce organizational efficiency and thereby interfere with the correct application of budgetary procedures and controls.

Fixed and Variable Budgeting

The fixed budget is a predetermination of a specific goal and the means of accomplishment. A company research program may be set up on the basis of a fixed budget. In this case a certain program of accomplishment is established, and the work progresses according to plan to this goal. No consideration has been made in the budgetary application for possible variations from the prescribed course. Possibly there is no need for concern with such variations. In some cases it is merely the managerial approach which places such absoluteness upon the situation.

A variable budget is a necessity for today's operations, for the usual firm finds that although it may anticipate the year's activity with more or less assurance, it must be prepared for variations in activity on day-to-day or some other basis of time. The variable budget procedure provides this element of flexibility without sacrificing the control aspects.

The variable budget anticipates that actual activity levels will vary; therefore, the budgetary procedure is one which provides a continuing comparison of budget estimates with actual performance. In order to install variable budgetary control, costs must be analyzed and their characteristics established. This type of analysis was discussed earlier in this chapter. With this knowledge of expense characteristics, as quickly as the forecast of operations is altered the anticipated costs can be reckoned. In this manner we have an extremely flexible means of estimating costs. Any variation in activity can be quickly translated in terms of the effect upon costs and other factors which are being subjected to budgetary control.

The income aspect of variable budgeting necessarily accompanies the determination of cost levels, for costs are incurred as a result of anticipated income.

Actual and Budgeted Costs and Income

If at any time actual performance varies from budget estimates, the difference is termed the *variance.* If it is budgeted that the labor cost for a particular volume of work should be $500 and the actual cost amounts to $540, the $40 variance is the signal for investigation. Whenever cost or income deviates from the predetermined plan, the uncovering of the reasons for the variance is of utmost importance. It provides management with a better understanding of the difficulties or irregularities of a situation and it also indicates areas of control which are inadequate or incorrect. Variance analysis is the means whereby better controls are established.

SUMMARY

The commonest language of the business world is that of dollars and cents. The businessman steers his venture toward a profit goal. Whether he makes his port depends in great part upon his understanding of costs, their behavior and interrelationships. Each department of the business harbors areas of potential cost improvement. These improvements are only had after management provides itself with the tools and ability to analyze its cost situations. The knowledge of the nature and characteristics of costs is the key to their control. The effect which variations in the level of company operations have upon the level of costs and income is seen in the lowering or increasing of the profit margin.

The interrelationship of cost and income is graphically seen in the form of the break-even chart. This device is a handy means of portraying the influence of cost and income upon profits. Its use embodies an accurate knowledge of cost and income data and the effect which higher or lower levels of plant activity have upon the cost of a unit of production. The spreading of fixed costs is of significance in this respect.

The materials and labor used in production usually are a lesser problem when it comes to assigning costs to production, for control systems used by management can provide direct information as to the costs of these items. Overhead, or plant burden, may involve use of some system of expense allocation so that units of production may be correctly costed.

The accumulation of the necessary data with which to establish cost controls and record the occurrence of expenses is the function of cost accounting. Job-order, process-cost, and standard cost are the three principal cost accounting systems used today.

Budgetary procedure embodies the principles of cost planning, estimation, recording, and control. Since the budget is an estimate, it is necessary that some means be used to estimate costs at various activity levels. This is where our knowledge of expense characteristics is used. In order to control our activity, costs and other information must be recorded as they occur and compared to the budget estimates. Any variance, above or below the budget estimate, is the signal for managerial investigation into the reasons why. This analysis is the means whereby the budgeting system is improved.

QUESTIONS

1. Why is the business manager concerned with costs?
2. How significant is the purchasing function from the viewpoint of cost improvement?
3. What is cost?
4. Differentiate short- and long-term costs.
5. What is a semivariable cost? A fixed cost? Illustrate.
6. What are the steps involved in expense analysis and estimation?
7. Analyze the following expense and estimate the total expense for 2,400 units.

	2,000 units	3,000 units
Total cost	$4,200	$6,000

8. What is the need for expense estimation?
9. What does the break-even chart portray?
10. Explain the principle of spreading fixed costs.
11. Explain expense allocation. List three overhead expenses and the basis on which they may be allocated.
12. List and explain briefly three systems of cost accounting.
13. What is a budget? What does it forecast? What is its purpose?
14. Differentiate: fixed and variable budgeting.
15. What is the importance of variance analysis?

CHAPTER 23

Financing the Enterprise

The business firm finds that its need for funds exists in two respects: short-term and long-term. The distinction is that between the need for funds to pay for labor and materials which daily enter into the production process and the need for funds which are invested in machinery and plant or other assets which are customarily financed over long periods of time. The existence of these needs can certainly be anticipated by virtually all business firms, but the extent and the time of need must necessarily be determined by orderly analysis. The work done by management in the analysis of costs and the installation of budgetary techniques and control is fundamental to the determination of the need for financing business. Devices used are the cash budget—which predetermines the flow of cash income and outgo, thereby establishing the time and amount of shortages or excesses of available cash—and the capital expenditures budget which sets up the program of asset purchase and payment in terms of the need for the asset and the availability of company funds or the need for outside funds for the payment thereof.

Nature of Capital Requirements

Working capital represents that amount of cash or assets that are converted into cash within a year of normal business operations. The assets of the firm which are bought and sold in the regular daily operating routine make up the firm's working capital. Inventory, receivables, and cash itself are the assets used to run the business from day to day. They represent the sources of daily receipts which are necessary to meet payrolls and creditor obligations. They are absolutely requisite as sources of funds in daily operations.

Every firm needs working capital; but how much? The retail or wholesale merchant who maintains a high inventory level and has a quick turnover of goods needs a relatively high amount of working capital.

Heavy industries require relatively little working capital, for their prime need is in terms of establishing plant and equipment.

The credit practices of the firm are another factor which determines working capital requirements. If it is the practice to offer long payment periods to customers and the same privilege is not enjoyed from creditors, the firm must increase its supply of working capital in order to finance this extension of credit.

The longer the merchandising or production cycle of the enterprise, the greater are the working capital requirements. If goods are tied up for long periods in the production process, and weeks or months pass before the finished goods are sold and payment received, working capital requirements are increased to support the firm during the interim. Likewise, a merchant who must store goods for a long while in anticipation of sales finds that he too needs extra working capital during the storage period.

Working capital requirements are often classified as (1) seasonal requirements and (2) normal requirements. The normal requirement is the minimum necessary to support operations even during the slowest part of the year. The seasonal working capital requirement is that amount over and above normal requirements necessary to support operations during the on-season when activity is at its highest levels.

In attempting to establish the level of these requirements the businessman is as likely to overestimate his needs as to underestimate them. Since he is always seeking the most efficient use of his funds, idle cash is as poor a situation as the shortage of funds. Excess working capital may prove beneficial at times by providing the firm with the means to support research or provide equipment replacements which may become necessary on short notice.

Fixed capital requirements are that amount of investment necessary to establish the physical facilities—plant, machinery, and equipment—and intangibles which are relatively permanent as part of the firm's investment, such as patents, trade-marks, long-term leases, etc.

The investment in these facilities is not to be converted into cash within the year. Although the assets may be sold, customarily the investment is of long-term duration. The value of the investments lies in the use of them, not the sale.

The fixed capital requirement varies greatly among firms. It is dictated by the nature of operations. Service and merchandising operations usually involve limited fixed capital requirements. Heavy industry and utilities usually have high requirements. Somewhere in between are the requirements of other industries, such as manufacturing.

The most important aspect of the financing of fixed capital requirements is its justification on a cash-return basis. The long-time period between the incurring of the financial obligation and a cash return carries with it a greater risk than does working capital financing which involves a short borrowing cycle. Funds acquired on a long-term basis and used to buy physical assets are thereby pretty well tied down. The assets so purchased can seldom be disposed of except at a significant loss; therefore the asset acquired must be capable of providing income sufficient to carry its repayment costs and operating costs, and to provide an element of profit. The possibility of the assets performing in this manner must be appraised by management prior to its assumption of the burden of a financial obligation in behalf of the asset purchase.

Sources of Business Funds

There are three sources of funds for the business firm. Capital may be secured from the owners of business, from lenders such as bondholders and banks, and from trade creditors through the mechanism of credit terms. See Figure 23–1.

The ownership of the firm as represented by stock investments or by proprietorship or partnership interests is the primary source of funds. Because efficiency in operations many times demands a supply of funds in excess of that available as owner investment, other sources of funds are needed. Owner investment is primarily of long-term nature and has certain characteristics which distinguish it from other sources of funds. First, the firm is under no obligation to pay a return thereon. Second, there is no stated date on which the funds must be returned to the investors. Third, the management of the firm is in the hands of those who provide the funds. This capital is often termed the "risk capital" of the firm. This indicates that the owners are undertaking greater risks than any other suppliers of funds.

The nonwithdrawal of profits from the business is another means whereby owners contribute funds to the business. Ploughing in the surplus is the term applied to this form of addition to the investment in facilities.

The decision to use borrowed funds should be made only after very careful consideration of the costs, anticipated income, and risks that are involved. Borrowing is engaged in principally because profits are anticipated from the use of the funds. Profits, however, are sometimes very slow in materializing. If the funds are destined for investment in physical assets, they probably will not be recovered except over a long-time period. Even so, there is no assurance of profits. The experience of the company or its industry provides the basis for profit estimation which is the starting point of evaluating financing needs.

When the business firm borrows, it gives a promise to pay. In addition the borrower may give the lender the pledge of particular assets as security for the loan. The terms of the loan involve some statement as to time

FIGURE 23–1

SOURCES OF FUNDS FOR LARGE CORPORATIONS

(Percentage Distribution 1946–1953)

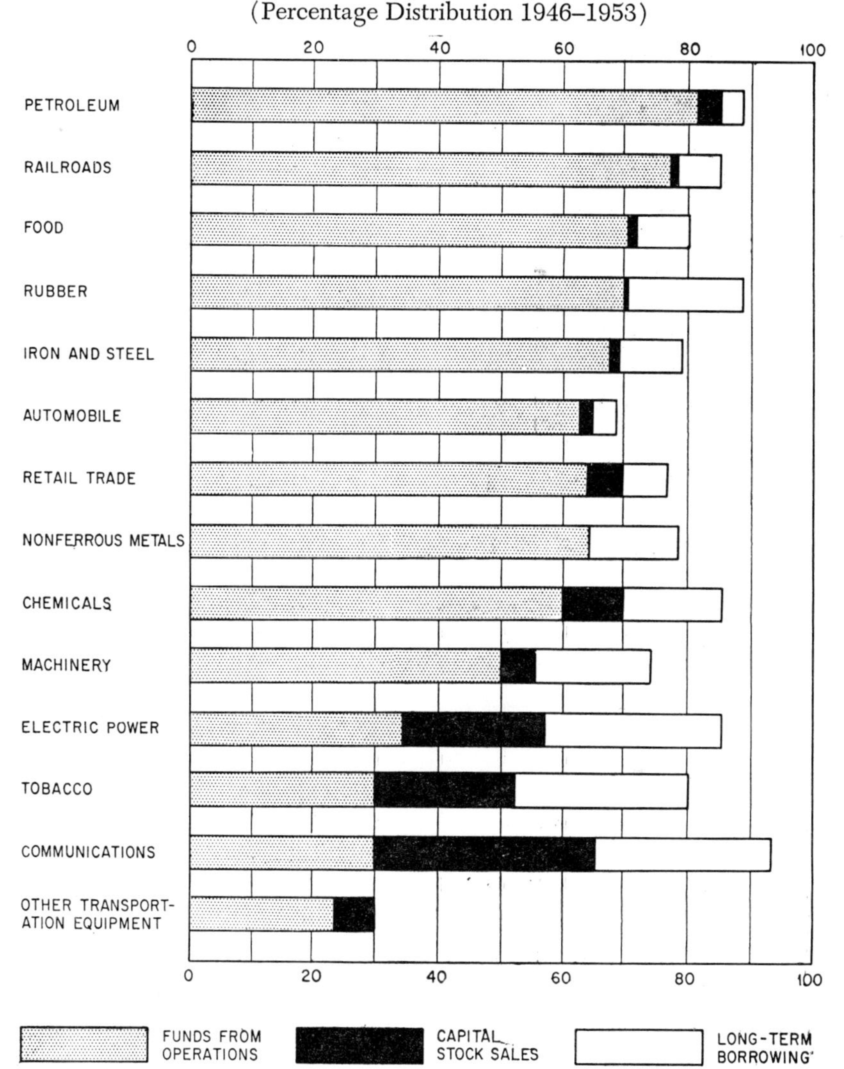

* Other sources: short-term borrowing, trade credit, prepayments, reduction of receivables, inventory liquidation. These amount to 17 per cent of all sources over the period 1947–53.

SOURCE: Board of Governors of the Federal Reserve System, *Federal Reserve Bulletin,* August, 1954, p. 816.

of repayment and contain terms as to interest charges and payments of principal. Banks' interest rates on secured loans tend to be higher than the rates on unsecured loans. This is evidence of the greater risk accompanying secured loans.

Short-term loans are those which mature within one year; and a long-term note is one which matures beyond one year. Sometimes businessmen like to classify certain of the long-term notes as intermediate-term borrowing. If the firm customarily borrows large sums over ten and twenty years, a loan negotiated for a five-year term may be classified as an intermediate-term loan. This designation is relative. It depends upon the prevailing borrowing activity of the firm. A five-year note may be long-term to one firm and intermediate-term to another.

Mercantile credit is an important form of short-term, or working capital, financing. This credit is that extended by one business firm to another in the course of normal business operations. A firm with sound reputation may enjoy credit terms which minimize its need for outside financing for working capital requirements. The firm with poor credit standing or one which is new in the field has an aggravated working capital position, for many times it may be called upon to prepay on its orders. This may necessitate borrowing from individuals, finance houses, or commercial banks.

Sources of Working Capital

The funds necessary for current operations are not always available in the firm's bank account. The firm may often be short of cash if its current assets are tied up in inventories and receivables. These short-term, or working capital, requirements may be satisfied by the commercial bank.

The smaller firms obtain most of their loan capital from commercial banks and finance houses. The firm which engages in seasonal operations may find that a line of credit with its bank will satisfy its need for working capital requirements. The line of credit is an arrangement whereby the availability of funds is established when and if borrowing becomes necessary. The borrower signs promissory notes as the funds are needed. Sometimes it is necessary for the borrower to maintain on deposit with the bank a percentage of the line of credit. If the firm finds that its needs do not recur on a seasonal or predictable basis, it should preferably make borrowing arrangements when the need specifically arises.

Fundamental to all borrowing is the establishment of a bank contact. The planning of the future of the enterprise should involve planning for the financing facilities with which the firm wishes to associate itself.

Short-term loans call for repayment within the year. Borrowers are expected to pay up their total indebtedness annually so that at some time during the year there is no outstanding obligation for the particular firm. This rule is not always enforced. Most short-term bank loans are secured, although more money is lent on the basis of unsecured loans. The security offered by the borrower may be in the form of inventories, receivables, stocks, bonds, equipment, or the security of its financial statement.

Another means of satisfying the cash requirements of the firm may be the sale of accounts receivable to a factor. The factoring company buys the accounts receivable, collects them, and charges the firm an interest and service charge on the basis of the outstanding balance of accounts. This procedure may be of great value to the smaller firm which is unable to utilize the security market in financing or is unable or unwilling to dilute ownership by seeking new investors. The arguments against factoring are that the procedure dissociates the firm from its customers, severs the contact had via monthly statements of accounts, and limits the freedom of sales arrangements which the company may at times feel justified in making. If factoring is a means of financing, greater attention must be paid to sales risks. Present practice calls more for the discounting of accounts or the assigning of accounts receivable as collateral for loans rather than factoring them. In either of these cases the responsibility for the accounts rests with the firm. The firm engages in the bookkeeping and collections work as it normally would.

Intermediate-term Capital Sources

The intermediate-term debts of business range from one to five or ten years. The arrangements for such financing may be in the form of term loans, installment plans arising out of installment purchases, or any other form of credit instrument which runs up to five- or ten-year maturity. These loans are usually payable on the installment basis and carry stipulated conditions as to payment and conditions under which the borrower may operate during the term of repayment. These loans are customarily extended by commercial banks and insurance companies, and the proceeds are used to finance purchases or for lease of facilities.

Long-term Capital Sources

The principal means of long-term borrowing are the real-estate-mortgage loan and the bond. Real-estate loans are made by commercial banks, insurance companies, and others. These loans carry higher rates than do other forms of loans and unless guaranteed or insured usually run up to 50 or 60 per cent of the appraised value of the property. Industrial property usually has a lesser loan value than commercial property; maturity of these loans is usually shorter; and the terms of amortization are more rigorous. The loan arrangements involve the note and mortgage instruments. The mortgage is generally regarded as lien on the property. In the event of failure to meet the terms of the note, the lender many times prefers to see financial reorganization rather than liquidation of the firm.

The bond is a long-term note and customarily has a maturity of ten years or more. It contains a promise to pay interest on stated dates and, usually, in stated amounts. The exceptions to this are the income bonds which pay interest only if income is earned. Bonds may be issued by an individual, a partnership, or a corporation. They may be registered as to principal and interest, or principal only, or they may be unregistered. In each case of registration, principal and/or interest payments are made by the borrower to the person whose name appears in the books of the borrower.

Bond financing is often coupled with mortgages, thereby creating the category of mortgage bonds secured by a mortgage on real property. If the bond is secured by other stocks and bonds, it is called a collateral trust bond. A bond which is unsecured is called a "debenture bond."

Borrowing by means of bonds is usually cheaper than borrowing by the issuance of preferred stock. In addition, the interest payments made are deductible for tax purposes. The disadvantage of any borrowing is the fixity of the payment schedule. The cost of borrowing becomes a fixed expense of the firm during the life of the indebtedness.

Leasing As an Alternative

Much more interest and activity have occurred recently relative to the leasing of industrial and commercial facilities as the alternative to outright purchase or long-term financing commitments. The leasing provisions eliminate or minimize the need for immediate availability of funds with which to set up the enterprise. Since plant, machinery, and equipment are all available on lease basis, a man may possibly undertake a business venture equipped with only as much financial backing as is necessary to secure lease arrangements and establish credit with vendor firms who will supply materials for the process. His working capital requirements depend upon the turnover of his finished goods and the speed of his production cycle. If the plant is capable of turning out finished goods in one day and credit terms are such that a good portion of his sales collections are made within one week, this income may be applied to meet operating costs such as payroll and other expenses which are most immediate in their demands upon cash funds. Other indebtedness may involve credit terms which provide ample time for the receipt of cash from the sales of goods to make payments within the trade terms.

It does not seem reasonable to assume that leasing arrangements are cheaper in the long run, for a return must be provided for the lessor which adds to the costs of the lessee. However, for the short-term or intermediate financing period the extra cost may be justified by the fact that the leasing arrangements made possible the establishment of the firm when other customary financing arrangements would not have been available.

Why Borrow?

Borrowing may be justified by stating that the need for funds exists; that equity financing is not desirable. Why? First, because there is greater freedom involved in making arrangements for loans than there is in arranging for the sale of stock. When we borrow, we plan our precise needs and so establish financing arrangements so that commitments cease when we wish. The sale of stock may establish a change in ownership structure which is undesirable and perpetual. Oftentimes it is cheaper and more expedient to finance with debts than with the sale of stock. Borrowing the funds with which to operate may make the investment in the firm appear better. The profit from operations as related to investments in the firm look much better if the total amount of investment is not increased by the sale of stock. The money borrowed entails a cost to the firm but does not enter into the participation of the additional profits which its use may bring about.

SUMMARY

The need for funds exists in two respects: short-term and long-term requirements. The short-term requirements are the working capital needs. These requirements depend upon the seasonal nature of the business, its credit practices, the turnover of goods, and the length of the merchandising or production cycle.

The long-term requirements, fixed capital, vary greatly among firms and are dictated by the nature of operations and the physical plant which is necessary. Fixed capital financing is most important from the viewpoint of justifying the investment on a cash-return basis.

Business funds arise from three basic sources: investors, lenders, and trade creditors. Investors are the principal contributors of business funds. However, it is very often necessary that the business firm apply to various sources for funds in addition to those available at any given time. These sources supply funds for short-, intermediate-, and long-term lending and use various credit devices to accomplish the lending. A line of credit, a short-term loan, and the sale or pledging of accounts receivable are some of the devices available for short-term financing. Intermediate-term financing is usually accomplished on the basis of term loans of five or more years' duration. Long-term financing is provided by means of real-estate mortgages or bonds.

As an alternate to financing, leasing arrangements are quite generally available; these minimize the need for funds or sources of funds on the part of the prospective business operator.

The firm engages in borrowing because it is cheaper and more expedient than equity financing, and involves no change in company organizational control.

QUESTIONS

1. In what area must fundamental work be carried on prior to determining the need for financing business?
2. What is the nature of business capital requirements?
3. How does the merchandising or production cycle time enter into the determination of working capital requirements?
4. What is the most important aspect of the financing of fixed capital requirements?
5. List three sources of funds for the business firm.
6. What considerations are preliminary to the borrowing of funds?
7. What is a line of credit?
8. What sort of security may be offered for short-term loans?
9. How does the factor satisfy the cash requirements of a firm?
10. How do factoring and assigning of accounts differ?
11. What is a term loan?
12. What are the principal means of long-term borrowing?
13. Real-estate-loan terms differ depending upon the nature of the property. How?
14. How does leasing minimize the need for financing?
15. List three reasons which justify borrowing.

PART SIX

Ownership and Development

The most important ingredients of our managerial recipe are yet before us. Up to this point we have identified the need for planning the organization of physical facilities, manpower, finances, and the provisions for servicing a market. Each of these parts has been examined as a unit, yet never without recognition of its interdependence with the others. To maximize the potential from all these areas of managerial concern the bonds of company organization and the methods of evaluation of performance must be established. Part Six is devoted to an examination of organizational structures and their characteristics and the examination of performance and its improvement. If performance is successful, and if conditions warrant, we foresee the development and growth of the enterprise. With business size comes the need for greater attention to the social and economic responsibilities of the firm and thereby the recognition of the significance of governmental relations with business.

The accomplishments of the business within the environment of competition and government are due to the efficiency of the management function. This function is most effectively promoted if there is first a statement of policy to serve as a guide, a clear picture of authority and responsibility, and a fulfillment of the areas of managerial concern.

CHAPTER 24

Types of Business Ownership

The owners of a business play a very important part in determining company policy, goals, and objectives, for as we have seen, the institution of private property gives owners the right to use their property as they see fit. The exact relationship between ownership and management of a business, however, will be determined by the type of ownership structure employed. In some instances owners are managers, and in others they are not. The type of ownership structure employed is important also in that it may determine the degree of control that the promoters will retain over the venture. The following discussion is designed to point out the strengths and weaknesses of the various types of business ownership.

THE RIGHT TO BUSINESS ORGANIZATION

Before a business can have legal status, it must first be of a form recognized in the eyes of the law. Just as certain types of business activity are illegal in our society, so are certain types of business organization. Business combinations such as the Standard Oil Company[1] and the American Tobacco Company[2] were considered to be operating against the best interests of society and were broken up under provisions of the Sherman Antitrust Act. It is a continuous function of the Justice Department to see that business does not operate against the public interest.

Business organizations, to be legal, must be sanctioned by law. The law which sanctions the business organization is either statutory law or common law. Statutory law refers to that body of law that has been created by our legislative bodies within the area of powers delegated to the governments by the people. Thus the Commonwealth of Massachusetts has created laws which regulate the establishment and operation of

[1] *Standard Oil Co. v. United States* 221 U.S. 1 (1911), 55 L. Ed. 619 31 Sup. Ct. 502.

[2] *United States v. American Tobacco Co.* 221 U.S. 106 (1911), 55 L. Ed. 663 31 Sup. Ct. 632.

the corporate form of business organization within the commonwealth.

However, all acts need not be spelled out in the laws to make them legal. In fact, all acts are legal unless prohibited by law. Over the years people may do things in such a proper manner that the courts and society look upon them as being legitimate. When the courts uphold or recognize such unwritten rules of conduct, they become part of the common law. Thus the courts have upheld the act of two or more individuals mutually entering a business to share profits and losses equally or in some predetermined ratio (partnership) or the act of an individual entering business by himself and doing business as a company (proprietorship). These are considered common-law types of organizations. Of the common forms of business ownership these two types are distinct because documented sanction by a government is not necessary to go into business. It must be remembered that if public health, safety, and welfare might be endangered by a new business, the government could always regulate to protect the public interest. These two types of business ownership are also distinct in that the business and the proprietor(s) are the same entity; what belongs to the business also belongs to the proprietor(s), and the debts of the business become the debts of the proprietor(s).

LEGAL FORMS OF ORGANIZATION

The Individual Proprietorship

More businesses in this country are formed on the individual proprietorship basis than on any other. (See Table 24–5.) It is the oldest form of business ownership and existed at the very beginning of business activity. There must be significant reasons why this type of ownership has lasted so long and retained its popularity. When a person enters a business, he should understand something about its formation, because his freedom of action as well as liability in business is based, in part at least, on the legal form of organization. The individual proprietorship is the simplest form of organization and is the easiest type to organize and operate. Frequently no formal action is required to start a proprietorship business. For example, John Jones decides to leave his employer and start an accounting service for small businessmen. He finds customers for his service and is then the sole proprietor of his business, John Jones, Accountant. What must he do to satisfy the law? In Massachusetts the answer is: nothing. He just goes into business; it is that simple. If John Jones decides to do business as Acme Accounting Service, then he must record, usually at city hall, the fact that he is John Jones doing business as Acme Accounting Service and pay a very small registration fee. Sometimes a permit or license is required if a person deals in certain commodities or services. A permit is usually required to sell gasoline, milk, tobacco products, and many other items. Except where this situation exists, a person is free to do business as he desires. As a result the individual proprietorship is the quickest and least costly type of organization to form, since there are no organization fees or annual reports to state agencies, and generally the services of an attorney are not needed when this type of business is organized.

The individual proprietor directs his business as he sees fit. He has no one to account to for his actions, if legal, except himself. There are no stockholders or directors to tell him what to do. All the profits earned by the business are his, and any losses incurred by the business are his personal losses, since the individual and the business are one and the same. When the individual proprietor wishes to go out of business, he simply stops doing business. Usually no reports are needed, nor is the approval of anyone required. There are some exceptions to this. If the individual becomes a bankrupt, or if he operates under the jurisdiction of a department of public utilities, for example, his exit from business can be regulated by law. When one examines the complicated nature of some ownership forms, he will be more appreciative of the simplicity of the individual proprietorship.

There are two significant drawbacks that are inherent in this form of ownership. The first pertains to the owner's liability. As mentioned above, the business cannot be separated from the individual; therefore, business losses become personal losses. If the business assets are not sufficient to cover any claims against the business, the personal assets of the proprietor can be taken to satisfy the claims of business creditors. This means that the proprietor's home, his car, and any other property which he owns can be taken to satisfy business debts.

Second, since the business cannot be separated from the individual, the business ceases to exist as such when the proprietor dies. To be sure, the heirs of the deceased may continue to operate the business; but actually it must become a new business with new owners, and certain legal processes must be administered before the heirs can make use of the property of the deceased.

In addition, there is generally a problem involved when one person tries to save or raise the capital needed to run a business. The problem of financing a business is discussed elsewhere in this text. The point here is that the individual proprietor must rely on his own savings or the savings of friends for his capital requirements. Since there is considerable risk with this form of business, individuals and financial institutions are reluctant to invest their funds in individual proprietorships, especially when there are more attractive investment opportunities elsewhere.

Finally, the success of the individual proprietorship rests on one person. The owner who knows his limitations does well to seek the advice of competent advisors when the need arises. However, if the owner does not possess managerial ability and cannot see the need for competent advice, his chances for success are reduced. When the enterprise is small, requires a small amount of capital, and lends itself to control by one man, then the individual proprietorship can be the ideal form of ownership.

The individual proprietorship is a socially desirable form of business since most proprietorship organizations are small in terms of capital, employment, and market covered, thereby reducing whatever danger may come of concentration of business in the hands of a few. Evidently our Federal government is interested in the continuance of this form of business for it has created several agencies to aid the small businessman. Among them is the Small Business Administration, successor to the Small Defense Plants Administration, created on July 30, 1953. This agency was established with "no primary function or interest other than the preservation and promotion of small business enterprise."[3] Accordingly, Congress specified that this agency "shall not be affiliated with or be within any other government or department of the federal government."[4]

The Partnership

Frequently more capital and/or more business ability than one man can supply is needed to operate a business successfully. When two or more individuals enter into business relations as coowners to share profits and losses equally or in some predetermined ratio, a partnership results. Since a true partnership rests on the intent of the parties concerned, it can be created by either express or implied agreement. It is, of course, much wiser to have a partnership agreement in writing to avoid subsequent controversies as to mutual rights and duties of the partners. Figure 24–1 illustrates a partnership agreement. The partnership agreement does not purport to provide for every possible contingency; it merely makes the partners' relations a matter of record. The partnership agreement cannot guarantee that one partner will not act to the detriment of all others.

The partnership is very similar to the individual proprietorship form of ownership. As noted above, it is a common-law institution and therefore has many of the strong and weak features of the proprietorship, and of course, it has the same legal status. The main difference is that two or more individuals join in the business venture rather than one.

There is one feature of the partnership that warrants special consideration; it is the subject of liability. Like the individual proprietorship there

[3] From a pamphlet issued by the Small Business Administration, 40 Broad Street, Boston 9, Mass., dated Sept. 9, 1953.

[4] *Ibid.*

FIGURE 24–1

ARTICLES OF COPARTNERSHIP

This contract, made and entered into on the second day of May, 1956, by and between Carl O. Johnson and Hector J. Bringle both of Dedham, Massachusetts.

WITNESSETH: That the said parties have this day formed a copartnership for the purpose of engaging in the general machine shop business under the following stipulations which are made part of this contract:

First: The said copartnership is to continue for 15 years from above date.

Second: The business shall be conducted under the firm name of Excell Machine Company at 26 Carlson Avenue, Dedham, Mass.

Third: The investments of the partners are as follows: $8,000 cash by each partner.

Fourth: All profits and losses shall be shared equally.

Fifth: A systematic record of all transactions is to be kept in a double-entry set of books, which are to be open for inspection by each partner. On June 30 and December 31 hereafter a statement of the business is to be made, the books closed, and each partner credited with the amount of the gain.

Sixth: Each partner will devote his entire time and attention to the business and engage in no other business enterprise without the written consent of the other.

Seventh: Each partner is to have a salary of $500.00 per month, the same to be withdrawn at such time or times as he may elect. Neither partner is to withdraw from the business an amount in excess of his salary without the written consent of the other.

Eighth: The duties of each partner are as follows: Carl O. Johnson is to have general supervision of the business and have charge of all records. Hector J. Bringle is to have charge of the machine shop, hiring all shop personnel and having charge thereof, scheduling of production and any other duties that pertain directly to the running of the shop.

Ninth: Neither party will become surety or bondsman for anyone without the written consent of the other.

Tenth: In the event of the death, incapacity, or withdrawal of either partner, the business is to be conducted for the remainder of the fiscal year by the surviving partner, the profits for the year allocated to the withdrawing partner to be determined by the ratio of the time he was a partner during the year to the whole year.

Eleventh: In case of dissolution, the assets are to be divided in the ratio of the capital invested at the time of dissolution.

IN WITNESS THEREOF

Carl O. Johnson ______________

Hector J. Bringle ______________

is unlimited liability for the owners; i.e., personal assets may be taken to satisfy business debts if the business assets are less than the total debts of the business. If both business and personal assets cannot satisfy claims against the partners, then the debts remain personal debts which may have to be paid in the future if and when the partners accumulate additional assets. Because there are two or more owners in a partnership, the problem of individual liability is more involved than in a proprietorship. According to law, partners are jointly liable for the debts of the partnership; this means that if a creditor should sue to collect a debt of the partnership, he would have to sue all partners jointly, not an individual partner. When partnership assets are not adequate to cover the creditor's claim, the creditor may then bring suit against any or all partners individually to gain satisfaction. This means that one partner with a large amount of personal assets might have to pay the share(s) of the other partner(s) if they do not have sufficient assets to cover their share of creditors' claims. The partner who had to pay could then bring suit against his fellow partner(s), but if they had nothing, he would have to bear the entire business loss. Great care should be exercised in the selection of a business partner, for in a partnership each partner is at the mercy of all others.

We understand that a partnership is owned jointly by the partners, but there remains the question of who actually controls the partnership. Each partner is entitled to a share in the management of the business. The partnership agreement should cover many of the day-to-day decisions that must be made, but there are bound to be times when decisions must be made relating to a new course of action. Ordinary partnership affairs are decided by a majority vote, with each partner having one vote. There are instances when a unanimous vote of the partners is necessary to establish a new course of action. Many partnerships involve only two individuals; therefore it is impossible many times to get a majority or unanimous approval. Unless one partner gives in, the operation may reach a stalemate.

The Limited Partnership

It is possible to reduce the liability of a partner by establishing a limited-partnership agreement. Since limited liability is not an inherent feature of common-law institutions, the limited partnership can be formed only in those states which have enacted enabling legislation. Under this type of agreement one or more partners must have unlimited liability as in the general partnership discussed above, but other partners may have their liability for business debts limited to the amount of their investment in the partnership. The limited partner takes no active part in the management of the business, and persons dealing with this type of partnership are entitled to know that certain partners have limited liability.

On the surface the limited partnership may appear to be a very satisfactory type of organization. However, if the statutes governing the limited partnership are not strictly complied with, the courts may treat all partners as general partners wherein all have unlimited liability. Since a limited partnership is formed under the statutes of a particular state, it is not free to transact business in other states as a limited partnership. It will be looked upon as a general partnership in all other states.

The Corporation

> A corporation is an artificial being, invisible, intangible, and existing only in contemplation of the law. Being a mere creature of the law, it possesses only those properties which the charter of its creation confers upon it.[5]

Chief Justice Marshall's definition of the corporate structure is considered by many the best yet given. Unlike the common-law institutions described above, all corporations are created by a state government. Except for special purposes, such as the organization of banks or export companies, the Federal government has not provided for the general chartering of corporations. Each state creates legislation which sets up the rules and regulations for the formation and operation of the corporation. There are, then, forty-eight different sets of laws governing the corporate form of business in the United States. Some states have made it easier to incorporate a business than others. This situation leads to some competition between states as each seeks to attract new corporate organizations which, of course, are a source of revenue. Delaware has long been the most popular incorporating state because of its low taxes and liberal laws. Attempts have been made to create a uniform business-corporation act which would result in a uniform set of laws for corporations in all states with modifications only to meet local conditions. It is doubtful, however, that such a code will be universally adopted. Since the corporation is a creation of the state, it naturally possesses only those rights and privileges that are expressed or implied in its charter.

A corporation generally gets its start after a group of promoters—three or more in Massachusetts—apply for a corporate charter. Their application states the purpose and location of the corporation, its proposed capitalization, and the names of those who are seeking the charter. If the state approves the application, a charter will be granted and the corporation created. Since a corporation is created under the laws of one state, it does not automatically have legal status in any other state. Thus a New York corporation does not automatically have any legal status in Illinois. This means that a New York corporation cannot bring legal action against a party in the state of Illinois. It should be noted that the common-law institutions mentioned above do have legal status in each and every state. Thus a proprietorship in New York can sue a person or

[5] Chief Justice Marshall, *The Trustees of Dartmouth College v. Woodward*, 4 Wheaton (U.S.) 518, 636 (1819).

a corporation in Illinois. This is because the business and the individual are the same and "the citizens of each State shall be entitled to all Privileges and Immunities of citizens in the several states."[6] However, through a rather simple procedure and the payment of a modest annual fee, corporations can obtain legal recognition in other states.

The corporate form of business is common where large amounts of capital are necessary to start and operate a business. Corporations are authorized to sell and issue shares of stock to anyone who wishes to buy them and invest in the business. Under certain circumstances this sale of stock is regulated by an agency of our Federal government. The person who owns or controls a majority of the voting stock of a corporation has control over its operations. If a person wishes to sell his interest in the business, he may seek out a buyer and sell his interest for whatever price the buyer is willing to pay. Thus the ownership of a corporation may change continually, and its life can be indefinite. A corporation also has the advantage of limited liability for its owners. Generally a stockholder's liability is limited to the amount that he has invested in the stock of the corporation. His personal assets will not be taken to satisfy business debts as in the case of common-law institutions. One exception to this principle is that if a person is a director of the corporation and is guilty of a fraudulent act,[7] his personal property may be taken to satisfy debts of the corporation.

The corporation lends itself to specialized management. Many times owners invest in a business for investment's sake alone; they have no interest in managing the business. The owners elect a board of directors to manage the business for them. The directors in turn obtain the specialized management talents that they need to operate the business profitably. Thus the corporation allows for diverse ownership and the utilization of the best managerial talent available.

Other Forms of Business Ownership

There are many other forms of business ownership of both common-law and statutory origin which are used today in business. They are not so widely used as the forms described above and for this reason will not be considered except for this listing:

1. Joint-stock companies
2. The Massachusetts Trust
3. Cooperatives
4. Holding companies

[6] Constitution of the United States, Art. IV, sec. 2, par. 1.

[7] Sec. 36, chap. 156, *General Laws of the Commonwealth of Massachusetts:* "The president, treasurer, and directors of every corporation shall be . . . liable for all debts and contracts of the corporation . . . if any statement or report required by this chapter is . . . false . . . and which they know to be false."

RELATIVE IMPORTANCE OF BASIC BUSINESS STRUCTURES

It was mentioned above that more businesses are formed on the individual proprietorship basis than on any other. (See Table 24–5.) One should not infer that the individual proprietorship is the best or most desirable form of organization. Each type of business structure has both good and bad features, good and bad applications. Because the small retailer is successful as an individual proprietorship is no reason to believe that others can use this form with the same success. Tables 24–1 through 24–5 show the relative importance of business structures in different lines of activity.

TABLE 24–1
LEGAL FORM OF ORGANIZATION
MANUFACTURING ESTABLISHMENTS IN THE UNITED STATES, 1947

	Number of establishments	Number of employees	Salaries paid in $1,000
Corporations	118,138	12,856,299	336,574,635
Individual proprietorships	69,519	585,514	1,183,808
Partnerships	50,787	757,140	1,686,684
Other	2,437	95,351	244,400

SOURCE: U.S. Department of Commerce, *Census of Business*, 1948.

TABLE 24–2
LEGAL FORM OF ORGANIZATION
RETAIL ESTABLISHMENTS IN THE UNITED STATES, 1948

	Number of stores	Per cent of total	Sales in $1,000	Per cent of total
Corporations	210,000	12	61,203,213	47
Individual proprietorships	1,321,127	70	44,813,592	34
Partnerships	322,223	18	23,422,224	18
Other	5,582	...	1,081,519	1

SOURCE: U.S. Department of Commerce, *Census of Business*, 1948.

Table 24–1 pertains to the area of manufacturing. In this field the corporation is more widely used than any other business form. This is to be expected because manufacturers generally have larger capital requirements than have the retail or service establishments. Corporate establishments employ eight times as many workers and pay more than eleven times the wages of all noncorporate businesses. On an average the corporate business has about 109 employees while the noncorporate averages about 12 employees.

In the retail field the individual proprietorship greatly outnumbers all

TABLE 24–3
LEGAL FORM OF ORGANIZATION
WHOLESALE ESTABLISHMENTS IN THE UNITED STATES, 1948

	Number of establishments	Per cent of total	Sales in $1,000	Per cent of total
Corporations	121,418	50	142,861,846	75
Individual proprietorships	77,416	32	20,189,425	11
Partnerships	42,815	18	24,150,901	14
Other	1,717			

SOURCE: U.S. Department of Commerce, *Census of Business*, 1948.

TABLE 24–4
LEGAL FORM OF ORGANIZATION
SERVICE ESTABLISHMENTS IN THE UNITED STATES, 1948

	Number of establishments	Per cent of total	Receipts in $1,000	Per cent of total
Corporations	28,570	5	2,983,405	35
Individual proprietorships	455,161	82	3,916,666	46
Partnerships	75,388	13	1,641,540	19
Other	440	..	36,551	

SOURCE: U.S. Department of Commerce, *Census of Business*, 1948.

TABLE 24–5
LEGAL FORM OF ORGANIZATION
ALL ESTABLISHMENTS IN THE UNITED STATES, 1947–1948

Establishment	Corporate	Ind. prop.	Partner.	Other
Manufacturing	118,138	69,519	50,787	2,437
Retail	210,608	1,231,127	322,223	5,582
Wholesale	121,418	77,416	42,815	1,717
Service	28,570	455,161	75,388	440
Totals	478,734	1,883,223	491,213	10,176

SOURCE: Tables 24–1 through 24–2.

other forms but is second to the corporation in volume of sales. (See Table 24–2.) This shows that there is a large number of establishments in the retail field, each with a relatively small volume of sales. In the service field much the same situation exists as in the retail field.

Table 24–3 shows that the corporate structure is more frequently used in the wholesale trade. It can be seen that the corporate form is most widely used in those types of business where large amounts of capital are required. However, the noncorporate forms are extremely important in the American business scene. They have been in the past and undoubtedly will be in the future.

THE FUTURE FOR SMALL BUSINESS

Reference has been made above to the small business organization and its desirability in the American system of free enterprise. It has been associated with the noncorporate business structure, as it should be. Perhaps it would be well to define what is meant by a "small business" before its role in the future is discussed. The term "small" is of course relative, and no specific definition of it can be given. A business is considered small when ownership and management are the same, when capital is supplied by one person or a small group of people, when its market is local and it has few employees. At the time of this writing the Committee for Economic Development classifies a business as small if it has fewer than 50 employees; the Department of Commerce sets the dividing line between small and large at 250 employees; while the Department of Defense calls a business small if it has fewer than 1,000 employees. There is no clear definition of a small business, yet there are definite differences between large and small, as noted earlier in this paragraph.

Quite often it is said that the small businessman does not have a chance in our business world which is dominated to some extent by highly integrated big business. In spite of the importance of many business organizations, General Motors for example, in American industry the small businessman plays an important but perhaps unknown role in our economic life. The small business is basic to the American system of free enterprise. Competition is stimulated and new developments encouraged through the small business unit. The small business unit adds so much to our economy in this way that we could not afford to let it play a minor role. There are several reasons why the small business is certain to play a dominant part in the American business picture in the years to come:

1. The Desire of So Many Americans to Be Independent. When a man has his own business, it gives him a feeling of being independent of any "boss."

2. *Government Recognition of the Problem of the Small Businessman.* The Small Business Administration,[8] an agency of the Federal government, has three principal functions prescribed by Congress—to see that small business (1) gets its fair share of defense contracts; (2) receives a fair share of critical materials; and (3) gets financial and technical assistance needed to participate effectively in defense and essential civilian production. During the year 1953 this policy was adhered to by the Ordnance Department in New England when 82 per cent of the $92,700,000 of ordnance was produced by small business establishments.

3. *The Interdependence of Large and Small Business.* Perhaps this is the strongest reason why the small business will continue to play an important role in American business life. Few if any organizations are so integrated that they can operate independently of others. General Motors has 26,000 suppliers; many are small businesses, located in every state of the Union. According to a statement by the General Electric Company,[9] small, independent firms supply materials, services, and many parts that go into General Electric products. General Electric calls on the abilities of more than 3,000 small businesses in its jet-engine program alone. Suppliers get nearly 60 cents of every dollar G.E. receives for defense equipment. This statement also refers to the fact that 82 per cent of the suppliers of jet-engine parts employ 500 or fewer workers.

Ninety-eight per cent of the business units in the United States today would be classed as small business according to the standards set by the Committee for Economic Development. While no measure is exact, this is more than an indication of the important role that small business is certain to play in perpetuating free competitive enterprise in our nation.

Statistics alone do not begin to tell the story of the importance of small business, for a business may be small in size and large in achievement. This was proved during World War II when very often small business was able to get into production faster and operate more flexibly than big business. In many cases small, specialized suppliers made possible the mighty output of the industrial giants.

Small business is just as important today as ever. When customers, at the retail level or manufacturing level, desire individual service or specialized products, small business frequently is able to do a better job than big business. Small business is a source of new ideas, new products, and materials brought about by their proprietors' intense desire to survive in a highly competitive business world.[10]

[8] See footnote 3, p. 380.

[9] From an advertisement of the General Electric Company which appeared in many national magazines, December, 1953.

[10] An excellent discussion of small business in the American economy appears in the semiannual report issued by the Small Business Administration.

SUMMARY

The ownership structure of a business organization is important in that it determines who will control and manage the operation. Since early business organizations were small, it is quite natural that the first types of ownership structure were the individual proprietorship and the partnership wherein the owners were the managers. As business organizations grew in size, a different type of structure evolved, the corporation. The individual proprietorship and the partnership are ideally suited to the small-business operation today, as they were in the past. The corporate form of organization is most popular in medium- and large-sized business. In determining the type of ownership structure to be used, the promoters of a venture should always keep an eye on the possibility of losing control to others. No form of ownership can be considered better than any other. In each instance the promoter(s) of a venture should determine the requirements of their operation and adopt an ownership structure that will allow them to reach their goals.

QUESTIONS

1. What group has ultimate control over company goals, policies, and objectives? How is this possible?
2. Why was the Standard Oil Company broken up in 1911?
3. Distinguish between statutory law and common law.
4. Describe how the proprietorship type of business is organized.
5. What are the strong features of the individual proprietorship?
6. What are the drawbacks of the individual proprietorship?
7. Why is the individual proprietorship said to be a socially desirable form of business?
8. What is the purpose of the partnership agreement?
9. Does a partnership agreement have to be in writing? Discuss.
10. Who controls a partnership? Discuss.
11. Describe the liability of individual partners in a partnership.
12. Describe the limited partnership.
13. What are the limitations of the limited partnership?
14. What is a corporation?
15. To what extent does the Federal government charter corporations?
16. What is meant by the statement that a corporation has no legal status in any other state?
17. Is this true of a partnership? Why?
18. What is the extent of the liability of a stockholder?
19. What is the extent of the liability of a director of a corporation?
20. Why is the proprietorship so popular in the retail field?
21. What is "small" business? Discuss.
22. What factors insure the continuance of small-business organizations?

CHAPTER 25

The Organizational Structure

The development of the organizational structure is an important element in the planning of the venture. The best of physical facilities and manpower are of little avail until a plan for their coordination has been developed. A good organization may offset the problem of inferior facilities; but on the other hand, the superiority of facilities can never substitute for organization.

The organizational structure is the backbone of the business concern. It establishes the outline of activity within which must be stipulated the personnel relationships which are deemed prerequisite to the achievement of business goals. These relationships establish the line, or flow, of authority and responsibility without which it would be impossible to achieve the direction, control, and coordination of the men, machines, and materials of the enterprise.

Organization, Administration, and Control

The management of an enterprise is confronted with various areas of concern as it plans and puts into effect its organizational scheme. The first is the act of organizing, the process whereby the relationships among individuals are so stipulated as to accomplish efficiently the purposes for which the group was established. These relationships define the activity between individuals and among the members of the group in respect to each other and to the group as a whole, and in respect to the physical elements of the enterprise.

By their nature the problems, and necessarily the solutions to the problems, which face an enterprise are ever-changing. The organizational structure must be sufficiently flexible to cope with new and varying business situations. Management caters to this need through administration, which is concerned with formulating the policies and principles on the basis of which the firm is operated.

Lastly, management is concerned with the means of supervising tasks so that assignments will be carried out according to the master plan of operational procedure. This we may refer to as the element of control.

Simplicity is a fundamental desideratum in creating the framework of company personnel relationships. However, in view of the complex and ever-changing situations which constantly attend the business scene, it is small wonder that organizational structure is many times the antithesis of simplicity. The businessman who attempts to create a singular organizational structure which is capable of dealing with any and all situations which may arise is fooling nobody but himself. An organizational structure in reality exists originally to satisfy one or a series of explicit objectives. When these objectives are modified or eliminated, the organizational structure must be modified accordingly.

Significance of Organizational Structure

A statement of the purpose(s) for which an enterprise is created must be made prior to the establishment of an organizational structure. The structure itself must be set up prior to the achievement of the purpose(s) of the enterprise.

It is necessary to establish the purposes or goals of the enterprise in order that the nature of the chief functions may be established and accorded positions in the organizational structure befitting their relative importance. These chief functions may be production, sales, purchasing, etc. If the company objectives involve geographical differentiations or diversified products, the functions may be established on geographical or product bases or on some other significant bases for organizational recognition and differentiation.

The goals of the particular firm determine the relative importance of each function. The supplier firm which is primarily concerned with sources of materials will establish the purchasing function as its most important activity. The manufacturer of precision equipment is vitally concerned with quality. This function, quality control, ranks high in terms of importance. The territorial divisions set up for sales purposes, each under the supervision of a district sales manager, have been so established because management considered the function important on a geographical basis. The importance of a function is most often reckoned in terms of its profit or cost significance.

The organizational structure seeks to bind the structural parts of the enterprise with links of authority and responsibility which best provide the desired results. The goals which are sought and the relative importance of the various company functions are subject to constant pressure for change. In the light of this, organizational structure and its plan of responsibility and authority must play a dual role. It must be cohesive but also dynamic. Each need for change must be met by change or else the company will lose ground.

VARIATIONS IN ORGANIZATIONAL STRUCTURE

The organizational structure of the firm evolves even as the scope and nature of its business activity vary and increase. With a given level and type of business operations there may be said to exist at a given time an ideal organizational structure to serve the needs of the venture. To create the "best" structure for a particular business situation could only be of significance to us if we were first to define completely the nature of the activities of this particular business situation. It must suffice for us at this time to consider instead the basic organizational forms and then recognize that any "best fit" will involve some adaptation of a basic form to suit particular or unique needs.

The structure of organization involves consideration of these three forms:

1. Line structure
2. Functionalization
3. Staff-and-service division

Line Structure

The simplest and oldest form of organization is the line structure. The title "line" is descriptive in that there exists a direct flow, or direct line, of authority through specific channels, and in that a flow of responsibility returns through these same channels.

FIGURE 25–1

SIMPLE LINE ORGANIZATION

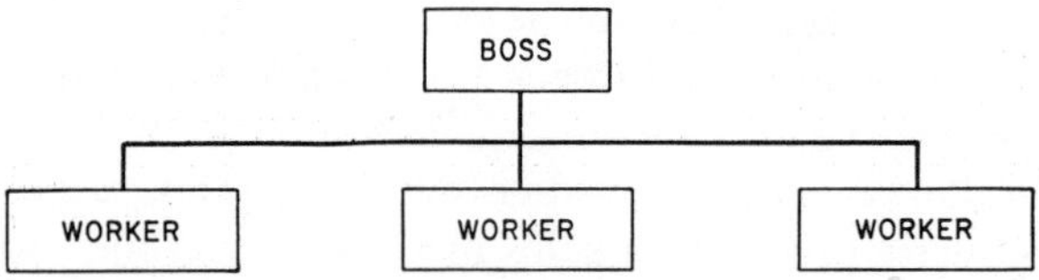

The line form embodies the most clean-cut and easily understood pattern of organizational relationships. It is the most basic of structures and is that form employed customarily by smaller firms and those which cannot afford the costs involved in maintaining a more specialized form of organization.

The graphic illustration of line organization, Figure 25–1, represents a two-level structure which would apply to a situation wherein the detail work of the business is of a homogeneous, or at least not too diversified, nature, and the extent of personal contacts is within reason. Because of these features, the individual designated as owner-manager is considered capable of dealing effectively and efficiently in his capacity as the top member of the organization. If the case were otherwise, if the details involved in carrying out the business routines were too many and demanded excessive time or personal relations on the part of the top executive, the line structure might yet suffice but with the addition of an intermediate level of authority. This situation is presented in Figure 25–2. What has occurred here is that there has been recognition of burdensome attention to details or realization of insufficient time on the part of top-level authority adequately to conduct the business. The intermediate level, in the illustration, is indicated as the establishment of a group of foremen who exercise authority over their respective groups of workers and thus relieve management of the need to devote excessive attention to details. In this illustration, the flow of authority stems from the top

FIGURE 25–2

LINE ORGANIZATION WITH INTERMEDIATE LEVEL

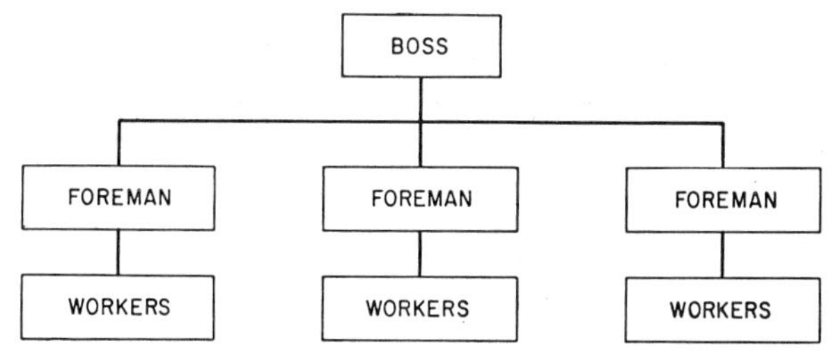

level to the various foremen and from each foreman to his respective work force. The flow of responsibility returns along the same lines. Again, the organizational pattern remains extremely clear, simple, and easily understood. In no case does the authority exercised by each foreman extend or overlap in any other area. Likewise, each worker is directly responsible only to his particular foreman. The foremen are all directly responsible to the top level authority.

The illustrations used in this case of simple line structures are not intended to give the impression that this form of organization is applicable only to smaller business units. Quite the contrary, for even the largest and most involved of corporate structures are built around a core or organization which is fundamentally line structure.

Certain advantages and disadvantages accrue to the use of the line type of organization.

Advantages:

1. Relationships are easily understood.
2. There is direct flow of authority and responsibility. Thus confusion is eliminated or minimized.

3. Quicker action is possible.
4. Discipline is more easily maintained.
5. "Passing the buck" and red tape are minimized.

Disadvantages:

1. It may be impossible to secure executives or supervisory workers who are sufficiently capable in all areas of business activity which they must direct. Therefore, inefficiency may exist to a greater degree than would be the case if fields of activity were narrowed and were handled by specialists rather than the "all-around" man.
2. If line structure is used in a company of considerable size, the attention which executives must give to varied details of operation may hamper their effectiveness as planners and controllers of the business.
3. Whenever an individual is endowed with too much authoritative control, there exists the possibility of an "all the eggs in one basket" situation. Incapacitation or loss of this individual can have drastic effects on the company operations. In a situation where excessive reliance is placed upon the top level, there is usually too little thought given by management to the need for eventual succession.

Functionalization

By reason of the defects which may be inherent in the line type of structure, it is natural that there be a successor form which will better serve managerial needs.

A company which engages in the manufacture or procurement of goods for resale will find that the areas of activity or the functions in which the firm must engage are production and/or procurement, finance and sales. These are the basic operational areas, each of which will have many specialized aspects. With simple line structure it was noted that the control of all activities in these various areas was very narrowly held. In our illustrations the control was held by one individual. Because of the pressure of competition, business must be conducted most efficiently from both the physical and administrative standpoints. Since the individual may be unable to cope with the many specialized problems which arise, either because of their complication or numbers, the form of organization must be adapted to meet each and every situation.

Pure Functionalization. The principle of functionalization is expressed as the use of individuals who devote their time and energies in narrowly defined areas of activity. These people are specialists. It is hoped that the best results will be forthcoming in terms of the various business problems with which each specialist is concerned.

Pure functionalization of organization involves an additional feature.

Not only are the activities of the business divided and assigned to specialists, but in addition the feature of authority flow is greatly modified. As a result of the division of activities, each person vested with the control of a specific function exercises his authority not only over his immediate staff but also over the activity regardless of the area of the business wherein it takes place. This feature is referred to as "functional authority." Thus, a division may be created which is assigned the area of material handling within the company. Authority or control over this activity will be had by the individual in charge of this activity whether material movement occurs in the production area, on the shipping platform, or in the storeroom. In this manner the authority of the division head is felt in many different areas by many different people.

Other specialized divisions in the performance of their particular functions have expression of authority in the very same areas as well as in different areas. Figure 25–3 illustrates the pattern of authority and responsibility flow which exists with pure functionalization. The figure does not present a complete picture of a pure functional organization, but it does allow for some insight into the maze of interrelationships which may exist.

Since a complete carry-through of functionalization involves the development of several "octopi of authority," it is usually found that discipline and control are weakened and thus rendered less effective. Each work-

FIGURE 25–3

PURE FUNCTIONALIZATION

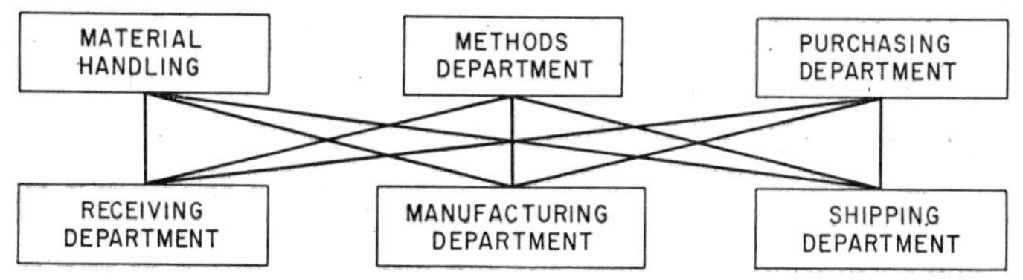

man finds that he has divided responsibility and receives his orders from any one or more of several persons. To serve one master well in itself may prove to be a difficult task; to serve a few or several masters may prove to be the undoing of the whole organization, for confusion may occur both as to the extent of authority and of responsibility. Although business recognizes the need for functionalization, it is probably never used in its pure form.

Practical Approach to Functionalization. The basic approach to functional organization is to assign certain defined areas of work to specialists. In this way several objectives are achieved. First, the tasks are expertly handled by specialists. Second, since the area of activity is narrow, training programs for personnel who are to do the necessary work are pin-pointed and to that extent are more easily accomplished. Third, a better knowledge of manpower needs is available. Fourth, the principle of division of labor is promoted. Fifth, functionalization is a step in the growth pattern of organization which serves the expanded needs of business.

The advantages of and the necessity for functionalization are well appreciated by businessmen. Figure 25–4 shows a typical functional breakdown of organization in terms of the basic areas of business activity and the creation of divisions to tend to these areas.

FIGURE 25–4

BASIC FUNCTIONAL ORGANIZATION

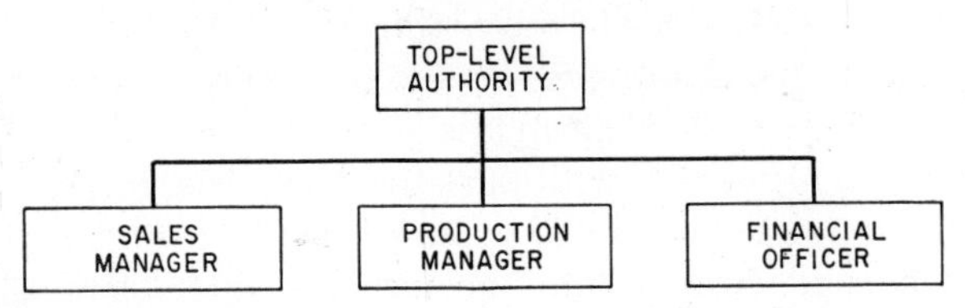

Neither the line nor the pure functional structure is in itself the answer to the organizational needs of most companies. On the one hand, the line structure masses authority in one or a few hands, while the pure functional structure disperses authority to a very great degree with an accompanying potential weakening of the sinews of organization.

Staff and Service Divisions

The combination of the best features of the line and functional types of organization results in that form of organization which is called the line-and-staff. The flow of authority proceeds along fixed lines from the top of the organization to the bottom. The need for specialists is tended to by the creation of divisions as in the functional type of structure. Here, however, the resemblance ceases, for the authority given to the specialist is usually restricted to his own department.

Activities which demand the services of specialists are assigned to staffs of specialists. Naturally we expect the basic functions—sales, production, etc.—to be assigned to capable personnel. However, beyond these basic functions there are many areas of endeavor, such as work and time measurement, wage administration, research, industrial safety, etc., which are specialty areas. The specialist staffs solve the problems assigned them or initiate improvements in the areas with which they are concerned. The solution to the problem is transmitted to the supervisor or officer of the division in which the problem arose. This supervisor or officer then exercises such authority as may be necessary to put the solution into effect in his work area.

In this manner, the supervisor maintains his position as a line officer and exercises immediate authority over his workers. This feature allows for the maintenance of discipline and control which are necessary for proper operations. The supervisor is involved fundamentally in issuing the orders for action within his department. He is relieved of the responsibility of solving the many specialized problems which arise in his area of supervision, for this responsibility is ably assumed by the staff division.

In its final form the picture of the organization of a firm consists of two areas. First, the line division which is engaged in carrying out the operations and procedures; second, the staff or service divisions which are assigned the solution of problems and the provision of necessary facilitating services.

Staff or service divisions of a business may, for example, be such departments as the following: production planning, cost estimating, research in sales or production, personnel, maintenance and repair, traffic, and inspection. As each of these departments is considered, it is obvious that the nature of their activities is not directly involved in the basic area of operation of the company. A company is organized to achieve production and sales of goods. The staff and service departments are the "helping hands" in this achievement.

Staff Assistants

The need for specialists' services is also found at the executive level. In order that policy makers may exercise their responsibilities competently, it is often necessary for them to have the advice and assistance of specialists available at all times. The position of staff assistant has been created out of this need. Today officers of many companies are assisted by personnel with specific types of talents. Thus, the president may have a legal counsel or a business economist who will each advise or prepare data for the use of the company officer. Organizationally, these staff assistants hold no position of authority; they may or may not have a staff of their own in the company.

These assistants serve to extend the abilities of the executive. They may handle problems involving details with which they are most familiar or they may serve as extensions of the executive by supervising the actions necessitated by his decisions or by interpreting his decisions so that actions will be facilitated. In no way is the assistant to assume executive authority. He is the "right-hand man."

Committee Use in Organization

The need for coordination amongst the various units of the business organization is well recognized. Without a concerted approach there is a less than desirable relationship which in itself means relatively inefficient operation of the business. To promote the necessary cooperation and coordination amongst the members of the company team, the committee device is most often used. The combination of line and staff structure facilitates the use of the committee.

In essence, the justification of the committee is felt to exist in the fact that the committee-room provides a common meeting place for men who have a common ultimate goal. It is hoped that individual goals will be unselfishly set aside in deference to this one common goal. This hope is easily stated but not so easily achieved.

Businessmen make use of the committee device at all levels of organization. There are five fundamental purposes which the committee may serve:

1. Investigation
2. Proposition or suggestion
3. Coordination
4. Education or information
5. Policy formation

The first four purposes listed above are common to committee use at any level in the organization structure. The last, policy formation, would be restricted to upper management.

It should be borne in mind that the committee is not a device of the elite of the organization. It can and must be used all the way down the ladder of rank, for any overlooking of the problems, the misinformation, the ignorance, or the noncooperation on the part of the lowest ranks, the workers themselves, strikes a severe blow at the roots of the firm.

The Committee in Operation. The committee is not usually considered as a formal unit of the organizational structure. It is a necessary facilitating or advisory unit in that it is intended to serve as a means of creating greater efficiency in the operations of the company. The committee customarily is not endowed with authority status.

The committee comes into existence as a result of a need being felt or expressed. It should not live in perpetuity nor beyond that period of time in which it has served its stated purpose. This rule is often violated and results in wasting the time of many men who are gathered together in pointless meeting.

Many times the work of a committee is in vain or at least hampered because of either a domineering or, on the other hand, a weak-sister chairman. In the first case, only one man's voice may be heard, and his impressions and conclusions may be forced upon the committee. In the second case, there may be no effective leadership in the group activity, and therefore unimpressive and delayed results may occur. These weaknesses are both organizational and human. The chairman is appointed to serve as the guide and inspiration of the group as the members work and maybe falter in accomplishing the scheduled task.

Since the committee is basically a discussion group, the size will depend upon the nature of the problems and the extent to which too large or too small a group will not serve adequately. There is no "best" number of committee members. Each case is an individual problem.

There is no reason to question the fact that there are potential benefits available from the use of any device which serves as a coordinating force in organization. In this respect the committee, wisely and capably used, has many times proved its worth.

FILLING THE ORGANIZATION RANKS

The task of filling jobs customarily falls to the personnel department. The task of filling organization ranks belongs to that group responsible for the planning, directing, and controlling of the enterprise.

There are three levels or ranks organizationally; work force, supervisory, and managerial. Each major function or department of the enterprise must have its scope of duties defined to facilitate the setup of the divisions and subdivisions within each department. This procedure sets off rank levels by earmarking work sections which will need heads or foremen or other supervisory personnel. In like manner divisional or department requirements for managerial positions may be ascertained.

At the work-force level men are primarily concerned with attention to details of performance most of which, if not all, have been worked out for them. The supervisors generally have their work fixed for them by rules, regulations and routines. Although they may have some leeway in dealing with details, for the most part they stick to an established procedure. Supervisors are responsible for the performance of work by others rather than the planning of the work. The higher one goes up the organizational ladder, the more so is it found that the ranks are filled with planners rather than doers. The emphasis at the higher ranks is a departure from the requirements of mechanical and manual skills and the ability to perform detailed work. At the higher levels the emphasis is placed upon initiative, resourcefulness, imagination, judgment, leadership, etc. The scope of work encompassed is much broader, and the significance of a single decision increases up to the position of the top executive who is responsible for the entire operation.

In many business concerns junior-executive or management-training programs have been established and are intended to provide men of desirable caliber as successors to today's top executives. These plans are of great variety and varying significance to the many firms which employ them. Both small and large firms find that long-term training programs for managerial candidates have merit.

The task of filling positions falls to the personnel department. This we understand. However, the significance of each position, organizationally, and thereby the necessary qualifications of the aspirants are determined via organizational planning and construction.

The preparation of workers for advanced positions is carried on at all levels. Worker training and indoctrination satisfy the position requirements at the lower levels. Managerial training, which extends to those in supervisory positions as well as those specifically designated as company executives or junior executives, and which is carried on either within the plant or by paid-for private educational means, is a device employed to fill the ranks of upper levels and to provide some assurance of a continuation of the supply of adequately prepared personnel.

ORGANIZATIONAL CHARTS

The organizational chart graphically portrays the relationship of functions and individuals and shows the level and flow of authority and responsibility. Charting is an aid in the visualizing and planning of organization. It does not solve the organizational problems; but many times, if the chart is difficult to establish, it is possible that the organization being

FIGURE 25–5 FIGURE 25–6

ORGANIZATION CHARTS

FIRST ILLUSTRATION SECOND ILLUSTRATION

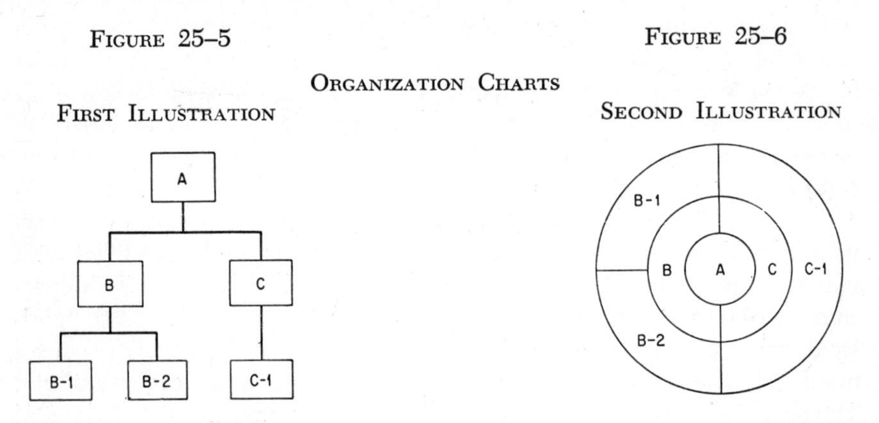

charted is deficient or confusing. The chart of organization may take different forms, some of which are illustrated in Figure 25–5 and Figure 25–6.

The vertical position of each block in Figure 25–5 is indicative of its rank in the organization. Thus, block *A* is the highest rank; *B* and *C* rank equally at a lower level; and the remaining blocks indicate equal rank at the lowest organizational level. The flow of authority proceeds from *A* to *B* to *B*-1 and *B*-2; and from *A* to *C* to *C*-1. The flow of responsibility returns along these same lines.

This simple organization may also be depicted by a circular chart on which the center circle depicts the top executive. (See Figure 25–6.)

In another form an organizational chart may appear as in Figure 25–7.

The usual chart consists of a series of boxes connected by lines. Each box represents a responsibility, and the lines represent the flow of responsibility as one looks up the line and the flow of authority as one looks down the line. (See Figure 25–8.) The chart cannot specify what this authority or responsibility consists of. This must be established pursuant to the study of organizational needs and the means of accomplishing the objectives of the enterprise. It is necessary that specific statements of authority and responsibility be recorded elsewhere, for the chart merely establishes the existence of the relationship and not the details. Customarily the specific details involved in organizational relationships are published in the form of an organizational manual or handbook. This book is often the first introduction which the employee has to the firm and to the significance and responsibilities of his job.

FIGURE 25–7

ORGANIZATION CHART—THIRD ILLUSTRATION

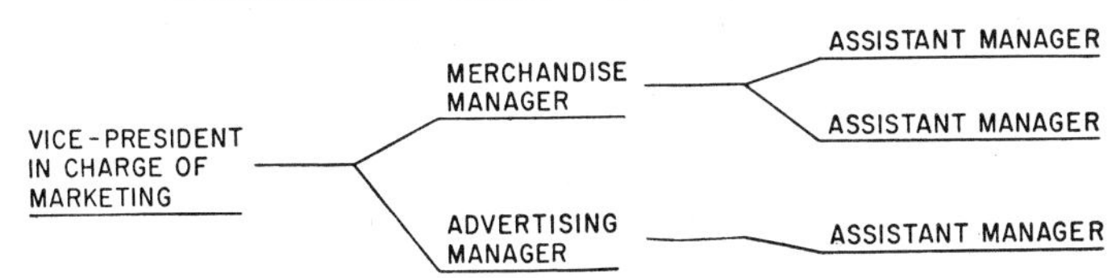

The organizational chart has its value and also its limitations. If the natures of position-to-position organizational relationships are quite varied, they are best disclosed by means of written statements to prevent misunderstanding which charting procedures may create. Some positions may carry complete authority or responsibility with respect to others. Some may carry partial authority. The chart cannot show all the possible variations.

SUMMARY

Organization is the process of establishing relationships among individuals which will help achieve the desired objectives of the enterprise. Organizational structure is the expression of these relationships, usually in the form of positions of authority and responsibility. Structure is necessary for the accomplishment of the purpose. The nature of the structure is determined by the purpose to be served. The administration of

FIGURE 25–8. LINE-AND-STAFF ORGANIZATION (Showing functions and authority levels; details incomplete)

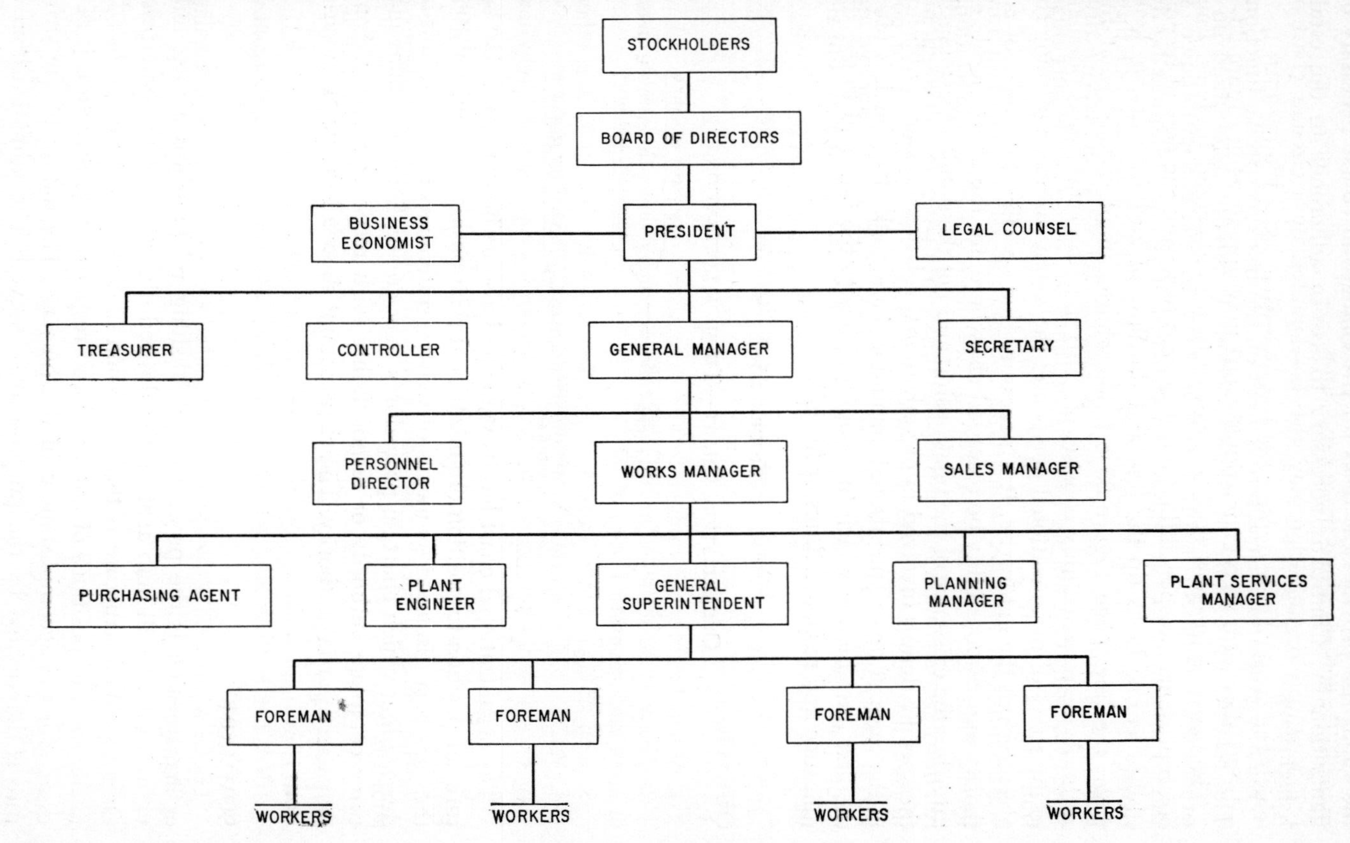

the enterprise provides the basis for the changes in course necessary organizationally. Control is necessary to assure adherence to the established plans.

Each organizational structure is built on the basis of specific functions. The relative importance of these functions is usually determined on a profit-and-cost basis. As the functions vary in relative importance, so should organizational purposes and structure. Organization must be dynamic. The structure of organization involves the consideration of three basic forms: line structure, functionalization, and staff and service divisions. Coordination among the various functions of a complex organization may be provided by means of committee organizations.

The filling of organizational ranks follows the establishment of rank levels. These are determined in the process of establishing organizational relationships necessary for control. The organizational chart, although not in itself a solution to organizational problems, is a handy device for portrayal and analysis purposes. Its various forms make it an attractive and understandable means of impressing employees with the nature and significance of company organization.

QUESTIONS

1. What does it mean to organize? To administer?
2. The purpose of the enterprise both precedes and follows the establishment of an organizational structure. Explain.
3. How do the three forms of organization evolve one from the other?
4. What are the advantages of line structures? Disadvantages?
5. Functionalization in its pure form is seldom if ever practiced. Why may this be so? What is the practical approach?
6. Customarily the staff or service division has limited scope of authority. Explain.
7. How do staff assistants fit into the organizational structure in terms of authority and responsibility?
8. What is the nature of a committee? What are the five fundamental purposes which the committee may serve?
9. How many members should be on a committee?
10. What is the difference between filling positions and filling organizational ranks?
11. Of what value is the organizational chart? Does it have any shortcomings or limitations?

CHAPTER 26

Basic Organizational Features

A good part of the success of any organizational structure is determined during the stages during which it is being planned. In order to develop a plan which will provide greater assurance of success in operation it is well to include consideration of some of the basic organizational features which should be "built in." These features, plus a means of effectively communicating within the ranks of organization, provide the substance for making organizational structure meaningful to the individuals involved.

Organizational successes stem from the soundness of plans and the effectiveness with which they are translated to those who operate the plan. Avenues of communication must be laid open to provide information to the work area and a means of expression from it.

BASIC ORGANIZATIONAL FEATURES

A business unit, depending on its size and scope, and the nature of its operations, will find that even as these features vary, so will the basic organizational needs vary. However, common to any type of organizational structure are certain features which must be built into the scheme. The aims which must be served are as follows:

1. Clarity
2. Completeness
3. Coordination
4. Authority commensurate with responsibility
5. Flexibility
6. Consideration of the human factor

Clarity

The aim of clarity can best be served by a detailed indication of the nature of the relationships which exist between people who make up the organizational ranks. This need for detail necessarily involves clear statement of such expressions of authority and responsibility as are associated with each personnel category of the organizational structure. Needless to say, the mere indication that two individuals are in the relative positions of supervisor and foreman within a particular area of the business is by no means a clear statement of the role which each person must play in relationships with each other. These roles must be expressed in terms of duties, authorities, and means of expressing control.

A common pitfall of the operating organization is what is called "overlapping authority." This term refers to actions that are contrary to expressed lines of authority. An instance of overlapping authority occurs when an individual oversteps his area of expressed jurisdiction and acts in a position of authority in an area which is not organizationally expressed as being within his province. The situation may arise for two fundamental reasons. First, the plan of organization may not in its construction have expressly or adequately delineated the spheres of activity and control. Second, the basic nature of a person may be such that usurpation of authority is his means of accomplishing an end; or his nature may be such that weakness in thought and power may result in the prevalence of "overlapping authority" on the part of others. Clarity as an aim of organizational structure is a means of overcoming the first reason stated above. The second reason involves the human factor of organization and will be explored below.

Completeness

The attempt to build into the organization a procedure for coping with every possible situation which may face a business is not the means by which completeness of organization is to be had. Regardless of the extent of the rules and procedures which may be elaborated upon in organizational structure, there eventually and inevitably will arise some occurrence for which specific handling instructions have not been formulated. Completeness in this case is achieved by providing a device whereby such unique and exceptional matters may be brought to the attention of those who are best prepared to analyze the problems and present the possible solutions.

We may define completeness of organization as that situation which exists whereby routine or anticipated areas of business procedure have been relegated to specific channels of action and, in turn, these channels have been specifically placed under the jurisdiction and control of organizational personnel.

This situation is amplified by the establishment of the "exception principle." The principle states that repetitive matters are best handled via established routines and channels, and therefore, only those situations which are "exceptional," or beyond the scope of customary activity, need be channeled to top echelons for evaluation and disposal. The need for practicing this principle becomes quite apparent when one conjures up the picture of top-management personnel constantly plagued with small, repetitive details of business operation and, therefore, being restricted in the devotion of their costly time to the more important aspects of their business.

The details of operation should be an increasingly larger part of an individual's job as he is assigned to progressively lower rungs on the ladder of organizational structure. This principle is described in the following illustration:

The Board President Officers	This is the area of concentration upon policy formulation and the art of administration.
Junior Management Supervisors Foremen	This is the area of management wherein policies are adhered to and procedures carried out.
Workers	This is the area of attention to details in the performance of the everyday routine of work.

Coordination

Since any and all areas of work within a business enterprise have a common goal, that is, success of the venture, it is necessary that the efforts of these various areas be concerted and coordinated. This necessity is easily understood in the light of business practice. However, an organizational structure is specialized to cater to the many areas of activity in which the firm is involved, and the problem of coordination amongst these several areas becomes aggravated. If but two of the divisions of a typical manufacturing firm, such as the sales and production departments, are to be considered in the light of their respective and immediate goals, it may be said that the sales department concerns itself primarily with the volume of sales, while the production department defines its first concern in terms of a quantity of acceptable production achieved with greatest practical economy. The fact that these separate goals may be incompatible is demonstrated in the case of the sales force, which constantly seeks new products or variations in old products to compete successfully in the market and woo its share of customers. The production unit, with its eyes ever focused on efficiency in production volume and costs, rebels at the fact that such product variation as the sales force may seek can be accomplished only with at least temporary losses in both productive and cost efficiencies. We have not lost sight of the fact that the ultimate goal of either department is over-all business success; but in terms of respective and immediate goals and successes, the two divisions are in opposition.

Organizational structure must, therefore, have built into it some device which will help mold the many specialized unit problems into the shape of a common problem and by so doing preserve the unity of goal. This effort presents a difficult problem in terms of finding the correct or even a workable solution. Attempts are made in industry to bridge this gap by employing such devices as the committee and conferences. By these means a common area of discussion, understanding, and evaluation is set up, wherein it is hoped that the individual goals set by each respective department or division may find place in the over-all goal of the enterprise.

Authority Commensurate with Responsibility

The failure of an organizational pattern may be traced directly to the fact that responsibility for some activity has been placed in the hands of an individual, but at the same time this individual has not been given sufficient authority to allow him to exercise command or control over men and machines so that this task for which he is responsible can be accomplished as management desires. It would seem foolish that such a situation could exist. The following illustration shows how easily this type of situation could arise and points out the weakness of inadequate authority.

Assume that an individual has the final responsibility of supervising a given production schedule. Whether this is production of goods or services is of minor importance in this illustration. Furthermore, assume that management has assigned a rigid deadline for the accomplishment of this production. If the deadline approaches and it becomes clear that the goal cannot be reached, is it not reasonable to assume that the individual responsible for the work output should have authority at his disposal to authorize overtime, reassignment of tasks, or some other suitable device, in order that the rigid schedule be met?

It is not consistent on the one hand for management to establish tight rules for performance and at the same time restrict the performer by limiting his authority.

There is no intention here of overlooking the natural question which should be asked at this point. Why was not the work accomplished within the normal work period? This presents another problem or area for investigation on the part of management. The answer may indicate another malfunction.

Besides having authority adequate for the performance of a task as specified, those given such authority need to know what specific areas of command are theirs. As basic as such a rule is, it is often violated; those responsible for delineating and publicizing the patterns of authority flow become haphazard, or at best ineffective, in giving any clear and complete indication as to the persons in whom particular authorities are vested. Both those assigned authority and those in positions of responsibility become better workers when authority flow is defined. Usurpation of power and dereliction of duties because of ignorance, actual or otherwise, are minimized when clear instructions are prepared and publicized.

Flexibility

When the element of flexibility in organizational structure is considered, two features should be kept in mind: first, the ability of the structure to mold itself to suit changing business needs, and second, the inclusion within the master plan of organization of attention to the need for succession and accession of personnel.

As to the first feature, since the patterns of business activity are potentially ever-changing, they must be subject to scrutiny and change if the organization is to best serve its purpose. A pattern once established should be considered as merely the start of a series of revisions, each of which is originated by the existence of some new need. The pitfall in organizational practice which may exist at this point lies in dependence on the attitude that an existing organization can shoulder additional or changed duties by simply adding or changing assignments. If there is either art or science in the scheme of building an organization, haphazard or makeshift delegation of work is a certain means of destroying its value. Flexibility may be achieved by reassignment, additional assignments, innovation, or elimination. Whatever the means, the desire is that it be accomplished only with due consideration of the final effect that it will have on personal relations and over-all organizational performance.

The second feature which we consider in connection with flexibility is that of succession of personnel. Succession refers to promotion within the organizational ranks. Accession refers to the additions to the organizational ranks.

There are various reasons why men vacate posts within a company. It is not these reasons which immediately concern us. We are concerned with the task of replacing these men.

Good policy in organizational procedures involves selection of individuals to fill vacated posts or newly created posts from existing personnel whenever possible. If, of course, after careful consideration of available personnel it is found that the necessary talents are not available, the company must resort to new employees.

The chart of organization must be viewed as a device which will indicate those areas in which the future need for promotion activity will arise. Every position will eventually need to be refilled. What operational procedures have been instituted which will aid in filling these needs? Some companies recognize that junior management will eventually replace senior management and that the positions of foremen will eventually be refilled from the worker ranks, and so forth. The need here is that those areas from which promotional material will be drawn have been assigned positions of preparation.

Therefore, if management recognizes that a feature of every job is that it is serving as a preparation ground for promotion, then it must follow that the necessary organizational environments which will best serve this purpose will be established.

Accession refers to the additions to or creation of organizational units. Even here, the problem is one of selection, orientation, and positioning of the new activity in relation to the existing structure.

Consideration of the Human Factor

The organizational chart posted on the wall of the executive's office is an impersonal thing. However, when the master plan is put into operation, the chart gains significance in terms of men and action. A good plan is of lesser avail unless the right men are placed in the correct positions. To accomplish this, there must be a means applied within the company correctly to evaluate and orientate available personnel. The basic desire is that the organizational ranks be filled as competently as possible. Personal evaluation will have its shortcomings since the subject and the object, man, are nonscientific. This fact should not be let to stand as a deterrent. The goal of evaluation is clear; the means of evaluation will become clearer.

The human factor must be recognized for what it seeks. Those employed, in any capacity, seek the answers to these questions:

1. What am I within this organization?
2. What status is available within the organization? What must I do to attain this status?
3. Who knows of what I do, and to what extent is there commendation or criticism due me for my work?

The office boy or the company executive should ask these questions of himself. If there are answers available, we may consider that the organization has cognizance of the human factor.

Each of these questions points to an area of human need and, if unanswered, of human frustration.

The first question recognizes that everyone, regardless of lot, wants to know where he stands in relation to others. He desires and needs a fundamental feeling of being part of something. Workers need to be a part of a team, a recognized and specifically assigned element in the structure of the organization.

The second question points to the need for a company policy of publicized information available to the workers regarding promotional opportunities and the necessary attainment qualifications. If this policy is fostered, the company has better assurance of a work force which will be interested and active in the area of self-improvement. It is simply a case of indicating the goals and specifying the means of attainment. Any policy which arouses the worker to the task of self-improvement in the hopes of his acquiring a better position results in a gain to management. As a result of learning, the worker is better able to serve management.

The third question is raised because of the desire on the part of the individual that he be recognized in terms of his own worth. Any organizational scheme which does not consider individual recognition must be considered deficient. Very few, if any, workers are of the type who get their confidence or assurance from within themselves. There is the need for the "pat on the back," the badge of achievement, the posting of exceptional production records, the hourly wage raise, the promotion, or some such device all of which are tools of recognition. The worker, since he is a sensitive being, is not, however, contented with continual praise which is not at some point materialized in terms of rank or monetary increase. Praise alone becomes insignificant and eventually spells out defeat as far as the employee is concerned. Eventual recognition must come in the form of improved status. Otherwise, all the verbal praises are lost in the worker's self-adopted attitude that the criticism which was not forthcoming must have greatly outweighed the expressed commendations.

Recognition and eventual promotion many times may cause a man to reveal capabilities heretofore not clearly recognized. On the other hand, promotion of a man may bring about unfortunate results if it is not recognized that the very interests which cause him to do an excellent job on one level may be too strong or specialized to satisfy the necessary qualifications for a succeeding position. For example, a salesman, extremely capable in his activity of selling the company products, may possibly be incapable of performing adequately as a sales manager or executive whose task may be to exercise authority and control over a sales organization. The necessary activities of a sales manager may be beyond the field of basic interest of the salesman.

The three questions raised above will, in their answers, provide some of the means necessary to assure management of a more contented and productive working organization.

COMMUNICATION WITHIN THE ORGANIZATION

The need for communication within the organization starts with the need for something to communicate. The nature of company policies, managerial philosophy, the objectives of the enterprise, and its principles of operation are subjects which may provide worthwhile information and establish a bond of understanding between the company as an entity and the workers as individuals. Inadequate communication with the workers may interfere with performance on the job because the worker is uncertain as to what to do in a given situation. It may also leave the workers cold as to their significance as members of the work force simply because they have not been included within the communicative system which could provide them with such a basic understanding.

Organizational structure is activated by communication. The success of operations is very much centered in the nature and adequacy of communication. The specific details of organizational relationships and operational procedures may be transmitted via channels, but the performance of individuals on the job depends upon the extent to which consideration of the human element has been included. Communication cannot be separated from employee relations, nor can it be separated from organizational relationships. It is vital as the connecting link between plans and action and a very significant determinant of the quality and adequacy of performance.

Means of Communication

Various approaches to establishing communication channels are used. Some companies place primary reliance upon "face to face" communication. In these cases the supervisory personnel are the important media of communication. Other firms use various publications, house organs, manuals, periodic reports, etc., or other visual aids, such as films. Other means employed to provide information and create understanding are staff meetings, group conferences, discussions by individuals, personal communication, and progress or activity reports. In each case the communication channel attempts to give information, check upon performance or reasons for nonperformance, and, most important, provide a means for worker problems to move upstream into supervisory and managerial levels where they can be objectively regarded and attended to. Suggestions systems are part of the communicative plan.

Supervisors As Communication Channels

Our introduction to organizational relationships was one which expressed the situation in terms of responsibility for performance and authority over performers and the details of work. Since communication cannot be separated from organizational relationships, we must recognize the variability in form of communication. Natural adherence to organization demands expression of orders from supervisory levels to workers and a return flow of communicated responsibility. In addition communicative needs are felt for the transmission of news, and for the handling of questions and complaints on the part of the worker. The supervisory level sometimes is used as the primary means of transmitting all information to the work force, whether the information pertains to work details, status, general company news, or official communication.

Ease of Communication

The availability of communication channels is a start in the development of the program. However, the availability or accessibility of those personnel who are assigned the task of listening as information flows upstream from the worker levels is probably the biggest potential weakness of the plan of communication. The instructions to workers may state that all complaints are to be reported to Mr. Smith or that all details of operation are to be cleared with Mr. Jones. If in either case the Smith and Jones people are unavailable or unapproachable, it would be just as well to have forgotten the provisions for communication at the outset.

The success of an operational plan depends upon more than the plan itself. People make the plan work. Plans establish the nature of relationships between people. The flow of communication provides the fuel for the operation of the organizational engine.

If communication channels are rigidly defined, there is the risk of an exceptional situation being left unattended to simply because no specific provision had been established for handling it. The channels of communication must leave some leeway for out-of-the-ordinary or emergency situations. The worker who wishes to register a complaint about his supervisor would feel that there was no recourse for him if his only channel of communication was through the particular supervisor in question. In this exceptional case the channels of communication should not adhere to the organizational pattern of authority and responsibility. When laying out the lines of communication, it is necessary to recognize the organizational relationships but at the same time not be bound by them. Communication channels should be set up which will provide the duodirectional flow of information which best serves the needs of the enterprise. If the channels thus established pay no heed to authority and responsibility relationships, it will only be because of necessity and the desired expediency.

Rewards from Good Communication

Communication channels are vital to the area of human relations. They are the means to a better understanding of the job to bc accomplished and an appreciation of the company and its policies.

Communication is essential to the development of sound personnel relations. It develops a confidence and understanding which results in a more competitive spirit within the organization.

If the supervisory work force is the mainstay in a successful communication program, it is found that a closer relationship exists between the worker and his supervisor and between the worker and his job. The supervisor is both the worker's outlet and his means of understanding what transpires around him. The supervisor is thus an effective instrument of the human relations program and cannot help but feel the significance of his position.

COST OF ORGANIZATION

The time and effort spent in the process of organization and the cost of operating the resulting organizational structure should be proportional to its utility. How to determine the cost of organization and its structure is virtually impossible, for it is a continuing activity. It is involved with today's activities and also with the plans for tomorrow. It is influenced and modified by each significant change or need for change internally or in the competitive structure of the industry. Its final utility may be measured by the amount of profits which result from operations. These profits may be the justification or proof of the organizational efforts. If the profits were achieved as a result of successful adherence to the plans as made by the administration of the firm, we may feel that organizational costs were justified.

In some cases we hear the expression that the organization is top-heavy. It is loaded with "brass." This means that the ability of the organization to earn profits is not equal to the task of paying for its organizational structure. Therefore, we may assume that the utility of the organization is not great enough.

SUMMARY

The built-in features of organizational structure determine its effectiveness. The basic features are clarity, completeness, coordination, authority commensurate with responsibility, and a consideration of the human factor.

Organizational structure is activated by communication. In order to communicate there must be something to communicate. Details of performance are part of the data communicated. The additional data are those which impart information and understanding to the worker as to the significance of his role and that of the company.

The cost of organization runs high but cannot in all respects be measured. At best, the structure of a firm is felt to be justified by the existence of adequate profits.

QUESTIONS

1. What features are common to any organizational structure? Briefly describe each.
2. What is overlapping authority?
3. Explain the exception principle.
4. What questions are raised by the employee pertinent to his being a member of the organization?
5. What is the nature of communication?
6. How does communication activate organization?
7. What are some of the means of communication?
8. Of what significance is the ease of communication?
9. What are the rewards from good communication?
10. How is the cost of organization to be justified?

CHAPTER 27

Measuring and Appraising Performance

A review of the discussions to this point will reveal a series of functions which, if properly appraised and executed, will make for a successful business venture. If management is unable to estimate future events accurately it cannot assemble and utilize the various factors of business, men, materials, machines and the like, in their optimum proportions. Somewhere along the line management is likely to adopt policies that are detrimental to over-all company goals. Such error may be due to poor judgment, misinformation, or lack of information. This is to be expected and cannot be completely avoided. There is, however, a limit to the number of mistakes that management can make and still survive in our highly competitive business community.

It has been mentioned before that management can minimize poor decisions through application of the principles of scientific management to its various problems. In addition, management can improve on its future policies by applying the lessons learned from the evaluation of its past performance. Such evaluation may indicate where company policies have been strong or weak and which individuals or what outside influences have been responsible for the turn of events. From this experience management can strengthen its future operating plan. This evaluation should encompass each and every segment of the organization. No segment is so unimportant that it precludes examination nor should the performance of any individual be excluded because of the preconceived notion that "the king can do no wrong." Only through a complete and unbiased appraisal of management's activities can the causes for success or failure be established.[1]

In business as in any other area of activity, success is always a relative concept; relative to other business organizations or relative to some pre-

[1] A complete appraisal of the management function appears in H. G. Benedict, *Yardsticks of Management*, Management Book Company, Los Angeles, 1946.

determined concept. The implication is that performance may be described as standard, above standard, or below standard; but before performance can be described as standard or otherwise it is first necessary that a rather specific indication of standard be established. Actually a standard should be established for virtually every area of business activity, sales, production, and profit to mention but a few.

Measuring and appraising performance involves several distinct steps. Specific goals or objectives must be established (these are the standards) and there must be some means of measuring the extent to which these standards have or have not been met. Analysis of the reasons why goals have not been attained or why they have been exceeded should always follow measurement to provide a better basis for planning future courses of action. In some instances goals have been met in spite of rather than because of the wisdom of management. Analysis also provides a basis for the final step in evaluation, the application of corrective action. The section, The Specific Appraisal Illustrated, page 417, provides a rather detailed application of these steps of measurement and appraisal.

THE SCOPE OF EVALUATION

The scope of the evaluation will of necessity vary from one organization to another based on its size and the multiplicity of functions involved. In a small job-order machine shop where labor costs amount to as much as 75 per cent of total costs, evaluation is quite simple. Success or failure for the organization will undoubtedly hinge on one factor, worker productivity. This is true because of the nearly complete reliance on individuals rather than machines to get things done. In other organizations evaluation may not be so simple. It is generally agreed that as the number of functions performed in an organization increases, and as the number of individuals having responsibility increases, the problem of evaluation becomes more involved and complex.

The scope of the evaluation will also vary in relation to the functions under consideration. A goal should be set for every phase of business activity; this point has already been established. The goal may relate to sales volume, profit, development of new products, or any other business function. The goal of an enterprise may be stated quite specifically, such as a sales volume of 1 million dollars and a net profit of 5 per cent after taxes; or it may be expressed in general terms, such as continued leadership in product research or the development of managerial talents. It must be pointed out that goals cannot always be expressed in specific terms. Because of this, measurement and evaluation in some instances will be quite general, while in others very specific.

The General Appraisal Illustrated

Let us assume that management wishes to measure and evaluate the performance of its personnel department. Is the personnel department doing the job that it should? When is the personnel department doing a good job? Obviously there is no single criterion that will answer the question; measurement must be in general or relative terms.

One method of appraising the operation of the personnel department is to establish a set of factors which reflect its performance.[2] An analysis of these factors will provide a basis for evaluation and the adoption of corrective measures if it is found that they are needed. The following factors are suggested:

1. What is the trend of labor costs?
2. What is the trend of labor turnover?
3. What is the trend of employee earnings?
4. What is the trend of absenteeism and tardiness?
5. What is the trend of the number and severity of accidents?
6. What is the trend of the quality of work performed?
7. What is the trend of the number of grievances filed?

The answers to these questions cannot, by themselves, be considered a valid appraisal of the personnel function. However, if labor costs are low, employee earnings are high, and little tardiness or absenteeism exists there is strong reason to believe that the personnel department is doing an effective job.

Through consultation with workers and supervision, top management can determine the reasons for the healthy climate of labor-management relations. High labor turnover on the other hand is a fairly sound indicator of labor unrest or an unhealthy work environment. The reasons for high labor turnover may be discovered in the answers to these questions raised above, e.g., low employee earnings. However, because of the nature of the general appraisal, the reasons why goals have or have not been achieved may not be forthcoming from a routine investigation and management may have to probe deeply to get at the root of the problem.

The Specific Appraisal Illustrated

The following illustration incorporates all the essentials for a complete evaluation; a standard is set, records are kept that provide an adequate description of performance and allow for its measurement. The measurement thus obtained is compared to the standard, deviations are meas-

[2] For a more complete discussion of this topic see Thomas J. Luck, *Personnel Audit and Appraisal,* McGraw-Hill Book Company, Inc., New York, 1955, chap. 4.

ured and then analyzed. The analysis provides a basis for applying corrective action.

Assume that management has established a cost standard of $10 to produce one unit of X. Cost records are kept, and during the month it actually cost $11.02 to produce a unit. Obviously the standard was not reached, but this is all that a comparison of these two cost values reveals. A cost standard set in terms of total cost is of little value to management for evaluation purposes because it is far too general. Actually the unit-cost standard is the total of three component standards, material, labor, and overhead. Let us assume then, that the standard is expressed as follows: material cost, $4; labor cost, $3.50; and overhead, $2.50; rather than simply a total of $10. Let us assume also that during the same month records were kept which showed that the cost of materials used was $5.02; labor, $3.50; and overhead, $2.50. We now know that the reason for not meeting the standard is that material costs were higher than planned. Although we are closing in on the real cause for the cost differential, we have not as yet arrived at the specific cause. The excess material cost can be attributed to two factors—the price paid may be higher than planned or more units of material may have been used than planned. For this reason the material standard must be expressed more specifically as, for example, 10 units of material A at 30 cents per unit and 4 units of material B at 25 cents per unit. Now suppose that the cost records showed that 14 units of material A costing 29 cents per unit ($4.06) were actually used with 4 units of material B costing 24 cents per unit ($.96). We are now able to determine specifically the reasons for not meeting the cost standard—too many units of material A were used per unit. We are also interested in the fact that the unit cost of materials used was below expectations. The variance in material cost can now be analyzed as follows:

Material quantity variance:

4 units of A at 30 cents per unit or $1.20 (This is an unfavorable variance since more than the standard quantity was used.)

Material price variance:

14 units of material A at 1 cent per unit, or $.14
4 units of material B at 1 cent per unit, or $.04
(These price variances are favorable since actual prices paid were less than the standard.)

The difference between the favorable and unfavorable variances, $1.02, equals the difference between the actual cost of materials used and the standard. Management can now evaluate its use of materials, saying that the quantity standard was exceeded costing an extra $1.20, while a favorable price variance resulted in a saving of 18 cents. Management now has a basis for applying corrective action. The excessive material usage may be the result of defective materials or the improper use of materials. In either event the creation of a specific standard and the subsequent measurement and evaluation of performance provide a basis for improving company operations. In general, all cost standards may be analyzed on the same basis as that used above.

AREAS FOR EVALUATION

The discussions above indicate that specific functions can be subjected to a more minute or exact measurement and evaluation than can general functions. As we have seen, when evaluation pertains to cost standards, which are very precise, the process of measuring and appraising is specific and direct. The more general the function performed, the more difficult it is to obtain an exact measurement. Frequently the general evaluation appraises the caliber of upper management levels, while the specific appraises the lower echelons of management.

General Evaluation

The nature of the general evaluation has been described above. The following paragraphs discuss additional areas where general evaluation is involved and point out several factors pertaining to the appraisal of each function.

Executive Evaluation. A business organization is limited in its growth, competitive position, profit-making potential, and in virtually every function by the caliber of its executive group. The thinking and actions of this group provide a basis for all policies governing company activity. We perhaps recognize the importance of competent executives, for our business history offers proof that success or failure arises within this area of management. When does an organization possess good executive talent? There is no specific answer to this question, yet there are several criteria that provide a basis for measurement and evaluation. Does the executive group work in harmony and as a team? Is there a definite plan for the development of successor management? Will nepotism be a part of the successor management program? Is the executive group interested in the role their organization plays in the community? Does the executive group have a long-range plan for the firm, and has it made provisions for carrying out this plan? These are some of the considerations that enter into an evaluation of the executive group. Executive evaluation should consider both current activity and the extent to which the foundation for the future has been formed.

Organization. Earlier discussions have pointed out the various types of organizational structure employed in business. Many variations in organization structures exist, primarily because of differences in emphasis. Size, nature of the markets, the relative importance of production and distribution, and the availability of personnel—each may require modification of a standard organizational structure. When does good organization exist? Generally, when there is "an uncluttered flow of authority and an effectiveness of executive communication."[3] The key to good organization rests in the ability of those in authority to communicate with others; the mere delegation of authority and placing of responsibility is not enough. Because all facets of a business organization are interdependent, because running a business is a joint effort, effective communication is essential to good organization. The essentials of good organization discussed in Chapter 26 are important considerations in evaluating the organizational structure.

Earnings. Business earnings have always been a popular basis for measuring and evaluating performance because of their relatively specific nature. Important though they may be, past and current earnings may be misleading and should be subjected to close scrutiny. The earnings or profit of a business organization for a period of time is the difference between incomes and expenses. However, the measurement of expenses especially requires the establishment of a policy which may be conservative or not, depending on the attitude of the executive group. A large profit may result through prolonging the period for depreciating fixed assets or from placing a relatively high value on closing inventory. The deemphasis of a maintenance or modernization program may reduce expenses temporarily and cause a high profit to be shown. Earnings must be examined to see if conservative and consistent accounting practices have been observed. Measurement on any other basis leaves much to be desired.

What are good profits? Again there is no absolute criterion, for good profits are relative. Profit goals may be set and earnings compared with the goal. Profit goals are commonly set as a per cent of sales, a per cent of invested capital, or a specific amount needed to pay dividends and to provide for expansion and contingencies. The profits of each company must be measured comparatively against the earnings of business in general and earnings in the industry, and also against the profit potential of the firm.

Fiscal Policy. Earnings are closely associated with, and in fact may be dependent on, fiscal policy. Whether profit goals are met or not depends in part on the degree of control maintained over company expenditures. The company that operates on a budget is considered to

[3] American Institute of Management, *Manual of Excellent Managements,* New York, 1955.

have better control over its finances than the one that does not. Reference is frequently made to sound financial management, and it is said that continuing success is dependent upon it. Good financial management is conservative and consistent. It is conservative in its depreciation policy, its policy of inventory valuation, reserve requirements, and requirements for future financial activity. These are the guideposts that may be used to evaluate the fiscal policy of an organization.

Research. While there is never complete assurance that profitable operations can be maintained in the future, a program of research and development can provide considerable protection of company profits. For this reason research is included in the general evaluation of the firm's performance. The gains possible from research are discussed elsewhere in this text. At this point we are interested in the effectiveness of the research program and the attitude of top management toward research effort. A research program is effective when it keeps a firm abreast or ahead of competition, when it enhances the company position through a continuous flow of new and useful products, and when it develops new processes and methods to improve production efficiency. This is the type of standard against which performance in research must be measured.

Specific Evaluation

Specific measurement and evaluation of performance occupies a dominant position in the well-managed firm. Standards or goals should be set for every business function that can be measured. Through the creation of standards greater control over company operations is possible. A discussion of some of the areas of specific evaluation follows.

Working Capital. Working capital is the excess of current assets over current liabilities. Current assets should always be greater than current liabilities, but there remains the question of how much greater. If working capital is too low, the firm may not be able to meet its obligations as they mature. This may impair the firm's credit standing. If working capital is too high, it may indicate that funds have been unnecessarily reserved for current activity that could be better utilized elsewhere in the operation. Experience may indicate that current assets twice the current liabilities is adequate for the firm's needs. Current assets in excess of this relationship would mean poor utilization of company resources.

Inventory Turnover. Whenever more funds are invested in any company activity than are absolutely necessary, it denotes waste. This is true with buildings, equipment, inventory, or any other physical asset. Inventory turnover, which compares the value of the average inventory with the cost of goods sold, provides a fair measure of the effectiveness with which funds invested in inventory are utilized. A retailer may find that an inventory turnover of two times a year is most desirable for him. A slower rate of turnover indicates that inventories, on the average, are larger than they need to be for the volume of sales or that some inventory items are not selling as fast as they should. A higher turnover might indicate that inventories are too low to provide complete assortments for customers and to take advantage of purchasing economies. In either event, if inventory turnover of a particular rate is necessary to maximize profits, then periodic analysis of inventory turnover must be a component of the measurement and evaluation of performance.

Turnover of Receivables. A large percentage of business organizations extend credit to their customers, but such credit transactions cannot be profitable unless the great majority of them are collected. Experience shows that the older an unpaid account becomes, the less chance there is to realize its full value. Turnover of receivables is a measure which indicates the average age of receivables and whether the volume of receivables at any given time is consistent with credit sales volume. To illustrate: if credit sales for a year were $120,000 and at year's end there were $10,000 of unpaid accounts, the conclusion is that the equivalent of one month's sales have not been paid for. If credit terms are net/30 days, then the receivables appear to be in good order. If there were $20,000 of accounts receivable at year's end, or two month's sales, then the conclusion is that receivables are too high, with $10,000 past due. The turnover of receivables provides a measure of the effectiveness of a firm's collection system.

Labor Turnover. An analysis of labor turnover may uncover strengths and weaknesses in a firm's selection techniques, in its supervision, or in many other phases of labor-management relations. Again, a standard for labor turnover may be established, and deviations from the standard analyzed so that corrective measures may be adopted.

Other Areas for Evaluation. Many additional areas for evaluation of a firm's operation are available, such as the use of sales quotas on a national, regional, and local level; analysis of cash discounts earned; the number of accidents occurring in the organization; the relation of net profit to sales and to net worth; and the utilization of production capacity. In each instance a standard is set to which actual performance is compared. This affords an opportunity to determine which segments of the organization are contributing to the success of the firm and which segments are not. The management that makes a bona fide evaluation of its performance has taken a great step toward the improvement of its operations.

EDUCATING AND INFORMING EMPLOYEES

Very often the difference between fair and good performance in the field of athletics is determined by the ability of the individual to follow through. This is equally true in the field of management. Fair management may become good management, and good management excellent, after each has mastered the art of following through with its plans, ideas, and controls. Follow-through for business management is obtained through a tried and proved plan of communication. We realize that if a businessman does everything himself there is little need for communication but modern business management requires a joint effort on the part of each member of the team from top management to the worker on the line. The measurement and evaluation of performance previously discussed will be ineffective unless those with authority have the desire and ability to communicate with others in administering the corrective measures. Communication is the main artery from the heart of management.

The Communication Program

Frequently thousands of people in their capacity as employees have a hand in determining whether or not performance will be up to par. Company goals may or may not mean much to the vast majority of workers, or they may provide a day-to-day challenge for the worker. The attitude of a worker toward company goals will be determined in large measure by the worker's understanding of these goals or the lack thereof. Since worker attitude plays such an important part in reaching goals it is essential to educate and inform the workers in terms of company goals and their significance. The attitude of workers toward their employer is another means of measuring and evaluating the effectiveness of management.

Management may set a goal which requires a reduction of 10 per cent in the unit cost of labor or an increase in production of 10 per cent for each worker. Normally workers would not welcome such a change. Management may introduce a new machine which eliminates the need for certain worker skills. Again, the worker would not welcome the change. However, if management takes the time to explain and justify its goals to the worker, there is far less opportunity for resentment and failure to meet goals. Management must recognize that company goals generally have a direct bearing on the work life of every employee. Workers need to know about the company's competitive position, its plans for new products, new plants, and new methods of doing things.

Workers should have some knowledge of basic economic principles and how they affect the firm's activity. American workmen want to know what the future holds in store for them, and they intend to find out. If management refuses to tell the worker why changes take place, if management ignores the value of consultation and the need for explanation to members of its team, it must expect that workers will go elsewhere for the answers to questions that affect them. They may seek answers from fellow workers "in the know" or from their union representative. In either event the sources may not be accurately informed nor necessarily sympathetic to management. The resulting misinformation can cause considerable employee unrest, whereas a program for educating and informing employees can be instrumental in building a loyal group of workers—the type of worker needed for top-flight performance.

The effectiveness of such a program will depend on management's attitude toward the endeavor and the methods employed. Management's attitude will reflect the quality of the program, while the methods employed will determine whether or not management actually reaches the worker.

The President's Letter. Many business executives feel that a periodic letter from the company president sent to each worker at his home is an effective device for telling the worker what has happened, what is to happen, and why. Coming from the chief executive, the letter speaks with authority; and since the worker has an opportunity to appraise the letter in the environment of his own home, his reactions are likely to be free from the bias that often permeates the work area. The president's letter can be an effective part of an educating and informing program, but one should not expect such an act to constitute the entire program.

The House Organ. The company newspaper or other periodical affords an opportunity to present a much greater volume of information to the worker than the president's letter. Since the house organ is often the joint product of both management and the workers, a two-way flow of information is possible. Workers can bring their thoughts to the attention of management through the same media used by management to communicate with them. The house organ is often the heart of a program for educating and informing the workers. It is a costly, time-consuming endeavor but can easily pay for itself through worker satisfaction.

Meetings. The president's letter and the house organ are perhaps too impersonal to be the sole means of contact with the worker. Workers want to meet their superiors and get information directly from them; they want to hear management say it. It is a source of satisfaction for workers that busy executives will take the time to communicate directly with them. The nature of these meetings must be determined by the physical facilities available; they may be company-wide or strictly departmental.

Bulletin Board. The bulletin board has become a major means of communicating with workers. Nearly all business organizations provide a bulletin board in an area easily reached by the worker; in fact, employers may require that workers examine the bulletin board daily and discover through this medium changes in policy or in operating plans.

Management is not limited to these few methods in conducting its education and information program; it is limited only by its imagination and common sense. Formal classes, movies, posters, in-plant broadcasts, and any other media that will do an effective job should be considered. Interest in the program must be maintained, and the media employed have considerable bearing on the retention of interest.

Evaluating the Program

There is little doubt that workers need to be educated and informed. Management should know, however, whether or not its program is producing good results and whether or not the time and money spent in this direction is worthwhile. Since the purpose of this type of program is to provide information for the worker, we must look to him for an evaluation. If worker morale has improved, if the worker appears to be more satisfied, if the worker's attitude toward his job, his superiors, and his fellow workers has improved since the adoption of such a program, there is reason to believe that it is effective. Individual workers may be approached directly or through questionnaire to determine their reactions to the program. If the workers are not at all interested in management's efforts in this direction, they are undoubtedly ineffective.

EDUCATING AND INFORMING STOCKHOLDERS AND OTHERS

In the case of the corporate structure where ownership and management are often separated, there is need for educating and informing the stockholders. The owners of a corporation, the stockholders, can change the management of their business if they so desire; therefore management needs to justify its policies and goals. Why was one course of action adopted rather than another and will it have a bearing on the return that owners receive now and in the future? Suppliers and dealers need to be informed about company plans because their livelihood may be dependent upon them.

Suppliers are primarily concerned with satisfying raw-material and component-parts requirements; dealers with the line of products, prices, and delivery. Suppliers may be informed through the purchasing division; dealers through the sales division. Stockholders present a different problem because of their varying degrees of interest in company affairs. The welfare of workers, suppliers, and dealers is tied in closely with company plans; whereas many stockholders regard their dividends as a minor part of their income. The holder of ten shares of American Telephone and Telegraph Company stock is undoubtedly far less interested in company plans for expansion or changes in operational methods than a switchboard operator who is employed by the company.

Since a large majority of stockholders may have only a general interest in company affairs, the methods of communicating with them are also quite general. The annual report and institutional advertising may be the only contact between stockholders and management unless major policy changes are contemplated. Stockholders who own a significant portion of the company's stock make it their business to become informed in company matters and will not rely on conventional methods of communication.

SUMMARY

The running of a business requires the performance of a wide variety of functions, all interdependent. If any function is inadequately performed, it will have a detrimental effect on the others. To prevent this situation, management sets standards or goals and compares actual performance with them. In this way management can maintain a high degree of control over its operation. Every aspect of business operation should be subjected to a periodic analysis to ascertain that it is contributing to business success in the way it should. The measurement and appraisal of performance provides management with a basis for setting future courses of action which can be justified to the workers, stockholders, and others interested in the endeavor.

QUESTIONS

1. "In business as in many other fields, success is always relative." Discuss the meaning of this statement.
2. What are the two basic components for measuring and appraising performance?
3. Why would a cost standard of $15 per unit be of little value to management in measuring and appraising performance?
4. Distinguish between general evaluation and specific evaluation. Present an illustration of each.
5. What is executive evaluation? How is it accomplished?
6. When does good organization exist?

7. Are earnings a good basis for measuring and appraising performance? Discuss.
8. What are good profits? Discuss.
9. How may earnings be dependent on fiscal policy?
10. What is good financial management? Explain.
11. Of what value is working-capital analysis?
12. What may be revealed through an analysis of turnover of receivables?
13. What is the purpose of a program to educate and inform employees?
14. How does a plan for educating and informing stockholders differ from the above plan?
15. Evaluate the various methods of educating and informing the workers.
16. How does one evaluate a program for educating and informing the worker?

CHAPTER 28

The Development of Business Size

The growth of business in the United States has customarily involved the development of large corporate organizations which enjoy a substantial portion of the market or control a major portion of the industry assets. Business units may achieve larger size by acquiring control or ownership of other business units or by self-expansion.

There are many reasons why a business unit may increase its size. Among these reasons is the desire to gain the economies of production, distribution, and finance which may come with larger size; or the desire may be to maintain the competitive position of the firm. Other reasons for expansion may be found in the desire to utilize more fully the existing personnel or skills which are available in the organization or to serve customers more adequately in terms of products and services. A firm may be forced either to expand activities or to sell out to larger companies. Some firms expand in search of the prestige which is associated with size.

Expansion of the business size may be closely geared to a stated policy. For instance, development may be undertaken only if management is able to recognize a distinct market advantage or some technical advantage in terms of know-how or production process. If the evaluation of expansion activity does not show such advantages to exist, management will not consider the subject.

PATTERNS OF INTEGRATION

Whether a business unit grows by self-expansion or by external means, the nature of the resultant expanded form is usually one or a combination of two patterns of growth. These patterns are called "horizontal" and "vertical" integration.

Horizontal Integration

If growth is accomplished by acquiring control or ownership of another firm, or by developing additional facilities which produce the same line of products or engage in sales activity at the same distribution level (see Figure 28–1), the resultant combination represents horizontal integration. Thus when a manufacturer of automobile tires buys out another plant which also manufactures automobile tires, or establishes a new facility for the manufacture of tires, the expansion which results is horizontal. When a group of retail merchants gets together and forms a chain-store system, the result is also horizontal expansion which, in this case, is based on a common level of distribution. If a manufacturer who operates his own distribution outlets adds to the number of these outlets, he is expanding horizontally at that particular level of his activity.

FIGURE 28–1

HORIZONTAL EXPANSION

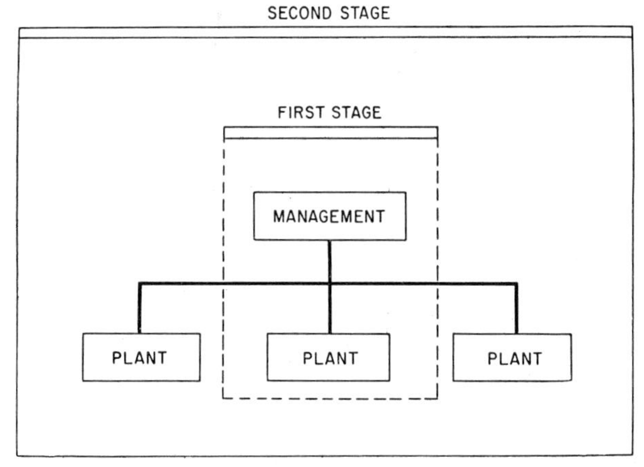

The question may be raised as to why a firm expands horizontally and what economic and managerial situations are involved. A firm which manufactures a given product or is engaged in sales activity at a given distribution level is already equipped with management that has the specialized knowledge necessary for operations in its field. Horizontal expansion for these firms does not involve the addition of foreign activities. It may, however, involve expansion of physical plant, personnel, and geographic coverage. All these additions are aimed at accomplishing the same activity but on a wider basis.

The management personnel involved in the business structure illustrated in Figure 28–1 will find that the specialized knowledge necessary to operate the business when it was in its first stage is equally applicable to operations in the second stage as long as each sales outlet handles the same products and sells to a common level of customer. Variations in either of these areas would involve management in new fields of activity. A greater volume of transactions and attentions would necessarily be part of the picture of expanded business size, but it is fundamentally the quantity aspects which are new and not the quality aspects or principles of control.

Horizontal expansion will allow better use of the managerial personnel who possess specialized talents but are being uneconomically used by virtue of the limited size of a company. Other advantages may exist in terms of ability to provide better service to customers, a larger market for the company, savings by virtue of the greater buying and bargaining power of the larger-sized firm, greater profit potential, expansion or contraction of company size with minor effect on over-all company status, less vulnerability since all dependence is not placed in a single area, and the ability to compare the performance of one unit with that of another.

Although horizontal integration does not necessitate a diversification of managerial skills, it does call for a greater amount of managerial skill. Without this, there may be no advantage in business expansion.

The amount of money invested will increase with the expanded scope of the firm's activities. Greater emphasis must be placed on the employer-employee relationships, for with the increase in the size of the company there is a lessening of the personal contact between those who own and manage and those who work. Small-firm attitudes and actions must give way to recognition of the wider scope of company responsibility to both the worker and the customer.

Vertical Integration

The combination of business units which are engaged in successive phases of the process of manufacture or sales is termed "vertical integration." (See Figure 28–2.) This type of integration occurs when a manufacturer buys out or combines with one of its supplier firms or combines with an organization which operates the sales outlets wherein the manufactured product is handled. By such means, the manufacturer may establish his own supply or sales facilities.

Expansion which involves the acquisition of supply sources is termed backward integration. Expansion which results in bringing the firm a step closer to the user of the product is called "forward integration." Thus, depending upon the stage of production or distribution at which the company originally finds itself, expansion activity may occur in either a forward or backward direction or in both.

FIGURE 28–2

VERTICAL EXPANSION

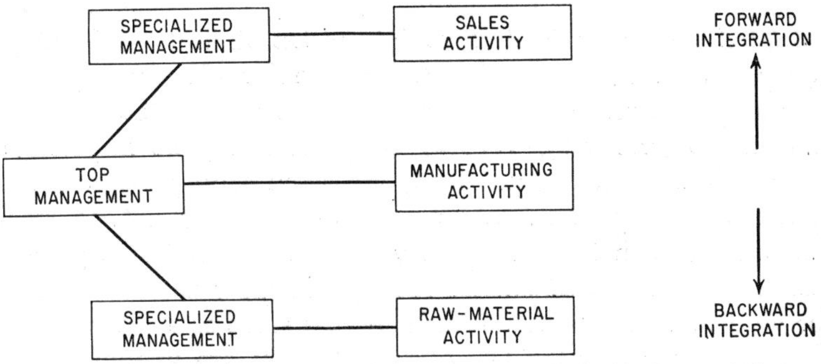

SPECIALIZED MANAGEMENT — SALES ACTIVITY

TOP MANAGEMENT — MANUFACTURING ACTIVITY

SPECIALIZED MANAGEMENT — RAW-MATERIAL ACTIVITY

FORWARD INTEGRATION

BACKWARD INTEGRATION

The automotive manufacturers and the steel producers have often been quoted as leading examples of vertical integration. In each of these two industries there are firms which own raw-material sources, processing and fabricating facilities, distribution facilities, and servicing facilities. In no case, however, does there exist an illustration of complete vertical integration. Such an illustration would involve the existence of an organization which was self-sufficient in every respect and, therefore, employed neither the personnel, services, materials, facilities, equipment, nor money of any other organization.

As a firm integrates vertically, it becomes involved in new areas. A producer may take up the selling of his product, or the newspaper publisher acquire ownership of paper-producing mills. The management group of the original venture may not have the necessary skills available to direct and control these new activities. Each differing area must be handled by specialists. Over-all control is exercised by top management, which places a great deal of reliance upon, and great authority in the hands of, the respective groups which control each area.

In Figure 28–2 the nature of activities has been diversified and their scope has been increased. Top management must exercise greater skills in the coordination of the diverse activities.

Expansion may occur along vertical lines because of desire to gain control over the quantity, quality, and availability features of raw materials. Other reasons may be that the firm wishes to gain a more favorable market position, or to ensure the degree of market effort being made, or to exercise better control over methods of distribution. It usually seeks the advantage of lower unit cost. The full scope of integration would provide control not only over the current scheme of operations but also over the destiny of the product(s) in terms of research and development emphasis.

Vertical integration involves great money investment and new areas of risk taking. The greater the variety of activities, the greater is the problem of over-all coordination. Size, in itself, is no assurance of success.

Restricted Capacities in Vertical Integration. A firm which integrates vertically is limited in its ability to provide for 100 per cent self-sufficiency at each level of integration. Complete vertical integration leads to unwieldy organization. Vertical integration may be impossible because of geographically or politically restricted supply sources. In some cases the ownership of necessary patent rights may not be available to the firm or such integration may not be economically practical.

Customarily a firm uses outside sources of supply and service to make up for its deficiencies. These outside sources serve as a margin of insurance in the event that the firm-owned facilities are unable to provide a part or all of their customary output. The development and maintenance of connections with supplier firms, even by those industry members that are leading examples of the vertically integrated combination, is an illustration of the principle of maintenance of flexibility in terms of source and quantity of needs.

FIGURE 28–3

RESTRICTED CAPACITY IN VERTICAL INTEGRATION

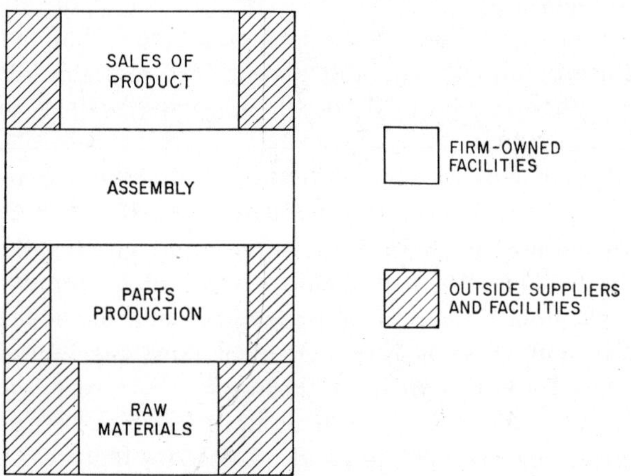

Figure 28–3 is a graphic portrayal of the nature of restricted capacity in vertical integration. The picture of the firm is presented in four stages—raw materials, production, assembly, and sales.

The illustration indicates that each preceding stage of activity prior to the assembly of parts is less capable of fully satisfying the needs of the succeeding stage of integration. To this extent, the balance of needs are supplied by outside sources of supply. At the top level of integration, sales, the indication is that the firm does not maintain sufficient sales outlets to handle the distribution of all the units which it assembles. Noncompany sales outlets are used. The taper of activity indicated in Figure 28–3 is but an illustration of the order of relationship. There is no set pattern as to the volume characteristics of each stage in the vertically integrated organization. Raw-material sources may provide more than enough materials for company needs, thereby creating the need for sales outlets for the excess materials. Similar situations could exist at the different levels of integration.

Variations in the Pattern of Integration

Customarily, as business units achieve size, we find neither a perfect pattern of horizontal nor vertical integration. Our automotive manufacturer, who may need greater quantities of a particular part than could be had from the production unit of his own organization, may acquire ownership of other firms which will satisfy his volume needs. In this case, the expansion would occur along horizontal lines in so far as there would be multiple units producing the same product. At the same time, the ownership and control of sources of supply is an indication of vertical integration.

A firm which expands its activities into unrelated areas is expanding laterally. Production and/or marketing facilities may be established to handle unrelated by-products or scrap products, or to allow the firm to make fuller use of facilities or know-how. Pure-research activities of a company may uncover new and varied products and lead the company into a program of lateral expansion.

Expansion which involves the addition of related or competing products to the company line is called "circular expansion." These additional products may be added by the firm in order to round out the variety offered the trade. The hope is that the greater variety offered is a service to the customer, thus a competitive advantage, and one which will result in a greater volume of sales. The fact that a company handles a variety of products may provide it with a measure of insurance in the event that there is a loss of market for any particular product. Circular diversification may sometimes occur because the firm grew even as Topsy grew. Management with idle funds or time may seek what appear to be good bargains and thereby acquire ownership or control in related areas.

MULTIPLE-PLANT ORGANIZATION

Many business firms are established on a multiple-plant basis. Rather than increase the plant size by physical additions at the original site, management may add new plants in different geographical locations. This procedure may be followed in order to provide facilities in important market areas or to minimize transportation costs to the markets. Other reasons may be that the company, as it seeks to diversify its activities, finds opportunities in scattered areas. Some firms separate their plants in fear of future warfare, or because they feel that many smaller units are more easily controlled than the single "king-sized" plant.

There are many characteristics which multiple-plant organization may assume. The company may find itself engaged in the production of diverse products or selling in diverse areas and dissimilar fields; the plants may be geographically scattered; or the pattern of activity may be extremely diversified. Each one of these characteristics indicates the need for specialized organization which caters to extracting effectiveness from the use of manpower and facilities. Out of this picture of varied characteristics there develop two patterns of organization suitable for use with multiple-plant operations. These are the centralized and decentralized control patterns.

Centralized Control

Centralized control of multiplant activities delegates authority over many stages or areas of operation to the hands of few people. If each person so entrusted with authority is responsible for a homogeneous activity, the control may be well established. If, on the other hand, the

FIGURE 28–4

CENTRALIZED CONTROL

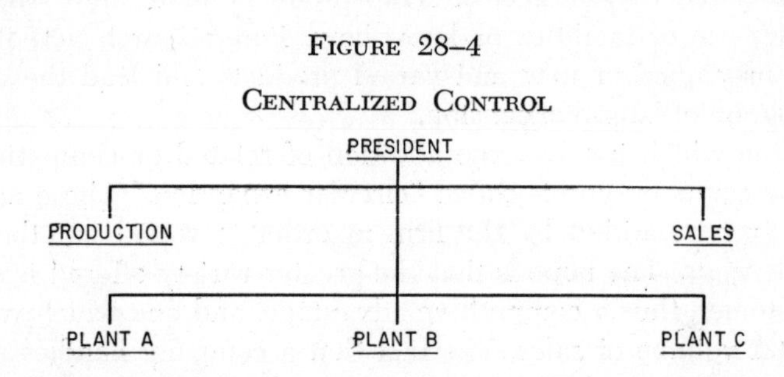

activity is of a heterogeneous nature, it is best that a decentralized control pattern be used.

Figure 28–4 represents the organizational form possible when all problems concerned in both the sales and production activities, respectively, of the multiple units are common. There must be assumed to be no differentiation by virtue of product, materials, processes, geographical areas, personnel, or scope of activities which would preclude adequate control from a central source.

Decentralized Control

The organizational form presented as Figure 28–5 recognizes the diversity of problems which may arise in one plant as compared with any other. In order that local conditions and differences may be more ade-

FIGURE 28–5

DECENTRALIZED CONTROL, NO. 1

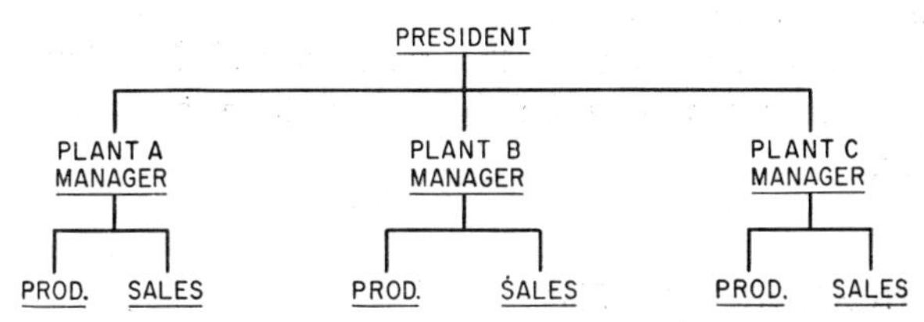

quately considered, the organizational control is decentralized. Each plant and each area of activity is controlled by its respective executive.

Figure 28–6 is representative of the firm which engages in production and sales activities in three geographical areas. It is assumed that each area has specialized problems involving the product, procurement of materials, the nature of sales activity, or some other function. However, finance and personnel have been designated as two activities which are better controlled on a centralized basis. It is most likely that financial matters could not be delegated to the individual areas while maintaining

FIGURE 28–6

DECENTRALIZED CONTROL, NO. 2

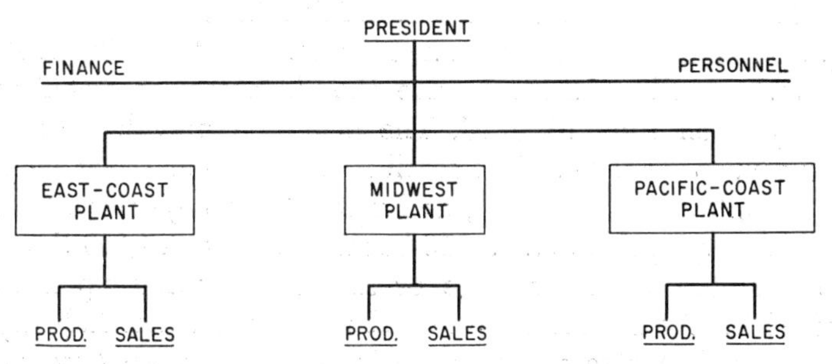

the effectiveness of the basic policy of the firm. Likewise, uniformity of personnel policies makes it desirable that the personnel activity be centrally controlled. In this case it must not be assumed that the routine activities of the personnel department, such as hiring and firing, are carried on by the central authority. The everyday routine of the department is rightfully handled by delegated officials at each plant. It is the policies which must be centrally established and controlled, and the exceptional matters which must be brought to the attention of the personnel officer at the main plant or home office.

The decision as to whether centralized or decentralized control is best suited to the business activity revolves around the following considerations:

1. The assignment of excessively diversified activities to a single area of control must be avoided.
2. With due consideration of the volume and location of activity, homogeneous areas may be delegated to a centrally responsible authority.

THE SIGNIFICANCE OF SIZE

What makes a business "big"? Does a million dollars of plant investment or a work force of three thousand men mean that a business is big? Can we measure size in terms of annual sales dollars or volume? Should we consider the concept of value added by manufacture?[1]

A new small-business-size standard became effective January 1, 1957. It was formulated by an interagency task force for procurement purposes and represents the unanimous judgment of the fourteen government agencies chiefly concerned with procurement procedures and the Small Business Administration. Under the new ruling, for purposes of government procurement, a manufacturing concern is considered a small business if (*a*) it is not dominant in its field of operations and, with its affiliates, employs fewer than 500 employees, or (*b*) it is certified as a small business by the Small Business Administration.

For purposes other than government procurement, the Small Business Administration will continue to use the definition of small business adopted by it on June 10, 1954. The definition provides: Any manufacturing concern is classified as small if it has 250 or fewer employees, including employees of affiliates; as large if it employs more than 1,000 persons. If it employs more than 250 but not more than 1,000 the concern may be classified as either large or small, depending upon the size standard which the SBA has developed for its particular industry.

For nonmanufacturing concerns the definition provides: Any wholesale concern is considered small if its annual dollar volume of sales is 5 mil-

[1] "Value added by manufacture is calculated by subtracting the cost of materials, supplies, and containers, fuel, purchased electric energy, and contract work from the total value of shipments . . . it approximates the value created in the process of manufacture. . . ." U.S. Bureau of the Census, *1947 Census of Manufacturers, Statistics by Industry,* vol. II, p. 18.

lion dollars or less; any retail or service-trades concern is considered small if its annual sales or receipts are 1 million dollars or less. (The regulation also provides certain exceptions.) The dividing lines between large and small for other industries are as follows: construction, average annual receipts of 5 million dollars or less for the preceding three years; trucking and warehousing, annual receipts of 2 million dollars or less with exceptions based on economic data in individual instances; taxicabs, annual receipts of 1 million dollars or less.

Regardless of the size of business, whether large with multimillion-dollar plant investments or small with but a few employees, there are problems which are common to management in all cases. Money matters, work-force problems, managerial talents, taxes, and selling are each major problem areas to any firm. The smaller businessman may be interested in borrowing only $15,000 while the large corporation is concerned with raising $15,000,000. These absolute amounts differ considerably, but in each case the problem of securing the funds may be relatively as severe to the respective managements.

Size is important in determining the ability of a business concern to compete in the market. Size is also important in so far as it may indicate excessive economic concentration and thereby be deemed an undesirable feature within a system which is trying to preserve the competitive aura. Governmental concern with industrial concentration has focused more clearly upon the problems involved in measuring size or concentration. With finer classification of industry groups, it is hoped that more realistic measurement of industrial-product concentration may be forthcoming. In addition, information will be available as to the share of manufacturing which is in the hands of a particular company or group of companies.

Feasibility of Large or Small Size of Firm

Entry into some areas of business is effectively restricted by virtue of the large investment necessary. The advent of a new automobile producer, aluminum producer, steel producer, or oil refiner is the exception rather than the rule. Entry into these areas is limited for two reasons. First, in order to operate on a technological basis comparable to that of established firms, the dollar investment in plant and facilities would have to be extremely large. Second, there would be little if any value in establishing a competing plant that would involve but a small or considerably lesser investment than those of its competitors. With varying degrees, increased size of business allows for more efficient operations. Therefore, depending upon the nature of the business, an effective competing unit must measure up to certain standards of investment, equipment, and output. These standards vary considerably from one type of business activity to another. A shoe manufacturer or garment manufacturer does not expand the size of his original unit indiscriminately, for added efficiency or lower costs would not, in this case, be had by establishing a larger plant. The smaller unit is just as efficient on a unit cost basis as is the larger unit. However, in order to accumulate a greater total profit, or for other reasons, the businessman would duplicate his facilities. This is tantamount to the establishment of a second unit rather than an expansion in size of the original.

The steel operator, in expanding size in the search for greater economies, lower costs, and greater profits per unit, may increase the size of his facilities rather than duplicate them. Thus, the blast furnace has greater capacity; the material-handling facilities are capable of handling greater volumes of materials; personnel are aided in their work by bigger and better instruments of production; rolling mills are of greater capacity; etc.

How far can we go in terms of size? At what point is it no longer feasible to consider increased size? Our answer must be found in an evaluation of the burdens imposed by the feature of size. We know that with a given state of technological development there are physical limitations to increased size. In terms of organizational control there are personnel limitations. In terms of money, the limitation is reached at the point where increased size detracts from the profitability of the venture. In terms of social implications, increased size imposes upon management the responsibility of satisfaction for added consumers, the responsibility for the welfare of a larger number of workers, and consideration of the impact of size upon the maintenance of our competitive system. Size demands that the firm accept many social and economic responsibilities.

SUMMARY

A study of American business organizations would undoubtedly reveal that a vast majority of them have grown in size since their inception. Growth is almost an inherent feature of American business. Growth, if properly planned, may result in production and distribution economies, larger markets, improved competitive position, and greater profits. Growth is accomplished through horizontal integration wherein the same functions are performed as before growth but on a larger scale; or it may be accomplished through vertical integration wherein a different level of activity is performed. When a new supermarket is added to a retail food chain, horizontal integration results. If the retail chain acquired a wholesale fruit-and-produce establishment or a cannery, growth would be through vertical integration since neither of these is a part of food retailing.

Horizontal integration requires larger portions of the same managerial talents, while vertical integration requires new and additional talents. Growth by any means can become unwieldy, but growth through continued vertical integration is more likely to become unwieldy because it requires that management venture into foreign fields. No organization should attempt to grow any faster than the management that directs it.

QUESTIONS

1. Why do business organizations increase their size?
2. Describe horizontal integration.
3. Describe vertical integration.
4. What is forward integration? Backward integration?
5. Is complete vertical integration feasible? Discuss.
6. Compare the advantages of centralized versus decentralized organization.
7. Define "value added by manufacture."
8. Distinguish between big and small business.
9. Why do garmentmakers refrain from developing to mammoth plant size?
10. Why are all automobile manufacturing companies large?

CHAPTER 29

The Government and Business

The American system of business was long characterized by the doctrine of *laissez faire*, as outlined in Chapter 1 of this book. This doctrine implies a minimum of government interference in the affairs of individuals and business organizations. We are aware, however, that a major function of any government is to protect the members of society from the oppression and injustice of others. It is understandable, therefore, that the established policy of our government toward business now lies between the two extremes of freedom and protection. Actually all business organizations are subject to varying degrees of governmental regulation.

The degree to which a business organization is regulated or controlled by the government is determined by the probability that the uncontrolled actions of a business organization will result in injury to large numbers of people. Virtually all business organizations are vested with some degree of public interest. There is some confusion as to what "public interest" means or implies but a fair appraisal has been given by Chief Justice Waite.

> Property does become clothed with a public interest when used in a manner to make it of public consequence, and affect the community at large. When, therefore, one devotes his property to a use in which the public has an interest, he, in effect, grants to the public an interest in that use, and must submit to be controlled by the public for the common good. . . .[1]

The amount of control exercised over business tends to vary in direct proportion to the degree of public interest involved. The involvement of public interest may result from the nature of business activity or from the size of the operation. Public utilities, banks, or railroads are vested with considerable public interest and, of course, are closely regulated. The corner shoe store and the watch-repair shop are not large enough to be involved with the public interest nor is the nature of their activity such that it warrants any great amount of control.

[1] *Munn v. Illinois,* 94 U.S. 113 (1876).

Some organizations are concerned with the public interest because of their immense size but size per se is not the only basis for the application of controls. A small entrepreneur-type establishment may be subjected to close government control, and undoubtedly there are many organizations of considerable magnitude that enjoy a bare minimum of controls. The following paragraph taken from the bylaws of a small town illustrates the extent to which controls may be applied to a small business venture.

> Every keeper of a shop for the purchase, sale, or barter of junk, old metals, or second hand articles, within the limits of this town, shall keep a book, in which shall be written, at the time of every purchase of any such article, a description thereof, the name, age, and residence of the person from, and the day and hour when such purchase was made; such book shall at all times be open to the inspection of the Selectmen or any person by them authorized to make such inspection. And every keeper of such shop shall put in a suitable and conspicuous place in his shop a sign having his name and occupation legibly inscribed thereon in large letters, and such shop and all articles of merchandise therein may be at all times examined by the Selectmen. . . . Such shop shall be closed between the hours of 6 o'clock P.M. and 7 A.M., and no keeper thereof and no junk collector shall purchase any of the articles aforesaid during such hours.

Whether this law is rigidly enforced or not is another matter; these provisions indicate the extent to which controls may be applied to a small business operation. The magnitude of this operation, therefore, is not the deciding factor. The significance exists in the nature of the activity and the potential injury to society if controls are not provided.

As a rule, however, the small businessman can carry out his everyday duties feeling little if any effect from government controls or regulations provided he has geared himself to the essential controls. This is not the case with the large organization whose activities can have considerable bearing on the economic life of the country for their management is under close and continuous scrutiny. Business organizations have become so gigantic that a single company could cause serious unemployment or a shortage of goods by its actions. The General Motors Corporation, the world's biggest manufacturer, can be used to illustrate this point. To gain some concept of its size and its importance in the American economy the following statistics are presented for the year 1956.

It produced 3½ million motor vehicles, more than one-half of the nation's output.

It sold over 10 billion dollars' worth of goods.

It employed 599,000 people, nearly 1 per cent of all workers employed in this country at the time.

It paid 2.9 billion dollars in wages.

It paid more than 1 billion dollars in taxes.

It paid over 5 billion dollars to some 26,000 suppliers.

When organizations become as large as this and control such a large portion of the supply of a variety of products, employ so many people, and are such an important element in our nation's economy, then the government should take precautionary steps to insure that the best interests of society are served by business organization. Despite its immense size, however, General Motors Corporation is subject only to those control measures that apply with equal vigor to other business establishments. In addition to General Motors there are more than twenty corporations in the United States each of which has in excess of 1 billion dollars of assets, and there are more than thirty corporations whose annual revenue exceeds 1 billion dollars. Such organizations singly could by their actions have a profound influence on the economic life of this country.

METHODS OF CONTROL

Whenever legislative authorities decide that the best interests of society can be served through control they must then lay down the rules of conduct to be followed by business organizations and provide for the enforcement of these rules. Rules that are not uniformly enforced cause great hardship to the law-abiding businessman and contribute little to the protection of individuals. An effective system of control requires the establishment of control methods to fit each activity being regulated. For this reason a variety of control methods are used.

Control through Statute

Business activity may be regulated through the enactment of specific laws. Violators of the law are brought to justice and if adjudged guilty of an infraction are reprimanded, fined, or imprisoned. Such laws cover a wide range of activity and apply to the businessman just as traffic laws apply to the motorist.

Control through Charter or Franchise

Most corporations are sanctioned by the issuance of a charter. Until the charter is granted the corporation does not exist. The charter extends certain privileges to the corporation which in turn is required to abide by established rules and regulations. An infraction of the rules may result in the revocation of the charter. If this is done, the corporation ceases to exist. Colleges, hospitals, and many social agencies are founded on the charter principle. Generally it is the state government that issues these charters.

A franchise, as the word implies, is a particular right and privilege given to a business by the government. The term also implies exclusiveness. Thus in the field of transportation the owners of a fleet of buses are given a franchise to operate a bus line over city streets or between cities. Intrastate franchises are granted by state governments and interstate franchises are granted by the Federal government. In return for this partial monopoly granted by the franchise, the holder agrees to abide by the rules and regulations laid down by the government. The rules may relate to schedules, fares, or safety precautions. Failure to abide by the franchise provisions may result in a suspension or revocation.

Control through Agency

There are dozens of state and Federal agencies that have been granted varying amounts of power in the making of rules—rules that regulate business. The Interstate Commerce Commission has issued volumes of rules and regulations that penetrate virtually every area of interstate activity. The Federal Trade Commission, the National Labor Relations Board, the Federal Reserve Board, and many other agencies are vested with the power to formulate rules that exert a profound influence on the actions of businessmen. Although many of these agencies are not clothed with any legal compulsion they may, in certain instances, enforce their rules through court edict.

Control through Taxation

From the businessman's point of view this is the most vicious of all control methods because it tends to undermine the financial foundation of a business or may cause the prices of commodities to rise to such a level that sales are curtailed.

Taxes are punitive in nature to the businessman just as they are to all taxpayers, and they tend to destroy the incentive to earn more. The main cry of the businessman is that prevailing high taxes make it impossible for a business to grow as fast as its needs dictate. The corporation that earns $75,000 in a year for example, must pay a Federal income tax of $7,500 on the first $25,000 of profit and $26,000 on the remaining $50,000 of profit, or a total of $33,500. On top of this there may be a state excise or income tax that can boost the tax burden upward to $45,000 or more. Dividends must also be paid to the owners or stockholders. Therefore, the businessman reasons, there is not enough left to provide adequately for business needs.

No attempt is being made here to criticize our tax system or the businessman's tax burden, rather the desire is to emphasize the businessman's reaction to taxation as a control device. Businessmen resent the fact that in some instances a large portion of the selling price of their product or service represents taxes, which if reduced would result in greater sales.

In some states one-third of the price of a gallon of gasoline is tax. The price of a fur coat is inflated 20 per cent by a luxury tax. The price of certain cosmetics is inflated by a 10 per cent tax, and so on. There are, then, many instances in which a significant portion of the selling price of commodities represents a payment of taxes. Such taxes do tend to control the sale of the product to varying degrees.

LIMITATIONS ON THE POWER TO CONTROL

Both the Federal and state constitutions contain provisions that limit the extent to which regulations and controls may be imposed on individuals and businessmen. The Bill of Rights guarantees certain basic freedoms that characterize the American way of life. The limitations placed on our governments are quite specific, but their meaning is given different interpretations to keep in tune with the changing times. We are well aware that the powers delegated to our governments are quite broad and that they have been loosely interpreted by our executive, legislative, and judicial departments. As our society develops, new and different demands are made on our governments which in turn expand the area in which they must participate. In the final analysis, except in emergencies, the people alone decide the nature and extent of government control.

Due Process of Law

The most important limitation on the power of the government to regulate is found in the Fifth and Fourteenth Amendments to our Federal Constitution. These amendments ensure that neither Congress nor any state government can deprive a person of his "life, liberty or property without due process of law." It is up to the courts to decide whether or not the due-process provision has been violated. Judicial interpretations have given us two specific implications of this principle. The guarantee of due process is not confined to procedural fairness but extends to the substance of the law, stating that it must be fair and reasonable. Actions that violate the due-process provision will not be upheld by the courts.

Equal Protection of the Law

No person shall be deprived of equal protection of the law by any state. This right is stated in the Fourteenth Amendment to our Federal Constitution but does not prevent Congress from such an act. Equal protection of the law does not mean that all persons or business establishments will be protected or treated alike, for "reasonable" application is permitted. Whether an application is reasonable depends on whether the nature of the application made bears a reasonable relation to the evil to be remedied or the object to be obtained by law. However, one businessman can expect the same treatment and consideration as another similarly situated. Laws cannot be created to arbitrarily give one business preferred treatment over another in a capricious way.

Obligation of Contract

No state may pass a law that will impair the obligation of contract. As a result, all contracts between private parties or business organizations are protected. Without this protection it would be difficult to make long-term commitments, for there would be little certainty that they would be fulfilled.

Freedom of Speech

Congress cannot pass laws that would abridge the freedom of speech or of the press or the right of the people to peaceably assemble. This right is guaranteed in the First Amendment to our Federal Constitution. For many businessmen this limitation has little application; for others, however, it may be of considerable significance. The employer who wishes publicly to express his feelings in a labor dispute, or the businessman who wishes to protest against government policy, both have considerable interest in their freedom of speech.

AREAS OF REGULATION

Article I, Section 8, of the Federal Constitution is an enumeration of the powers of Congress. It is from this enumeration of powers that the bulk of regulatory measures have been made. Outstanding as a source of regulatory power is paragraph 3, which gives Congress the power to regulate commerce between states and foreign nations. The broad interpretations made of the term "commerce" have resulted in a wide variety of regulations and controls.

Business Combinations

In some instances there is an advantage if two or more business organizations can combine forces for production and distribution economies. In general there is no law that will prevent such combinations. However, in several instances there have been business combinations designed to create a private monopoly at the expense of society. The Sherman Act of 1890 was passed to do away with business combinations that operated in an unreasonable restraint of trade. The Clayton Act of 1914 carried this philosophy further through statement of specific forms of conduct that are prohibited. The Robinson-Patman Act of 1936 dealt with price discrimination. Price discrimination can reduce competition and/or create a monopoly situation. This law requires that differences in prices charged by a vendor must be justified through differences in the cost of manufacture, selling, and delivery, caused by difference in methods of producing a product or differences in cost resulting from varying quantities sold. The Federal Trade Commission (1914) was created to enforce the provisions of these and other laws on the subject. In general the law is designed to do away with unfair business practices which could ultimately work to the detriment of society. Congress has the power to regulate business combinations and business practices through its power to regulate interstate commerce.

Patents, Copyrights, and Trade-marks

Article I, Section 8, paragraph 8, gives Congress the power to "promote the Progress of Science and useful Arts, by securing for limited Times to Authors and Inventors the exclusive Right to their respective Writings and Discoveries." Such protection is absolutely necessary to protect a businessman's investment in product research and development. The holder of a patent is given the exclusive right to manufacture, use, and sell his patented device for a period of seventeen years. In other words, the holder of a patent has a legal monopoly. The law does not require that the holder of a patent actually produce or sell the patented item, nor does law grant the holder of a patent any special privilege regarding pricing or price fixing. After seventeen years the patent expires and the discovery becomes public property.

Copyrights are granted to authors, composers, and the like to guarantee them the exclusive right to their writings or compositions for a period of twenty-eight years, with a privilege of a renewal for a like period.

Trade-marks differ from patents and copyrights inasmuch as the Federal government has no direct regulatory power over them. Congress can regulate only if the trade-marks are used in interstate commerce. A trade-mark does not have a limited life; it can be used as long as desired.

Should another person infringe on the protection granted under patent, copyright, and trade-mark laws, the person who has been injured can bring the infringer into court and may obtain damages caused him by the unfair actions of others who have improperly used his property.

Regulation of Production

During periods of emergency we expect the government to regulate production in certain fields to further the best interests of the nation. In several instances in the past the Supreme Court has held invalid laws that limit or control the level of production in any industry. Today, however, we find that the Federal government regulates production during peacetime in agriculture, petroleum, and several other areas.

Pricing

The price of a good or service is simply the amount that the seller charges and the amount that the buyer must pay. The purpose behind price-regulating laws is to prevent a seller from obtaining an exorbitant price for the goods he sells, especially where there is a shortage of that good, or it may be to prevent a seller from charging a price that is too low in the eyes of the law.

Price regulation is practiced by both state and Federal governments. The right of the state to regulate prices stems primarily from its police power which allows a state to pass laws to protect the general health, safety, and welfare of the people. In addition to the regulation of public-utility rates, it has been held by the Supreme Court of the United States (*Munn v. Illinois*)[2] that a state may regulate prices in those businesses that operate in the public interest. In this case the state was allowed to fix the rates charged by grain-elevator operators. Later, in 1932, New York State established a Milk Control Board with the power to fix both maximum and minimum retail prices of milk. It appears that in this industry unrestricted competition is not desirable and that the best interests of the community can be served through price regulation. The right of the state to regulate the price of milk was upheld in the Supreme Court of the United States in the case of *Nebbia v. New York*.[3] These two cases have pretty well established the fact that the state may control prices where it is in the public interest to do so. In Massachusetts it is a violation to sell popular brand cigarettes for less than 25 cents per single pack. Attempts have also been made in this state to regulate the price of gasoline.

Under the commerce clause Congress has the power to regulate interstate commerce. From this power Congress has been able to regulate the price of several commodities that move in interstate commerce. Congress can regulate the price of milk and coal and can fix the rates for the interstate transmission and transfer of electricity and natural gas.

The wartime powers conferred on Congress are much stronger and more far-reaching than its ordinary ones. Under such powers Congress may fix the price of any and all commodities including wages and rents. Today this power is extremely important to the businessman, for the nation need not be engaged in hostility with any foreign nation for war powers to apply. In sustaining the right of the government to build the TVA, the courts held that the law providing for its construction may be valid even though there is no reason to believe that there will be a

[2] 94 U.S. 113 (1876).
[3] 291 U.S. 502 (1934).

particular war. The war powers have been construed to cover preparation in case a war does break out.

Price Fixing

Should a manufacturer be allowed to set and enforce the retail price at which his goods will be sold, or should the individual retailer be able to adjust the price to suit his own particular situation? Since different retailers have different costs of operation, perhaps they should be allowed to set prices at their own discretion. In 1937 Congress, by passing the Miller-Tydings Act, legalized resale price maintenance in interstate commerce for trade-marked products. In addition, forty-five states, all states with the exception of Missouri, Texas, and Vermont, have passed Fair Trade Laws which make legal contracts between manufacturer and retailer for establishing the retail price of a commodity. That is to say, a manufacturer of branded goods has the power to indicate the price at which his branded merchandise will be sold. Thus if a manufacturer sets a Fair Trade price of $4.95, a retailer must charge this price if he wishes to sell this manufacturer's product.

In addition to the Fair Trade Laws, some thirty states have passed laws that regulate retail prices by requiring that at least a minimum mark-up be applied to the cost of an item. Such laws are designed to prevent retailers from selling goods below their actual cost.

SUMMARY

As our society develops into a more highly complex state where business, people, and the government are more dependent upon one another, we must expect that the government will continue to play a very important part in the relation of business to society. The government depends upon business; people depend upon business; and business itself depends upon other business. It is in the best interests of all concerned that the government exercise some control over the activity of businessmen. How far will the government extend its controls and regulations in the future? This depends to a great extent on business itself. Governments tend to regulate and control when it is in the best public interest that they do so. If business conducts itself in an appropriate manner, we need not fear additional controls except in cases of national emergency. The intent of the courts seems to be to have the government regulate only when necessary. The opinion of Chief Justice Taft in the case of *Stafford v. Wallace*[4] expresses the attitude of courts in interpreting regulatory statutes.

[4] 258 U.S. 495 (1922).

Whatever amounts to more or less constant practice and threatens to obstruct or unduly to burden the freedom of interstate commerce is within the regulatory power of Congress under the commerce clause, and it is primarily for Congress to consider and decide the fact of the danger and meet it. The court certainly will not substitute its judgment for that of Congress in such a matter unless the relation of the subject to interstate commerce and its effect upon it are clearly nonexistent.

QUESTIONS

1. What is the meaning of *laissez faire?* What are its implications?
2. What determines the extent to which business organizations will be regulated?
3. What is the meaning of the doctrine of "public interest"?
4. Should a business organization be regulated simply because of its size? Why? Why not?
5. Who is responsible for the controlling of business?
6. Distinguish between a charter and a franchise.
7. List five types of business organizations that operate on a franchise.
8. How does control through agency operate?
9. How can taxation be a control over business?
10. What is meant by "due process of law"?
11. What is meant by the term "obligation of contracts"?
12. What is the purpose of the Sherman Act?
13. What is the function of the Federal Trade Commission?
14. Where does the Federal government get the bulk of its power to regulate? Discuss briefly.
15. Where does the state government get the bulk of its power to regulate? Discuss briefly.
16. According to Chief Justice Taft, what should be the attitude of Congress toward business regulation?

CHAPTER 30

The Managerial Roles

The tasks of planning, organizing, and operating the business firm have by this time been presented in detail. Throughout the content of the preceding chapters attention has been directed toward the nature of business activity and its environment. It is time that we must directly draw the strings and bring the various elements of our concern together in some manner which will designate the managerial structure which cements the parts. The phase on which we are about to embark represents an advanced level in the study of business management. The real problems are yet ahead, for although our study to this point may have provided us with many sound working tools, the talent of management is the element which coordinates their use and is the determinant of success.

Necessarily all our endeavors in industry are directed toward accomplishing specific goals. This oneness of purpose must be stated and understood by those whose concern will be the management of activity. Our continued stress on the need for goals, or objectives, is justifiable at this time, if not previously, as we consider that each of the managerial roles plays a part in tying the business functions together so as to accomplish these goals. Without such direction, the effort of management is at best haphazard.

The importance of managerial roles varies as a business firm goes through various stages of transformation. Critical stages in the growth of the firm lay varying stress upon the importance of the managerial functions. As we have already noted in our treatment of company organization, the development of the small one-man firm into a larger organization involves the delegation of work and authority to others. This is the first critical stage, for herein the owner assumes more exclusively the role of a manager. As the need for a more formal and specialized organization is felt, there must be resort to much more detail in terms of records, reports, control devices, planning and coordination. When size or variety and complexity of activity make their presence felt, unwieldy management structure is the pitfall or bogey. Consultation and coordination among great numbers of specialists, each of whom has a hand in molding the future design of operations, become the basic problems of top management. When organization becomes highly specialized there may arise the tendency to consider people as numbers and titles and to depend too much upon the rendering of reports as the means of coordination. This of course raises a favorite topic of many business executives, for the problem becomes one of finding time to read through the myriad reports, let alone separate the wheat from the chaff.

As the firm structure develops in size and unwieldiness many questions are raised pertinent to its future course and management development. Pertinent questions as to the advisability of decentralization, the use of staff roles in organization, types of control which should be instituted, and the type of executive needed are common at this time.

THE EXECUTIVE STRUCTURE

Characteristics

Although the number depends largely upon definition, there are probably about 500,000 executives in the 100,000 corporations that account for almost all this country's production.[1] This number includes many junior executives who represent the supply from which will be drawn the top-drawer executives of tomorrow. The selection task presents a complex problem for today's top management. All junior executives cannot possibly achieve senior status, nor are all so deserving. The separation process therefore becomes something of vital significance, for within this process is the seed of future success.

To discriminate between the good and the bad, it is necessary that a basis for such discrimination be established. This must take the form of a statement, or at least an understanding, of those qualifications which are requisite for the executive officeholder. These abilities may be most neatly put in terms of three words—ability, integrity, and industry.

It is felt that complete reliance upon a single factor as being demonstrative of executive talent is the most frequent shortcoming of the selection program. Each factor listed above is significant in its own right, and in conjunction they provide what is deemed a rounded appraisal basis. The ability of a person in terms of professional skill, leadership, and intelligence is more readily identified than either integrity or industry. The ease of measurement and the indication of great ability are neither one an assurance that the possessor will exercise such ability.

The American Institute of Management recognizes integrity as the factor most difficult to appraise but also as the most important of the

[1] American Institute of Management, *The Corporate Director,* October, 1956, vol. VI, no. 7.

three. Integrity includes honesty and a sense of responsibility. Intellectual sincerity and civic responsibility are inherent in the appraisal, for responsiblity must be carried beyond the aspect of company loyalty, and honesty must include the recognition of a man's independent thinking and free expression of ideas. Management which is deficient in integrity is management in poor moral health.

Industry consists of efficient application of initiative and diligence. It involves the ability to discriminate between minor and significant items to the extent that achievement is in terms of the more important things. The existence of industry as a trait among the executives can instill the same qualities in others and thereby enhance the dynamic force within the firm.

Managerial Roles in Organization

In a corporate structure the role of management commences at the board of directors' level. The members of the board are chosen by the vote of the stockholders and are entrusted with the direction of the activities of the corporation within the limits of its charter. This board is responsible for the establishment of basic policies concerning production, marketing, financing, and public relations. Many of those who hold board positions have gained them in recognition of influence or knowledge in other fields. The chief executive of the firm, the president, is chosen by board action and is usually a member of the board.

The president is the responsible, acting head of the enterprise. With the cooperation of subordinates, and within the framework of basic policies as determined by the board, he establishes operating policies and is responsible for the coordination of the enterprise as a whole. At times the large organization may see fit to relieve the president of many managerial activities in order that he may devote his time to more significant areas such as price fluctuation, market trends, governmental relations, etc.

Production. The member of management entrusted with control over the production function usually finds several activities within his jurisdiction. There is no standard relationship which must be maintained, for each function must have its respective significance determined on the basis of its own merits. However, we may realistically include the following within the realm of the production executive:

1. Supervision of production from receipt of order through delivery. This includes the schedule of manpower, equipment, and materials needs and flow.
2. The development of production standards and controls.
3. Control over facilitating services considered essential to efficient production.

4. Responsibility for production research, plant layout, and economic appraisal of expenditures.
5. Coordinating with the sales department in terms of quantity, variety, and product development.

In the manufacturing concern the production function is of major importance, and the individual in charge usually reports to the president.

Sales. The sales executive is concerned with the measurement and development of the market. In so doing he finds many functions are assigned to him:

1. Market research and market planning.
2. Product development.
3. Participation in the development of price policy.
4. Establishment of distribution channels.
5. Creation of sales territories and assignment of personnel.
6. Development, training, and compensation of a sales force.
7. Advertising and promotion.
8. Sales planning and control.
9. Coordination of sales and production.

The executive responsible for the sales function reports to the top executive, the president.

Financial. The officer entrusted with the financial function, usually called the treasurer, is concerned with the following activities:

1. The formulation of financial policies and general control of financial matters.
2. Receiving and disbursing company funds.
3. Paying taxes, insurance, and as instructed by the board, dividends.
4. Responsibility for the procurement of capital.
5. Responsibility for the purchase and sale of company property.
6. Custody of company funds and legal papers which have financial importance (such as contracts, leases, insurance policies, patents, notes, bonds, etc.).

The financial officer reports to top management, such as the chairman of the board. Subordinate to him is the controller who is responsible for the methods and procedures involved in financial and statistical record keeping. He also has charge of general accounting, cost accounting, statistical analysis, auditing, and perhaps credits and collections. Many times he is the general officer manager and is concerned with inventories, time keeping, payrolls, tax reports, and other like matters. He is an important executive if such over-all understanding and association are assigned as his function.

Within the area encompassed by the basic functions elaborated upon above exist many facilitating departments. The significance of these service functions depends upon the purpose of the organization and the extent to which the particular activity has a profound bearing upon accomplishment.

To illustrate, no union shop can relegate the function of personnel and industrial relations to any indiscriminate level of importance. In some cases the nature of problems associated with the area may be so weighty that the function may be one of prime importance and rank high. Therefore the job may assume executive status. On the other hand, there may be little if any problem in the area to merit such high-level delegation of responsibility for the function. If such were the case, the function might well be assigned in a position subordinate to the manufacturing activity or whatever major function is most concerned with the personnel and industrial relations roles.

Likewise, the roles of purchasing, research, public relations, and others must each be reconciled to their respective positions of importance within the statement of basic company purpose and thereafter assigned to whatever major function or executive level best promotes the attainment of the stated purpose.

THE MANAGEMENT FUNCTIONS

The preceding section has attempted to portray the nature of specific tasks assignable to the various managerial roles. To attempt a complete listing of functions and tasks would serve no real purpose since these roles vary in importance and assignment from company to company. However, an approach to the understanding of the managerial role may be had in terms of recognizing those over-all functions which become the responsibilities of top management regardless of their specific tasks.

The functions of management are, by some, termed the "elements" of management and are listed as planning, organizing, command, coordination, and control.[2] In another interpretation these functions are listed as planning, organizing, staffing, direction, and control.[3]

Planning is the executive function which involves the selection, from among alternatives, of enterprise objectives, policies, procedures, and programs. Planning is fundamental to all activity and is a requisite function of all levels of management. The *organizing* function of the manager involves the determination and enumeration of the activities required to achieve enterprise purposes, the grouping of these activities, assignment of them to subordinate management, and the delegation of authority to

[2] Henri Fayol, *General and Industrial Management,* Pitman Publishing Corporation, New York, 1949.

[3] Harold Koontz and Cyril O'Donnell, *Principles of Management,* New York, McGraw-Hill Book Company, Inc., 1955.

carry them out. Within the organization there must be established the provisions which permit the desired type of coordination.

Staffing comprises those activities which are essential in manning the executive posts and keeping them manned. This involves not only the filling of positions but also the provision for succession. *Direction* is concerned with the guidance and supervision of subordinates. The supervision employed here must involve an appreciation of alternative means of direction and an appreciation of the psychological factors involved in establishing effective leadership. The *control* function includes those activities which are designed to compel events to conform to plans. Since the establishment of a plan is not a guarantee of achievement, the control function is established to serve this purpose.

There is no question but that the need for *coordination* exists throughout the functions of management as executives and throughout the overall plan of company operations. Coordination of objectives and the means of achievement is the never-ending responsibility of management.

COMPANY POLICY

Policy is generally regarded as a means for directing and controlling an enterprise. A clear statement of policy is recognized as a most important tool of management. A definition of policy is as elusive as the Scarlet Pimpernel, but at least management is able to discuss its own policy as it sees it. This discussion provides a listing of the main ingredients of policy and in summary may allow the following definition: Policy may be said to be the guides of conduct established by a company's management to direct decision and action within the enterprise toward predetermined objectives.[4]

Unfortunately, many firms feel that company policy is essential only in the area of personnel and public relations. Other firms merely state the major goals of the business and let that suffice as their statement of policy. In some cases management interprets policy to include a detailed summary of methods and procedures to be used in the accomplishment of objectives. In spite of these varied concepts of policy, there is general agreement on the role of policy as a guide to management action.

The size of the firm does not apparently minimize the need for policy statement, but as the firm becomes larger, the areas of coverage become more extensive and the need for a formalized, written policy becomes

[4] Booz, Allen, and Hamilton, Management Consultants, in a report entitled *The Making of Company Policy*, New York, 1956, p. 4, offer this summary definition of policy. This report also contains the results of a preliminary excursion into the field of company policy making.

apparent. The executives filling the top management functions are the policy makers and should be responsible for the periodic review of policy and for its updating if necessary.

The establishment of policies provides many advantages:

1. The dependence upon experience and judgment as the basis for action is preferable to trial and error procedure. Policy is the means of transmitting experience.
2. Policy is a means of drawing people into a coherent organization.
3. Policy sets a basis for the maintenance of consistency in action.
4. Policy provides a guide to action and thereby affords some certainty that the activity will take place within the plan as conceived.
5. Policy regulates activity to the extent that routine matters may be delegated to subordinates, thus relieving executives for attention to more significant matters.
6. A program of policy formulation forces the company to consider its goals and future actions.
7. Policy facilitates the making of decisions and also serves to back up action.

There is group executive participation in the formulation of policy. This teamwork activity is focused upon the chief executive's office. The areas wherein policies are formulated need not be delineated, for there may be universal applicability of policy within the firm.

CONCLUSION

The establishment of a plan or objective, an investigation of the business environment, the creation of policies to guide, the establishment of facilities, specific operational plans and controls, and the breath of life which is organization and staffing are the ingredients which we have explored throughout this text. These provide us with our finished unit, the operating establishment. The secret of success lies not simply in the list of ingredients but far more in the understanding of their blending.

Bibliography

PART ONE. BASIC PLANNING

Appley, L. A.: "A Current Appraisal of the Quality of Management," *Progressive Policies for Business Leadership,* American Management Association, General Management Series, no. 156, New York, 1952.

Bethel, L. L., F. S. Atwater, G. H. E. Smith, and H. A. Stackman: *Industrial Organization and Management,* McGraw-Hill Book Company, Inc., New York, 1956.

Boyd, H. W., Jr., and R. Westfall: *Marketing Research,* Richard D. Irwin, Inc., Homewood, Ill., 1953.

Bratt, E. C.: *Business Cycles and Forecasting,* Richard D. Irwin, Inc., Homewood, Ill., 1953.

Brown, L. O.: *Marketing and Distribution Research,* The Ronald Press Company, New York, 1955.

Cornell, W. B.: *Organization and Management in Business and Industry,* The Ronald Press Company, New York, 1947.

Fayol, H.: *General and Industrial Management,* Pitman Publishing Corporation, New York, 1949.

Filipetti, G.: *Industrial Management in Transition,* Richard D. Irwin, Inc., Homewood, Ill., 1953.

Hertz, D. B.: *The Theory and Practice of Industrial Research,* McGraw-Hill Book Company, Inc., New York, 1950.

Hurley, M. E.: *Elements of Business Administration,* Prentice-Hall, Inc., Englewood Cliffs, N.J., 1955.

Ireson, W. G., and E. L. Grant: *Handbook of Industrial Engineering and Management,* Prentice-Hall, Inc., Englewood Cliffs, N.J., 1955.

Knowles, A. S., and R. D. Thomson: *Industrial Management,* The Macmillan Company, New York, 1944.

Koontz, H., and C. O'Donnell: *Principles of Management,* McGraw-Hill Book Company, Inc., New York, 1955.

Larson, G.: "Developing and Selling New Products," U.S. Department of Commerce, 1950.

Roscoe, E. S.: *Organization for Production,* Richard D. Irwin, Inc., Homewood, Ill., 1955.

Samuelson, P. A.: *Economics,* McGraw-Hill Book Company, Inc., New York, 1955.

Taylor, F. W.: *The Principles of Scientific Management,* Harper & Brothers, New York, 1923.

Terry, G. R.: *Principles of Management,* Richard D. Irwin, Inc., Homewood, Ill., 1953.

Umbreit, M. H., E. F. Hunt, and C. V. Kinter: *Fundamentals of Economics,* McGraw-Hill Book Company, Inc., New York, 1952.

PART TWO. PLANNING FOR PHYSICAL FACILITIES

Alford, L. P., and J. R. Bangs: *Production Handbook,* The Ronald Press Company, New York, 1945.

American Management Association: "Significant Factors in Plant Location," *The Management Review,* New York, January, 1947.

Apple, J. M.: *Plant Location and Material Handling,* The Ronald Press Company, New York, 1950.

Dewhurst, J. F., and Associates: *America's Needs and Resources,* Twentieth Century Fund, Inc., New York, 1948.

Hoover, E. M.: *The Location of Economic Activity,* McGraw-Hill Book Company, Inc., New York, 1948.

Immer, J. R.: *Layout Planning Techniques,* McGraw-Hill Book Company, Inc., New York, 1950.

Ireson, W. G.: *Factory Planning and Plant Layout,* Prentice-Hall, Inc., Englewood Cliffs, N.J., 1952.

Losch, A.: *The Economics of Location,* Yale University Press, New Haven, Conn., 1954.

Neuhoff, M. C.: *Techniques of Plant Location,* Studies in Business Policy, no. 61, National Industrial Conference Board, Inc., New York, 1953.

Shubin, J. A., and H. Madeheim: *Plant Layout: Developing and Improving Manufacturing Plants,* Prentice-Hall, Inc., Englewood Cliffs, N.J., 1951.

Stocker, H. E.: *Materials Handling,* 2d ed., Prentice-Hall, Inc., Englewood Cliffs, N.J., 1951.

U.S. Department of Commerce: *Basic Industrial Location Factors,* Sept. 30, 1946.

Woos, R.: "Where to Put Your Plant," *Fortune,* vol. LIV, no. 1, pp. 100–104, July, 1956.

PART THREE. MANAGEMENT OF MANPOWER

American Management Association: *Measuring Results of Personnel Functions,* Personnel Series, no. 111, New York, 1947.

American Management Association: *Organizing the Personnel Function Effectively,* Personnel Series, no. 158, New York, 1950.

Aspley, J. C. (ed.): *Employee Relations Handbook,* Dartnell Corporation, Chicago, 1955.

Belcher, D. W.: *Wage and Salary Administration,* Prentice-Hall, Inc., Englewood Cliffs, N.J., 1955.

Black, J. M., and J. G. Picolle: *Successful Labor Relations for Small Business,* McGraw-Hill Book Company, Inc., New York, 1953.

Dubin, R.: *Human Relations in Administration,* Prentice-Hall, Inc., Englewood Cliffs, N.J., 1951.

Gardner, B. B., and D. G. Moore: *Human Relations in Industry,* Richard D. Irwin, Inc., Homewood, Ill., 1955.

Ghiselli, E. E., and C. W. Brown: *Personnel and Industrial Psychology,* 2d ed., McGraw-Hill Book Company, Inc., New York, 1955.

Gomberg, W. A.: *A Trade Union Analysis of Time Study,* Science Research Associates, Chicago, 1948.

Gregory, C. O.: *Labor and the Law,* rev. ed., W. W. Norton & Company, Inc., New York, 1949.

Harbison, F. H., and J. R. Coleman: *Goals and Strategy in Collective Bargaining,* Harper & Brothers, New York, 1951.

Heinrich, H. W.: *Industrial Accident Prevention,* 3d ed., McGraw-Hill Book Company, Inc., New York, 1950.

Lytle, C. W.: *Job Evaluation Methods,* 2d ed., The Ronald Press Company, New York, 1954.

Maier, N. R. F.: *Principles of Human Relations,* John Wiley & Sons, Inc., New York, 1952.

———: *Psychology in Industry: A Psychological Approach to Industrial Problems,* rev. ed., Houghton Mifflin Company, Boston, 1955.

Peters, R. W.: *Communication within Industry,* Harper & Brothers, New York, 1950.

Pigors, P., and C. H. Myers: *Personnel Administration,* 3d ed., McGraw-Hill Book Company, Inc., New York, 1956.

Planty, E. G., W. S. McCord, and C. A. Efferson: *Training Employees and Managers,* The Ronald Press Company, New York, 1948.

Randle, C. W.: *Collective Bargaining Principles and Practices,* Houghton Mifflin Company, Boston, 1951.

Scott, W. D., R. C. Clothier, and W. R. Spriegel: *Personnel Management,* 5th ed., McGraw-Hill Book Company, Inc., New York, 1954.

Shartle, C. L.: *Occupational Information,* 2d ed., Prentice-Hall, Inc., Englewood Cliffs, N.J., 1952.

Stone, C. H., and W. E. Kendall: *Effective Personnel Selection Procedures,* Prentice-Hall, Inc., Englewood Cliffs, N.J., 1956.

Thorndike, R. L.: *Personnel Selection—Test and Measurement Techniques,* John Wiley & Sons, Inc., New York, 1949.

Whitehill, A. M., Jr.: *Personnel Relations,* McGraw-Hill Book Company, Inc., New York, 1955.

Yoder, D.: *Personnel Management and Industrial Relations,* 4th ed., Prentice-Hall, Inc., Englewood Cliffs, N.J., 1956.

PART FOUR. PRODUCTION

American Management Association: *Planning for Efficient Production,* Manufacturing Series, no. 206, New York, 1953.

Barnes, R. M.: *Motion and Time Study,* 3d ed., John Wiley & Sons, Inc., New York, 1949.

Cady, E. L.: *Industrial Purchasing,* John Wiley & Sons, Inc., New York, 1945.

Carroll, P., Jr.: *Time Study for Cost Control,* 2d ed., McGraw-Hill Book Company, Inc., New York, 1943.

Enrick, N. L.: *Quality Control,* 2d ed., The Industrial Press, New York, 1954.

Feigenbaum, A. V.: *Quality Control,* McGraw-Hill Book Company, Inc., New York, 1951.

Gilbreth, F. B.: *Motion Study,* D. Van Nostrand Company, Inc., Princeton, N.J., 1911.

Goetz, B. E.: *Management Planning and Control,* McGraw-Hill Book Company, Inc., New York, 1949.

Heinritz, S. F.: *Purchasing: Principles and Applications,* Prentice-Hall, Inc., Englewood Cliffs, N.J., 1951.

Juran, J. M.: *Management of Inspection and Quality Control,* Harper & Brothers, New York, 1945.

Landy, T. M.: *Production Planning and Control,* Richard D. Irwin, Inc., Homewood, Ill., 1950.

Lewis, H. T.: *Industrial Purchasing,* Business Publications, Inc., Chicago, 1951.

———: *Procurement Principles and Cases,* Richard D. Irwin, Inc., Homewood, Ill., 1952.

Maynard, H. B., G. J. Stegemerten, and J. L. Schwab: *Methods-Time Measurement,* McGraw-Hill Book Company, Inc., New York, 1948.

Moore, E. G.: *Production Control,* McGraw-Hill Book Company, Inc., New York, 1951.

O'Donnell, P. D.: *Production Control,* Prentice-Hall, Inc., Englewood Cliffs, N.J., 1952.

Ritchie, W. E.: *Production and Inventory Control,* The Ronald Press Company, New York, 1951.

Voris, W.: *Production Control,* Richard D. Irwin, Inc., Homewood, Ill., 1956.

Westing, J. H., and I. V. Fine: *Industrial Purchasing,* John Wiley & Sons, Inc., New York, 1955.

Whitih, T. M.: *The Theory of Inventory Management,* Princeton University Press, Princeton, N.J., 1953.

PART FIVE. SELLING AND FINANCING

American Management Association: *Building and Marketing a Profitable Product Line: Planning—Pricing—Distribution,* Marketing Series, no. 98, New York, 1956.

American Management Association: *The Sales Department Looks at Costs—with a Paper on Legal Pitfalls in Marketing,* Marketing Series, no. 90, New York, 1953.

American Management Association: *Strategic Areas in Cost Reduction,* Manufacturing Series, no. 215, New York, 1954.

Brown, G. H. (ed.): *Readings in Marketing from Fortune,* Henry Holt and Company, Inc., New York, 1955.

Cowan, D. R. G.: "The Functions of Management in Marketing," *The Annals of the American Academy of Political and Social Science,* vol. CCIX, Philadelphia, May, 1940.

Crisp, R. D.: *How to Reduce Distribution Costs,* Funk & Wagnalls Company, New York, 1951.

Dean, J.: "Pricing Policies for New Products," *Harvard Business Review,* November, 1950.

Doris, L.: *Business Finance Handbook,* Prentice-Hall, Inc., Englewood Cliffs, N.J., 1953.

Gardner, F. V.: *Profit Management and Control,* McGraw-Hill Book Company, Inc., New York, 1955.

Heckert, J. B.: *Analysis and Control of Distribution Costs,* The Ronald Press Company, New York, 1940.

Heckert, J. B.: *Business Budgeting and Control,* The Ronald Press Company, New York, 1946.

Howard, P. B., and M. Upton: *Introduction to Business Finance,* McGraw-Hill Book Company, Inc., New York, 1953.

Maynard, H. H., and H. C. Nolen: *Sales Management,* The Ronald Press Company, New York, 1950.

Nystrom, P. H. (ed.): *Marketing Handbook,* The Ronald Press Company, New York, 1948.

Oxenfeld, A. R.: *Industrial Pricing and Marketing Practices,* Prentice-Hall, Inc., Englewood Cliffs, N.J., 1951.

Payne, B.: "A Program for Cost Reduction," *Harvard Business Review,* 31, September–October, 1953.

Prather, C. L.: *Financing Business Firms,* Richard D. Irwin, Inc., Homewood, Ill., 1955.

Rowland, F. H., and W. H. Harr: *Budgeting for Management Control,* Harper & Brothers, New York, 1945.

Tosdal, H. R.: *Introduction to Sales Management,* 4th ed., McGraw-Hill Book Company, Inc., New York, 1957.

PART SIX. OWNERSHIP AND DEVELOPMENT

Barnard, C. I.: *The Functions of the Executive,* Harvard University Press, Cambridge, Mass., 1938.

———: *Organization and Management,* Harvard University Press, Cambridge, Mass., 1948.

Brown, A.: *Organization of Industry,* Prentice-Hall, Inc., Englewood Cliffs, N.J., 1947.

Dale, E.: *Planning and Developing the Company Organization Structure,* American Management Association Research Report, no. 20, New York, 1952.

Davis, R. C.: *Fundamentals of Top Management,* Harper & Brothers, New York, 1951.

Drucker, P. F.: *The Practice of Management,* Harper & Brothers, New York, 1954.

Gillmore, R. E.: *A Practical Manual of Organization,* Funk & Wagnalls Company, New York, 1948.

Holden, P. E., L. S. Fish, and H. L. Smith: *Top Management Organization and Control,* McGraw-Hill Book Company, Inc., New York, 1951.

Jamison, C. L.: *Business Policy,* Prentice-Hall, Inc., Englewood Cliffs, N.J., 1953.

Koontz, H., and C. O'Donnell: *Principles of Management,* McGraw-Hill Book Company, Inc., New York, 1955.

Martindell, J.: *The Scientific Appraisal of Management,* Harper & Brothers, New York, 1950.

Metropolitan Life Insurance Company, Policyholders Service Bureau: *A Management Audit for the Small Company,* New York. N.D.

Metropolitan Life Insurance Company, Policyholders Service Bureau: *Outline for Management Audit,* New York, 1947.

Newman, W. H.: *Administrative Action,* Prentice-Hall, Inc., Englewood Cliffs, N.J., 1951.

Urwick, L. F.: *Problems of Growth in Industrial Undertakings,* Winter Proceedings 1948–49, no. 2, British Institute of Management, London, 1949.

Index